To Foreign Shores

TO FOREIGN SHORES

U.S. Amphibious Operations
in World War II

JOHN A. LORELLI

NAVAL INSTITUTE PRESS   ANNAPOLIS, MARYLAND

LIBRARY OF CONGRESS CATALOGING-IN-PUBLICATION DATA
Lorelli, John A., 1946–
  To foreign shores: U.S. amphibious operations in World War II / John A. Lorelli.
      p.   cm.
  Includes bibliographical references and index.
  ISBN 1-55750-520-9
  1. World war, 1939–1945—Amphibious operations.   2. United States. Navy—
History—World War, 1939–1945.   3. United States. Marine Corps—History—
World War, 1939–1945.   I. Title.   II. Title: U.S. amphibious operations in World
War II.   III. Title: United States amphibious operations in World War II.
D769.45.L67   1994
940.54'5—dc20   94-32014
                                                                              CIP

Printed in the United States of America on acid-free paper ∞

9   8   7   6   5   4   3   2
First printing

Dedicated to

Anthony John Lorelli
Courtney Megan Stevens
Andrew Dane Lorelli

with the wish that they will always live in a world at peace.

Contents

FOREWORD

I became involved in amphibious operations shortly after I received my commission in 1943. I was initially assigned to train assault boat crews for the Normandy invasion. Soon my base was selected to train crews for the Landing Ship Medium (LSM). As an impressionable 22-year-old, I was very excited when handed the book of plans for this class of ships so new that the first one had not yet been launched. I methodically concentrated on visualizing this oceangoing ship. I wanted to understand what crew training was going to be necessary because I was now on the engineering school staff. I was eager to do my part well. But like the hundreds of thousands of young Americans then in the amphibious forces, I did not truly appreciate the significance of the endeavor in which I was taking part.

In the years following World War II, I discovered that among the thousands of books on military history there was not a single authoritative volume on the total scope of U.S. amphibious operations in that war. Never before (and one hopes never again) will we see amphibious operations on such a worldwide scale. In my mind, this unique aspect of World War II had been overlooked by military historians. Although my civilian life was absorbed in founding and growing a sizable manufacturing company, I vowed to do what I could to remedy that unfortunate oversight. Thus began this book.

In early 1991, I retained Samuel Loring Morison, grandson of the famous historian Rear Adm. Samuel Eliot Morison, to begin the extensive research necessary for this ambitious project. Within a couple of months I realized I would need a skilled and enthusiastic author to translate this raw research into the finished product I envisioned. Having read *The Battle of the Komandorski Islands*, I was greatly impressed with the writing style of John Lorelli. After only one meeting he agreed to join us in the project. In short order he immersed himself wholeheartedly in the task, in spite of his regular, full-time job. As the manuscript went through its various iterations I was pleased with the direction it took. I thank John for sharing in my vision of this book and for skillfully making it a reality.

The thrill I felt as I held the book of plans for the LSM pales in comparison to the thrill I feel as I hold this manuscript. I hope this book will help the reader comprehend the magnitude, complexity, and marvelous execution of this aspect of World War II.

ROLF F. ILLSLEY
SANTA ROSA, CALIFORNIA
SPRING 1994

PREFACE

What was it like in World War II to cross the line of departure as an LCI skipper, LVT crew chief, or Higgins boat coxswain, running at full throttle toward a fiercely defended beach? Historian John A. Lorelli provides both macro and micro views of every Allied amphibious assault conducted during that war, from top-level strategic imperatives to the noise and confusion of the assault waves during the final, desperate moments counting down to H-hour.

Amphibious warfare is that dimension of naval warfare in which an attack is launched from the sea by naval and landing forces embarked in specialized ships and craft against a hostile shore. Risky and complex, an amphibious assault is one of the most difficult of all military operations. Seaborne assaults have been employed by warriors since at least the Greco-Persian Wars of the fifth century B.C., but the emergence of rapid-firing weapons earlier in this century raised serious questions about the continued military utility of opposed landing operations. Indeed, the eminent British strategist Sir Basil H. Liddell Hart concluded in 1939 that technology had rendered future amphibious assaults "almost impossible."

Fortunately for the Allied cause in the war to come, a small group of American military officers rejected this conclusion. Instead, they devoted much of the 1930s to developing a rudimentary doctrine for joint amphibious operations. As Mr. Lorelli relates, these visionary pioneers contributed significantly to the art of war. America may have been ill-prepared for global war in 1941, but at least it had in hand a sensible set of guidelines—and prototype landing craft—for projecting naval power ashore against hostile fire.

The author relates how this innovative doctrine received a true baptism of fire starting with the 1942 landings in the Solomon Islands and North Africa. From tentative beginnings, American armed forces refined the doctrine, the ships, and the assault craft that made possible the massive amphibious landings at Leyte, Normandy, Iwo Jima, and Okinawa in 1944–45. Lorelli provides the texture of each assault, drawing upon his extensive research into oral histories, war diaries, and combat reports. Once the amphibious task force steams into each objective area, the veterans' accounts take over. Time and again we witness the disintegration of carefully prepared landing plans into chaos as a result of enemy action, hydrographic obstacles, or human frailties. Somehow, in every case, some iron-willed survivor—a beachmaster, landing team commander, or naval control officer—steps up to take charge and restore the precious momentum of the assault. Today, we can only marvel and ask: Where did we get such men?

The author is a Navy veteran of the Vietnam War and a gifted historian, author, speaker, and teacher. He spent years conducting research and collecting personal vignettes to prepare this comprehensive history of what rightfully has been called "The Golden Age of Amphibious Warfare." *To Foreign Shores* provides not only a valuable account of Army, Navy, and Marine Corps amphibious developments in World War II; Lorelli's book also provides lessons applicable in coming decades to joint operations by our maritime nation against the littoral features of potential enemies.

JOSEPH H. ALEXANDER
COLONEL, USMC (RET.)

Acknowledgments

This book has been a long time in the making. Like most works of its length, it has been both a labor of love and a test of endurance. It began as one thing, became something else, then changed again. Like most people who are interested in modern naval history, I fancied that I knew a lot about amphibious warfare. While preparing this book, I discovered I knew very little about it, a situation I have since redressed. I have done my best to make that learning experience into an enjoyable read.

This work could not have been done without considerable help. Rolf Illsley brought me the original kernel for the book. He soon showed that his interest in the subject was more than transitory. Without his significant financial backing, there would be no book. There would also not be a book without the peerless efforts of Samuel Loring Morison. Sam is an accomplished writer of naval history and a nonpareil researcher: if a document exists, I believe he can find it. His mental catalogue of World War II naval facts is encyclopedic. I have relied on him for advice more than once and he has never let me down.

Numerous other people have contributed help for which I am grateful. Among them are Col. Joseph H. Alexander, USMC (Ret.), Scott Martin, and Liz Auchincloss. Joe Alexander is not only an exemplary Marine Corps officer, he is a gentleman and a scholar as well. I am deeply grateful for all the material contributed by veterans of the amphibious wars: R. Samuel Dillon, Bud Farmer, William Fox, Harry Heckman, Johnny Huggins, Lt. Gen. Victor Krulak, USMC (Ret.), Stan Newland, Alan Pace, John Stewart, and Gene Watts. Official records are invaluable but do not compare to the immediacy of personal accounts. My old friend Capt. J.F.B.

Johnston, USN (Ret.), once again took time to explain the intricacies of a gunnery problem to me, showing me just how difficult it is to hit something like an island gun emplacement from a moving ship. I also want to thank Paul Stillwell of the U.S. Naval Institute. Every ten years he appears like a genie and offers a helping hand. Mark Gatlin of the Naval Institute Press gets my thanks for shepherding this manuscript through an arduous review process and all the subsequent modifications. He showed remarkable grace in listening to my protestations against cutting pages from the manuscript. I know of no writer who believes his prose to be anything but perfect or who happily accepts having that prose edited. An editor thus needs both the skills of a diplomat and the ability to smooth sometimes tortured syntax into readable form. Charles Neighbors, who edited this book, is good at both.

I have done my best to ensure accuracy in this account and am confident that I have presented a fair picture of events. Any errors of interpretation are mine alone.

JOHN A. LORELLI
VENTURA, CALIFORNIA

SELECT CHRONOLOGY OF U.S. AMPHIBIOUS LANDINGS DURING WORLD WAR II

OPERATION NAME	DATE	LOCATION	ASSAULT FORCE
Watchtower	8/7/42	Guadalcanal Is.; Solomon Is.	USMC
Torch	11/8/42	North Africa	USA
Landcrab	5/11/43	Attu Is.; Aleutian Is.	USA
Toenails	6/30/43	Rendova Is.; Solomon Is.	USA
Toenails	7/2/43	New Georgia Is.; Solomon Is.	USA, USMC
Husky	7/10/43	Sicily, Italy	USA
Cottage	8/15/43	Kiska Is.; Aleutian Is.	USA
Postern	9/4/43	Lae, New Guinea	USA
Avalanche	9/9/43	Salerno, Italy	USA
Postern	9/22/43	Finschaven, New Guinea	USA
Goodtime	10/27/43	Treasury Islands	RNZA
Dipper	11/1/43	Bougainville Is.; Solomon Is.	USMC

OPERATION NAME	DATE	LOCATION	ASSAULT FORCE
Galvanic	11/20/43	Butaritari Is. (Makin); Gilbert Is.	USA
		Betio Is. (Tarawa); Gilbert Is.	USMC
Director	12/15/43	New Britain Is.; Solomon Is.	USA
Backhander	12/26/43	New Britain Is.; Solomon Is.	USMC
Dexterity	1/2/44	Saidor, New Guinea	USA
Shingle	1/22/44	Anzio, Italy	USA
Flintlock	2/1/44	Roi, Namur, Kwajalein Is.; Marshall Is.	USMC, USA
Catchpole	2/17–19/44	Eniwetok, Parry, Enbegi Is.; Marshall Is.	USA, USMC
Brewer	2/29/44	Los Negros Is.; Bismarck Is.	USA
Persecution	4/22/44	Tanahmerah Bay, New Guinea	USA
Reckless	4/22/44	Aitape, Humboldt Bay, New Guinea	USA
Hurricane	5/27/44	Baik Is.; Schouten Is.	USA
Overlord	6/6/44	Normandy, France	USA
Forager	6/15/44	Saipan Is.; Marianas Is.	USMC, USA
Forager	7/21/44	Guam Is.; Marianas Is.	USMC
Forager	7/24/44	Tinian Is.; Marianas Is.	USMC
Typhoon	7/30/44	Sansapor, New Guinea	USA
Dragoon	8/15/44	Southern France	USA
Stalemate	9/15–17/44	Peleliu, Angaur Is.; Palau Is.	USMC, USA
King II	10/20/44	Leyte Is.; Philippine Is.	USA
?	12/15/44	Mindoro Is.; Philippine Is.	USA
Musketeer II	1/9/45	Luzon Is.; Philippine Is.	USA

OPERATION NAME	DATE	LOCATION	ASSAULT FORCE
Detachment	2/19/45	Iwo Jima; Bonin Is.	USMC
Victor III	2/28/45	Palawan Is.; Philippine Is.	USA
Victor IV	3/10/45	Zamboanga Is.; Philippine Is.	USA
Iceberg	4/1/45	Okinawa, Ryukyu Is.	USMC, USA
Victor V	4/17/45	Mindanao Is.; Philippine Is.	USA

To Foreign Shores

INTRODUCTION

The events of World War II, now a half century past, continue to hold our interest. A benchmark in American history, the war defined an entire generation and set the nation on a course that it steered for almost fifty years. The war had a profound effect on American perceptions of its military men. The war transformed the armed services from afterthoughts into full-fledged participants in the nation's political and economic life. The years 1941–45 have assumed almost mythical status as the last time when all Americans were so united in a common purpose.

Millions of us grew up hearing our fathers and uncles, and sometimes our mothers and aunts, telling tales of the South Pacific, of that day over Regensburg, or simply of what they were doing when news of victory arrived. Pearl Harbor, Midway, Normandy, the Battle of the Bulge, and V-J Day were all part of our historical experience. On a less-personal level, Americans generally know the war began with the disaster at Pearl Harbor, progressed through a slow comeback, and ended with two atomic bombs dropped on Japan.

Many images of the war are familiar, too. Among the more memorable: Battleship Row aflame at Pearl Harbor, huddled infantrymen about to leave their landing craft at Omaha Beach, and that knot of marines raising the colors on Iwo Jima. The latter two photos are central to this narrative. Those soldiers about to land in Normandy and the marines on Iwo were participating in the greatest amphibious campaign ever conducted. Everyone interested in World War II history knows American soldiers and marines made many amphibious landings, often against fierce opposition. But most people know little about how the specialized tactics of amphibious warfare were developed and put into practice. The reason amphibious forces have remained comparatively unsung is clear: amphibious warfare is simply not glamorous. Ships that lift assault forces are large and clumsy, lacking the sleek lines of destroyers or the formidable presence of an aircraft carrier. While combat and news photographers were usually present in droves to record landings, far fewer stayed to cover the mundane task of unloading supplies. This book seeks to redress that imbalance.

Amphibious warfare doctrine, like carrier aviation, was still in its formative stages when the United States entered World War II. Landing soldiers or marines across a beach was not a new experience for the Navy, but none of America's services had ever assaulted a fortified beach or atoll. Preparations to do that had begun before the war started, but even so, every landing that followed was a learning experience. Large-scale amphibious capability was crucial to Allied strategy; without it there was no way the Allies could reenter Europe, or the Americans could cross the Pacific. Considering competing demands for aircraft carriers and other warships, building the necessary thousands of amphibious ships and landing craft represented a significant and vital commitment of scarce resources.

Producing the many different craft needed for amphibious operations involved thousands of workers who had never been near a shipyard. Typical was the workhorse Landing Ship, Tank, better known by her naval acronym LST. Two-thirds of the LSTs delivered to the Navy were built at new shipyards on the Ohio and Illinois Rivers. The Missouri Valley Bridge & Iron Company of Evansville, Indiana, built 166 LSTs, the wartime record. The yard was built from scratch beginning in February 1942 and launched its first ship only eight months later. As the neophyte shipbuilders in all the yards became more experienced, on average an LST was being launched every day. Without these efforts the amphibious campaign on so many fronts would never have achieved the momentum so crucial to its success.

As the number of available ships increased, amphibious forces became the cutting edge of the global Allied offensive. Assaults launched from the sea decided the war, but the Allied capability of striking from the sea wherever they chose to shortened it considerably. Had there been no amphibious doctrine in place before hostilities commenced, the war would surely have lasted years longer, because victory in World War II was clearly a combined-arms result. With their Marine Corps and Army comrades-in-arms, the Navy's amphibious forces were central to victory.

This is the story of how amphibious doctrine developed and how it was put into practice during World War II. Although the book is written mainly from the naval viewpoint, the Army and Marine Corps are well represented. As much as possible the narrative incorporates reports written at the time as well as the recollections of participants.

There were mistakes, of course, and some inter-service bickering, and the inevitable ego clashes among talented and confident officers. Nonetheless, the story of U.S. amphibious operations in World War II reflects credit on many who gave their best to solve difficult problems under the most arduous and dangerous circumstances. Our country was fortunate to have had so many visionary and dedicated citizens, whose accomplishments are no less noteworthy more than fifty years later.

1

IN THE BEGINNING

Just before dawn 15 February 1945, most of the 23,000 Japanese comprising the Iwo Jima garrison are still asleep in the hundreds of tunnels and bunkers they have painstakingly dug into the island's volcanic soil. In one of scores of positions deep in the slopes of Mount Suribachi, a Japanese sentry wonders whether the bombers or the ships will attack today. After two months of steady U.S. bombing, Tokyo has warned the island that the American fleet is at sea—invasion is imminent.

For the hundredth time of this long watch, as on many before it, the sentry peers across the beaches of black ash and lapping surf, searching the vast ocean for any sign that the Americans are at hand. Peering through his bunker firing slit he sees that on this morning as on so many others all that meets his studied gaze is the silent, rolling sea.

As he turns away, he wishes the universal soldier's wish: that he was home. The sentry's wait will soon be over. Tomorrow's dawn will bring a fleet of American warships and the beginning of a thunderous three-day bombardment. More threatening to him would be knowing that two-days' sail behind the men-of-war an armada of less-graceful ships is bearing right for him carrying all the sinews of twentieth-century war. After more than three years of war with the United States, the defenders of Iwo Jima have no illusions about the strength of the coming attack. Their commander knows an amphibious assault is a most difficult military operation to carry out. He has driven his soldiers hard to prepare their defenses; if the Americans can be stalled at the waterline, the landing will fail. The defenders are therefore ready to endure the bombardment they know will precede the assault. They are under strict orders not to fire a shot until that decisive moment when troop-laden landing craft arrive at the beach.

Neither are there any illusions among the more than 80,000 American marines packed into the approaching ships. They know from hard experience that their enemy is skillful and willing to fight to the last man. They also know the coming battle will be hard, though few are prepared for its eventual cost.

In a global war that saw many D-days, the assault on Iwo Jima epitomized the amphibious war so integral to that larger conflict. Successfully landing and sustaining troops on a well-defended shore far from support bases demands detailed planning, determined and experienced leaders, adequate means, a high degree of training, flawless coordination among naval, ground, and air forces, and the sort of valor that will not accept even the possibility of failure.

The annals of warfare include stories of invasions from the sea that either meanly failed or gloriously triumphed. A particular fierceness seems to attend battles waged at the water's edge—perhaps caused by the defender's knowledge that to succeed, he has only to prevent the invaders from gaining a foothold. Meanwhile, the invader lands knowing that a retreat into the sea is a most desperate proposition. In the battle for Iwo Jima, more than 22,000 members of the Marine Corps, Army, and Navy were killed or wounded; only 1,200 Japanese survived from the garrison of 23,000. More men and more ships had participated in the Normandy landings the previous June, and even more would be involved in the Okinawa landing only a few weeks later. In Normandy the invaders suffered particularly heavy casualties on one of the five landing beaches; the defenders of Okinawa would not even fight for the beaches, choosing instead to concentrate their efforts well inland. The ferocity of the battle for Iwo Jima was acknowledged later by Fleet Admiral Chester Nimitz: "Uncommon valor was a common virtue." Iwo Jima was the culminating act of a long and especially bitter war that had no historic precedents in its scale.

During three bloody years of combat, American fighting men had amassed an unsurpassed knowledge of the problems inherent in amphibious warfare and developed previously undreamed-of solutions. Strange and awkward ships in the hundreds were built, and doctrines devised to govern their use. Hundreds of thousands of lawyers, teachers, truck drivers, farmhands, and boys with high school fight songs still ringing in their ears donned navy blue and took the new ships down to the sea. Joined by their army and marine comrades-in-arms, they sailed their ships from the rivers and ports of the United States into every distant corner of a world at war.

Place names like Guadalcanal, Mehedia, Licata, Anzio, Tarawa, Biak, and Peleliu forever became part of America's military history. Of the thousands of sailors and marines present at Iwo that February day, only the professional military men among them appreciated that they were witnessing an operation that had progressed from theory to practice in just over ten years. The ships carrying marines to Iwo Jima and the landing craft that put them ashore were the offspring of a doctrine formalized only in 1934. Secretary of the Navy James Forrestal recognized the long road traveled by that force of marines who erected an American flag atop Mount Suribachi on 23 February when he turned to Marine Gen. Holland M. Smith and said, "Holland, the raising of that flag on Suribachi means a Marine Corps for the next five hundred years." The path to the summit of Mount Suribachi had been fraught with difficulties.

The United States Navy before World War II was no newcomer to the challenges of amphibious warfare. For almost two hundred years, American soldiers and marines had landed across beaches from Maine to the Philippines. Neither was the Navy unaware of the obstacles other navies and armies had encountered. The 1915 failure of the British landing at Gallipoli cast such a long shadow after World War I that many military planners believed amphibious assaults were no longer feasible. The realities of the well-armed and revolutionary nationalism inspired by the Treaty of Versailles dictated that the amphibious puzzle had to be confronted and solved, no matter how much America craved "normalcy." The doctrine that evolved in the twenties and thirties responded to a modern need. The invasion fleet massing off Iwo Jima that late-winter morning in 1945 had its antecedents almost two centuries earlier, in the days before the American Revolution.

THE FIRST AMPHIBIANS: 1704–1915

Americans began participating in amphibious landings even before they had a navy, much less a country. Before the Revolution, American colonists cooperated with the Royal Navy in operations against the French. When the war for independence broke out, Continental forces mounted an abortive amphibious assault against a British fort at Casco, Maine, that ended in disaster with the American ships destroyed and their naval commander cashiered. American marines scored an early amphibious success when they landed in the Bahamas to seize a British fort. Americans were on the receiving end of amphibious operations when the British exercised their control of the sea to mount several assaults against the colonists. In the years after the Revolution the new American Navy put small landing forces ashore in defense of American economic interests. Even so, it wasn't until the Mexican-American War that the Navy had to deal with the problem of delivering a large body of soldiers onto a hostile shore.

In the spring of 1847, the Navy landed 12,000 men at Vera Cruz.

Naval officers and men showed considerable ingenuity in providing landing boats and the Navy got a first-hand lesson in the power of steam propulsion. The next exposure to large-scale amphibious operations came during the Civil War. While choking off seaborne access to the ports of the Confederacy, federal forces conducted extensive amphibious operations. With no recent experience, and an army and navy greatly diluted by volunteers, not all these landings were equally successful. All were integral, however, to the eventual success of the federal blockade that deprived the Confederacy of foreign trade and foreign arms. With the end of that war, large-scale amphibious warfare vanished from the U.S. Navy's corporate memory for more than thirty years.

The Civil War did not change overall American naval strategy. The huge Union Navy deteriorated quickly as the nation returned to commercial pursuits. What ships remained settled into the traditional routine of showing the flag and subsisting on sparse appropriations. While Britain's Royal Navy was steadily building steel ships, the wooden frigates of the United States Navy grew older and dowdier. The naval memory of riverine and combined operations grew ever dimmer. A reformist movement began in 1873 with formation of the U.S. Naval Institute, but not until 1883 were any modern, American steel ships laid down. The Naval War College was created in 1884 and began classes in 1885. Though Congress authorized the first battleships in 1886, the conceptual change to a modern navy really began in 1890 with publication of Alfred Mahan's *The Influence of Sea Power on History*. The U.S. fleet that grew eventually out of Mahan's thesis soon discovered it needed more than the seamanship to fight fleet actions. A global-power navy also had to know how to put ashore large numbers of troops far from home.

The first test for the new steel navy came in 1898. Months of jingoism over Cuban independence created such a public furor that President McKinley reluctantly opted to declare war on Spain. The fleet engagements that destroyed Spanish naval power are well recorded. Not so well known is that a battalion of marines landed at Guantánamo Bay on 10 June; another 16,000 American soldiers landed eighteen miles east of Santiago between 22 and 25 June. Fortunately for the American invaders of Cuba, the landings were unopposed. A marine officer writing years later thought the only notable aspect of his landing was its disorganization. Another 13,400 troops were landed in the Philippines and in Puerto Rico. As part of a war that saw the United States entering the ranks of the colonial, big-navy powers, these landings planted the seeds of future amphibious doctrine.

In the victorious afterglow of the Spanish-American War, naval leaders faced some new and unexpected issues. If the United States Navy were to defend national interests against other big-navy powers, it had to prepare for fleet action on a scale larger than any previously conceived. To be a successful colonial power, the U.S. would have to defend its Philippine possession. To give this new foreign policy teeth, the United States would have to project its will all the way to the wharves of the great Chinese trading ports. The steel, big-gunned fleet had proved itself a powerful instrument of war, but it was short-legged and needed close-at-hand bases to recoal. Any campaign fought across the vastness of the Pacific would necessarily entail seizing and defending an advanced base. Mahan's disciples realized that to secure these bases, the Navy would need a specialized land force to accompany the fleet. That perceived need couldn't have come at a better time for the Marine Corps; some naval officers believed the Marines no longer had a purpose in the steel navy. Developing a specialized landing force would give the Corps new definition and a true mission.

Planning a naval strategy to employ the new fleet properly became the province of the Navy's General Board, established in 1900. Three years later, the Joint Army–Navy Board was created, charged with coordinating planning. Four officers from each service served on the Joint Board and despite considerable bickering contrived to work out a series of war plans that shaped American strategy. Each potential enemy was given an identifying color, so the Joint Board's efforts were known as the "Color Plans." War Plan Orange, assigned to Japan, became a main force driving development of amphibious warfare doctrine.

At the tactical level, the General Board directed the Marines to establish a school dedicated to solving problems of seizing and defending fleet bases. The next few years saw varying levels of attention and funding devoted to the advanced base issue. By December 1913, however, navy and marine planners had decided upon a 2,600-man marine brigade sufficiently equipped to repel an enemy landing force. The planners chose the islands of Culebra and Vieques off Puerto Rico as the training grounds for evaluating the new ideas they had formulated.

After intensive organization and training, the Marines tested the advance base force concept in an exercise carried out on Culebra in January 1914. Three weeks' hard work later the troops landed equipment, dug in, then defended their positions against mock attacks from units of the Atlantic Fleet. Observers judged the Marines successful at defending the bases, thus validating the theory of advance-base operations. Though not amphibious assault training in the strictest sense, these exercises were a first step toward preparing for what was coming.

However, amphibious warfare receded into the background during late summer 1914, when the attention of the Marine Corps was drawn to events in Europe. Nationalism and an unrestrained arms race had brought on the first general war since the defeat of Napoleon. World War I is well known for stalemated trench warfare. Marines were brigaded with soldiers and fought valiantly, with one Army division even commanded by a Marine general. Of particular importance to Marines was the dismal failure of the British landing at Gallipoli, Turkey.

A large British invasion force was bottled up on a small beachhead and eventually forced to withdraw after severe losses. A leading British naval officer said Gallipoli proved amphibious operations conducted in daylight were "folly." "All our amphibious operations after this, whether attacking or evacuating, were carried out with as many hours of darkness at hand as possible and also have a regard to the vital importance of surprise. . . ."[1]

Although some American marine and naval officers viewed the operation differently, the disaster at Gallipoli caused a general belief among all military planners that massed amphibious assaults were impossible. Even as the world recoiled from the horrors wrought by the war, farsighted military thinkers were contemplating the future. The revolution in Russia gave new impetus to the forces of nationalism everywhere. Technological developments had placed ever-more-destructive and capable weapons in the hands of existing powers. Fortunately for the United States, some Americans were among those visionaries.

PLANNING FOR A DANGEROUS FUTURE

Few civilians in any nation can understand why professional soldiers and sailors are always planning for the next war they might be asked to fight. This process is not born from any desire for war, but from the need to be prepared if war should come. Not only are old enemies included in these plans, but new ones, alone and in combination, are considered, too. Following World War I, German naval power had been expelled from the Pacific by treaty, leaving the vast ocean mainly to Britain, the United States, and Japan. Although there were U.S. war plans for a conflict with Britain, the countries' shared interests and cultural affinity made that event unlikely. If there were to be a war in the Pacific, most military planners were certain it would be with the Japanese, whose militant nationalism and commitment to a large, modern navy were apparent after their victory in the Russo-Japanese War. The threat was the Imperial Japanese Navy, geography dictating that control of the Pacific peoples and their resources demanded control of the sea.

The basic American strategy evolved before World War I, envisioning a decisive fleet battle fought in the Western Pacific. Executing that strategy, however, called for the U.S. fleet to advance across the Pacific, presupposing a forward base in the Philippines from which the fleet could be supported. Two major problems confronted American war planners: The Philippines were much closer to Japan than to the United States, suggesting that no advanced base could be defended there. The second problem made solution of the first more difficult: During World War I, control of the Marshall, Caroline, and Mariana Islands had passed from Germany to Japan. If the Japanese established air and naval bases in their new mandate, the route across the Central Pacific would be effectively barred to any American advance to the Philippines or the home islands of Japan. American distrust of Japanese intentions increased when Western access to the new island possessions was strictly limited by Japan. Naval planners could see that for an American fleet to advance across the Central Pacific, it would first have to reduce the new Japanese outposts.

Those Americans who believed a war with Japan was a distinct possibility had the company of a keenly interested British writer. Hector Bywater believed the United States and Japan were fated to fight for control of the Pacific and recorded his thoughts in two books, *Sea Power in the Pacific* and *The Great Pacific War*. Bywater's books, especially the latter, garnered attention from professional officers of both Pacific navies. The British writer predicted war would begin with a surprise strike by the Japanese designed to overcome American superiority in numbers. This strike would be coincident with well-planned amphibious operations aimed at the Philippines. Contrary to what most Americans felt at the time, Bywater was certain the Japanese would initially be successful in defeating the U.S. Navy and seizing the Philippines. He did not believe, however, that the United States would accept such a defeat.

After a difficult year and a half, Bywater predicted, the Americans would make a counterthrust across the Central Pacific aimed at capturing the Marshall and Caroline Islands. Faced with penetration of their defensive perimeter and a direct threat to their home islands, the Japanese would be forced into a decisive naval battle that they would lose. Although the first edition of *The Great Pacific War* featured battleships as the decisive weapon, Bywater was astute enough to recognize the growing importance of the aircraft carrier and amended later editions accordingly. The effect Bywater's writings had on Japanese war plans has recently been the subject of scholarly debate; the actual course of the war followed the author's scenario uncannily.

Bywater was not the only one predicting the course of the coming war. Interestingly, a marine officer had foreseen the need to drive the Japanese from their new island bases, and he created a blueprint for the future. Lt. Col. Earl "Pete" Ellis had predicted as early as 1912 that Japan would someday attack American territory in the Pacific and an American counteroffensive would have to cross the Central Pacific against strong opposition. In 1920–21, Ellis put forth his ideas in "Advanced Base Operations in Micronesia," a paper describing in detail how an American amphibious campaign should be conducted. Specifically, Ellis said a campaign against

Japan should be directed first through the Marshall and Caroline Islands, then at the Japanese home islands.

Tactically, Ellis insisted the landing force should be completely organized and loaded before leaving port. He believed transfers at sea were impractical and counterproductive. Ellis advised against night amphibious operations, too, preferring attacks at first light, with the Navy's role to guard the flanks of the landing area, providing heavy gunfire support as needed.

The paper called for air support to be provided by a naval air arm, for approaches to the beaches to be cleared of obstructions, for the beaches themselves to be properly marked and controlled, for specialist troops such as artillerymen and signalers to land with the first wave of attackers, and for naval gunfire support to be directed by trained spotters. Ellis stressed that rapid ship-to-shore movement of troops was essential, with their deployment on a broad front crucial. Ambivalent about smoke screens, he feared they would mask the enemy more than they protected the invaders.

Ellis concluded that offensive amphibious operations should be the primary mission of the Marine Corps. His paper found ready acceptance in July 1921 by Maj. Gen. John Lejeune, commandant of the Corps. Lejeune came to his office determined that the Marines would distinguish themselves from the Army by always being ready to take the field. If the Japanese were to be the chief enemy, being ready to mount an amphibious assault seemed a logical focus. Lejeune and other like-minded officers, among them Holland M. Smith, therefore championed Ellis's ideas. Both Lejeune and Smith were tireless and outspoken in their efforts to convince their naval counterparts that neither the mere presence offshore of a large fleet nor the traditional ad hoc landing parties of sailors and marines was sufficient to meet the needs of twentieth-century warfare. As usual, change was incremental.

Reinforcing and holding the Philippines remained the keystone of American strategic planning in the Pacific. Even so, Lejeune exerted enough influence on the Joint Board so that it assigned to the Marine Corps the specific task of conducting amphibious operations.[2] What the Marines had to do next was convert theory into practical doctrine and usable hardware. An exercise on 1 February 1924 showed how much work the Navy and Marines had left to do if they were to make Ellis's ideas a reality.

As part of Fleet Problem Number 4 in February 1924, 1,700 marines landed on Culebra Island after an hour of simulated bombardment by battleships. As Marine Brig. Gen. Eli Cole reported in the aftermath, all was not well: "chaos reigned. The boat officers had not been informed of the designated landing beaches. There was no order maintained among the boats carrying the landing party. Certain boats became lost for a time and landings were made on beaches which had not been designated for certain units."[3]

There were other significant problems as well. The transport was not loaded properly, the boats were considered to have been under fire too long, and food was slow coming ashore. Fairness dictates that despite the Navy's predominant institutional bias toward a big-gun fleet, developing amphibious doctrine was not the sole purview of the Marines.

The commander of the naval attack force at Culebra later concluded, "the Navy should develop a doctrine on the seizure, defense and attack of naval advanced bases [and] . . . should undertake training for the solution of such problems. . . ."[4] In 1925, Rear Adm. Robert Coontz said that developing specialized landing craft and proper naval gunfire-support technique was essential to the success of American war plans:

> use of regular ships' boats for . . . transporting landing parties ashore, when opposition is to be encountered, is a hazardous undertaking and little likely to succeed. . . . it [is] of the utmost importance that experiments be continued . . . to determine what type of boat is best. . . . a landing operation is likely to [be a] disaster if the officers in charge of the boats are not experienced. . . .[5]

Solutions to these problems developed slowly for several reasons, chief among them that most of the Marine Corps was busy protecting America's colonial interests in Central America and China. Second, there was resistance within the Corps; many marine officers were wedded to the style of warfare they had experienced in France during World War I. On the naval side, there was a decided lack of interest among all but a few officers. As Rear Adm. Walter Ansel remembered years later, "[amphibious warfare] wasn't the way to promotion and pay. The way to rise was to take ships to sea and go squads right and squads left and do sea maneuvers and fight play actions against another outfit with guns, torpedoes, and so on."[6]

The twenties and thirties were also a period of extreme fiscal hardship for the services; the traditional American dislike of military expenditures was strengthened by the apparent success of the Washington Naval Treaty and a strong anti-war, isolationist sentiment. One naval historian estimates that in 1935, only $40,000 was available for development of landing craft.[7] Despite inertia and competing claims on scarce resources, Ellis's ideas managed to inch closer to fruition.

The Culebra exercises saw the first experiments with landing craft built solely for that purpose. All landing exercises to that point had been hampered because no equipment larger than what could be manhandled over the gunwales of a standard ship's boat could be moved ashore. A prototype 55-ft., wooden-hulled boat with a steel cover was built in 1923, but proved highly unwieldy, its steel cover promised mainly to "prevent a hundred

Marines or so from getting out if the boat capsized or sank."[8] A cumbersome device known as boat-rig A was eventually devised that allowed vehicles to be landed from a standard 50-ft. motor launch, but the rig weighed 4,700 lb., took eight men ten minutes to erect, and so overloaded the boat that it could be used only under the most favorable conditions. No production hardware resulted from these early tests, but they were the first steps toward developing practical landing craft.

The Marine Corps School at Quantico increased the amount of lecture time devoted to amphibious operations from two hours in the 1924–25 course to forty-nine hours in 1926–27 and two hundred hours in 1927–28.[9] A committee of four marine majors and Navy Lt. Walter Ansel put much of the accumulated experience into writing in 1932. Entitled *Marine Corps Landing Operations*, it was the first American military publication devoted solely to amphibious problems. The crystalline moment for the modern Marine Corps arrived in January 1933, when the Joint Board issued a general doctrine covering the conduct of joint Army-Navy overseas operations.

Among other things, "Joint Overseas Expeditions" addressed the problems of amphibious operations, the primary responsibility for which had been previously assigned to the Marine Corps. Ellis's and Lejeune's followers were quick to seize the moment: Maj. Gen. John Russell outlined a plan to Marine Commandant Ben Fuller for the formation of a standing body of marines trained and equipped for expeditionary operations in support of the fleet. No longer would marine troop strength be splintered among assignments to shore stations, expeditionary forces, and ship detachments. On 7 December 1933, Navy Department General Order 241 created the Fleet Marine Force, replacing the former Marine Corps Expeditionary Force. Even while this organizational change was taking place, the doctrine that would guide it was being formalized.

Commandant Fuller had seen in the issuance of the Joint Board doctrine an opportunity to deflect another challenge to the existence of the Corps. Army Chief of Staff Gen. Douglas MacArthur had reawakened the old cry for the Marines to be absorbed into the Army. Something was needed to set the capabilities of the Corps so distinctly apart from that of the soldiers as to make the Marines' continued existence certain. To realize that goal, Fuller suspended classes and ordered the staff and students of the Marine Corps School to develop a detailed plan for conducting amphibious operations. Led by Col. Ellis Bell Miller, the school went to work, studying the past for clues to what might be done in the future.

Their labors produced a document issued in January 1934 as the *Tentative Manual for Landing Operations*. That its creators got it mostly right in what has been called a "remarkable document" is demonstrated by what the original manual spawned: After one metamorphosis as the *Tentative*

Landing Operations Manual in 1935, it became the Navy's *Fleet Training Publication 167, Landing Operations Doctrine, U.S. Navy* in 1938. Further proof of its influence is found in the manual's almost verbatim adoption by the Army as the basis for its own field manual on amphibious operations. Even after three revisions, in May 1941, August 1942, and August 1943, the tenets of the original manual remained operative throughout World War II. In only a few months, a handful of dedicated officers had created the operational guidelines for the most complex and far-ranging amphibious operations the world would ever see.

The new manual and its revisions addressed the component parts of an amphibious operation with specific answers. The naval commander had authority over all parts of the task force, amphibious and support ships alike, as well as all embarked personnel. Experience would cause some changes, but the age-old problem of who commanded what in a joint expedition seemed to have been answered. The manual then asserted that despite the known limitations on capability and control of naval gunfire, such support was essential for any landing to succeed. More effective ammunition and methods of fire control would have to be developed to overcome deficiencies and existing capabilities would have to be maximized. Naval officers would be assigned to shore fire-control parties to direct ship gunfire.

Air support was recognized as an important component of a successful assault. Naval and marine airmen would range ahead of the assault force on scouting and softening-up missions. The manual writers believed what was lost in surprise by aerial assaults would be more than made up by increased offensive punch. Once the invasion began, the airmen would prevent enemy air power from intervening, spot for ship gunfire, and disrupt defender reinforcements. There was considerable discussion and some argument about the role of airpower, but the framework was in place for what eventually evolved as doctrine.

The new manuals envisioned ship-to-shore movement in a much more coordinated and powerful attack than ever before. The basic assault unit was a marine infantry battalion integrated with supporting arms and all necessary equipment embarked. Transports carrying the assault force would anchor opposite the landing beach and disembark troops into assault craft carried to the scene by the transports. The assault craft would proceed in a group to the line of departure and from there to the beach in line-abreast formation. Landing boats would be armed and capable of putting down enough fire to keep the beach defenders' heads down. Artillery and light tanks were to be included in the earliest possible phase of the landing. Once the first-wave troops were ashore, follow-up waves of infantry and support elements were to be coordinated and directed by a naval beach party and a shore party made up of army or marine personnel.

Specific directions described combat loading of the transports. Supplies that would be used first were loaded at the top of the hold in the order needed. Less essential items were loaded farther down with the least essential at the bottom. Tables were worked up listing cubic dimensions of all equipment; quartermaster officers used these tables and plans of ship holds to figure loading schemes for each transport.

If the *Tentative Manual* missed anything, it was adequate emphasis on logistics. It did not mention follow-up supply efforts and no provision was made for permanent shore parties. This oversight was corrected in FTP 167. Even with thirty-two pages of instructions, logistics would long remain the stepchild of amphibious operations.

DEVELOPING THE TOOLS: 1935–1941

Obviously, there is a difference between laying instructions out on paper and putting them into action. The Fleet Landing Exercises, annual events conducted from 1935 through 1941, subjected every section of the manuals to the rigors of operational testing. While there was significant artificiality associated with the exercises, they nonetheless acquainted a generation of planners and soon-to-be generals with real problems of delivering large forces onto a hostile shore. Besides the familiar beaches of Culebra Island, the Marines began maneuvers at San Clemente Island off the coast of Southern California.

During these exercises, observers confirmed that armor-piercing naval shells had little bombardment value against exposed troops or open defensive positions like artillery emplacements. The exercises demonstrated that the technical difficulties inherent in the flat trajectories of naval guns were not insurmountable; a ship could compensate by changing firing positions and by intensive gunnery training. Meanwhile, the Navy's efforts to develop an effective dual-purpose gun resulted in an unexpected benefit for the amphibious forces: The new 5-in./38-caliber gun had ballistics better suited to indirect fire than existing weapons. Furthermore, the gun fired a thin-walled projectile with a comparatively large bursting charge fusable for air or surface detonation, making it lethal against personnel and exposed positions. Along with these advances in hardware came an accompanying evolution of doctrine.

Various targets and gunfire missions called for specific types of ships. Destroyers seemed best for close-support fire missions like beach defenses and coastal artillery batteries. Cruisers and battleships got the jobs of deep support and long-range missions associated with neutralizing an enemy's artillery positions, harassing reserve areas and supply lines, and disrupting communications. To aid shipboard observers and the shore fire-control parties, aviators got considerable practice in spotting for naval gunfire, a task made a lot simpler by development of the gridded map. Aviators also de-voted considerable effort to learning the fundamentals of effective ground support.

The need for specialized landing craft was reconfirmed, as ordinary ship's boats remained unsuitable for rapid landing and deployment of large numbers of assault troops.[10] In 1937, Marine Lt. Victor Krulak saw what he immediately recognized to be the answer to the problem. Krulak was serving with the 4th Marines in China, where the Japanese were waging a full-scale war of conquest. He was able to observe a Japanese assault land-ing that included the use of "exactly what the Marines had been looking for—sturdy, ramp-bow-type boat capable of transporting heavy vehicles and depositing them directly on the beaches. What we saw was that the Japanese were light years ahead of us in landing craft design."[11] Among the few naval officers who were trying to meet the challenge was Walter Ansel. He remembers the frustrations of the early days:

> As a low lieutenant, I stomped around the Navy Department, at the behest of the Marines, to work up an interest in the development of the craft. We had three primitive types and we wanted to try them out. We had some exercises, and we went high and low stealing rum-runners' boats and other things of that sort . . . and trying them out in these small exercises. I couldn't get a flicker of interest in the Navy Department on developing a landing craft, or any interest in landing operations.[12]

Ansel's words gain added confirmation from Krulak's recollection of what became of the "enthusiastic" report he had filed from China about Japanese progress in developing landing craft: "two years later, in July 1939, upon returning to the United States, I spent a day hunting for my report in the files of the Navy's Bureau of Ships. Finally unearthed, I was chagrined to read a marginal comment from some bureau skeptic, that the report was the work of 'some nut out in China.' "[13] Krulak's experience was typical of the time; while he watched the Japanese employ a variety of mission-built landing craft, the Marines were able to convince the Navy to purchase only a single design from a New Orleans–based boatbuilder named Andrew Higgins. That one-boat buy was the fortunate beginning of a relationship between the Marine Corps and Higgins that would have important consequences for the development of amphibious warfare.

An energetic, self-made man of considerable talent, Higgins developed an affinity for the Marines. Krulak believed that Marine determination to have the proper boats struck a chord with Higgins's own straight-ahead directness in solving a problem. It would be unfair to say that the Navy was making *no* effort to prepare for what was coming: the drumbeat ap-proach of war was beginning to have some effect. The Secretary of the Navy created the Continuing Board for the Development of Landing Craft in 1937; funds remained scarce but at least a mechanism was in place dedicated to solving this problem. One result was that several experiments begun under the "Special Boat Plan" of 1938 would over the next three years put some extremely useful hardware into the hands of the Navy and Marines.

Along with technical advances came further doctrinal developments for solving the major amphibious problem: night landings were difficult to control and carry out. Cargo nets draped over the ships' sides replaced gangways for loading assault troops into landing craft, a technique used throughout World War II and since. Although combined Army–Marine Corps operations were few, they did demonstrate to the Marines that the Army field radios were superior to theirs. Unfortunately, durable, reliable radios would remain an unmet goal of the amphibious forces for some time. This lack of clear, effective communication would impair more than one landing.

Tonnage tables advanced combat loading by giving loading officers the basic information they needed. The Marines also argued that pending development of specially modified and equipped destroyers, warships or lightly armed transports should no longer carry troops. Beginning with conversions of some old four-stack destroyers, many destroyer-transports (APDs) were eventually built. But large transports remained the principal means by which assault troops traveled to the scene of action. Diverting warships from their primary job of protecting the transports and providing gunfire support for the troops ashore was also recognized as a waste of assets. There were other developments.

Army observers were present from the outset of the Fleet Landing Exercises, but army units first participated in the 1937 and 1938 exercises. Although Army amphibious doctrine had been slowly evolving in parallel with that of the Marines, that service had no Pete Ellis or Holland Smith to give it clear direction. There were also doctrinal differences between the services about command and tactics that stemmed from their unique perceptions of the amphibious problem. Marine focus was primarily on assaulting defended islands in the Pacific, an operation that presented a quite different military problem from forcing entry onto a continental landmass to open a large-scale campaign.

An amphibious planner of the time would probably have looked at the problem this way: when an island base was assaulted, the enemy was assumed to be cut off from reinforcement or resupply. His garrison had finite materiel and manpower, little or no air cover, and severely restricted mobility. The attacker could rely on naval gunfire and carrier-based air support, so he didn't have to bring along a large mass of armor or artillery with the assault force. The probable avenues of assault were known equally to attacker and defender, so surprise was not considered essential—thus, the marine belief that daylight landing operations were preferable to night. Finally, as long as the attacker controlled the sea approaches, his supply line was secure. An assault on a continental landmass, something the Army had to consider, presented an entirely different, far more complex set of problems.

As events in Europe unfolded, the German blitzkrieg graphically proved that an armored force combined with air power imbued an army with previously unknown striking power. Assaulting a landmass controlled by such an army meant the attacker *had* to include considerable armor and artillery in the landing force if he was to counter the mobility and firepower of the defenders. Given the limitations of carrier aviation at the time, considerable land-based air cover would be needed to suppress beach defenses and interdict enemy rear areas. Army planners believed surprise was essential and could be best achieved by making the landing under cover of darkness. As events would show, the Army justifiably believed that such an assault would be a shore-to-shore movement. Common to both services were the difficulties associated with putting ashore a small-to-medium-sized force for the sole purpose of conducting a raid. The legitimately different perceptions of the larger tactical problem were also complicated by other issues.

The 1935 update of the Joint Board's *Joint Action of the Army and Navy* attempted to address the issues of combined landing operations, but even after the Germans overran Western Europe and threatened to invade England, the Army still had no document on a par with the *Tentative Manual*. Even as late as 1940, the Army War College was devoting only three lecture hours each year to amphibious warfare. Most high-ranking army officers considered amphibious problems not especially difficult, an attitude that delayed a well-defined amphibious doctrine.

In fairness, Army energies were largely being devoted to rearming, developing an armored force, and absorbing the large mass of draftees flooding into the service. The publicity garnered by the Marines during their World War I service with the Army also contributed to resentment among Army leaders. Thus, Marine accomplishments in developing amphibious doctrine and equipment got less than their full respect in the Army. Only the clear prospect of war prompted the War Department to confront amphibious operations with greater urgency.

Despite their differing perceptions of the problem, Army commanders were impressed enough with what the Navy and Marines had accomplished to initiate the process that eventually saw FTP 167 adopted almost unchanged in June 1941 as the Army's Field Manual 31–5, *Landing Operations on Hostile Shores*. That the Army adopted a Navy manual did not eradicate some profound differences in perception about the nature of amphibious warfare: there would be some vicious bureaucratic battles over division of labor and the manner in which soldiers were to be landed on a hostile shore. Nonetheless, the progress represented by FM 31–5 was well timed. Europe was again engulfed in an all-out war and the Japanese were threatening to export their war with China to the rest of Asia.

DISTANT THUNDER: 1933–1941

The growth of Japanese naval strength and national ambition had not gone unrecognized by American military strategists. As early as 1933, navy planners began to reorient traditional American thinking away from a rush to the Philippines and more toward Ellis's ideas of a phased advance through the Central Pacific. A revised Plan Orange came out in 1935 that was supported by the Army, some of whose leaders had begun to believe the Philippines were indefensible. Concurrently, the increase in German military strength under Hitler forced army planners to broaden their own focus. A 1937 visit to Berlin by the Army's deputy chief of staff convinced him the Germans were the ultimate danger and that American war plans should be reoriented toward Europe. This fundamental disagreement with the offensive-minded Pacific orientation of the Navy led to a five-month review of American war plans over the winter of 1938–39. A new series of joint contingency plans, known as Rainbow 1 through 5, were outlined and accepted by the Joint Board in June 1939.

Three months later, President Roosevelt reached deep into the ranks of the Army's generals and chose George C. Marshall as the new chief of staff, the officer responsible for turning these plans into reality. Marshall's reputation for integrity and his ability as a planner were peerless. He was ambitious and possessed of a fierce temper that he controlled with the same discipline that marked his dedication to duty. He also had the important quality of recognizing excellence in subordinates and placing them in positions of responsibility. While Marshall was not personally close to the president, the two men forged a working relationship based on mutual trust and admiration. Marshall's sterling character and clear strategic vision would soon be of the utmost importance.

By the summer of 1940, continental Europe was under German control. The British retreated to their island and appeared to be tottering on the brink of defeat. Rainbow 2 had envisioned the United States confronting Japan while Britain and France kept Hitler in check, but that was clearly no longer a valid idea. Faced with a decided shortage of resources and a far different scenario, U.S. military planners shifted their attention to Rainbow 4 and began to think about simply defending the Western Hemisphere.

President Roosevelt did his best to help Britain, stall the Japanese, and provide resources for the military. General Marshall applauded the passage of conscription legislation, but recognized that the expected one-million-plus draftees did not constitute a combat-ready army. The misgivings of the Army's leadership were so great they warned the president not to provoke the Japanese. The Army generals were too aware that an army that could not field a single fully equipped division was grossly unprepared for a confrontation with Germany, much less a simultaneous war with Japan. Navy planners shared the apprehension of their Army counterparts. When asked by the Secretary of the Navy if the Navy was ready for war, the General Board responded with a resounding "No." Nonetheless, Roosevelt continued to press ahead; in October 1940, he directed the Secretary of the Navy and the Chief of Naval Operations to develop a comprehensive plan for cooperation with the British if America entered the war.

Working with Capt. Richmond Kelly Turner, Chief of Naval Operations Adm. Harold Stark put his thoughts into a paper titled "Memorandum on National Policy." Without knowing it, the CNO outlined the strategy America would follow throughout World War II. Stark clearly believed Germany was the threat that must be confronted first. His plan called for the United States to absorb Japanese blows in the Pacific while concentrating the bulk of American forces against the Germans. As Stark put it, "If Britain wins decisively against Germany, we could win everywhere; but . . . if she loses, the problems confronting us would be very great; and, while we might not lose everywhere, we might possibly not win anywhere."[14]

In his plan, the CNO declared that a large army of Americans would have to be transported across the Atlantic and landed in Europe to decide the issue. Once the Germans were defeated, the full weight of a United States offensive would be brought to bear in the Pacific, crushing the Japanese in their turn. To the surprise of the Navy men, Marshall agreed with Stark's conclusions and directed that his unchanged plan be the basis for future Army planning. Neither Stark nor Marshall foresaw the enormous investment in amphibious warfare resources that would be required to make this Plan Dog a reality. Stark's support for Britain was also consonant with Roosevelt's—FDR authorized joint British-American planning to begin quietly, as soon as possible.

At the end of January 1941, a British military mission slipped into Washington. The conference lasted until 27 March; fourteen meetings took place during which a framework of strategic cooperation was agreed upon despite the differing imperatives of both sides. With Stark's plan as the philosophical underpinning of the American participants, the conferees agreed that the weight of the allied effort was to be against Germany. Of profound importance to the entire course of the war was the British revelation of Ultra, the closely guarded ability to read German codes. What the meetings left undefined was the exact shape of how a possible war in the Pacific would be fought. American plans soon rectified that omission, defining the shape of the amphibious war.

The United States would prepare to fight the war's decisive campaign in Europe, Africa, or both. Sufficient forces would be allocated to the Pacific to deny the Japanese the resources of Malaya and the Dutch Indies as well as access to the Indian Ocean, defend but not reinforce the Philippines, and keep the sea lanes open to Australia. The planners assumed that the scheme would not go into effect before 1 September 1941. There were to be some intensely fought differences of opinion about adherence to the plan, but thereafter it was the operational guideline under which the United States fought the battles of World War II. There were some changes; the scope and circumstances of the war guaranteed that. The four men most responsible for changes were President Franklin Roosevelt, Admiral Ernest J. King, and Generals George Marshall and Douglas MacArthur.

Roosevelt's ideas about the course to follow in the Pacific had the most immediate impact. His main sympathies continued to lie with England, but he demonstrated a growing unwillingness to grant the Japanese a free hand. Roosevelt persuaded Congress to expand the Lend Lease Act of March 1941 (which opened a pipeline of free arms to the British) to provide similar aid to the hard-pressed Chinese. Even after the Germans invaded the Soviet Union in June 1941, Roosevelt's greater concern that summer was with the Japanese.

In July, he ordered creation of a new command in the Philippines and placed it under former Army chief of staff Douglas MacArthur, who was recalled to active service. MacArthur would become one of the most controversial personalities of American military history. He had gone to the Philippines in 1935, where he assumed command of the fledgling Philippine armed forces with the somewhat grandiose title of field marshal. His considerable abilities were more than matched by a colossal ego, a Machiavellian talent for political intrigue, and an almost messianic belief that America's chief sphere of interest lay in Asia. These qualities would figure prominently in the Pacific war.

MacArthur accepted the president's appointment and accompanying promotion to lieutenant general though it represented a demotion from his Philippine rank. That MacArthur was arrogant and his contemporaries thought him difficult were ignored. No one denied his talent, which the country needed. Roosevelt directed Marshall to reinforce MacArthur's forces in the Philippines, despite the strictures of Rainbow 5. Roosevelt also responded to Japanese seizure of French Indo-China (Vietnam) by freezing Japanese assets in the United States. As Kelly Turner had warned the chief of naval operations, war with the Japanese was thereby assured;

their intense nationalism would not permit concessions to the Americans. Ominous as it was, the storm gathering over the Pacific was not the only one threatening to burst over Americans.

War inched closer during September 1941, when President Roosevelt ordered the Navy to begin escorting convoys bound for England. After a U-boat fired on the destroyer *Greer*, he issued orders to shoot on sight any Axis unit. Within six weeks, a German torpedo hit the destroyer *Kearny*, killing eleven sailors. Another sank the destroyer *Reuben James* with 115 dead out of a crew of 149. The storm was breaking.

LAST-MINUTE PREPARATIONS: JANUARY–DECEMBER 1941

The problems of reconciling national policy and grand strategy are seen from their individual perspectives by the people at the forefront of creating the plans. Similarly, they are seen altogether differently by those not privy to the plans. The predominant perception of most Americans was that the United States should avoid involvement in the European war. So strong was this antiwar sentiment that a renewal of the conscription law passed the House by a single vote. An interest group known as America First staged rallies whose isolationist theme was cheered by thousands. Though the administration had quickly declared American neutrality in September 1939, the urgent need to be prepared was obvious to America's military professionals. They knew it was one thing to formulate plans and talk about offensives, but something else entirely to create the means to accomplish those plans. American strategic planners envisioned moving 413,900 men overseas within six months of commencing hostilities; every responsible officer in the War and Navy Departments knew there weren't enough trained men or transports to move that many.

During the first half of 1941, the drive to get the Navy and the amphibious forces ready was given added impetus through a fortunate combination of events. The most extensive in its consequences for the future was Roosevelt's January promotion and appointment of Admiral King to command the newly designated Atlantic Fleet. King was both a driven man and a driver of men. Upon taking command of the Atlantic Patrol Force in December 1940, he wasted no time emphasizing to his officers and sailors that they were preparing for war. His ships were darkened at sea, exercised constantly at general quarters, and were under strict orders to remain adequately provisioned and fueled. His uncompromising demand for excellence was soon felt throughout the fleet.

His sense of discipline also extended to his own actions: as was common in the Navy of that time, King was a hard drinker. By his account, he swore off hard liquor in March 1941, "for the duration and, very likely, after."[15] King's reputation was such that when Cdr. Ruthven Libby told a friend he had been ordered to King's staff, the friend said, "Well, what have you done to deserve this?"[16]

King's greatest attributes were his insistence that his subordinates use their initiative and his belief that they were "competent in their several command echelons unless and until they prove themselves otherwise."[17] He was ruthless in weeding out those who "proved themselves otherwise." George Dyer discovered just how ruthless after King became commander in chief. Then a commander on King's staff, Dyer was called into the boss's office and summarily told to relieve a rear admiral who was serving as intelligence officer and to have him out of the Navy Department by 1630 that afternoon.

Another vital component in American preparation for amphibious war was the steady rise of Marine Gen. Holland Smith. Smith was an early adherent to the gospel of amphibious warfare. He was an outspoken perfectionist who not only drove himself and his subordinates hard, but also drove his superiors with equal bluntness. Smith recorded in his memoirs that he first considered the problem of amphibious warfare in 1920, when he was assigned to the Naval War College after combat duty in France. What he found to be the naval approach to the problem did not impress Smith:

> Most naval minds refused to contemplate the endless new problems that must be solved to make a landing successful. Even the bitter lessons the British learned at Gallipoli had little effect on the War College. Let us consider the primary considerations involved. No special troops existed which had been trained for this task. Not a single boat in the naval service was equipped for putting troops ashore and retracting under its own power.[18]

The naval attitude "made [Smith's] blood boil."[19] As he rose in rank and responsibility, his unceasing and vocal demands for proper equipment and professional respect for the Marine Corps would in turn boil the blood of more than one admiral.

Smith took command of the 1st Marine Brigade in 1939, a position from which he unsparingly worked to convince the naval establishment that adequate resources and support must be allocated to amphibious warfare. In common with other officers, he recognized the need for purpose-built landing craft. After Krulak saw what had become of his report on Japanese landing craft, he built a wooden model of a ramp-bowed landing boat and brought it to Smith. Smith took one look at the model, said "That's it," and took Krulak and his handiwork in to see the commandant. The battles over design and procurement of landing craft that would occur over the next two years also made Smith one of Andrew Higgins's strongest backers. Smith's efforts were not limited to lobbying for landing craft; he also worked hard training the 1st Brigade.

The future received some definition in February 1941 when the brigade became the nucleus of the newly constituted 1st Marine Division. Smith's determination came to public attention when *Time* magazine gave him the nickname "Howlin' Mad." His biographer maintains that his supposed anger was a device to keep himself focused and to ensure that no one took him lightly. The same outspokenness that seemed so colorful to reporters brought Smith early on into conflict with an equally determined admiral named Ernest King. His relationship with King was stormy but later stood him in good stead.

Like many naval officers of his generation, King believed himself competent in military as well as naval matters. King was quick to announce that he considered amphibious forces an integral part of the fleet. He also soon made it clear that he believed he was as qualified as Smith to direct their employment. Smith was subordinate to King, a fact that did not prevent numerous arguments. The Marine general was neither cowed by King's reputation nor abashed in standing up for his beliefs. Their many disputes came to a head in early summer 1941, when King attempted to dictate to Smith the manner in which a proposed landing in the Azores would be conducted. Smith listened to the admiral with growing impatience.

> [Smith] finally exploded at King and told him he was going to issue the orders and he would determine the scheme of maneuvers for any operation, that no admiral was going to give orders to the Marines and tell them how to go and fight. That was his job. King replied heatedly, "I am commander-in-chief of the fleet, I'll have you relieved." "Relieved or not," Smith replied, "as long as I am in command, I am going to command."[20]

Apparently the argument was over Smith's selection of a landing beach. After this outburst by Smith, King allowed him to make his own selection, provided it was different from the one for which Smith had been fighting. King's compromise worked and he did not have to face relieving Smith. Admiral and general thereafter viewed each other with mutual respect; when King became commander in chief of U.S. Fleet, he was one of Smith's staunchest supporters.

Further groundwork for amphibious war was laid in May, when Congress authorized the Navy to acquire 550,000 tons of shipping for conversion to troop transports and cargo ships. Another important event was the 6 June 1941 creation of the First Joint Training Force and the appointment of Holland Smith as its commander. A like command was set up on the Pacific coast under Maj. Gen. Clayton Vogel.

Smith used the time remaining before the United States entered the war to push his amphibious corps, which consisted of the 1st Marine Division and the Army's 1st Infantry Division, to a higher state of readiness. More than 16,000 soldiers and marines participated in intensive exercises that took place at the new training ground at New River, North Carolina. The exercises again showed how unpolished amphibious technique continued to be. The troops embarked at widely scattered locations, troop commanders thought the Navy transports were too cramped and unsanitary, and shore parties were hopelessly overworked and disorganized.

But there were positive achievements. The "Special Boat Plan" of 1938 began to bear fruit: orders were placed for an armored, machine-gun-armed support craft (LCS) to accompany the landing boats. The first models of the new bow-ramped landing boat (LCP(R)), were successfully tested as was its new, larger cousin, the landing craft, mechanized (LCM). Andrew Higgins built both of the latter boats. The LCM was available only because Holland Smith and other Marines waged a long battle with the entrenched bureaucracy of the Navy's Bureau of Ships. The bureau had designed its own tank lighter, about which Smith disgustedly observed:

> In the 1941 Caribbean exercises, the Bureau of Ships supplied us with three, 45-foot tank lighters of its own design, capable of carrying one 16-ton tank or two 6-ton tanks. After the exercises I reported; "The Bureau type tank lighters are heavy, slow, difficult to control, difficult to retract from the beach and equipped with an unpredictable power plant." They were unmanageable and unseaworthy in heavy surf. One capsized.[21]

Despite these criticisms, the Bureau pressed ahead with its plans to produce the lighter. A chorus of Marine complaints finally convinced Admiral Stark to give Andrew Higgins a chance to produce a more capable boat. Higgins took a shallow draft boat intended for a Venezuelan company and modified it to Marine specifications in less than three days. The resulting boat proved far superior to the bureau design and, after intervention by Senator Harry Truman, entered into production as the LCM.

The development of the amphibious tractor (LVT) mirrored that of Higgins's LCM. The boat-hulled, tracked vehicle was originally designed by Donald Roebling for use in the Florida Everglades. An article in *Life* magazine eventually brought the craft to Marine and Navy attention: the vehicle seemed the perfect conveyance to get men safely over coral reefs or through the surf zone and onto the beach. The Marines made a formal request to the Navy in 1938 to buy one of Roebling's creations for evaluation. Acquisition was apparently as slow then as it is now; a tractor wasn't available until 1940. Victor Krulak was among the men who put the LVT through a series of strenuous tests that revealed its many shortcomings. Krulak believed all the defects to be correctable; in his enthusiasm to show what the tractor could do, he had the unenviable experience of stranding Ernie King on a coral reef.

At General Smith's request that he take a ride in the new craft, King reluctantly agreed but with the admonition that he had time for only a short run. Krulak wanted to show the admiral what the tractor could do and attempted to take it across a reef. As luck would have it, the LVT broke a track, leaving the fleet commander stranded beyond reach of a boat. King was quick with a few choice comments remembered by Krulak as "not intended to contribute to my long-term peace of mind." Dress whites notwithstanding, the admiral and his flag lieutenant clambered over the side and waded ashore through chest-deep water. After repairing the broken track, Krulak took the LVT back alongside the flagship. Telling his two crewmen that they might "never see him again," Krulak went aboard to report to Holland Smith. Smith listened to the sad tale and quietly told his lieutenant, "I took the heat."[22] Krulak's career fortunately survived, the bugs were worked out of the LVT, and deliveries began in July 1941.

By the end of September, the amphibious forces had 680 landing craft in hand and another 1,396 under contract or actual construction. These were not large numbers by later standards, but they represented a significant jump over the forty-six assorted landing craft in Navy hands only eighteen months before. By late October, there were also forty-seven transports and cargo ships in commission or in the process of conversion from civilian liners. Again, not large numbers, but an increase of twelve ships over the previous six months.

The problems of purpose-built small landing craft had been worked out by Smith, Krulak, and others, but the pressing need for specially designed ocean-going ships was not seriously addressed by the Americans until the last hour. Churchill had written a plan in 1917 that said "*tank-landing lighters should be provided, each carrying a tank or tanks. . . . By means of a drawbridge or shelving bow* [the tanks] *would land under* [their] *own power. . . .*"[23] At Churchill's instigation in the summer of 1941 the British Chiefs of Staff forwarded to their American allies the concept for a large ship that could land tanks directly on a beach. They requested that Americans take responsibility for its development and mass production. Scarcely one month before Pearl Harbor, John C. Niedermair, a civilian ship designer at the Bureau of Ships, prepared a rough sketch of what eventually became the Landing Ship Tank (LST). In February 1942, detailed designs were available and contracts were let. Nowhere was America's much-vaunted mass production capability better demonstrated than in the ensuing shipbuilding program. In less than a year from the time of Niedermair's sketch the first LST was commissioned. Over 1,000 were produced during the war, mostly by inland shipyards never before involved in classical naval ship construction.

The LST was more than merely a means to land tanks. It was 328 feet long, had a full load displacement of 4,080 tons, a speed of 11 knots, and accommodated 13 officers and 106 enlisted men. Besides vehicles, it carried supporting troops and assorted cargo. Concurrent with the LST building program, two other specialized designs were put into mass production. The Landing Craft Infantry (LCI) was 158 feet long, had a full load displacement of 387 tons, a speed of 14 knots, and accommodated 8 officers and 21 enlisted men. As many as 205 troops could be carried for a couple of days, then landed over ramps directly ashore. Including several variants, approximately 1,000 were produced, with the first commissioned slightly before the first LST. Finally, the Landing Craft Tank (LCT) was designed to bridge the gap between the LCM and the LST. It came as the 114-foot-long Mark V and the 119-foot-long Mark VI. Both had a full load displacement of approximately 300 tons, a speed of 10 knots, accommodating 1 officer and 10 or 12 enlisted men respectively in the Mark V and Mark VI. The LCT was the first of the three new designs to be commissioned, and including variants, almost 1,500 were produced.

Previous exercises had proven the weaknesses inherent in assigning randomly chosen ship's officers to control shore bombardment. Their lack of familiarity with marine doctrine and the tactics of infantry combat combined with poor radio technology to make fire support a haphazard affair. The solution suggested by Holland Smith was creating a pool of specially trained naval officers who would work with a trained artillery officer to direct fire support. With King's approval, the Marines opened a training course at Parris Island. Students learned infantry tactics and the capabilities of naval guns. They practiced spotting artillery fire and drilled extensively in radio procedure. The first of the new naval gunfire liaison officers completed training in time to participate in the July 1941 exercises. Some difficulties remained, but the basic format for controlling naval gunfire had been established. Much was left undone, but as fall 1941 waned, the days of an uneasy peace finally ran out.

WAR

When Japanese dive bombers began to plummet out of the Sunday morning sky over Pearl Harbor on 7 December 1941, the armed forces of the United States were not yet ready to conduct any kind of offensive operations, much less amphibious. Fortunately, a good start toward readiness was under way. The doctrine that would govern operations was in place and had undergone a series of practical tests. The ranks of the military had grown dramatically during the previous year. Many problems arising from inexperience and the complex character of amphibious warfare were identified and being addressed. Much of the specialized landing craft and transports and other equipment needed for amphibious warfare was under construction. Most important, strong and determined leaders were ready to direct the coming campaigns. There would be some bitter fights about priorities and the politics of fighting within a coalition, but rarely has a nation gone to war with so many gifted officers already holding positions of responsibility.

Despite its relative military unreadiness for war, four factors made the United States a formidable enemy. The first was the enormous store of natural resources available to the country within its own borders and in the Western Hemisphere. Modern war demands vast supplies of steel, oil, and a hundred other resources; with a highly developed industrial economy and a bounty of natural resources, most were available right at home. Second, the food supply of the United States was secure. Unlike the British or Japanese, dependent on massive importation of food across war-torn seas to sustain themselves, American workers would never suffer the debilitation of an inadequate diet. Third, despite the advent of the long-range bomber and the aircraft carrier, the United States enjoyed relative security behind her ocean barriers. No Coventry, Hamburg, or Hiroshima would be inflicted on American cities.

The final factor was the American people. Americans profess to value peace above most other ideals, but war has always been an element of the national experience. American politicians have been equally masters of idealistic denunciation of war and warrior guardians of the national interest. They have been supported in their efforts by a people whose abhorrence of a large, standing military has been matched by enthusiasm for soldiering when called upon. The attack on Pearl Harbor swept aside all the tinny paeans to pacifism and aroused America's traditional combativeness. The enormous energy Americans had invested in commercial pursuits was about to be unleashed in an outpouring of violence backed by vast natural and industrial resources. In keeping with the evolution of American military thought, this war could not end until either the United States or her enemies were defeated. There would be stumbling blocks along the way; the first were revealed soon after Pearl Harbor.

2

THE AMPHIBIANS GO TO WAR

"Luck can be attributed to a well-conceived plan carried out by a well-trained and indoctrinated task group."

FLEET ADMIRAL CHESTER NIMITZ

FIRST DECISIONS AND FIRST MOVES

Fortunately for a nation still reeling from the catastrophe at Pearl Harbor, the Navy's compelling need for a strong war leader did not go unfulfilled. President Roosevelt's instinct told him George Marshall was the man he needed to build and direct a wartime army; in mid-December, that instinct told him the same thing about Ernest King. The president's decision had a profound effect on the way the Navy fought the war and by extension, on the course of the amphibious war.

Secretary of the Navy Frank Knox called King to his office and offered the admiral the position of commander in chief of the United States fleet. Despite some initial reluctance, King was not the kind of man who hesitated to make a decision; he told the secretary he would take the job. Nor was he afraid to ask for what he wanted. He insisted that his headquarters be in Washington rather than afloat, as was customary. He further asked for control over the administrative side of the naval establishment, which he viewed with the disdain of a lifelong fleet sailor. Roosevelt agreed to all but control over the bureaus, which would need hard-to-get congressional approval. As did Marshall, King had access to the president at any time.

On the debit side of King's many strengths were a few important faults. He apparently considered it a normal course of action to keep operational information from the Secretary of the Navy and he focused too much on events in the Pacific. He also devoted too little time to logistical matters, expecting his chief assistant to supply the material needs of the fleet while he concentrated almost exclusively on operational matters. Despite his faults, King clearly was the right man at the right time.

American worries about the Pacific came into sharp relief when Churchill and his military staff began a visit to Washington late in the month. The Arcadia Conference of 23 December 1941–14 January 1942 established a theme that ran throughout the many wartime meetings of the Anglo-American alliance. Both sides hewed to their agreement that the Germans remained the priority. Still, the principle of protecting "vital interests" in the Pacific meant one thing to the Americans and another to the British. To King in particular, the Pacific was close to paramount. In common with most other officers of the Navy, his orientation was by instinct and training toward the Pacific and the Japanese. He was also in command of a navy that was smarting with humiliation and rage over Pearl Harbor. King recognized and agreed with the validity of defeating Germany first; however, the focus of his professional life was on the Pacific. The sooner he could tear into the Japanese, the better. He was supported in his wishes by the American public, which wanted nothing so much as to repay the Japanese for their perfidy.

This need, coupled with King's naturally stiff demeanor and innate distaste for the British, led quickly to friction within Allied councils. King insisted that the conferees agree on language that called for denying the Japanese areas containing natural resources. He also insisted that the seizure of "points of vantage" was a legitimate goal of Allied operations. The Combined Chiefs agreed to this language but the British still believed no major offensive against the Japanese could begin before 1944.

Opposing priorities were not the only problem. Differing national philosophies caused by previous experiences in war came into focus during the discussions. The Americans needed to come to grips with the Germans as soon as possible while the British preferred a peripheral approach designed to wear down the Third Reich. The American Civil War had imbued American military thought with the belief that the best way to win a war was to go directly for the enemy's army and destroy it. The British chiefs of staff had been junior officers during World War I and remembered the tremendous cost in blood. Given the disparity between German and British manpower, they knew their country could not afford the cost of a direct assault. Churchill summed up the difference between the two positions when he noted that Americans preferred logically organized plans carried out on a large scale. In contrast, the British gave greater importance to opportunism and improvisation. The philosophical differences noted by Churchill would lead to more than a few heated exchanges during the coming years.

The operational decisions that resulted from the ARCADIA conference were that the lines of communication to Australia would be kept open, and that a landing in North Africa was to be carried out late in May, if possible. On the planning side, the conferees agreed that the Combined Chiefs of

Staff would coordinate all efforts and that the British and Americans would make the necessary operational decisions. The net effect of the coalition's initial wartime meeting was to give an inkling to all concerned just how vast the scale of warfare had become. Equipment and men in undreamed quantities and numbers were going to be needed.

The American chiefs of staff immediately realized that the integrated British staff system was far superior to their own. If the American heads-of-service were to persevere in discussions about strategy, they would have to coalesce into a combined body equally well supported and speaking with a unified voice. To that end, the Joint Chiefs of Staff came into ad hoc existence on 23 January 1942. Rather than having the War and Navy Departments planning separately and often at cross purposes, the new system was intended to coordinate American efforts and provide the strategic direction needed to fight a global war.

There were some problems involved with the start-up of the new system, but the basic organization was in place, dealing with the day-to-day exigencies of a nation at war. Strategic decisions and organizational changes aside, there was one other lasting consequence of the ARCADIA conference.

The arguments between the wartime Anglo-American alliance have been duly noted and commented upon. There were disappointments on both sides and personality conflicts abounded. Yet, despite their profound differences in outlook, the Allied commanders were always able to put aside nationalism and reach agreements necessary to successfully prosecute the war. The military chieftains of both countries often had to follow orders with which they disagreed; they did so confident in the knowledge that whatever reservations they harbored had been heard.

Allied military leaders enjoyed a cooperative process unmatched by their Axis enemy. The apparent strength of a centralized authoritarian system was in fact undermined by the inability of Hitler's generals to make themselves heard. Those who persisted often did so at considerable risk. So also with the Japanese, whose decisions were made independently by the Imperial Army and Navy without civilian participation or often without joint planning. Much of Japan's war effort was thus dissipated by unrealistic or uncoordinated plans. The first wartime conference of the two great allies set a precedent unequaled by their enemies and one that contributed significantly to the eventual victory.

Between 7 December 1941 and 30 March 1942, 90,000 American soldiers moved to the Pacific theater. Japanese control of the sea precluded any reinforcements reaching the Philippines, so 57,000 went to Australia. The remainder were sent to Hawaii or to garrison the islands lying astride the sea lanes between the United States and Australia. This movement of men and materiel considerably disrupted the planned flow of American strength to England. Shipments to the Pacific represented 50 percent of American overseas movements and graphically showed how important shipping would be to the war effort. The need to move so many men also showed how the vast openness of the Pacific would demand untold numbers of transports and freighters.

The sea distance from San Francisco to Brisbane is 7,500 miles; from New York to Liverpool, 3,500 miles. The same shipping needed to transport 40,000 men to Australia and keep them supplied would transport and supply 100,000 men in England. The need to keep Lend-Lease supplies flowing to the Soviet Union further diluted the shipping pool. A staple of British and American thought throughout 1942 was that unless the Soviets could be kept in the war, Germany would be invincible. Both Marshall and King would have to juggle their pressing demands for resources against Roosevelt's insistence that all possible materiel be sent to the Soviets.

The basic equation of time and distance was further aggravated because in the first four months of war, German U-boats sank eighty-seven assorted tankers and merchantmen off the east coast of the United States alone. Not only were there competing demands, but Allied shipping was going to the bottom at a rate that made all plans problematic. It caused Brig. Gen. Dwight Eisenhower to enter a prophetic comment in his diary: "Ships! Ships! All we need is ships!"[1] The movement to the Pacific also caused Marshall to order prioritizing of what was possible. Eisenhower got that task and his subsequent report reconfirmed the Germany-first approach.

Eisenhower said the United States must concentrate on what was necessary, not what was desirable. In this vein, he was unsure if holding Australia was essential. Despite the understandable desire to hit back at Japan, Germany was the stronger of the two and the supply line to Europe was shorter. An attack on the Japanese homeland was impossible and one on the defensive periphery demanded too much effort for too little return. This was not good news to MacArthur, by then evacuated out of the encircled Philippines to safety in Australia. MacArthur left his command by direct order of the president, but upon his arrival in Australia uttered his well-known promise to the Filipinos, "I shall return." His vow and his belief that the strategy of Germany-first was ill-conceived was to be the basis of his demands for priority in resources in the coming years. When Marshall advised him that the strategy of concentration in Europe meant he was to receive only two divisions in the immediate future, the information did not sit well with MacArthur. Neither was he the type of person who could sit by quietly and wait while others made grand strategy. He soon made his dissent known through a deluge of telegrams, adding to the pressures being felt in Washington.

Events on the political front, meanwhile, were adding significantly to King's influence over events. At the urging of Marshall and King, Roosevelt suggested that the British and Americans divide the war theaters into areas of responsibility, with the United States taking the dominant role in the Pacific. Churchill agreed and after that the British and Americans shared responsibility for Europe, the British commanded in Southeast Asia, the Americans in the Pacific.

Within the American chain of command, the Pacific was divided into the North Pacific, the Pacific Ocean Area, the South Pacific, and the Southwest Pacific. The latter area was assigned to MacArthur, the others to Adm. Chester Nimitz. Although there were to be many outstanding personalities among the naval officers who fought the war in the Pacific, Nimitz would dominate. He was another case of the right man in the right place at the right time. Secretary of the Navy Knox sent him to Hawaii after the Pearl Harbor disaster to replace Adm. Husband Kimmel as commander of the Pacific Fleet. Edward Beach describes Nimitz:

> As a commander, he was brilliant; as a leader, without a peer. He never shirked responsibility when things went badly, and he always exhibited a form of good-humored self deprecation when they went well. He was a student of naval affairs, and had thoroughly grounded himself in Plan Orange at the Naval War College. On top of this, he was invariably considerate of those serving under him. No sentimentalist, he understood the capabilities and shortcomings of his men and always did his best to improve conditions or compensate for them as the situation might require.[2]

Nimitz would also have an impact on the course of the amphibious war in the Pacific. As King's executive, he would be responsible for implementing King's preferred strategy of a Central Pacific offensive. King had certain reservations about Nimitz, believing him to be too ready to compromise. Because of those reservations and because MacArthur was actively promoting a competing strategy for the Pacific theater, King would meet with Nimitz numerous times through the course of the war. His purpose was to remain abreast of events at first hand and to offset any influence MacArthur might be able to exert on Nimitz. Despite his reservations, King never interfered with Nimitz's command prerogatives. Nor did Nimitz fail to render his opinion about strategic matters. With regard to the command setup in the Pacific, Nimitz was directly over the Central Pacific and operated through subordinate commanders in the other two areas.

Both Nimitz and MacArthur answered to the Joint Chiefs, who issued orders through the respective heads of services. This command structure and the geography of the theater were favorable to King's desire to initiate action. His own prerogatives had been powerfully enhanced on 26 March 1942, when Roosevelt appointed him chief of naval operations. King was thereafter in a position unrivaled before or since. The Navy's contribution to strategic planning began at King's desk, he had unquestioned authority over the operational forces of the entire fleet, and he was in charge of a massive shipbuilding program. He also had Roosevelt's promise to remove anyone in the naval bureaucracy who proved unable to sail with the prevailing wind. King's ability to influence the course of events would soon be felt.

Most of the demands for action being heard that spring in Washington war councils came from King. He firmly believed the United States should take the offensive when possible and that Australia was essential to future operations. Throughout the late winter and spring of 1942, he continually pressed for action in the South Pacific. In a conversation with the president early in March, he told Roosevelt that with sufficient forces, the Japanese could be driven back through the Solomon Islands and away from Australia. His philosophy is shown in a memo written to the president that included these words, "No fighter ever won his fight by covering up—by merely fending off the other fellow's blows. The winner hits and keeps hitting even though he has to take some stiff blows in order to be able to keep on hitting."[3]

King was reacting to the steady Japanese advance toward Australia. During the period January through early May, the Japanese bombed Darwin and drove small Australian garrisons out of the Bismarck Islands, most of New Guinea, and the Solomon Islands. Japanese air power was now based less than 700 miles from Australia, a fact worrisome to King. He had done what he could to forestall the Japanese advance, sending small carrier task forces to carry out a series of raids in the South Pacific; unfortunately, the Japanese had been only marginally inconvenienced. King's unswerving insistence that the garrisons of the islands lying between Hawaii and Australia be reinforced brought him into conflict with Marshall and Army planners. None of them shared King's sense of urgency about defending the southern continent.

King was undeterred; his desire to strike at the Japanese was focused by a memorandum prepared by Rear Adm. Richmond Kelly Turner that laid out a four-stage plan of attack. The second stage of Turner's plan specifically called for "a combined offensive by United States, New Zealand and Australian amphibious, naval and air forces through the Solomons and New Guinea to capture the Bismarck Archipelago and the Admiralty Islands."[4] King used April to set various wheels into motion that eventually brought the name Guadalcanal into the American lexicon.

At Nimitz's suggestion, he appointed Vice Adm. Robert Ghormley commander of the South Pacific Area. He started the 1st Marine Division on its way to New Zealand and called for establishment of an amphibious force in the South Pacific. He also approved the detachment of Kelly Turner from his staff, a move that launched Turner on his way to being Ghormley's amphibious force commander. Turner reputedly told King that he knew little about amphibious warfare, to which King answered, "You will learn." Late in the month, King ordered Nimitz to San Francisco for the first of their wartime meetings. There he told his Pacific Fleet commander to begin preparing an amphibious offensive.

King's demands for action became even more pronounced in May after intelligence learned the Japanese had established a seaplane base at Tulagi in the Solomon Islands. Navy code breakers also warned King that the enemy was about to launch an amphibious assault on Port Moresby, the last Australian outpost on New Guinea. King thought it obvious that the Japanese were positioning themselves to cut off Australia, a situation he could not allow. King's intuition was correct; the Imperial Navy intended to sever Australia's link with the United States. The Japanese understood that an American counterattack was inevitable but were convinced it could not come before 1943. Their ultimate aim was to expand their defensive perimeter to the maximum practicable extent and wear down the American will to fight long before the home islands could be threatened.

These plans resulted in the Battle of the Coral Sea, 7–8 May, which saw a Japanese invasion force turned away from the planned assault on Port Moresby. A month later came the Battle of Midway, 2–6 June, which cost the Japanese the heart of their carrier strike force. Faced with these catastrophes, the Imperial Naval general staff ordered the existing perimeter to be strengthened. In the Solomons, these orders sent construction troops to Guadalcanal. They were burning the grass off Lunga Plain by 20 June as they prepared to build an airfield. In Washington, meanwhile, there were fires of a different kind burning.

Eisenhower had privately shrugged off King's demands to garrison the South Pacific as an effort by the Navy to "have a 'safe' place to sail their ships."[5] He did caution that unless the Germany-first plan "is adopted as the eventual aim of all our efforts, we must turn our backs upon the Eastern Atlantic and go, full out . . . against Japan!"[6] Eisenhower's conclusions dovetailed with Roosevelt's desire to get American troops into combat against Germany as soon as possible and with plans already forming in Marshall's mind. Those plans were revealed to the British early in April when the Army chief of staff flew to England.

THE LANDING CRAFT DILEMMA: SPRING 1942

Marshall went to London to share with the British the projected scale of the American buildup in England. Code-named Bolero, the plan was intended to do two things: stem the flow of men and resources to the Pacific and mass enough American fighting power with the British to permit Operations Sledgehammer or Roundup. The former was strictly an emergency measure intended to draw German forces away from the Russian front, where it still appeared the Red Army might succumb. Roundup was intended to be the decisive blow that would eventually drive the Germans out of France. Marshall's planners believed that the minimum American force sufficient to invade the continent was an army of 600,000 men with supporting air elements. As the combined planning staffs confronted the problem, two increasingly familiar restraints exerted their pull. While the planners estimated that 890,000 U.S. soldiers would be available by 1 April 1943, they also estimated that the cargo shipping available by 1 January could support only 252,000. Even if shipping schedules could be juggled, there simply weren't enough landing craft.

The problem that bedeviled the planning stage of almost every amphibious landing of World War II was making itself known. When the number of landing craft of all types required for Roundup was tallied, the total came to more than 4,000, an undreamed-of quantity. The British were quick to point out that American plans did not provide for the construction of sufficient numbers of ocean-going landing ships, something they felt essential to the success of any cross-Channel assault. By their estimate, the United States needed to build 765 assorted landing ships by 1 March 1943 if Roundup was to have a chance to succeed. These figures were not well received by King; in his view, so many ships and the manpower needed to provide crews must necessarily be a subtraction from the Pacific. Marshall determinedly advised his naval colleague that if necessary, the Army would do the job alone. Both men benefited from talks with Lord Louis Mountbatten, whose commandos were pestering the Germans with amphibious raids along the French coast.

Marshall reportedly asked Mountbatten, "How can I get into this game as soon as possible?" Mountbatten's reply reinforced what Marshall was learning. "Double all the orders you've already given for landing craft." Mountbatten described the need for an infantry landing craft (LCI) that could put 250 soldiers ashore at once. "How many would you like?" asked Marshall. The American's quiet determination was well received but there was still no hardware. King also spoke to Mountbatten, who advised the American as one naval officer to another that unless King fully supported an invasion of France, the Army would necessarily usurp the Navy's function.[7]

Though the British committed themselves in principle to both operations, the shortage of landing craft was insurmountable. These discussions further illustrated a truth to the Americans: even with many landing ships and boats on the building ways and under contract, more would be needed. The priorities accorded the building programs would also have to be reviewed. President Roosevelt had authorized the construction of 300 tank landing ships (LSTs) and 300 tank landing craft (LCTs) in January. Unfortunately, they were not scheduled for completion until 1944.

The Joint Planning Committee concluded in a March meeting that the shortage of landing craft was one of three decisively limiting categories of war materiel and that a construction program with specific priorities was required to meet the needs for 1942. Late in April, Navy planners decided that Pacific requirements alone would be 4,000 landing craft. Part of the problem lay in King's control of the shipbuilding program, which did not emphasize landing ship production.

The low priority accorded the production of landing craft was a reflection of several factors. Foremost was the Navy's total lack of experience in amphibious warfare. There was simply no scale against which naval planners who had never before organized an actual amphibious campaign could gauge demand. Second, there was the pressing need for warships of all categories, particularly destroyers and destroyer escorts. And last was an unspoken institutional bias: duty in any amphibious assignment was considered second-rate. Amphibious ships were considered auxiliaries, not on par with more glamorous duty in battleships or destroyers. Thus, in January 1942, landing craft remained in the eighth group of the Navy's Shipbuilding Precedence List, far behind destroyers. In March, they fell to tenth place.

For neither the first nor the last time in naval matters, President Roosevelt chose to exercise his constitutional fiat as commander-in-chief. He had once served as Assistant Secretary of the Navy, a period he afterward referred to as "when I was in the Navy." He thus considered himself well qualified in all issues before the Navy. For the most part, he allowed King to run the naval aspect of the war. FDR was not averse, however, to taking a hand when he saw fit, and the shortage of landing craft was one of those times. The president attempted to use his influence in April, when he ordered a higher priority for landing craft. He directed the Bureau of Ships to deliver 600 LCTs by 1 September.

But not even presidential directives can solve the problems inevitable in the start-up of a production run. The last of the 600 were delivered in late November, though without engines. By July, the projected need for more than 12,000 landing craft finally moved the Navy to put their construction on a par with combatants. Capt. Daniel Barbey, then on King's staff, noted that $100 million had been appropriated for the construction of amphibious ships.[8] With the upcoming invasion of North Africa no doubt on his mind, Roosevelt showed his continuing concern about the production of landing craft in August, when he instructed the head of the War Production Board "that landing craft were of such urgency that the program 'should interfere, when necessary, with any other program where such interference could not be avoided.' "[9] The next two years would see some fiercely fought battles between competing bureaucracies, but the allocation of materiel and the production of landing craft were thereafter always the highest priority. The unforeseen upshot of the landing craft bottleneck was effectively to kill Sledgehammer and Roundup. Operation Bolero would continue, though events in the Pacific soon took center stage.

The immediacy of war served both to increase the pace of preparations for amphibious operations and to add a healthy dose of reality. A joint Army-Marine landing exercise was scheduled on Cape Cod in January. Holland Smith was adamant in his belief that German submarines presented too much of a menace. To the comments of an admiral who suggested that damaged ships could be salvaged, Smith angrily retorted, "Admiral, how in hell are you going to salvage those soldiers and sailors who may be blown up with those ships?"[10] The landings were rescheduled within the safer confines of Chesapeake Bay but proved to be unsettlingly disorganized. No Army unit landed on its assigned beach; one even landed outside the exercise area. Recriminations between Army and Navy commanders were plentiful but the threat of a senate investigation caused the furor to subside. For his part, Holland Smith was unsparing of marines, soldiers, or sailors in his critique of the operation. The marines of the 1st Division and the soldiers of the 9th Infantry Division got no respite in the relentless drilling intended to prepare them for what they would soon face.

Later that spring, Smith's need for realism and adequate facilities resulted in the purchase of Bloodsworth Island. Safely within Chesapeake Bay, it was the first full-time, amphibious-gunfire training range. His efforts were mirrored on the West Coast, where the Navy bought 132,000 acres of scrub-covered California hills and beachfront property north of San Diego soon to be known as Camp Pendleton. In April, King and Marshall signed a memorandum of understanding agreeing that army divisions would be assigned the amphibious assault role in Europe while marine amphibious operations would be confined to the Pacific. At least one historian believes that the underlying Army sentiment was to keep the Marines out of Europe and thus avoid sharing the limelight.[11]

King used the elation that resulted from the Midway victory to continue his campaign for an offensive in the South Pacific. A 25 June memo shows his continued proselytizing of Marshall:

> As you know, it has been my conviction that the Japanese will not stand still . . . and will not let us stand still. Either they will press us with an extension of their offensive, seeking weak spots in order to break our line of communications, or we will have to be pressing them. It is urgent, in my opinion, that we lose no time in taking the initiative ourselves.[12]

Perhaps his words to Marshall convinced King that enough time had been lost; without approval from either the JCS or Roosevelt, he issued a same day preparatory order to Nimitz for the seizure of Tulagi in the Solomon Islands. Nimitz was to use elements of the 1st Marine Division available in New Zealand as the assault force. The Joint Chiefs recognized the validity of King's stance on 2 July when they agreed to a limited counter-offensive in the South Pacific. The first step in the plan would be to recapture Tulagi.

INTERLUDE: SUMMER 1942

Before any units could actually be set into motion, King found himself involved in two disputes with the Army. One had to do with who would command the South Pacific offensive. The other involved which service had primary responsibility for landing assault troops. King naturally made Marshall aware of his plans; Marshall's reaction was that since the Solomons fell within the Southwest Pacific Area, command should reside with MacArthur. In keeping with the recent agreement that the Navy would be responsible for amphibious operations against islands and the Army against continents, King reminded Marshall that he had acceded to an Army commander in Europe and would not accept an Army officer controlling what was essentially a naval operation. He further stressed that if the Army was unwilling to cooperate, the Navy would carry out the assault on its own. It was at this moment in a tempest among commanders that Douglas MacArthur chose to demonstrate his single-mindedness.

MacArthur had been feeling slighted for several months. He had already made known his beliefs that he considered the Pacific the decisive theater of combat and that he expected a commensurate commitment of men and materiel. Beginning with his arrival in Australia in March, he had issued a constant stream of demands for more of everything. When told by Marshall that his ground forces would be limited to two divisions, he had gone so far as to express his "bitter" disappointment to Australian Prime Minister John Curtin. He further suggested to Curtin that Churchill be requested to divert two divisions of British troops and additional British shipping to Australia. The ensuing rebuke MacArthur received from Marshall did nothing to temper his demands.

MacArthur next told Roosevelt that "a 'full-scale' offensive should be launched from Australia. It would serve, 'not only to secure Australia and India, but would also open up a second front which would be of incalculable aid to Russia.' "[13] To accomplish this grand design, MacArthur asked for 1,000 combat planes and three "first class" divisions. On 8 June he weighed in with a plan for an attack on the main enemy base at Rabaul on New Britain Island. The plan called for a single-division assault supported by two aircraft carriers. The Navy from King on down was unwilling to put any of its few carriers under MacArthur; Marine Commandant Lt. Gen. Thomas Holcomb reportedly said that MacArthur should never "be permitted to command either the fleet or ship-to-shore aspects of an amphibious operation."[14] More to the point, the Chiefs considered MacArthur's scheme impractical and beyond American capabilities.

On 28 June, MacArthur fired another volley, claiming that King's planned assault in the Solomons was part of a scheme to reduce the Army to little more than a garrison force for the Navy. He also insisted that he possessed the better and more capable staff. Marshall suggested to Mac-Arthur that he fight the Japanese instead of the Navy. Working closely together, the two service chiefs worked out a compromise. The Tulagi/Guadalcanal area would be included in the South Pacific area and thus come under Nimitz. Subsequent offensives through the upper Solomons and New Guinea, and ultimately toward Rabaul and the Philippines, would come under MacArthur. The command dispute was momentarily settled, though it would not be the last heard from MacArthur. King and Marshall were also able to come to an agreement about which service was responsible for the naval aspects of an amphibious assault.

Few people are aware that before and during World War II, the Army owned and chartered a large "fleet" of troop transports and other water craft. This military intrusion into what seemed a clear naval function came about because of interservice rivalry and was given apparent legitimacy by wording found in *Joint Action of the Army and Navy*: "Neither Service will attempt to restrict in any way the means and weapons used by the other Service in carrying out its function."[15] Under Rainbow 5, the Navy was to take over the Army's ships and had actually begun to do so during the spring of 1941. But transports and cargo ships generally required large crews; King was reluctant to man them because his priority was the new combatants that were beginning to emerge from American shipyards. The inevitable manpower crunch meant there were not enough sailors to take over all the Army's transports. The Coast Guard was called upon to man some ships, but the Army remained in the shipping business then and throughout the war.

Manpower problems and the continuing shortage of ships also dictated that the Navy charter transports. Charters were effected through the War Shipping Administration and although each ship remained under a civilian master, its movements conformed to naval requirements. A small contingent of naval personnel was placed aboard to perform the strictly military functions of manning guns and landing craft. There were problems, of course, stemming chiefly from the differing perspectives and pay rates of unionized, civilian merchant sailors and Navy men who were in for the duration. Officers commanding the naval detachments found their diplomatic skills as important as their military skills. Chartered transports would serve on the front line in several amphibious operations, including nine assigned to Operation Galvanic in fall 1943. Approximately forty vessels were eventually under charter, making an important contribution to the Navy's amphibious effort.

Army resistance to joint action with the Navy also figured in the procurement of landing craft and amphibious training. The Army had done some work on landing craft designs and had, like the Navy, turned to Andrew Higgins for prototypes. The Navy's inability to provide either boats or trained boat crews led the Army to establish the Engineer Amphibious Command in June 1942. Eight Engineer Amphibious Brigades were planned, with the mission of conducting any shore-to-shore operations that might be required. Because the Army program was recruiting from the same pool of civilian boatmen and drawing boats from the same manufacturers, it naturally had a deleterious effect on the Navy's crushing need to prepare its own forces.

Potentially even more damaging to a cohesive joint effort was the insistence in some quarters of the Army that soldiers should receive all amphibious training from their service. An Army report of February 1942 contained "a frank criticism of naval command, constituting a powerful indictment of the theory and practice of joint action." On 3 April, Marshall received another report "expressing dissatisfaction with the training received by the 3d Infantry Division . . . and recommending a straight unilateral approach to the problem."[16] Even so, the Army effort brought a divided response from within the naval establishment: those who held amphibious warfare to be a diversion of naval manpower hoped the soldiers would take on as much of the work as they could. Others saw the Army program as usurping a purely naval function. The press of operational matters was such that no decision was reached. Conflicting ideas between the Army and Navy continued to simmer and aggravate but no resolution was found until the following spring.

The argument over who would command the first American offensive in the Pacific was only one among several problems facing the Joint Chiefs during the summer of 1942. The foreign minister of the Soviet Union visited Washington seeking assurances that the Allies would open a second front against the Germans that year. Roosevelt's acutely attuned political instincts recognized the vast imbalance between American and Soviet contributions to the war against Germany. Attended by Marshall and King, he therefore sent the Soviet foreign minister home with the unequivocal promise that a second front would be opened in 1942. The man whose assistance Roosevelt would most need to turn his idealistic but poorly conceived promise into reality arrived in Washington a week later.

Churchill and Field Marshal Sir Alan Brooke, chief of the Imperial General Staff, arrived in Washington on 18 June with the aim of clarifying Allied strategy and commitments for 1942 and 1943. The visit made it clear to the Americans that British support for a cross-Channel assault in 1942 was no more than illusion. The possibility of landing in North Africa again reached the table but both King and Marshall were against it, though for different reasons. Marshall considered any operations in the Mediterranean as wasteful diversions of strength away from the main theater in Western Europe. He believed a landing in North Africa would make an invasion of France impossible in 1942 and probably 1943 as well. On the other hand, Marshall knew that landing craft production was far enough behind schedule to make American plans for a landing in France problematical. Only 238 landing craft were available in England and planned deliveries would only support a landing force of 16,000 men. King was against North Africa because it would divert strength away from the Pacific, especially the upcoming attack in the Solomons.

At Roosevelt's behest, the discussions continued in London the next month. In contrast to the apolitical nature of American military leaders, the president's desire for a decision was driven by very strong political motives. Roosevelt knew Churchill was strongly in favor of a landing in North Africa. Furthermore, Congressional elections were scheduled for November, making it imperative that his administration should be seen to be actively prosecuting the war. He therefore put heavy pressure on his commanders by giving them unequivocal instructions that they were to reach a decision within one week that would commit American troops to action against Germany in 1942. Marshall's frustration with the course of events grew when, in the face of British refusal to commit to a cross-Channel assault, he realized that there would be no landing in France in 1942 or 1943. The root of American impatience lay in the fact that they simply could not grasp what the past meant to the British.

As First Lord of the Admiralty, Churchill had been primarily responsible for the World War I disaster at Gallipoli. He remembered the cost only too well and knew that if he committed the British army to a premature assault on the Continent, all might be irretrievably lost. Marshall showed his distaste for what he felt was British unwillingness to come to grips with the Germans by suggesting to the president that the United States shift the focus of its efforts to the Pacific. King naturally supported this suggestion, but Roosevelt emphatically refused to consider the idea.

Knowing that the American leader was eager to get U.S. troops into action, Churchill again brought up the subject of North Africa. King and Marshall found themselves in a bind—the British would not support an attack into France and Roosevelt adamantly wanted Americans in action against the Germans somewhere. Since one condition of the alliance was that any major operation had to have the unanimous agreement of the Combined Chiefs of Staff, what Churchill was now calling Operation Torch appeared to be their only option. Both sides agreed that supreme command of Torch should fall to the country providing most of the troops. They also agreed that the final decision to mount the operation would be made by 15 September.

Roosevelt learned of the agreement from a telegram containing the single word, "Africa." His reply to Churchill was equally cryptic: "Thank God." Any notion on the part of Marshall or King that Torch was still tentative was dispelled by Roosevelt when he told his assembled commanders that "he, as Commander in Chief, had made the decision that Torch should be undertaken at the earliest possible date. He considered that this operation was now our principal objective, and the assembling of means to carry it out should take precedence over other operations."[17]

WATCHTOWER: JUNE–AUGUST 1942

Far away from the conference rooms of London and Washington, Navy plans were moving ahead for an offensive in the Solomons. Nimitz issued orders on 27 June to assault and seize Tulagi. At the request of Kelly Turner, Nimitz added Guadalcanal to the order on 5 July because reconnaissance had revealed the construction of an airstrip there. Responsibility for the actual assault now devolved onto Admiral Ghormley. He had arrived in New Zealand only one week before Nimitz's order. Ghormley was doubtless surprised, for he later recalled King telling him as part of his April briefing, "In time, possibly this fall . . . we hope to start an offensive in the South Pacific."[18] In war, imagination and daring can compensate somewhat for lack of experience or instructions that are not entirely clear. It is also axiomatic that to be successful, any military commander must believe in what he has to do.

Ghormley had no experience in amphibious warfare nor was he daring. He also quickly made it known that he had little faith in the planned assault, codenamed Operation Watchtower. Both he and MacArthur issued gloomy appraisals of the possibility of success, citing the paucity of land-based air cover and the Japanese capability of bringing their airpower to bear. After his 8 July conference with MacArthur, Ghormley sent the following message to King:

> The two commanders are of the opinion, arrived at independently, and
> confirmed after discussion, that the initiation of the operation at this
> time without reasonable assurance of adequate air coverage would be
> attended with the gravest risk . . . it is recommended that this operation
> be deferred.[19]

Perhaps Ghormley was remembering what King had told him in Washington only two months previously: "you have a large area and a most difficult task. I do not have the tools to give you to carry out that task as it should be. . . ."[20] Ghormley had a reputation as a planner so it is in character that he was also bothered by the distances and lack of logistical support. He believed that Washington did not understand adequately the difficulties inherent in operating across vast expanses of ocean. As he put it, "Our planners were not personally familiar with the geographical set-up in the South Pacific area."[21] Ghormley's remarks are given credence by George Dyer. "Our recent naval intelligence in regard to the Solomons was zero point zero due to the fact that about a year and a half before we went in there Admiral Stark had gotten out an order saying, 'In no way was the Pacific Fleet to show any interests in the Solomons.' "[22]

King was of sterner stuff and would countenance none of Ghormley's objections; the landings were to take place no later than 1 August. Unlike the amphibious juggernaut that would appear off Okinawa three years later, the first American landing of World War II was anything but a polished affair. Although King reportedly told doubters the operation would work because Holland Smith said it would, Watchtower was a desperate gamble. The Navy did not control the sea, making communications anything but secure, and American combat power was stretched thin. Planning was hastily done, there was little intelligence, and logistical support was more idea than reality. Nowhere is the ad hoc nature of the operation more evident than in the cobbled-together command arrangements.

Ghormley was overall commander but was content to remain in his flagship tied up in Noumea harbor, New Caledonia. Ghormley's actions have caused speculation that he was unsure what Nimitz had assigned him to do: was his primary task defending the lines of communication to Australia? Or was the assault on Guadalcanal foremost? Whatever the case, he kept at a distinct remove from the operation. Vice Adm. Frank Jack Fletcher was expeditionary force commander, flying his flag on the aircraft carrier *Saratoga*. Fletcher was also tired and extremely conscious that the three carriers under his command represented the remaining striking power of the Pacific Fleet. He was unwilling to risk them, despite the patent need of the Marines for air cover. Fletcher had never worked with Ghormley before nor with Kelly Turner, who had arrived in Auckland on 15 July.

Turner was on the scene as amphibious force commander. He was didactic, imperious to an extreme, and possessed of a fiery temper that he often made no effort to keep in check. He was what is now called a workaholic and he found it almost impossible to delegate; it is said he could not ride in a small boat without telling the coxswain how to manage the craft. He had long sought action in the Solomons, but only learned of the impending assault when he arrived in Pearl Harbor on 5 July. Typical of the nascent state of amphibious warfare in the U.S. Navy, no officer on Turner's newly formed staff had any experience with the task at hand. Another glaring omission was the absence of a single trained supply corps officer on the staff. Turner's second-in-command was a Royal Navy officer who had been assigned despite his objections that he did not think it proper for a somewhat junior Allied officer to be over so many Americans. Worse yet, he had never before met Turner.

Maj. Gen. Alexander A. Vandegrift commanded the 1st Marine Division. Vandegrift was burdened because his division was incomplete and not fully trained. He arrived in Auckland on 12 June and learned of the operation from Ghormley on 26 June. Vandegrift had been expecting six months to train his men, but suddenly discovered he had only six weeks. The regimental commander of the First Marines would later write: "[They] have had less than three months of battalion training. Not once have we had a regimental problem, much less training with planes, tanks, and other units." Reflecting on the youth of his marines, he added, "Maybe we can make up in guts what we lack in training."[23] What they had to learn first was not field skills, but how to load the ships taking them to combat.

The transports carrying the division's second echelon had not been combat loaded because the attack was ordered after their departure from the States. Beginning on 12 July, therefore, twelve ships had to be unloaded, nonessential equipment sorted out, and the ships reloaded for the assault. The plan was for each ship to carry one combat team and enough supplies to support the team for thirty days. The hurry-up nature of the task is illustrated by an entry in the transport *Barnett*'s war diary noting that unloading was completed at 1100 on 14 July and reloading commenced at 2200. King's timetable lagged further behind because only five ships could be accommodated at once at the Wellington quay. Pioneer battalions existed but their numbers were too small; the backbreaking work of reloading was assigned to 300-strong gangs of marines who had not enlisted to serve as longshoremen.

The round-the-clock task was aggravated by a persistent rain that drenched men's spirits and supplies alike. Some sense of the work involved can be deduced from a partial listing of the stores and equipment loaded in the transport *Zeilin*:

27 trailers, 10 tractors, 18 trucks
8x90mm guns
1 ice machine
110,000 lb quartermaster stores
72,000 lb clothing
100,000 lb .30/.50 caliber guns and ammo.[24]

Combat loading is less efficient of space, so divisional equipment was divided into thirteen categories, each pared to the barest minimums.[25] The completion of loading saw 75 percent of the division's vehicles, a third of the rations, and half of the ammunition left behind. This less-than-optimum use of space, inherent in combat loading, shows up in the action report of the cargo ship *Libra*; she had 3,200 tons of equipment and supplies aboard, but the load was only a third of her capacity.[26] The work lagged far enough that Ghormley and Vandegrift asked for a delay until 7 August, a request granted reluctantly by King. The transports finally sailed from Wellington on the morning of 22 July, destination Koro Island, where a rehearsal was scheduled. Even at this late date, most of the marines did not know where they were bound. They had been told there was to be a routine landing exercise, but it was clear to all hands that something was in the air.

Uncertainty was not confined to the ranks. Despite radio intelligence and the reports of coastwatchers suggesting a large Japanese presence on Guadalcanal, estimates of their strength varied widely. Ghormley's staff said there were 3,100 enemy troops on Tulagi and Guadalcanal, while Turner's posited a strength of 7,125. Vandegrift's intelligence officer told him there were approximately 8,400 enemy troops on the island, including 2,000 labor troops. Ghormley's estimate was the more accurate; there were approximately 3,400 Japanese in the target area, but 1,700 were labor troops.

Intelligence about enemy troop strength was not the only gap in American knowledge. Scant information was available about the topography of the island or the nature of Japanese defenses. The division intelligence officer mounted an effort to locate and interview people who had been on the island, but their descriptions of the terrain were no substitute for real-time intelligence. Only outdated maps were available. An Army Air Force B-17 carrying two Marine officers flew a reconnaissance mission over Guadalcanal and Tulagi, and photos taken during this mission were used to produce a map of the planned landing area. Lack of intelligence was only one of many concerns for General Vandegrift. As the transports plodded northward through heavy weather, he could only hope that the rehearsal would provide his partly trained men with enough of a tune-up to get them ashore without too many problems.

The many different courses steered by ships coming from San Diego, Norfolk, Pearl Harbor, and Wellington converged the morning of 25 July when the assault force rendezvoused enroute to Koro Island in the Fijis. Koro had been chosen because it was 1,100 miles from Guadalcanal, far enough to avoid the prying eyes of Japanese air reconnaissance. A conference convened on the twenty-sixth was the only time the various commanders met as a body; Ghormley did not attend. Admiral Fletcher showed little faith in the operation. He began by castigating the plan as the offspring of someone who knew nothing about the realities of combat. He then stunned the assembled commanders when he announced that despite

Turner's stated need for five days to unload the transports, the carriers under his command would provide air cover for only two days before withdrawing.

Vandegrift attempted to sway Fletcher by explaining that this was not a "hit and run" raid but a division-sized assault. One of Turner's staff officers recorded his impressions of the meeting, leaving the clear record that it was anything but a harmonious council of war:

> The conference was one long bitter argument between Vice Admiral Fletcher and my new boss. Since he kept implying that [the landing] was largely Turner's brainchild, and mentioning that those who planned it had no real fighting experience, he seemed to be doubting the competence of its parent. Fletcher's main point . . . was the operation was too hurriedly and therefore not thoroughly planned, the Task Force not trained together, and the logistic support inadequate.[27]

There was also some friction between Turner and Vandegrift; Turner's order that two battalions of marines be kept in reserve for a peripheral operation nettled the Marine general, who wanted all possible strength ashore. Turner did agree that he would give the transports and cargo ships four days to unload before pulling them out. One of Fletcher's objections, that logistical support was too limited, was well merited. Tulagi lies 1,200 miles from Australia, 800 from New Caledonia, and 550 from Espiritu Santo. Distance is not necessarily an impediment, but every American installation was newly established, shipping and air transport were scarce, and the scale of materiel supplies was limited. The rehearsal did little to assuage the uncertainties.

Security remained intact, but much of the rehearsal's intended value was thwarted by coral reefs that prevented full-scale boat landings. Turner had only 475 landing craft in his transports and was careful to husband this scant resource. Only a third of the embarked marines made it into boats, but none of the valuable landing craft were lost and considerable maintenance was carried out. Another disadvantage was that radio silence prevented the airmen and air liaison parties from practicing. All the men in Turner's new command had one profound learning experience; they discovered that their commander was a stern, no-nonsense taskmaster. All hands, from ships' captains to boatswain's mates, learned that Turner's sharp tongue spared no one.

General Vandegrift believed that the troops and boat crews gained valuable experience in debarking into the boats, in the timing of debarkation intervals, and the coordination of boat movements. Still, all had not gone according to plan when the transports set course for the six-day slog to Guadalcanal and Tulagi. Meanwhile, Turner fretted over the words of British strategist B. H. Liddell Hart, who had declared in a 1939 book that modern air power made amphibious operations "almost impossible." As if Liddell Hart's scenario wasn't bad enough, Turner had another worry: in an apparently glaring breach of security, the prime minister of New Zealand delivered a speech on 31 July in which he publicly stated that an Allied offensive was about to begin in the Solomon Islands. For all Turner knew, the Japanese would be waiting at the beach.

THE LANDING AND OTHER PROBLEMS

After all the hurried planning, the gathering of men and ships, the brief rehearsal, came the night before the landing. One marine who was there gives his impression:

> Aboard all the troopships the men went below. They descended to holds far below the water line, [some] to chaplain's services, others to write the last letter home, and some to lie fully clad on their bunks . . . alone with their reveries or their forebodings. In the heads, where the air was blue with tobacco smoke and loathsome with the reek of human refuse, the "showdown" games were being held between the lucky—or skillful— hands into which most of the money had finally settled.[28]

By 0600 on 7 August, seventy-six assorted ships of the assault force had arrived undetected off the shores of Guadalcanal, Tulagi, and the islets of Gavutu and Tanambogo. The twenty-three amphibious ships of the task group had 23,000 marines embarked. No account of the landing fails to mention the lush tropical beauty of the islands; what was about to occur was beautiful only in the most terrible sort of way.

There were five fire-support groups, but unlike later years, these groups numbered only a single heavy cruiser or two destroyers each. The first American amphibious assault of World War II began at 0613 when, to the complete surprise of the Japanese garrison, the guns of the bombardment ships opened up on Guadalcanal. Twenty minutes into the barrage, the command "Land the Landing Force" sent the marines scrambling down the nets into their boats, an exercise that was not as easy as it looked in the movies:

> In those days you went down a sort of landing net, a webbing made out of stout rope which they would otherwise use to load cargo. They put these nets over the side and we'd use them as a rope ladder to go down into the Higgins boats. Even with a fairly medium-sized sea the Higgins boats would go up and down, and to try to get down that swaying cargo net with about eighty pounds of equipment on your back without killing yourself or getting jammed between the Higgins boat and the ship was quite a stunt.[29]

Of course, getting into the boats was only the first step. Once loaded, each boat proceeded to an assembly area where it joined all the other boats assigned to a particular wave. When the control ship determined that the proper number of boats was present, they formed into line-abreast formation and proceeded toward the line of departure. In this first American landing of the war, destroyers had been assigned to control the boat waves, a practice post-invasion analysts would condemn as a waste of precious fleet and gunfire-support assets. After the first wave of landing craft was in formation and began to make the 5,000-yard run to the single designated landing beach, the warships of the support group poured more than 1,500 rounds of shellfire into the area around the 1,600-yard-wide landing area. By later standards, this barrage was in the proportion of a spring shower to a monsoon. Still, it probably seemed impressive to the approaching marines.

Further contributions to the cacophony of noise came from the bombs and gunfire of the fighters and dive bombers wheeling overhead. The fliers had the task of knocking out gun positions, ammo or supply dumps, and blasting any vehicles they found. Beginning fifteen minutes before sunrise, they attacked what they could see, but the lack of intelligence limited their efforts. In the words of George Dyer, "The carrier pilots, not specially trained for this exacting and difficult air-support chore, did not always come up to the expectations of the Marines, their own desires, or the desires of the top commanders."[30] The bomber controller was embarked in the transport *McCawley* while the fighter controller was in the heavy cruiser *Chicago*. Technical problems and inexperience hampered these efforts, too.

First among the communications problems was that the *McCawley* was not built as an amphibious flagship. The demands of providing communications, including the need of the air controller to coordinate air support, overwhelmed her inadequate radio facilities. None of the units ashore had any direct contact with the aircraft orbiting overhead. Any request for support against a specific target had to be relayed to the *McCawley*, then to the senior air group commander circling overhead, and thence to the attacking aircraft. Trouble with the *McCawley*'s radio equipment limited her range to only 8 miles, requiring a destroyer as a relay ship. Events also quickly demonstrated that to be effective, the shipboard air controllers had to remain within radio range of both the aircraft and the ground units.

Despite difficulties, 11,000 marines landed on Guadalcanal without hindrance from the surprised Japanese. Twenty miles away across Sealark Channel, resistance to the landings on Tulagi and Gavutu varied from isolated shots by snipers to an assault under a hail of machine-gun fire. Only one destroyer provided fire support at the latter place, and her bombardment served mainly to alert the defenders that an assault was imminent. The prospect of combat was no doubt a relief to at least some marines; the 14,000-yard run-in to the landing zone at Gavutu took more than two hours and left many men seasick. The Japanese allowed the first wave to land with little interference, but met subsequent waves with such deadly effect that one man in ten was killed or wounded.

Two days of intense fighting followed before the connected islets of Gavutu and Tanambogo were declared secure. Several ships provided gunfire support to the marines as did dive bombers from the carriers. The troops were grateful for the support, but two misdirected American bombs killed and wounded several marines. The fighting on Tulagi was also fierce, but the attackers' preponderance in numbers and firepower had the situation well enough in hand by the end of the second day to allow some units to reinforce the battle on Gavutu and Tanambogo.

This first confrontation of marines and Japanese showed the Americans what the coming years would bring. The Japanese demonstrated their proficiency in the construction of defensive positions. Bunkers built of coconut logs and earth, guns emplaced in caves and tunnels, all proved nearly impervious to anything but a direct hit from a bomb or naval shell. Jeter Iseley sums up the problem: "The . . . naval gunfire ships repeatedly used high-capacity ammunition where armor-piercing alone would have done the job. It was like blasting hard rock with dynamite placed on the surface, where a drill hole packed with TNT was required."[31] Unfortunately, this lesson was not taken to heart and would have deadly consequences in 1943.

That the Japanese soldiers and naval landing troops of 1942 were true inheritors of the samurai code of Bushido was made bloodily evident. Of the 886 Japanese combat troops and laborers present on the three islands, only twenty-three were captured. General Vandegrift later wrote of the "astonishing" tenacity of the Japanese and their willingness to die rather than surrender.[32] Because the Japanese fought under a completely different set of rules, their behavior was incomprehensible to Americans. Every Japanese serviceman knew by heart the Imperial Rescript for Soldiers and Sailors: "Be resolved that honor is heavier than a mountain, and death lighter than a feather." The few words of the Rescript signified a vast cultural gap that engendered a level of savagery unlike anything seen in Europe. The Japanese soldier had but one mission: destroy his enemy completely or die in the attempt. Marine casualties on Tulagi came to 115 killed and 163 wounded. Many thousands more would follow from both sides.

Once ashore, the problem facing the amphibious invader is to remain there. Not only must the inevitable counterattacks be fended off, but reinforcements and logistical support must be readily at hand. The Japanese commander on Tulagi immediately called for help along with a pledge to fight to the last man. By 0930, his comrades on Rabaul had dispatched a fifty-nine plane attack force that included some dive bombers without the range to make the return trip. The first torpedo bombers arrived over the invasion area around 1315 and scored no hits while losing five of their number to defending fighters and antiaircraft (AA) fire. The dive bombers arrived later and scored a hit on a destroyer while losing five to intercepting fighters. As would so often be the case, enemy air attacks would disrupt but not halt the landing.

The raid illustrated another important facet of the war with Japan. Damage claims by Japanese fliers were far more than they really achieved, a practice common to airmen of every nation. But as Army historian John Miller observed,

> there were two important differences between American and Japanese claims. First, Japanese claims were wildly exaggerated whereas American claims were merely exaggerated. Second, Japanese commanders apparently took the claims seriously, as the nonexistent victories often served as the basis for decision. On the other hand American commanders, taking human frailty into account, evaluated and usually scaled down claims so that decisions were normally based on more realistic estimates of damage.[33]

This penchant for overstatement would cause the Japanese to claim more than once during the amphibious war that they had repulsed a landing.

The Japanese air raids seriously disrupted efforts to get Marine supplies ashore. Each troop commander was responsible for providing sufficient men to work cargo holds on a twenty-four-hour basis. However, when the air raid warning sounded, the ships had to cease unloading and get underway to maneuver, slowing what was already a tedious process. All supplies had to be winched out of the deep holds and into the landing craft. Once at the beach, the supplies were hand-carried from the boats to temporary stacks above the surf line. At that point one of the major problems of the operation developed.

All hands knew they were working against the two-day deadline when air cover would be withdrawn. Cargo was therefore being handled at maximum speed, which meant the boats were able to bring supplies to the beach faster than they could be moved into permanent dumps. The pioneer battalion doing the work found itself completely overwhelmed; although the op-order directed the shore party commander to seek assistance from unoccupied troops, of which there were many in the beach area, no commander took the initiative of assigning them to the job.[34] Robert Leckie's account gives a picture of confusion and disarray:

> Untrained coxswains brought rations to beaches marked for fuel, or medical supplies were mixed in with ammunition. Sailors could not help,

because, as they rightfully maintained, it was their job to bring material ashore and the Marines' to get it off the beach. Many Marines not committed to action might have helped, but they merely watched their comrades of the shore parties melting under the strain. "Hell, Mac, we're combat troops," they sniffed. "You unload the goddam stuff."[35]

As late afternoon turned into night, loaded boats began to back up until there were nearly 100 at the beach and another 50 lying off waiting their turns. One ship's captain was unsparing in his criticism, pointing the finger primarily at the Marines. Turner agreed: "There were two primary reasons for failure to completely unload. First the vast amount of unnecessary impediments taken, and second a failure on the part of the 1st Division to provide adequate and well-organized unloading details at the beach."[36] Even the heaps of supplies presented a hazard to the success of the operation:

> Most of the 1st Division's available supplies were piled high on the Guadalcanal beachhead, constituting a heaven-sent target for the Japanese planes and . . . destroyers which for two solid weeks roamed freely night and day above . . . and on the surface of the waters between Guadalcanal and Tulagi. Had the Japanese set fire to the supplies towering high on the Guadalcanal beachhead, . . . "the consequences might well have been incalculable and ruinous."[37]

These critical comments all came later, with the clear vision of hindsight. With the enemy present in unknown strength and disposition, troop commanders were more concerned with establishing a secure position than unloading supplies.

The second morning saw the boat crews and pioneers dealing with the problem at hand. Their efforts were again interrupted at mid-morning when a large force of torpedo bombers skimmed in to launch an unintercepted attack. Adroit maneuvering and heavy AA fire from the transports and screen smacked several bombers into the sea and prevented all but a single torpedo hit. That the amphibious ships were on the front lines was shown by the experience of the *Barnett*. One bomber bore down on the ship, apparently intent on crashing into her. The plane began to climb at the last second, clipped the ship's signal mast and crashed into the sea. One shot-down bomber crashed into another transport, turning her into a blazing torch.

On the downside, the transports remained under way until after 1700, seriously interrupting the flow of supplies going ashore. In the *Libra*, the pressing need to refuel some of the destroyers again interrupted unloading; her log records the *Southard* alongside for a drink of black oil at 2130. Two days of air attacks had been brushed off with small cost. As nightfall began to descend on that second day, the threat manifested in the air raids was about to take on a far more menacing and deadly shape.

A HARD LESSON

Land-based air support for Watchtower was coming from a multinational bag of squadrons. Some were operating under the control of Ghormley's air commander and some under MacArthur's. Part of their assigned duties was to search the sea approaches from the large Japanese base on Rabaul. It is not surprising that given the divided nature of command and control, the task was poorly carried out. On the morning of 8 August, patrol planes made two separate contacts on a group of Japanese warships headed toward Guadalcanal. More than seven hours passed before the airmen filed their only report, itself unclear about the types of ships sighted. The subsequent delays in encoding and rebroadcasting the report meant that Turner did not receive the information until approximately 1900.

Although Turner personally reviewed the message and made an estimate of Japanese actions, most students of the campaign feel he made the error of mentally projecting what the Japanese were going to do rather than what they were capable of doing. His undoubted concern was most likely overridden by a more immediate problem: Fletcher had been fretting all day about the torpedo bomber attack that morning. His fears got the better of him that afternoon, leading him to put his carriers on a course taking them away to the southeast. He then asked Ghormley for permission to withdraw completely, citing 20 percent attrition in his fighters and the large number of enemy torpedo planes and bombers operating against his ships.

When Turner saw Fletcher's message asking to withdraw, he faced a cruel dilemma. He knew there was a Japanese surface force of undetermined strength and composition approaching. Now he had to consider the dangerous reality of the transports remaining off Guadalcanal without air cover. He therefore called his subordinate commanders to a late conference aboard the *McCawley*, where he disclosed to them that he planned to take the transports out of the area the following morning. General Vandegrift requested that the withdrawal wait until he could find out the status of his units on Tulagi, which Turner granted. Unknown to the American commanders, their decision was about to be made for them by a Japanese admiral named Gunichi Mikawa.

Mikawa's cruisers were the ships sighted earlier in the day and about which Turner was warned. Mikawa's mission was straightforward: break up and destroy the American invasion force off Guadalcanal. Fortune supposedly favors the bold but fighting a tired and inexperienced enemy also helps. The Japanese were about to sail among an American task force yet unbloodied in ship-to-ship combat, totally unprepared for a night battle, whose sailors were reeling from the exhaustion of operating at fever pitch the previous two days.

Between 0132 and 0216 on the morning of 9 August, Mikawa's well-trained and experienced sailors showed the mettle of the Imperial Navy as they slipped undetected between the American picket destroyers and fell upon the support force. In less than three-quarters of an hour, they reduced four heavy cruisers to flaming pyres off Savo Island. There was thereafter nothing to keep Mikawa from slaughtering Turner's transports, something one of his captains importuned him to do. Mikawa was certain that dawn would bring American carrier planes eager to exact retribution and he also considered his clear victory a night's work well done. The Japanese ships turned for home, leaving the U.S. Navy smarting from another defeat but more important, leaving the amphibious force intact. Not that the men in the transports didn't know that something big was going on.

Gun flashes and flares descending out of the night had sailors and marines wondering what was happening. In the logs of the various amphibious ships, there's a sense of nervous unease as the reflected glare and rumble of heavy gunfire is noted. Like sheep catching the scent of a marauding wolf, the amphibious ships got underway and steered away from the distant fight. It was a sign of the times that even in their unease, many Americans automatically decided that any battle taking place would be a victory for the U.S. Navy. The truth was hard to accept. Savo Island was galling to the Americans, but it is important to remember that it could have been worse.

If the transports had been sunk, the 1st Marine Division would inevitably have been destroyed, a catastrophe of far greater consequence than the loss of four cruisers. The immediate upshot of the Japanese victory occurred at 1330 that afternoon, when Turner led his amphibious task force away from Guadalcanal. The *Barnett* bore with it the debris of the defeat at Savo. Several hundred survivors of the sunken cruisers *Vincennes* and *Canberra* were aboard, but the inevitable toll of war saw many of them buried at sea over the next two days.

Turner had originally planned to go ashore and assume command of the operation from Guadalcanal, but decided that not only were communications facilities ashore inadequate, he also would be better able to organize resupply and reinforcement from Noumea. Of more immediate concern to Turner was the logistical battle to supply the Marines. From his vantage point on King's staff, George Dyer made this observation:

> there was no real planning at the COMINCH level about what would
> happen one week, three weeks, or six weeks after the troops had landed.
> After the marines had gone ashore at Guadalcanal, no one at the highest

level had figured out where the next thirty days' rations or the next thirty days' supply of ammunition, or anything was going to come from or how to get it there way across the Pacific. This was not planned for at COMINCH.[38]

Fortunately, Kelly Turner was up to the task. The *McCawley* let go her anchor in Noumea Harbor on 13 August. Turner had already been arranging for all available supplies to be forwarded to Guadalcanal. Although the main depot at Auckland lay 1,825 miles from Guadalcanal, the Marines received their first shipment on 15 August and another on 21 August. Of greater importance was the herculean effort that made the uncompleted airfield available to American planes by 20 August. The planes were few and inadequately supplied, but they would make the difference between survival and defeat. The battle for Guadalcanal was not over; there followed a bitter six-month struggle as each side attempted to reinforce its forces ashore faster than the enemy could.

The issue remained in doubt for some time as the U.S. Navy battled to wrest command of the sea from the Japanese, and in doing so suffered severe losses. Among the casualties of Guadalcanal was Admiral Ghormley. Nimitz came to the conclusion, albeit one that was personally painful, that Ghormley had to go. Nimitz relieved him on 18 October, replacing him with Vice Adm. William F. Halsey.

Uncomplicated, a hard drinker, salty in demeanor and expression, Halsey was a fighting sailor in the simplest sense. Among his first actions after taking command was to have a large sign erected greeting newcomers to Tulagi with the exhortation, KILL JAPS, KILL JAPS, KILL MORE JAPS. Nor was he averse to expressing his contempt for the Japanese: "When we first started out I held one of our men equal to three Japanese. I now increase this to twenty. They are not supermen, although they try to make us believe they are. They are just low monkeys. I say monkeys because I cannot say what I would like to call them."[39] His presence would dramatically change the tenor of operations in the Solomons.

One person intimately aware of the pace of operations was Kelly Turner. His South Pacific Amphibious Force worked hard to carry supplies and reinforcements to the battle area. It was a task that allowed them to put into practice the lessons they were learning. A large reinforcement convoy ran in to Guadalcanal during the period 8–15 November, and Turner's operations order is illustrative of the experience he and his sailors had gained.

Point by point, Turner told his men what he expected: each ship was to hold four rehearsals before reaching the transport area; as many cargo nets as possible were to be loaded beforehand; shore parties were to be the first men on the beach; each transport was to provide a salvage boat; each ship's beach party was to clearly mark its designated section of beach with an 8×6-ft. sign; cargo was to start ashore "at the earliest possible moment, and move as fast as possible"; every ship was to be kept in use continuously and all cargo nets were to be employed. Turner made sure all hands were aware of the stakes. "It must again be stated, in the most emphatic terms, that the safety of our [Guadalcanal] position, our ships, and our troops and crews, depends directly on the speed of unloading." He further emphasized his concern to his captains by encouraging them to "Give wide publicity to . . . this plan, and to the expectancy of battle. Drill thoroughly in all measures of preparation."[40]

American industrial production, organizational ability, determination, and valor eventually prevailed in the battle for Guadalcanal. The larger importance of the fight lies in that it was the beginning of the counteroffensive that the Japanese did not expect before 1943. Thereafter, the Japanese fought at places of American choosing. They had to attempt to defend everywhere, with accompanying dispersion of men and materiel. Given the disparity between Japanese and American resources, the eventual outcome could hardly have been different. Guadalcanal was an epochal battle that taught the Navy and Marine Corps much about amphibious warfare and the nature of their enemy. Six months of vicious fighting showed the Americans what had to be endured. While the battle raged, ships and landing craft were beginning to flow from American shipyards and factories in an increasing stream. Guided by the body of experience gained at Guadalcanal, they would soon be employed in other South Pacific operations.

Turner, meanwhile, was also being forced to deal with the unpreparedness of the Navy's logistical establishment and the competing demands for resources by other commanders. He was first pressed in September when both Nimitz and King wanted him to release some of his marines and amphibious ships for other operations. MacArthur wanted a regiment of amphibious-trained troops as well as the shipping needed to support them. Turner pointed out that Guadalcanal was the only place where they could be found and he could not afford to weaken Vandegrift's already slim strength. Curiously, Turner did approve of one practice that had a negative effect on his amphibious ships throughout the war. After the conclusion of an assault, several ships had to transfer several landing craft and crews into a local boat pool. This practice had the effect of constantly draining the amphibians of experienced boat crews.

Still other demands were made on Turner by King, who wanted, and would get, ships for Operation Torch. Although Turner was realist enough to admit the validity of what he heard, he was no doubt irritated when Air Force commander Hap Arnold reported to Marshall that "Navy planning and operations to date have demonstrated a definite lack of appreciation of the logistic factor, and as a consequence, operations to date have lacked continuity by reason of the shortage of essential supplies and installations to support military operations."[41]

While Turner was fighting the Japanese and everyone else who crossed his path, two amphibious raids served to teach the Americans and their British allies some painful lessons about the dangers inherent in amphibious warfare. One raid took place in the Central Pacific and was intended to draw Japanese attention away from Guadalcanal. The other took place on the French shore of the English Channel and saw the bloody rejection of a British attempt to seize a defended port.

THE RAIDS ON MAKIN AND DIEPPE: AUGUST 1942

Defending against invasion is not the only problem faced by a military force charged with guarding a shoreline. If the enemy retains his freedom of movement on the sea, he always has the capability of unexpectedly putting ashore a raiding party at a place of his choosing. Installations can be destroyed, casualties inflicted, prisoners snatched, intelligence gathered, and daily routine turned to nervous peering into the night. A raid won't decide a campaign, but it can divert the attention of the occupying force and cause the raided place to be reinforced at the expense of other locations. That was the purpose of an assault mounted against Makin Island in August 1942.

The Gilbert Islands, of which Makin atoll is a part, lie in the Central Pacific some 2,000 miles southwest of Pearl Harbor. Plans for the raid originated in Nimitz's headquarters; the idea was to dissuade the Japanese from sending any reinforcements to the Solomons, where the battle for Guadalcanal was about to begin. The 2nd Marine Raider Battalion was alerted for the operation; 222 men embarked in the large transport submarines *Nautilus* and *Argonaut* and departed Pearl Harbor on 8 August. It took eight days for the tightly packed subs to make the transit to Makin.

Both submarines arrived off Makin and conducted a periscope reconnaissance of the landing site. They surfaced in the midwatch darkness of 17 August, and immediately the raiders began embarking in rubber boats. They had some trouble loading, but all eighteen boats eventually reached shore, where they made an undetected landing. Action was forced upon the Marines when someone accidentally fired a weapon. The ensuing fight was difficult for the raiders; Japanese aircraft from neighboring islands made several attacks throughout the day and one seaplane even attempted to land reinforcements. The *Nautilus* made a valiant effort to give support with her deck guns but poor portable radios made communication difficult at best. Since his orders called for reembarkation no later than 2100 on 17 August, Lt. Col. Evans Carlson made the decision that his force would have to forego the planned destruction of Japanese installations. The raiders therefore withdrew to the beach, recovered their boats, and made ready to push through the crashing surf. Doing so proved to be a task more easily put into an operations order than executed.

Heavy surf drowned the boats' gasoline engines and only effort borne of desperation got some of them through the waves. Several others overturned, dumping weapons into the sea and drowning several marines. When the coming day brought the urgent need for the submarines to dive, there were still 120 mostly unarmed marines stranded on Makin. To their relief, they discovered there were only two live Japanese on the island; the garrison had resisted almost literally to the last man. The marines spent an anxious day destroying buildings and equipment. The submarines resurfaced at nightfall and having been advised that there were no Japanese left on the island, moved around to the lee side where it proved far easier for boats to clear the beach. Thirty of the raiders were missing and those not known to have been killed in action were thought to have drowned. Incredibly, nine of the missing men were alive and somehow were left behind.

Action Reports of the time put the best face possible on the raid, but it accomplished little other than the destruction of the small garrison and a few buildings. No Japanese forces were diverted from movement to the Solomons; as events would show, the raid actually cost the Americans dearly. Reinforcements poured into the Gilberts and their defenses were substantially increased. As for the nine unfortunate men left behind, they were captured and eventually beheaded in a ritual samurai execution.

More was gained, though at a far greater cost, by the British raid on Dieppe. After the Germans drove British forces out of continental Europe in the summer of 1940, Churchill was quick in his demand that the enemy not be allowed to rest easily anywhere on the conquered shore. The British Army and Royal Marines formed elite commando units whose sole purpose was staging raids along the vast coastline from Norway to the Spanish border. After several months of sporadic, small-scale raids that put tactics and equipment to the test, British planners reached an initial decision to try a large-scale raid against a port. With no experience of providing large amounts of supplies across a beach, doctrine of the time held the seizure of a port essential. Planners chose Dieppe because of its size and because it lay within range of aircover from England. Approximately 9,800 British and Canadian military personnel and sixty U.S. Army Rangers were assigned to Operation Jubilee. After several delays, the raid was scheduled for 19 August 1942.

The assault force made the Channel crossing without incident and arrived off Dieppe in the early morning darkness. Very little after that went right. There was no prelanding air bombardment because the planners believed it would destroy the element of surprise and make the streets of the town impassable to tanks. There was thus no reduction of the defenses, which soon cost the invaders dearly. A chance meeting between several landing craft and a German convoy caused many defenders to be alerted; those who weren't at their posts came quickly to their guns as the assault began. Naval gunfire support was scant as only four destroyers armed with 4-in. guns were present. The ability of the gunfire ships to support the soldiers was further limited because observers couldn't get forward. Defensive fire was extremely heavy, destroying or disabling all twenty-seven tanks that landed, as well as thirty-three landing craft, and sinking one destroyer. A few units were even unable to approach the beach due to the heavy volume of fire.

The necessity of controlling the air over the invasion area was violently demonstrated by unceasing German air attacks that sank many smaller landing craft. Communications with Royal Air Force headquarters in England were good but there were lags between calls for air support and the arrival of planes overhead. Only one beach objective was taken, a coast defense battery on the west flank of the landing area. Casualties among the troops were disastrous: 3,300 of 5,000 Canadians engaged were killed, wounded, or captured. British forces suffered another 1,200 casualties.

As a test, the raid was costly in the extreme, but it did have two important strategic consequences. German military authorities knew the attack was no more than a raid. Ironically, Hitler convinced himself the defenders had repulsed an actual attempt to invade France. Many of the Germans' vast defensive efforts centered thereafter on ports, leaving the beaches relatively open. The influence on Allied planning was manifold. The intensive review issued by the British concluded that the cost of achieving surprise was too high and made several specific recommendations to correct the problems. Naval gunfire resources should be sufficient to provide a heavy bombardment and overwhelming firepower during the landing phase. Air support should be continuous and heavy. Permanent naval units dedicated to amphibious warfare should be formed and trained to the standards of any front-line unit. The whole operation suffered from poor communications, so another recommendation called for outfitting specialized amphibious command ships. Finally, the review recommended that specialized armor be developed to penetrate beach defenses.

An American Marine assigned as an observer also forwarded a few observations to Marine Corps headquarters. Col. Franklin Hart suggested dive bombing was more effective than horizontal bombing in reducing beach defenses, that smoke screens actually protected the defenders from suppressing fire rather than concealing the invaders, that spotting from ashore or from the air was essential for naval gunfire to be effective, and that a successful withdrawal under fire was a virtual impossibility for an amphibious operation. No further mention was made on either side of the Atlantic of assaulting a port as a prelude to entering Europe.[42]

Dieppe was costly, but the assault had opened wide the eyes of planners already contemplating the difficulties of putting ashore a large army in France. The lessons learned that one bloodily chaotic morning in 1942 would have a significant payoff on another morning two years later, when the Allied invasion fleet hove to off the beaches of Normandy. More immediately, planners on both sides of the Atlantic were spending long hours at their desks as they sought to convert into reality Franklin Roosevelt's orders for a landing in North Africa.

3

ACTION IN AFRICA

An amphibious operation, in order to succeed, you've got to roll; it's got to grow. If you get sealed off on your beachhead, you may be safely ashore all right, but you're not going anywhere.

VICE ADM. RICHARD CONOLLY

TORCH: SEPTEMBER–NOVEMBER 1942

War was no stranger to the Mediterranean shores of North Africa. The German Afrika Korps and the British Eighth Army had been vying for control of Libya and Egypt for two years. By early August 1942, the front lay in uneasy stasis just west of the Suez Canal. A visit to the area by Churchill brought the genesis of a plan intended to end the seesaw struggle definitively. Therein lay the direct military objective of Operation Torch. Far to the west of the combat zone, behind the Afrika Korps, lay the French colonies of Morocco, Algeria, and Tunisia. The first two possessed modern ports, Casablanca and Algiers, through which a large army could be supported for a drive against the German rear. The Afrika Korps would be ground out of existence between the converging Allied armies.

The relationship of military and political matters is foregone, so it is no surprise that Churchill saw the destruction of the Afrika Korps as part of a larger, decidedly political scheme. After his visit to the Eighth Army, he flew to Moscow to try to explain to Stalin why the Allies would not be opening a second front in France in 1942. Soviet bitterness and suspicion were extreme; Churchill therefore had to put what would now be called the proper "spin" on the Allied decision to mount Torch instead of invading France. Roosevelt's need for action and Churchill's promise that the North African venture would be a major operation thus locked the Americans into a far greater effort than they wanted. There were a few obstacles to be overcome.

The first was who would command the operation. It seems ironic that King suggested an Army officer who eventually would have supreme command of one of the largest amphibious forces ever assembled. Marshall had appointed Dwight Eisenhower as United States commander of the European Theater of Operations on 11 June. By the time Torch was settled, Eisenhower had developed a solid rapport with the British, especially Churchill. King's suggestion that Eisenhower be placed in command of Torch therefore met with no opposition. Eisenhower had been strongly against the plan, but once in command, he dedicated his efforts to making it succeed. He gathered a staff comprised in equal measure of British and Americans whom he drove hard to create a plan of operations. The arduous weeks of conferences and trans-Atlantic travel that followed not only hammered out a plan for Torch, but also gave Eisenhower his baptism in the difficulties of commanding a coalition.

Eisenhower's merits as a military commander have been discussed often and at length. Judgments ranging from great to mediocre have been rendered, although the nationality of his appraiser always had a bearing. There is no question, however, that whatever his failings as a strategic thinker, no officer in the panoply of Allied generals who fought World War II could have done as well managing the intrigues and competing imperatives of the Anglo-American coalition. Eisenhower's dedication to the coalition was complete; he expected anyone assigned to his staff to put aside national differences and work for the common good. A directive issued by the British War Office to the commanders assigned to Torch shows the trust placed in Eisenhower by his allies:

> The First Army has been placed under the Supreme Command of . . .
> Lieutenant General Dwight D. Eisenhower, United States Army. You will
> carry out any orders issued by him. In the unlikely event of your receiving
> an order which . . . will give rise to a grave and exceptional situation,
> you have the right to appeal to the War Office, provided that by so doing
> an opportunity is not lost, nor any part of the Allied Force endangered.[1]

Operation Torch was crucial to Eisenhower because it allowed him to begin learning the skills he would need two years later. High on the list of questions facing Eisenhower's planners was the location and scale of the assault. The British favored concentrating the assault on the Mediterranean shore as far east as Bône to forestall German reinforcements being sent to Tunisia from Sicily and Italy. The Americans wanted to seize Casablanca as insurance against the Germans' cutting the supply line through the Straits of Gibraltar. Marshall was also mindful that the Germans had far the shorter distance to cover in reinforcing their position. The biggest problem was that there simply wasn't enough shipping available to support all the proposed landings.

The compromise worked out by the combined staffs planned landings on the Moroccan coast at Mehedia, Fedhala, and Safi. The main objectives were the large, modern airfield at Port Lyautey and the port of Casablanca. Four landings on the Mediterranean coast of Algeria had been posited, but the availability of shipping limited the effort to two, one at Oran, the other at Algiers. Churchill and Roosevelt again exchanged some short telegrams: "Hurrah!" wired the president. "O.K., full blast," the prime minister replied.

The compromise about the number of landing sites came about only after intense pressure was exerted on King. With his main focus already on the Pacific and Watchtower about to get underway, he was not particularly receptive to diverting precious ships to the Atlantic. He knew of the political imperative behind Torch, but was too well aware that releasing any of the transports in the Pacific would shorten the already long odds facing the Marines on Guadalcanal. Furthermore, the loss of four cruisers at Savo Island stretched gunfire support assets even thinner. He was also growing increasingly irritated by a seeming lack of concern with security, not only within the Navy Department, but especially among the soldiers. He sent George Dyer to find out how many people knew about the still highly secret operation. When Dyer told King that sixty-one naval officers had knowledge of Torch, King exploded. He tempered his fury the next day when he discovered that more than 1,300 Army personnel were in the know.[2]

King's insistence that there were no ships to spare was one of Eisenhower's biggest headaches and caused him to warn two officers sent to England by King that

> the U.S. Army and Navy were both under the President's explicit orders making Torch an operation of the highest priority, that the British armed services were in a parallel position, and that the Combined Chiefs of Staff would require that the navies of both countries overcome all obstacles in executing the operation.[3]

With the president so deeply involved in the planning for Torch, King inevitably had to relent. On 3 September, Marshall was able to tell Eisenhower that enough ships would be available. This was not the last time the battle over allocating naval resources between the Atlantic and the Pacific would be fought.

Another serious concern was whether the proposed landings would be opposed. Morocco and Algeria were under the administrative control of the collaborationist Vichy French government, which had pledged to the Germans that the colonies would be defended against any invader. In addition, anti-British feelings ran very high among the French military. Eisenhower's planners therefore decided that considering the historic American alliance with France, the assault force would not open fire until fired upon and British participation would be masked as far as possible through subterfuges such as flying American colors over British ships.

The intertwining of political and military spheres so evident in the choice of North Africa as a landing site was manifested in a series of cloak and dagger machinations that took place before the invasion. The brain trust at Allied Force Headquarters in London decided that a high-ranking American officer from Eisenhower's staff would be landed from a submarine at Algiers. There, he would secretly contact supposedly sympathetic French civil and military officials and attempt to convince them that resistance was useless; fighting would also be criminal considering America's traditional relationship with France. The mission took place, but essentially came to naught. While some French officers were loath to fire on Americans in defense of Vichy, duty is often the stronger imperative. These efforts notwithstanding, the assault force commanders were under no restrictions should the defenders open fire. Once the assault was under way, any movement at all by French military units was to be treated as hostile.

Operational details were more clear cut. The U.S. Navy had responsibility for the Atlantic coast landings, and the Royal Navy had responsibility for operations in the Mediterranean. Thirty-four thousand American troops were assigned to make the landings in Morocco. A large naval task force would bring them directly from the United States to the landing area. Three separate attack groups were designated within the task force: one to take Safi, another for Fedhala, the last for Mehedia. Forty-nine thousand other Americans already assembled in England had the job of taking Oran and Algiers. Twenty-three thousand British soldiers were in the Algiers assault force.

GATHERING THE RESOURCES

The large scope of Torch meant that a vast armada of ship types would be needed to transport, support, and protect the forces coming from the United States and England. It took King until 9 September to tell his task force commander what ships would be available. Newly converted transport and cargo ships had to be formed into groups, gathered at the ports of embarkation, and provided with escorts. Gunfire-support ships had to be scheduled into task forces. The job of providing air support off the Moroccan beaches fell to the fleet carrier *Ranger* and three new CVEs. Expediency was sending the new carriers to war, for neither their crews nor their air groups were fully trained or ready for combat.

The same could be said of most of the ships comprising the transport groups. Thirty-three transports and cargo ships were in one task force, but only fourteen were commissioned naval vessels on 1 August. Ten merchantmen had to be acquired in August and their conversion to naval service hurriedly begun. Converting a former civilian merchant ship into an amphibious assault ship was not without its difficulties. Conversion still took less time than it took green sailors to learn, practice, and become polished at the specialized skills in cargo handling and seamanship that amphibious warfare demanded. Most boat crews called upon to put soldiers ashore only began learning their craft in June and even those efforts suffered from too many coxswains needing training and not enough boats to provide it.

Stan Newland was among the thousands of new sailors about to learn the rigors of amphibious warfare. He was assigned to the recently converted transport *Florence Nightingale*, soon to be known to her men as "Flossie":

> September 17, 1942, was commissioning day; a day of mass confusion! So many of us were green. We had never seen an ocean before, let alone been on a ship. The chow on board ship was nothing to write home about! One item I do remember fondly is the terrific peach pies. We got underway finally for an unknown destination and soon experienced our first taste of rough seas. Machinist Worden told me I had better secure for sea as he expected we would have some rough weather. So, I did what I thought was a pretty good job of lashing things down. Not good enough as I found to my dismay. When I went to the storeroom, there was Mr. Worden surveying it and shaking his head in disbelief! Large glass jars of distilled water had smashed, cans of grease and flake graphite had fallen on the deck and mixed with the water and glass. My next assignment was the machine shop, where I was supposed to be in the first place.[4]

As with any amphibious assault, intelligence was a particular preoccupation of the Torch planners. Analysts estimated the French had 55,000 to 60,000 troops in Morocco, but their general quality and willingness to fight was uncertain. The French navy was known to be pro-Vichy and willing to fight; there were enough men-of-war in Moroccan ports to pose a serious threat to the invasion. As one recap of the operation stated, the French navy in Morocco was "well trained, well equipped, thoroughly disciplined and the leadership is energetic and able." The same report stated, "That the rank and file of the French Navy would resent any interference in French affairs, no matter how well intentioned, was a foregone conclusion among all competent observers."[5]

The Americans also feared a possible German attack against Gibraltar, the base from which land-based air support would be funneled into the invasion area. Another question mark was the landing beaches; there was an ample supply of locally gathered intelligence about the defenses, but besides British-supplied aerial photographs, there were no charts of the Moroccan beaches. Meteorologists knew that surf conditions on the Atlantic coast could run up to fifteen feet, creating an extreme hazard for the landing craft. None of these questions could be answered until the moment when the invasion waves began to approach the beaches.

The principal American commanders who had to cope with these problems were Rear Adm. H. Kent Hewitt and Maj. Gen. George S. Patton. Hewitt was intimately aware of many problems he would face in putting the Army ashore in North Africa. He had transferred to Torch from his post as commander of the Amphibious Force Atlantic Fleet, a job in which he had been living every day with the associated problems of training a vast assemblage of landlubbers into the mysteries of conducting an amphibious assault. His staff had also anticipated the possibility of a landing in North Africa and had begun studying how to overcome the obstacles. A lesser of those obstacles was that Patton's staff was in Washington, D.C., and Hewitt's was in Norfolk. Of greater concern were the difficulties caused by Army ideas.

Hewitt was constantly aggravated and irritated by the Army's openly stated position that "training of Army elements as landing forces was essentially a unilateral matter and that the Navy should take a supporting role and provide the ships and craft for such training."[6] The Army's separate training program drained personnel off Hewitt's joint effort, causing him to ask King for assistance. King took the problem to Marshall, who demonstrated his commitment to the common goal. Marshall agreed that joint needs should come first; he directed that Hewitt was to be consulted before any disruption of the training schedule.

Hewitt had problems on the operational side as well:

The main difficulty for the Moroccan landings was the availability of the troops and shipping. Some of the transports we were to use were held until the last moment; some of the troops weren't on hand. The 3d Division . . . had had some amphibious training on the West Coast. They were given some of the rudiments there but it was unfortunate in some respects because they knew just enough about it to think they knew it all and they didn't. There was always a lack of time and facilities but above all the serious lack of any opportunity for landing in the surf, in the open sea.[7]

The truth of Hewitt's comments is shown in the elementary nature of some training. Because there were few boats, a portion of the 3d Division's "amphibious" training consisted of drills in which "automobiles riding over artificially undulating ground took the place of small boats. Beaches marked off were then occupied and unloading operations performed with as much realism as possible."[8] While there is room to question the "realism" of such an exercise, it was typical of the creative energy that would be applied to solving the problems created by inadequate resources.

At the other end of the spectrum from Hewitt was Phil Bucklew. In the summer of 1942, he was one of many newly enlisted sailors who were learning the art of handling a small boat in the open sea. Bucklew and his comrades were being prepared to reconnoiter in advance of the landing and to mark the approaches to a beach. He had an experience indicative of the thrown-together nature of training that first wartime summer:

> we were working in Chesapeake Bay one cold night in the middle of summer. . . . I was in a rubber boat . . . a half mile offshore. In the boat with me was an army captain named Pettigrew. I asked Captain Pettigrew how, as an army officer, did you get into this with the Navy. And he said, "It's very simple. For many years prior to WWII I was a rum runner. When war came along I applied to the navy saying that I have as much knowledge of shoreline silhouettes and . . . of landing as any man you will find. It is proven by the fact that I have never been arrested or caught. The navy turned me down cold. So I told the same story to the army and they commissioned me . . . and sent me over to train naval personnel."[9]

Bucklew paid attention to what Captain Pettigrew was teaching.

There was evidence of the continuing evolution of amphibious warfare practice in other preparations for Torch. Naval shore fire-control parties specially trained for the task were formed and plans made to assign them to advance elements of the invasion force. A joint communications school was established on the new amphibious training base at Little Creek, Virginia. There was still no amphibious command ship, so the heavy cruiser *Augusta* drew the assignment; she got extra bunks, extra radios, and the designation force flagship. Despite the joint nature of much of the preparatory work, many Army men were decidedly doubtful about the Navy's amphibious skills.

Hewitt's Army counterpart was Major General Patton, an officer who was then still somewhat unknown. Patton had a jaundiced view of the Navy's ability to put his troops ashore anywhere near the objective. At the last conference of commanders before sailing, Patton voiced both his reading of history and institutional bias when he told the assembled audience, "Never in history has the Navy landed an army at the planned time and place. If you land us anywhere within fifty miles of Fedhala and within one week of D-day, I'll go ahead and win."[10] Patton's boastful persona was not yet the stuff of media legend nor had his generalship been put to the test of combat, so his comments no doubt rankled some naval officers present.

Patton's force consisted of the 3d Infantry Division, units of the 9th

Infantry Division, the 2d Armored Division, and miscellaneous supporting units. None was completely trained in amphibious warfare and there were no boats available capable of landing medium tanks across the invasion beaches. Doctrinal differences also diverged on the loads each soldier should carry. Army ideas held that the troops should take as much ashore as they could carry while Navy doctrine believed that assault troops should be lightly burdened with only what they needed in the attack. These differences in turn dictated varying schemes about the loading of transports. The loadout of the transport *Harris* is illustrative of these differences in doctrine.

The ship's load was 1,837 soldiers, 2,100 tons of cargo, and 180 vehicles. The problem with the load, which was put aboard under the supervision of the Army Transportation Service, was that it was too large for proper combat loading. The ship's Action Report also notes that because the troops embarked in alphabetical order, it took two days to reberth them in assigned combat teams.

The limited number of days available before the scheduled landing put the ideal solution to all the problems out of reach. Fully trained or not, 37,305 soldiers had to be embarked in their transports. Thirty thousand tons of supplies and 2,953 vehicles were crammed into the tightly packed holds of the Western Task Force. The landing craft were hoisted and secured to davits. Included among the landing craft were six prototype rocket-armed support boats. The third week in October saw the 100-plus ships of the task force slip their moorings and begin the long trek to war.

Departure was an especially hectic time for the crew and passengers of one transport. The ship developed last-minute engine trouble, requiring the transfer of her entire load to the *Calvert*, a job accomplished in forty-eight hours. Accompanied by two escorts, the *Calvert* put to sea in the wake of her brethren. Heading east from Casco Bay in Maine, from Norfolk, Virginia, and from Bermuda, the other transports, covering group, and air group meanwhile rendezvoused and formed into a huge convoy. Their destination lay two work-filled weeks away across the U-boat infested Atlantic.

The revelation of their previously secret destination occasioned a round of intership radio traffic that brought an admonition from Hewitt, "to whom it sounded 'more like a Chinese laundry at New Year's than a fleet going to war.' "[11] The Navy's official historian, Lt. Cdr. Samuel Eliot Morison was embarked in the light cruiser *Brooklyn*. Morison's personal notes reveal a sense of high purpose and exuberance among the *Brooklyn*'s men, as if setting out for war was no more than a visit to an amusement park. At supper time on the first night out, the *Brooklyn*'s captain announced, "I'm god damn glad to tell you we are going into battle." Morison's diary entry for 26 October notes the disgust of the men on hearing some news from the States; "Over the radio this afternoon or evening, the 'Washington Merry-Go-Round,' Drew Pearson announced that American troops would be in Casablanca within ten days. Everyone thinks he ought to be shot."

On 29 October, he recorded, "In the evening we had the film 'A Yank at Eton.' Very jolly—and strange how these movies do take one outside oneself. I looked around afterwards as in a dream—can I really be in a fighting ship in the greatest fighting force the USA has ever sent abroad?" And like the scribe who recorded the tropical lushness of Guadalcanal, the life-long sailor in Morison could not help but take in the beauty of the setting in which the task force was sailing. "A beautiful sunset with great, high dramatic clouds, and moonlight too. The kind of day that would send a clipper ship along at 15 knots."[12] Of course, not all was so prosaic in a fleet that was sailing into battle.

The problem of maintaining security while in transit was addressed in clear terms in one report:

> Neutral merchant vessels and aircraft which are met at sea shall . . . be boarded and set on the quickest course that would take them out of sight. If necessary to insure secrecy, they might be detained in an Allied port. Flagrant violations of the rules against unneutral service might lead to capture and even sinking. Aircraft were to be shot down.[13]

The report of the *Harris* gives the impression of constant training. Scale models of the transports and landing craft were built and maneuvered on deck to familiarize coxswains and boat crews with the relative positions of the transport area and the beaches. A color painting of Safi harbor was also done on the deck and the contour of the shoreline as it would appear from a boat was applied to the adjacent bulkhead. Training was also a necessity for the American troops in England. In common with the rest of the U.S. Army at that time, they had little to no amphibious training. The Army's 1st Engineer Amphibious Brigade conducted a few exercises at British facilities in Scotland, but the terrain was so dissimilar and time so short that what was done had little practical value.

The combined assault force of more than 73,000 American and British soldiers embarked in two groups of ships that formed a fast and a slow convoy. The Royal Navy's Force H, under the command of Adm. Sir Andrew Cunningham, escorted and supported both. The convoys passed through the Straits of Gibraltar the night of 5–6 November and began their approach to the Algerian assault areas. German agents watching from Spanish territory reported the passage, but their assumption was that the convoys represented British reinforcements for Libya.

The impending approach of action got sudden punctuation early on the morning of 7 November when a transport was hit by a torpedo and brought to a halt 155 miles west of Algiers. The escort commander detached a corvette to stand by while the remainder of the convoy pressed on toward its destination. Far to the west, the task force was also nearing the end of its journey as it approached the Moroccan shore.

NORTH AFRICA: NOVEMBER 1942

One wild card thrown into the planning of any amphibious assault is the weather. The Torch planners knew that after the first week in November, winter surf conditions along the Moroccan coast were likely to preclude any chance of a landing. The World War II planners did not have the advantage of satellite pictures and computerized weather data banks. Historical records and best-guess estimates provided the basis for their decisions, so anxiety ran high in the flag quarters when the weather began making up on 4 November. Weather reports from Washington and London added to the gloom, seeming to suggest that the assault would have to be diverted to a fall-back landing on the Mediterranean shore. Hewitt's fleet meteorologist was more optimistic, convincing the worried admiral that the weather would abate enough for the landing to be carried out as planned. Task Force 34 therefore continued its steady advance toward its assigned objective.

One skill Hewitt's sailors did not need to polish was their navigation. The *Augusta* began a radar search for the expected landfall off Fedhala at 2100 and made first contact at 2137. After a passage of 4,500 miles and some Ultra-generated course changes, the three separate assault components began approaching the transport areas around 2300 on 7 November. The bright glow of lights ashore sent a wave of excited anticipation through the task force as the men realized the long crossing was over and their objective was at hand. Anticipation was quickly replaced with subdued apprehension as Casablanca plunged suddenly into blackout, leaving the assault force to maneuver by the faint glow of starlight. While some transports found themselves badly out of position, most anchored in the correct place with little difficulty.

Despite the few problems, the transport groups at Safi and Fedhala anchored six to eight miles off their respective beaches by 2400 on 7 November. The transports carrying troops assigned to the initial assault waves anchored in lines nearest to the beach and those assigned to subsequent waves farther away. At Mehedia a freshening wind forced the ships to remain under way. Shortly after the transports anchored, the first American attempt to get ashore without resistance was put into play. At 0130, the BBC began broadcasting a message from Roosevelt announcing the landings and asking French forces to come over to the Allied cause. The broadcast was not widely heard, had no effect on those who did hear it, and aggravated thousands of American soldiers and sailors who believed it compromised the element of surprise.

Attention then turned to accomplishing what the landing force had come so far to do. The op-order called for a four-hour period during which marker boats would be posted off each designated beach to guide the incoming waves of landing craft, the necessary boat groups would be formed, the initial assault elements embarked, and the boat waves started shoreward. The inevitable divergence between what has been planned and what really occurs under operational conditions soon revealed itself.

The lack of training in basic boat handling skills, the extreme difficulties inherent in coordinating boat movements at night, and the unfamiliarity of the soldiers with debarking quickly proved it was going to take far longer than expected to get the troops into the boats. First came the problem of forming boat pools. The number of soldiers assigned to the first wave far exceeded the boat capacity of any given transport. The solution appeared to be simple: pool the total available boats and assign enough to each front-line transport to do the job. Given the scale of the operation and the greenness of the men, the op-plan fell into disarray.

It is easy to understand the confusion considering the example of the *Harris*: forty-nine boats from six different ships were assigned to unload her. Since this situation was common to all the front-line transports, it is not surprising that too few boats showed up to lift the first wave. The captain of the transport *Charles Carroll* was critical but understanding in his comments:

> The most glaring deficiency of Operation Torch was the lack of discipline in boat crews. It is believed that this inadequacy will have to be shared by all those in the chain of command . . . through the commanding officers of transports to those in higher authority who placed a Herculean responsibility on such immaturely trained men. They were unskilled in handling their boats, they were unlearned in even the simplest elements of seamanship. The supreme test of their training was made under conditions where only experts could hope to succeed *part of the time*. No one should be made to take the blame for this condition, for no blame is intended here to attach to anyone.[14]

The timetable was further delayed by the loading process being excruciatingly slow.

Afterward, neither service was averse to blaming the other for problems. The Army believed the delay in loading stemmed from poor positioning of the transports and a general lack of trained boat coxswains. The Navy countered that the pooling of boats needed to accommodate the Army's excessive demands for men on the beach was the main problem.

The Navy also argued that the soldiers were far too "sluggish" in embarking in the boats. The skipper of the *Harris* wrote, "It must in fairness be said . . . that many of the troops had practically no training and they carried a tremendous amount of equipment on their backs. Much too much and too heavy."[15] Rope nets stretching and fouling boat propellors slowed debarkation while the wire nets proved slippery and often cut the soldiers' hands.

The *Harris's* executive officer also noted that improper stowage of cargo greatly delayed unloading. In several instances, material needed in the first wave was stowed as deep as the fourth deck instead of the first where it should have been. Unloading off Mehedia was complicated by wind conditions that forced the transports to remain under way. Troops disembarked to the lee side as the ships tracked slowly back and forth across the wind. There is a kernel of truth in the arguments of either side, but the real crux of the matter is that both services were still new to the business of amphibious warfare.

As at Guadalcanal, destroyers served as control ships for many boat waves. By 0515, slightly more than an hour late, the boats of the first wave crunched ashore at Mehedia. There was a similar delay at Fedhala, where the first troops touched down around 0500. The centerpiece of the Safi attack was a direct assault against the harbor by troops debarking from two APDs. That attack began slightly after 0400 when the *Bernadou* began her approach to the harbor entrance. She and her sister ship *Cole* each carried 197 soldiers whose job was to secure the harbor so the Army's medium tanks could be landed at pierside. Both ships had their upperworks cut down to reduce their silhouettes, but in the event both were seen and taken under fire by the harbor defenders.

The *Bernadou* and a fire-support destroyer replied quickly; their return fire was so heavy that all the French guns were silenced by 0514. The battleship *New York* and the light cruiser *Philadelphia* helped by pummeling a nearby shore battery into silence. Finding the way to her intended landing pier blocked, the *Bernadou's* skipper neatly grounded his ship alongside a stone jetty onto which the soldiers scrambled and began going about their tasks. The *Cole* followed and came smoothly alongside her assigned pier and immediately began spilling ashore her load of soldiers. Safi was effectively in American hands by daylight and by late afternoon vitally needed tanks were coming ashore.

The landings across the various beaches were generally successful, but each had its share of difficulties. There were expected failures in execution: some scout boats were out of position, landing craft missed their rendezvous points, and other boats landed hundreds of yards, even miles, from their assigned beaches. There were collisions, engine failures, faulty compasses, and boats holed by rocks. A war correspondent who accompanied the troops to Fedhala recorded what it was like in one boat that experienced difficulties:

> Then came a grinding crash as our landing craft smashed full speed into a coral reef. From its ripped front ramp the water climbed to our shoetops, then surged to our knees. "Every man overboard," said the boat commander. We plunged from the sides of the settling craft up to our armpits in the surf. Waves washed over our heads, doubling the weight of our 60-pound packs with water, but sweeping us nearer safety. I grabbed an outcropping of coral. Twice the surf pulled me loose and twice it returned me. My strength was ebbing fast when another soldier pulled up the man before me and lent me a wet hand to safety.[16]

The captain of the transport *Thomas Jefferson* later reported that the beach marking boat from his ship was delayed because someone had partially cut through the lashings on a debarkation net. There was even a spectacular burst of flame alongside the transport *Dorothea Dix* as an Army truck being hoisted over the side spilled gasoline from a punctured can onto the hot engine of the boat below. The resulting explosion and fire convinced everyone that the *Dix* had been torpedoed and brought some wild gunfire from the green gun crews of the neighboring transports. Excepting Mehedia, enough troops were ashore to assure that the landings could not easily be repulsed.

Surf conditions varied from excellent to moderate but the inexperience of most coxswains immediately began to take a toll on the landing craft. One ship lost eighteen of twenty-five boats employed in the first wave and of the remaining seven, five were lost when the second wave came ashore. Except for two ships manned by the Coast Guard with a more solid core of experienced boat handlers, the other transports suffered disproportionately high losses of landing craft. Besides the normal difficulties of beaching a landing craft, the large number of inexperienced coxswains had been asked to beach on an ebbing tide, a problem of seamanship that was beyond most of their capabilities. George Dyer sheds some light on the mechanics of beaching:

> It is very difficult in any kind of weather at all to hold small landing craft perpendicular to the beach . . . as the waves strike the stern. You're held forward by the fact that you're aground. In any kind of swell, and in the case of delays, it is difficult to unload without getting broached [or] . . . sideways to the beach. . . .[17]

On the other hand, some coxswains had a natural talent for the job. Bud Farmer remembers that the task of beaching a landing craft wasn't "that hard." In his quiet Tennessee drawl, he said the trick was to keep the boat going slightly ahead as the load came off, thereby staying firmly on the beach. Farmer held the problem to be particularly easy on a sandy beach; "If you hit sand, it's nothin'—stick it in the sand."[18] Another frequent problem was boat crews lowering the bow ramp too soon, flooding the boat. These difficulties would be addressed with more intensive training, the formation of boat salvage groups, and the fitting out of a designated repair and salvage ship. On its part, the Army would make salvage part of the training syllabus for engineer units assigned to beach duty.

Fortunately for the Americans, French confusion and uncertainty made initial resistance to the landings sporadic. The Safi attack came under fire immediately, but French shore batteries at Mehedia only commenced firing about thirty minutes after the first landing; those at Fedhala did not open up until fifty minutes after the first troops dashed ashore. The opening shots from shore presaged an active day for the gunfire-support ships of the Torch task force.

RESISTANCE

Several shore batteries of differing calibers defended the invasion areas. When they began to drop shells around ships of the support group and the landing boats, the typically American code phrase "Batter Up" let the various task group commanders know that all hopes for an unopposed landing were in vain. The response was quick: within seconds of hearing "Play Ball," gunnery officers were laying their main batteries on target. Typical of the problems faced when ships fight it out with shore batteries was the duel between the *Augusta*, four destroyers, and some guns at Fedhala. Between 0710 and 1035, each ship in turn opened fire on the battery; though they managed to destroy the French fire control equipment, they never silenced the guns.

The *Brooklyn* was more successful in her fight with another battery. She inundated the French gunners with a rapid-fire deluge of 6-in. shells that destroyed the battery fire-control gear, wrecked one gun, and caused many casualties among the gunners. The fire of a battery defending Mehedia fell close enough to chase the transports to a safer anchorage fifteen miles offshore. Nonetheless, the naval gunners were able to suppress French fire enough for the landing boats to complete their mission successfully. The gunfire-support ships were aided by naval shore fire control parties whose only previous experience had been calling fire missions down on Solomons Island, Maryland. Even though their radios proved notoriously susceptible to failure, 60 percent of the fire control parties were eventually able to establish and maintain contact with the ships offshore.

The shore fire control parties were helped by spotters in float planes launched by the battleship *Massachusetts* and the cruisers. One pilot showed the stuff that makes ground troops cheer when he took his slow-moving biplane down to bomb an advancing column of French tanks. Once the troops landed, it was often only a matter of hours before the shore batteries were overrun. The general commanding the troops at Mehedia did go into the operation with some preconceptions about the effectiveness of naval gunfire support. Lucian Truscott was so skeptical about the ability of the Navy to hit shore targets that he permitted only a minimum of call-fire missions. His was a common attitude that would undergo slow but drastic change over the next two years.

More threatening to the success of the landing was the fight put up by the Vichy-dominated French navy. There was a sizable naval force available to the defenders; loyalty to their commander-in-chief and a perverse code of honor dictated that the French sailors would fight. Among the weapons available was the unfinished battleship *Jean Bart*, moored in Casablanca harbor. Although immobile, she demonstrated her ability to shoot when she dropped a salvo 600 yards off the starboard bow of the *Massachusetts*. There were also a number of cruisers, destroyers, and submarines available to the French naval commander at Casablanca. He wasted no time ordering them to sortie against the invasion fleet; at 0641 one of the *Augusta*'s spotting planes reported two submarines under way and proceeding toward the harbor entrance.

The *Massachusetts* and the heavy cruiser *Wichita* meanwhile took the *Jean Bart* under fire and hit her solidly enough to jam her only operable turret. The downside was that in their maneuvering, the ships of the covering group put themselves twenty-five miles away from the transports they were there to protect. Seven speedy, well-armed French destroyers and a single cruiser seized the moment to emerge from the harbor and break for the transport area. As they raced northward, they opened fire on the landing boats clustered at the shoreline, disintegrating one with a direct hit. A greater disaster loomed if they were able to get among the amphibious ships, however briefly.

While the transport sailors stood to their guns and steeled themselves for what appeared to be coming, Hewitt ordered the *Augusta*, the *Brooklyn*, and two destroyers away from their gunfire-support duties and into action against the onrushing French force. General Patton was just about to embark in a landing craft swinging from the *Augusta*'s davits when the call to battle arrived. He was able to retrieve his trademark ivory-handled revolvers but muzzle blast from the main battery destroyed the rest of his personal effects. Firing as fast as the guns could be served and laid, Hewitt's ships caused the French to reverse course and retire under a smoke screen. Hewitt meanwhile ordered the ships of the covering group to join the action and eliminate the threat. The *Massachusetts* and the heavy cruiser *Tuscaloosa* came charging into the ring and quickly blew up one French destroyer. While the other French ships continued to evade the torrent of shellfire aimed at them, the submarines that had sortied earlier made their presence known. Both the *Massachusetts* and the *Brooklyn* had to put their helms hard over to comb the tracks of torpedo salvoes. Luck was with the Americans; none of the torpedoes hit and American fire finally began to score on the French warships.

In an hour and a half, the French force was reduced to a single undamaged destroyer. The others were all sunk, beached, or immobilized by a combination of ship gunfire and bombs from the *Ranger*'s aircraft. Though shore batteries continued intermittent fire at the American ships, the French naval threat no longer existed. Three American sailors were killed and five ships hit, none with serious damage. For the sake of a dubious honor, the French navy lost four destroyers, eight submarines, and 490 dead. Fortunately for Hewitt's men, the French had shot their bolt; ammunition expenditure among the American ships was so high that another battle would have left them with empty magazines. The need for a large fleet supply train was becoming ever more evident.

One especially bright spot of the day's action had been the quality of air support. No amphibious operation of World War II was planned without the question of air cover being foremost among the problems to be solved. No landing could hope to succeed if the defenders were able to exert extended control over the landing beaches. There was a disparity in numbers between attackers and defenders; Hewitt's carriers bore 172 planes with them to oppose an estimated 315 available to the French. Whereas the Navy fliers had the multiple tasks of providing cover over the beaches, close support to the troops, and antisubmarine patrol, the French fliers had the single task of attacking the landing force. The successes that his fliers turned in on the first day must therefore have lifted a little of the burden from Admiral Hewitt's shoulders.

Though French air attacks destroyed forty-three landing craft, Navy fighters shot down a combined total of fifty-five French planes over the beach areas. Determined strafing attacks also turned much of the enemy air threat into flaming wreckage on the ground. Dive bombers and fighters joined in attacking French shore and AA batteries. Air support for the troops ashore was coordinated by naval air liaison parties that accompanied the advancing units. In a process more streamlined than at Guadalcanal, the air liaison parties were able to radio their requests for support directly to their assigned carrier, which directed its airborne planes to the target. Air support thus coordinated helped break up several French attempts to mount counterattacks.

French resistance had not ceased as the day ended on 8 November, but there was no doubt in American minds that at Safi and Fedhala they were ashore for keeps. Mehedia was a different story. One objective of the assault had been to cut a wire boom blocking access to the Wadi Sebou, a river leading inland to Port Lyautey airfield. Unfortunately, the defenders drove off the boom-cutting party with heavy machine gun fire. Nor were the beach landings an unqualified success: the plan of maneuver was completely disrupted by troops being landed in the wrong place. Confusion resulted when command ashore proved incapable of sorting out mixed units and maintaining order on the beaches. The natural consequence of so many landing craft being destroyed or rendered inoperable was ever greater confusion.

Supplies were slow getting ashore as fewer boats struggled to maintain the unloading plan. Enterprising sailors from the transport *George Clymer* tried towing a cargo net loaded with fuel cans and drums but their effort failed. The engineers and Navy beach parties working to keep the supplies flowing inland quickly realized the need for adequate prelanding reconnaissance. A road had to be graded through more than a mile of soft sand to give incoming supplies a route off the beach. It was also clear that not nearly enough bulldozers had been included in the engineers' equipment tables. Even nature contrived to add to the problem; by nightfall, the surf at Mehedia began to mount, eventually reaching 15 feet, making landings hazardous in the extreme. Not only had the initial D-day objective of Port Lyautey airfield not been reached, the official Army history characterized the situation there at nightfall as precarious.

Sufficient troops were ashore at Fedhala but the scene at the beach was one of men working desperately to avoid chaos. Cargo handlers worked through the night of 8–9 November; a situation reminiscent of Guadalcanal resulted. What was coming ashore was not getting off the beaches or piers either quickly or in an organized way. Army shore parties had been established, but as with the Marine pioneer battalions in the Pacific, their numbers were too few and their organization flawed. The Navy beachmaster at Fedhala endured considerable criticism from assault unit commanders as he altered the landing plan to conserve the dwindling supply of landing craft. General Patton later said that the "[beachmaster] saved the whole Goddamned operation."[19]

Patton went ashore from the *Augusta* at 0800 on the 9th to check on the progress of unloading and found the situation ashore,

"a mess," with leadership negligent. He personally ordered a launch sent out to intercept the boats and to direct them into the port instead of letting them ride to the beach through the towering surf. The Army shore parties seemed to him neither energetic nor resourceful in moving the materiel already on the beach. In a state of exasperated frustration over the slackness that he observed and over some cases of fright during a French air attack about 0800, he remained on the beach until after noon.[20]

Naval working parties from the transports joined the Army men, but the work lagged. The op-plan gave no single officer sufficient authority to exert proper control over the combined effort. Communication between beaches was also a problem as the Navy radios proved completely unsuitable for the rough treatment they received. Among post-invasion recommendations were that the beach parties should be provided and commanded by the Army and that any naval shore parties be equipped with Army radios. A good deal of the congestion was caused by too few bulldozers to free bogged-down wheeled vehicles, and a shortage of trucks to move the supplies to dumps; 90 percent of the assault troops were landed on the first day, but only 16 percent of the vehicles. Though local labor was belatedly recruited into service, there would be little respite for the hard-pressed working parties until the transports finished unloading. The Army response to its experience in North Africa was to beef up the number of men and increase the handling equipment assigned to shore parties.

The logistics problem was also present at Safi, though not to the same extent. Space in the harbor was limited, but most of the unloading was accomplished at pierside rather than across beaches. The same problem of insufficient motor transport plagued efforts at Safi and resulted in a jumbled mountain of supplies piling up open to pilferage and exposed to enemy action. While this logistics problem was being resolved, other landings were taking place on the Mediterranean coast.

ORAN AND ALGIERS

Except for one group that was out of position by 2¼ miles, the transports arrived off Oran shortly before 2300 on 7 November and immediately began swinging out landing craft. There was no prelanding bombardment because the same rules applied as in Morocco. Difficulties followed, though on a lesser scale. A small coastal convoy blundered into one transport group; sorting out the confusion put the force an hour behind schedule. The solution was to move the transports closer to the beach to reduce landing craft run-in time. There was still the delay inherent in getting troops into the boats. Here the divergence between Marine and Army doctrine was again highlighted; each soldier carried up to 90 lb. of gear, making descent into the bobbing landing craft arduous and time-consuming.

Except for one four-ship division, the transports were British-manned. Royal Navy amphibious techniques differed from American practice in forming and directing boat waves, depending more on guides than expecting individual coxswains to be skilled at navigation. Beacon submarines were stationed at the transport areas to provide piloting teams for each beach. Once the transports were in position, the subs moved closer inshore to launch marker teams in boats that took position only 400 yards off each beach. By 0057, the landing craft were putting ashore troops of the U.S. 1st Infantry Division against no resistance. Units flowed across the beach in quick succession, helped in small part because after the first wave was ashore, British practice called for the transports to be moved within a mile of the beach. The basic demands of seamanship do not change however; different techniques still could not make up for inexperience. Operational boat losses at Oran and Algiers were of the same unacceptably high proportion as in Morocco.

There were the usual mishaps. At one Oran beach, the LCMs grounded on a sandbar parallel to the shoreline. The 5-ft.-deep water between sandbar and beach became a concern only after the first vehicles off the boats crossed the ramp and sank out of sight. Though not a common occurrence at Oran, one medical unit was scattered across a three-mile stretch of beach. The landing also enabled Americans to witness three of the prototype British LSTs in action. These vessels had been converted from shallow draft oilers designed for work on Lake Maracaibo and were thus known to the British as "Maracaibos." They had the soon-to-be-familiar bow doors of the LST and were capable of carrying twenty-two medium tanks. Once grounded on the beach, they also carried a 60-ft. pontoon to bridge any gap to dry land.

Despite resistance that in some places was determined and well led, while in others was ineffectual and more symbolic than real, most of the troops scheduled to be ashore were landed by day's end 8 November. The one dark spot on the day's record was a disastrous frontal assault on Oran harbor.

Mirroring the daring attack at Safi, the assault on Oran included a hotly debated scheme that called for two British cutters loaded with American troops to enter the harbor at 0245, overwhelm the defenders, and prevent the French from damaging any port facilities. There were two fatal flaws in the plan, code-named Operation Reservist: the French navy defended the harbor and the operation was scheduled to begin after the beach landings, when the defenders would probably be on alert. The mission was planned by a British officer and hotly contested by the Americans, who believed the delayed starting time made it suicidal.

The 430 American soldiers, marines, and sailors assigned to the mission were embarked in two Royal Navy cutters, the *Hartland* and the *Walney*. The two ships arrived off Oran harbor under cover of darkness and awaited the appointed hour to begin the assault. In keeping with the other attempts to keep French guns silent, both ships were flying large American flags at the fore besides the white ensign of the Royal Navy. The disguise didn't work; when a searchlight beam fell on the *Walney*, the defenders opened fire. The slender thread by which the fate of any amphibious operation hangs was dramatically demonstrated. Both ships were quickly pounded into flaming wreckage, pyres for 189 American soldiers, 3 sailors, and 2 marines. One hundred thirteen British sailors also perished with their American allies. The survivors had to endure a captivity of only two days, but the mission was a costly failure.

Though the French were able to scuttle several ships in the harbor and inflict some damage on the cargo-handling facilities, most resistance to the landings had ended by nightfall. Three Royal Navy carriers ably provided air cover. Additional land-based air support staged in from Gibraltar beginning late in the afternoon of 8 November, while naval gunfire support came from a battleship, several cruisers, and destroyers. Once the troops were ashore, the familiar litany of problems associated with managing the flow of supplies was also present at Oran. There simply weren't enough troops trained in logistics to handle the problem. The Allies were again fortunate that resistance was fragmented. French honor was satisfied by 1230 on 9 November, when Oran formally surrendered to American forces. Work immediately turned to making the port operable to ease the shoreward flow of supplies and prepare for the coming campaign toward Tunisia.

Despite the effort invested in the Morocco landings, the seizure of Casablanca was secondary to Algiers; that city, with its port, was the administrative center of French rule in North Africa. Algiers was much closer to Tunisia and the Afrika Korps rear, so there was doubtless considerable relief among the Allied command echelons when the beach landings at Algiers proved somewhat easy. Troops landed across three separate groups of beaches. Surf conditions were initially favorable, and except for sporadic fire from some shore batteries and localized firing at the landing craft, resistance was almost nonexistent. Gunfire support from British warships was effective and well directed, as was the air support provided by two more Royal Navy carriers. The presence of HMS *Bulolo* showed the Americans the value of a dedicated command ship in an amphibious task force.

The lack of concerted opposition meant more problems resulted from units landing on the wrong beaches than from enemy action. One group of boats got so mixed up it took six-and-one-half hours to get ashore, then they landed twelve miles from its true destination. There was the continuing problem of excessive wastage of landing craft, leading the commanding general of the 34th Infantry Division to suggest that the Army should take charge once the troops got into the landing craft.

General Eisenhower's response was in keeping with his desire to keep efforts focused on the real enemy: he reminded his subordinate that the Navy had control until the troops were ashore, then the Army took over. No unnecessary interservice squabbles for Ike. The Algerian beach landings were halted at 1800, when port facilities became available.

Particular valor was shown that first day in another thwarted frontal assault on a harbor. The same goal of seizing port facilities intact that created Operation Reservist produced Operation Terminal, a similar plan for the port of Algiers. Almost seven hundred men of the 34th Infantry Division embarked in two British destroyers, HMS *Broke* and HMS *Malcolm* to make the assault. The attack began after the beach landings and again, the defenders were waiting. The *Malcolm* was badly shot up and forced to withdraw. The *Broke* pressed valiantly into the harbor, ramming her way through a boom and drawing alongside a quay where her troops poured ashore. The French brought more guns to bear on the *Broke*, finally making her position untenable. Her whistle sounded to recall the soldiers, but only about half were able to rejoin the ship. The *Broke* then made her way out of the harbor behind a smoke screen. The stranded troops were surrounded and eventually taken prisoner, though their captivity lasted only two days. Casualties for the operation were far lighter than at Oran, with ten killed. Consolation for the failure was found in the courage with which the assault was pressed and because the French did not wreck the port as they did at Oran.

Fighting ended in Algiers first, followed by two days of byzantine negotiations. While Adm. Jean Darlan, the French commander in chief, temporized, fighting continued in Morocco and German reinforcements poured into Tunisia without hindrance from the French. After a series of secret communcations with the Vichy government, Darlan agreed to a complete cease fire to take effect on 11 November. His decision came none too soon, for events had almost removed the power of choice from his hands.

ALLIES AND ENEMIES

While Darlan vacillated, the shooting continued in Morocco. At Mehedia, the battleship *Texas* probably made true believers of some Army men when she broke up a French attempt to truck some infantry to the front. The old battlewagon scattered the convoy when she dropped several thunderous 14-in. salvoes into their midst from 17,000 yards. The light cruiser *Savannah* also demolished a French attempt to mount an armored counterattack with a blistering barrage of air-spotted 6-in. fire. There was one jarring note when a Navy plane mistakenly dropped a bomb on some advancing American troops. The fliers redeemed themselves the morning of the tenth, when dive bombers arrowed their loads onto the last French stronghold with enough accuracy to convince the defenders the time had come to quit.

The four-stack destroyer *Dallas* mimicked the success of the Safi attack by delivering an assault force of Army Rangers nine miles upriver to the

Port Lyautey airfield. The *Dallas* rammed her way through a boom, partially cut during the night of 9–10 November by a small boat crew from the transport *George Clymer*. The *Dallas* ran a gauntlet of fire and headed upriver. So shallow was the water at one point that she was making turns for 25 knots but actually moving at 5. She ran aground farther upriver but an exploding artillery shell helped lift her over the obstruction and into deeper water. She arrived off Port Lyautey airfield around 0737 where she was able to land her complement of soldiers; their presence swung the balance at the airfield in the Americans' favor.

Patton assumed command ashore on the ninth, relieving Hewitt. Other units were meanwhile pressing inland from Safi and Fedhala to envelop Casablanca. An assault on the city was planned for the morning of 11 November and supporting naval forces were preparing to carry out their missions. While the soldiers prepared to continue the battle, unloading the transports continued despite the growing fatigue of the overworked boat crews. Less than 2 percent of the cargo had been brought ashore on the first day, creating a crying demand for rations, ammunition, and communications gear.

The efforts to get everything ashore combined with deficiencies in organization to create a supply officer's nightmare; food was piled with ammunition while gasoline nested with medical supplies. The Army Engineers' record of the campaign notes that handling supplies suffered from cartons being poorly marked, by the inadequacy of cardboard packaging for across-the-beach handling, and by some items being too bulky to be manhandled out of boats. All hands were greatly relieved when news arrived that a cease fire would go into effect on the eleventh. In a gesture of amity, General Patton hosted a luncheon for the French commanders in Casablanca. Relief was short-lived because a new enemy arrived that evening.

Two strong imperatives drive the unloading of an amphibious task force: the first is the pressing need forces ashore have for reinforcements, vehicles, and supplies to sustain the momentum of their assault. The second is that a fleet of transports tied to a single geographical location is too tempting a target to be ignored for long. The defenders know that if the transports can be destroyed or forced to withdraw, the landing must fail. The men-of-war defending the transports are made more vulnerable by curtailment of their ability to maneuver. French attacks on the transports had been thwarted, but the efforts of the more efficient and well-equipped Germans were not to be denied.

The French made Fedhala harbor available to Admiral Hewitt on 8 November; the larger facilities at Casablanca had to await arrangement of the 11 November cease-fire. French authorities offered every available berth the same day, but Hewitt decided the harbor must be left open for the follow-on convoy due 13 November. At the moment when Hewitt and his staff were discussing these plans, a German U-boat was approaching the transports and other ships anchored off Fedhala. Shortly before 2000, torpedoes began slamming into the American vessels. Three ships were hit, among them the transport *Joseph Hewes*. The *Hewes* sank with almost all her cargo, but the other two ships were saved.

This attack still did not move Hewitt to send the transports into the safety of Casablanca harbor, a decision that was costly. Late in the afternoon of 12 November, sharpshooting U-130 sent a salvo of torpedoes blasting into three anchored transports. All three sank enveloped in flames, taking more than a hundred sailors with them. The remaining ships moved into the harbor on the thirteenth, where unloading proceeded in relative security.

The Luftwaffe appeared over Algiers on the evening of 8 November with a combined dive bombing–torpedo attack. The transports remained anchored and blazed away at the attackers. None of the Germans were downed, but a torpedo hit the transport *Leedstown* and the Coast Guard–manned *Samuel Chase* reported two near misses. The transports moved into Algiers harbor the next day, but the *Leedstown* was immobilized and fell victim to renewed attacks that same afternoon, the last ship sunk off the invasion beaches.

Beginning 12 November and continuing through the fifteenth, the ships of all the Torch assault forces completed unloading and began the long voyage back to the United States or England. The captain of the *George Clymer* had run afoul of Admiral Hewitt by entering Casablanca harbor on the wrong side of the channel buoy. When the ship joined the homeward-bound convoy she was forced to signal that, "due to a foul bottom," she was unable to maintain formation speed. Back came the reply, "Your ship is lucky to have a bottom. Standard speed 15 knots. Hewitt."[21]

There is no doubt that Torch diverted valuable Allied resources away from Western Europe. The Germans realized that to prolong the battle in North Africa reduced the number of men and ships available for operations elsewhere. On the other hand, Torch was an invaluable proving ground for American amphibious techniques. The military authors of a study done in 1953 believed that Torch broke through psychological barriers hampering the conception and conduct of amphibious operations.

> the significance of the first joint amphibious operation . . . Torch, cannot be over-emphasized. Doubts which existed in the minds of nearly all officers were, to a large degree, dispelled by the success of Torch, even in spite of its many shortcomings. This operation gave impetus to landing force training which, from the psychological standpoint, was immeasureable. An initial tendency towards underestimating the need for an elabo-

rate and comprehensive training program for landing forces was dispelled from the minds of participating commanders.[22]

Just as Guadalcanal showed the mettle of the Japanese, so did the desert campaign teach Americans that the Wehrmacht was a formidable enemy. North Africa was not decisive, but ultimately it cost the Germans far more than a simple accounting of casualties might suggest.

While U.S. soldiers learned their trade in the Tunisian desert, the amphibious forces gained a respite of several months before American soldiers again got into landing craft and headed for a hostile shore. In the meantime, the planners would have time to pore over reports of those engaged and ponder the cautionary words written by some participants such as the executive officer of the *Harris*. Reflecting on conditions at Safi, he noted that had there been less than ideal weather conditions and no effective resistance from the beach, "the assault would inevitably have resulted in terrific losses of personnel and equipment and possibly complete failure."[23] These thoughts and other lessons of Guadalcanal and North Africa would be digested and incorporated into preparations for the next operation.

A typical conversion from civilian passenger liner to military transport, the USS *Hunter Liggett* (APA-14) entered naval service in June 1941. (Courtesy, Samuel Loring Morison)

USS *Aquarius* (AKA-16). Commonly known as "attack" cargo ships, the *Aquarius* and her sisters lifted much of the material needed by an invasion force. An LVT is on the pier just forward of her bridge. (Courtesy, Samuel Loring Morison)

A heavy load of landing craft in davits and stowed as deck cargo on the USS *Crescent City* (APA-21). (Courtesy, Samuel Loring Morison)

LST 556 carrying a pontoon causeway on her starboard side. (Courtesy, Samuel Loring Morison)

LST 19 with an LCT on her main deck. (Courtesy, Samuel Loring Morison)

An "aircraft carrier": LST 16 with runway mounted for army artillery-spotter planes. (Courtesy, Samuel Loring Morison)

Another variation of the LST aviation role: LST 776 outfitted with Brodie gear for launching and recovering spotter planes. A plane is poised on her midships catapult. (Courtesy, Samuel Loring Morison)

The high-speed destroyer transport was a mainstay in the South Pacific. USS *Clemson* (APD 31) was an early conversion of an older, four-pipe destroyer no longer suited for fleet service. (Courtesy, Samuel Loring Morison)

As the amphibious war progressed, more specialized landing ships became available. Coast Guard-manned LCI (L) 95 on her return to the United States after service in Europe. (Courtesy, Samuel Loring Morison)

Another development of the amphibious war: the Landing Ship, Dock (LSD). Note the well deck aft, capable of floating loaded LCMs and LVTs. The USS *Fort Marion* (LSD-22) is pictured. (Courtesy, Samuel Loring Morison)

A smaller relative of the LST, LSM 291 unloads at Marcus Island. (Courtesy, John M. Daly)

Demands for adequate staff working space and communications facilities resulted in development of the amphibious force flagship. On the USS *Appalachian* (AGC-1), the large number of antennae illustrate graphically her extensive communications suite. (Courtesy, Samuel Loring Morison)

Support craft were integral to amphibious operations. SC 1306 typically served as a boat control vessel and LCI (G) 16 delivered close-range gunfire in support of landing craft. (Courtesy, Samuel Loring Morison)

En route somewhere in the South Pacific. The LST in the background tows an LCT. The embarked troops have rigged canvas for shade. (Courtesy, the family of Capt. G. A. Sinclair)

Nighttime unloading. Late in the war, unloading proceeded around the clock under the glare of flood lamps. (Courtesy, the family of Capt. G. A. Sinclair)

In the shadow of Mount Suribachi, Iwo Jima. Five LSTs and an LSM discharge onto the hard-won beach. (Courtesy, Samuel Loring Morison)

After the war is over— LSM(R)s awaiting disposal at Little Creek, Virginia, early 1946. (Courtesy, Bernard J. Shumacher)

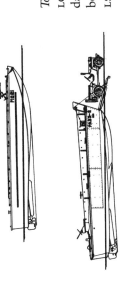

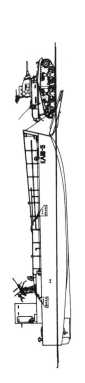

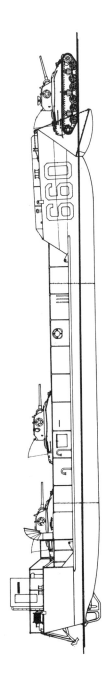

Top to bottom: An early LCP, an LCVP, an LCM, and an LCT. The first three were usually davit launched, while the LCT was either borne to the scene on the main deck of an LST or towed for short distances.

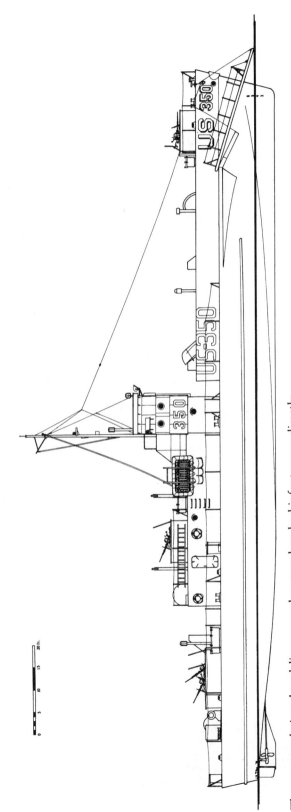

The LCI was designed to deliver more than two hundred infantrymen directly onto the beach. Note the personnel ramp lowered from the bow.

Vice Adm. Ken Hewitt, who directed landings in North Africa, Sicily, Salerno, and southern France; with Lt. Gen. Mark Clark, Fifth Army commander. (Courtesy, U.S. Naval Institute)

Vice Adm. Richmond Kelly Turner, who fought the amphibious war in the Pacific from Guadalcanal to Okinawa. (Courtesy, U.S. Naval Institute)

Vice Adm. Richard L. "Close in" Conolly, who participated in landings from Sicily to the Marianas. (Courtesy, Samuel Loring Morison)

Vice Adm. John L. Hall, who participated in landings in the Mediterranean, Normandy, and Okinawa. (Courtesy, U.S. Naval Institute)

Vice Adm. Daniel Barbey (*right*), considered by some the best practitioner of amphibious warfare in the U.S. Navy, with one of his LST flotilla commanders, James Van Zandt. (Courtesy, U.S. Naval Institute)

Rear Adm. Alan G. Kirk, who commanded the U.S. naval component of Operation Overlord. (Courtesy, U.S. Naval Institute)

Rear Adm. Theodore S. Wilkinson, who replaced Kelly Turner in the South Pacific. Wilkinson's III Phib Force coordinated closely with Barbey's VII Phib to keep the Japanese perpetually off balance. (Courtesy, Samuel Loring Morison)

Rear Adm. Harry Hill (*right*) discussing the situation with Admiral Nimitz on Iwo Jima, spring 1945. (Courtesy, U.S. Naval Institute)

In this aerial shot of a Leyte beach, no fewer than eight LSTs can be seen discharging cargo. (Naval Historical Center)

Army troops disembark from LST-450 on Saipan. Note the LCT on the main deck of LST-341 in the background. (Naval Historical Center)

4

CHOICES TO BE MADE: WAR ON MANY FRONTS

"Okay lads, that's it. That's what we'll do."

VICE ADM. WILLIAM HALSEY

THE CONFERENCE IN CASABLANCA: JANUARY 1943

Casablanca again became the focal point of Allied planning in January 1943. Although the campaign in Tunisia was not going as smoothly as hoped nor was the outcome yet in sight, it was clear to Roosevelt and Churchill that plans had to be laid for future operations. The American chiefs had been wrangling among themselves throughout the fall of 1942 without coming to any firm conclusions. In part, they were not yet accustomed to joint planning nor to working with the British. They were also somewhat hesitant to commit to future operations with the battles for Guadalcanal and North Africa still raging. The president and the prime minister forced the issue by agreeing to a January meeting.

They chose Casablanca because it was close to the field commanders and gave them a chance to be close to the scene of action. The Americans in particular were concerned that the initiative that had been so painstakingly gained should be maintained. Code-named Symbol, the meetings that began on 14 January soon showed that there remained significant differences between British and American perceptions about the direction of the war. The Americans also believed they had yet to prepare themselves properly to defend their position in the inevitable arguments.

As usual, the British arrived fully prepared to argue their position, with ample staff and well-developed studies to buttress their arguments. The American chiefs assembled with a minuscule staff and without a clear-cut consensus for directing the war effort. King gathered them to ask that they negotiate with a united front, demanding that the British agree to an overall strategy. He specifically wanted a commitment of men and resources to the

Pacific. Minimally prepared, the Americans ventured forth to meet their allies.

To Marshall's irritation, the British remained adamantly opposed to a landing attempt in France. Gen. Alan Brooke was quick to point out that insufficient troops and shipping would be available in 1943 to make an invasion possible. With Churchill in the forefront of the argument, the British wanted to continue operations in the Mediterranean. Rather than tying up shipping by moving all the troops in North Africa back to England once the campaign ended, the British believed they should be launched against the Italians, with the specific intent of knocking Italy out of the war. If Mussolini's reluctant warriors could be induced to quit, the Germans would have to occupy Italy, thereby further diluting their strength. Furthermore, the British estimated that 225 transports and cargo ships would be freed for other operations if the Allies controlled the Mediterranean.

While there was some merit to the British position, Marshall's chief reaction was frustration. He wanted a firm commitment to a landing in France, which he believed was the decisive theater in the war against Germany. He wanted to focus on what he called the "main plot" and did not want to get bogged down in what he believed would be "interminable" operations in the Mediterranean. He believed so much shipping would be lost there as to further delay a landing in France.

King was vexed, too. He wanted a greater allocation of resources to the Pacific to continue the counteroffensive begun at Guadalcanal. He believed the British granted too little consideration to Japanese capabilities: the British view was that the Japanese were extended to the limit of their resources and could go no farther. Because King rightly believed the Japanese to be steadfastly offensive minded, he considered the ongoing threat to Allied communications with Australia to be real. He also knew that the longer the Japanese had to prepare the defenses of their conquered territories, the higher the cost to reclaim them.[1]

King knew the war against Germany had primacy but pushed for a 70–30 split of resources, an increase of 15 percent over what he said had previously been going to the Pacific. Both King and Marshall were also concerned that the war against Japan not drag on too long. With Roosevelt, they understood intuitively that the American public wanted the war over as soon as possible. Despite these arguments and their belief that King's control over the production of landing craft could be used against them, the British would not be swayed from the Mediterranean. Ruthven Libby, one of King's staff officers, said his boss became so vexed with British indifference to the Pacific that he flatly asked, "Well, who's going to fight the Japanese?"

Libby formed the opinion, shared by many others, that Churchill's renowned eloquence was able to sway Roosevelt in a way that adversely affected the course of the war in the Pacific:

> Winnie Churchill would butter Roosevelt up one side and down the
> other . . . just to get him purring and convince him that he was the
> greatest man that ever lived and then he'd ask for the fillings out
> of Roosevelt's teeth and get them. That's one of the reasons that 99
> percent of our production went to the British, you see.[2]

Churchill attempted to mollify the Americans by offering a treaty promising full commitment of British resources to the Pacific war once Germany was defeated, but Roosevelt brushed aside the gesture as unnecessary.

There were as yet insufficient resources for mounting an invasion of the Italian mainland, so attention turned to the large islands lying off the Mediterranean coast of Italy. The British posited an attack on Sardinia, but the American response was summed up when King reportedly grumbled that invading Sardinia was "merely doing something just for the sake of doing something."[3] Sicily then entered the picture: only 90 miles across the Mediterranean from Cape Bon, Tunisia. Fighters from airfields on Malta could cover an attack aimed at seizing the ports of Catania and Syracuse. Furthermore, once the many airfields on Sicily were captured, a further leap into Italy would be within range of land-based air cover. With Marshall's pained acceptance, an amphibious assault against Sicily was scheduled for September. But Roosevelt and Churchill wanted the operation accomplished sooner so the planning staffs redid their figures and came up with July. This date won approval, but Churchill asked for the date to be advanced to June through "contrivance and ingenuity." Next to be settled was the matter of command.

Eisenhower remained as supreme commander, but Alan Brooke's lack of faith in the American as a combat leader was reflected when he insisted that British officers be appointed as deputy commanders. Gen. Sir Harold Alexander, whose experiences during the North African campaign had given him a less-than-favorable impression of American soldiers, became assault commander. Admiral Cunningham remained in command of Allied naval forces in the Mediterranean, and Air Chief Marshal Arthur Tedder took over as air commander. With operational commanders selected, the Combined Chiefs ordered planning to begin immediately.

To Walter Ansel, serving as a staff officer at the Naval Base, Oran, the push to assault Sicily in June was

> frightening: nobody trained in landing operations or craft or landing
> doctrine. We'd only had this one landing and it was against no opposition
> and we were now landing against Germans. I can remember making out
> a schedule of training for one division, and that it would take six to eight

weeks to even give these soldiers a taste of getting into boats, the right boats, landing, getting out of them and setting up their beachhead. If it took that long to do one division and they wanted three divisions landed ... more time was needed. Finally they settled on July. I still thought that that was too early.[4]

Ansel would have been even more alarmed if he had known Sicily was not the only landing on the timetable that summer. Because the Americans had been unequivocal in voicing their intention to maintain the initiative in the Pacific, the British agreed to a limited offensive in the South Pacific and a concurrent offensive in the Central Pacific. They added the stipulation that operations against the Japanese could not be allowed to jeopardize the war in Europe.

Local campaigns thus decided, the conferees struggled to formulate the grand strategy King had argued should be resolved first. Defeating the German U-boats was high on the list; no assault into France was possible unless the sea-lanes to America were open. At Marshall's insistence, staff studies for a possible spring 1944 invasion of France were to begin and a chief of staff appointed to guide the effort. Churchill called the tentative operation Overlord.

King never did get the formal allocation of resources he wanted, but would use the agreed-upon term "adequate numbers" to his advantage. He also got the green light for the first steps toward the Marianas. The initial move in that long Pacific voyage, however, was not west but north, to the cold reaches of the Aleutians.

INTO THE LAND OF THE WILLIWAW: DECEMBER 1942–MAY 1943

The Aleutians are a desolate string of wind-swept islands stretching westward from the tip of the Alaskan peninsula. The war came to the Aleutians in June 1942, when Japanese forces seized the islands of Attu and Kiska as part of the Midway operation. The new holdings supposedly would be the northern anchor of a patrol line that would prevent a recurrence of the Doolittle raid. They were also intended to block any possible American assault against the Kuriles and northern Japan. Such was the hysteria of the early months of the war that many Americans believed a Japanese invasion from the north was imminent. American reinforcements rushed to Alaska and the Aleutians, where they found themselves engaged in a sporadic war of attrition with the Japanese and with the miserable weather.

Though King recognized that the Japanese position in the Aleutians was of no military consequence, he wanted them expelled, so in October

1942, he sought and received agreement from Marshall to assault Kiska. No immediate operation could be mounted because of the need to replace naval losses incurred off Guadalcanal. By 18 December, the situation had improved enough for the Chiefs to authorize planning for the Kiska operation. Rear Adm. Francis Rockwell got the job of putting together the invasion. He assembled a joint staff at San Diego in January 1943 and set to work.

Typical of many amphibious operations of the war, there was a serious impediment to truly integrated planning. The overall commander of the operation was in Alaska, the commander of the assigned Army troops was in Monterey, California, and the amphibious task force commander was in San Diego. Keeping these headquarters working together required considerable liaison. Rockwell's first question was asked of Holland Smith. The admiral wanted to know how many troops would be needed to assault Kiska. Intelligence being sparse, Smith suggested a force of 27,000. The Army's 7th Infantry Division, training in the California desert, moved to Fort Ord, California, to begin amphibious training. In recognition of his expertise, Smith was assigned to direct the soldiers' preparations. One tool in his hands was the newly issued publication, FTP 211—*Ship-to-Shore Movement, U.S. Fleet*, which drew upon the recently accumulated experience of wartime operations to standardize training for both Atlantic and Pacific amphibious forces.

While Rockwell was taking up the reins of his new job, Nimitz sent Adm. Thomas Kinkaid to take command of the Aleutian area. Kinkaid immediately gave the forces under his command the dual tasks of softening up Japanese positions and cutting their supply line from the Kuriles. This effort resulted in the Battle of the Komandorski Islands in March, when an American task force intercepted a heavily escorted Japanese convoy attempting to run reinforcements to Attu. The Japanese turned back, leaving the garrisons of both Attu and Kiska to face the coming onslaught with only the forces on hand.

Kinkaid had meanwhile been forced to confront the problem familiar to every American commander tasked with mounting an amphibious operation: there wasn't enough shipping available either to conduct training properly or to carry out the planned assault. Nor would enough become available in time. Therefore, he suggested that Attu alone be substituted since the garrison there was smaller. The benefit would be twofold: Kiska would be completely cut off and fewer ships would be needed for the assault. On 10 March, the JCS accepted Kinkaid's suggestion for Operation Landcrab.

Intelligence estimates had originally put the Attu garrison at 500 men, but aerial reconnaissance and the large volume of flak put up by the defenders caused that number to be revised upward. The plan to use the full

7th Division on Kiska was scaled down by Kinkaid to a single regiment of infantry plus supporting artillery against Attu; the revised estimate of enemy strength caused the assault force to be increased to 11,000 men. Seven transports and cargo ships were available for the job. In common with the marines who landed on Guadalcanal, the soldiers headed for Attu were literally sailing into unknown territory.

As stated in the official U.S. Army history, "Seldom has an operation been planned with less knowledge of the conditions the troops would have to face."[5] The only map available extended only 1,000 yards in from the beach and bore the notation that ships should come no closer than 1,000 yards from the shoreline. In contrast to the tangled jungles of the South Pacific, the Aleutians were nearly barren, having only a spongy crust of plant life known as muskeg growing over wetter areas, or a matted layer of grasses known as tundra clinging to the volcanic rock. Vehicles and men often broke through the muskeg, then found themselves mired in a boggy muck of peat and volcanic ash. The Aleutians are also subject to rapid and violent weather changes. Especially bothersome is fog, which can change crystal-clear visibility to impenetrable gray in minutes. Weather would play a major role in the conduct of the Aleutian campaign.

The Attu transport force assembled in San Francisco Bay late in April 1943. The Navy's global reach was revealed by the presence in the assault force of the *Zeilin* and the *Harris*, the former a Guadalcanal veteran, the latter of North Africa. Because of the limited number of available transports, both were laden with men and equipment far in excess of proper combat loading. The hard school of war recorded in *Zeilin*'s War Diary hints at the preparations for the Attu landing: March saw her boats participating in practice landings at San Clemente Island on the twentieth, off Oceanside on the twenty-third, and at Monterey on the twenty-seventh.[6] Moving north to San Francisco, the *Zeilin* loaded 1,819 men of the 17th Infantry Regiment while the *Harris* took on 1,873 men of the 32d Infantry. Army Commander Maj. Gen. Albert Brown and his staff were aboard the *Zeilin*.

On 24 April, all the transports left San Francisco to rendezvous at sea with ships of the covering force. Three battleships, including the resurrected Pearl Harbor veterans *Pennsylvania* and *Nevada*, were among the men-of-war assigned to cover and gunfire support. The new CVE *Nassau* was along to provide air cover. Concealing the destination of any task force was always a security concern; in the Attu task force, one security measure was to hide the large stock of winter clothing from unfriendly eyes. This had an unfortunate consequence, as William Mack relates:

> The Army division which was to go to Attu was not trained in cold weather operations at all—it was not allowed to have its equipment,

parkas, boots, and so forth so that they could condition their men to wearing this equipment. We were not allowed to make preparations by pulling cold-weather gear out and so forth. They found out they had the wrong kind of shoes. The Army wanted to wear leather boots ashore and they had a lot of frozen feet.[7]

Mack also notes that the staff was well equipped with cold-weather gear bought from L. L. Bean.

The task force arrived in Cold Bay, Alaska, on 30 April. Ruthven Libby was there, released from staff duty and commanding a squadron of destroyers. He remembered the arrival in Cold Bay: "We were all shivering and shaking on the bridge as we put into Cold Bay, and here came this tug out to greet us with the crew of the tug in their undershirts, so apparently they were pretty much polar bears. It was warm weather for them."[8] After a three-day layover during which the assault force commanders decided which of five alternate landing plans would be chosen, the task force sortied for Attu.

The landing was to take place on 8 May, but a typical Aleutian blow kicked up, forcing a series of delays until the eleventh. The same weather put a kink in Army Air Force plans to bomb Attu for ten straight days in support of the invasion. No attacks were possible during the four days preceding the landing and due to heavy fog none of the planned air support could take off on D-day itself. The assault force made a careful, radar-guided approach through dense fog on the morning of 11 May. Two separate landings were planned, at Holtz Bay on the northern side of the island, and at Massacre Bay on the southern side. The transports anchored six miles off the beach and by 0800 the troops were embarking in their boats. It was fortunate the water was calm because the soldiers were in for a long day in the boats. With visibility less than 200 yards, it was impossible for the boats to form into waves and maintain contact with the control ship. They circled slowly in their assembly areas, waiting for the fog to lift.

Scouts embarked in two submarines meanwhile rowed ashore in rubber boats and began their search for the enemy.[9] The battleships opened up with a radar-directed bombardment using both main and secondary batteries to saturate suspected Japanese positions. Because weather was grounding the Army Air Force fliers assigned to close-support duties, planes from the *Nassau* swooped in to bomb and shower the Japanese with leaflets demanding surrender.

More than seven hours after they got into the landing craft, the soldiers finally moved shoreward. The fog had not lifted completely, but Admiral Rockwell was growing increasingly concerned to get the men ashore during daylight hours. The spare language of official records notes that the boat waves formed in tight Vs to facilitate control in visibility that seldom exceeded 300 yards. The control ships were totally dependent upon radar as they groped their way toward the beach. Somewhat more colorfully, Ruthven Libby remembered the scene:

> We got out and finally found our way into the transport area more by guess and by God than any other way. Because we had this radar aboard the *Phelps*, we were sort of mother hen. We would get the boats from the transports and lead them in to the landing area, then go back with the boats to the transports, and we spent the night running back and forth in this absolutely dense fog leading the boats in to the shore. We would get as close to the beach as we dared—maybe something like 2,000 yards—and tell them, "go that way."[10]

There was no resistance at the water line but at least four soldiers drowned when the ramp of one landing craft was lowered too soon.

In typical Aleutians fashion, around 1600, visibility suddenly lifted to 1,500 yards. The first soldiers landed around 1630 and by 2130, 3,500 men were on the island. They soon contacted the first of the Japanese outposts: because of the limitations imposed by the tundra on digging any emplacments, the enemy had entrenched themselves on the ridges dominating the harbor areas, from where they intended to sell themselves dearly. The fighting became a hard, uphill slog for the Americans. As usual, there was also much hard work for the sailors of the amphibious ships.

Clearly, the increased level of training was paying off, for few boats were wrecked during the actual course of the landing. The effort to put supplies ashore was a different story; the old problem of inadequate shore parties erupted again. This time the terrain added an additional burden. Moving supplies away from the beaches was very slow: the *Zeilin* was able to unload only a third of her cargo by the end of the second day. In the *Harris*, an effort to relieve the strain on her boat crews backfired. Fifty-five supposedly trained coxswains and other boat crewmen came aboard in San Francisco; after one day's operations, they had wrecked so many boats they were relieved. The *Harris* also attempted to make life a little easier for the shore parties by sending hot food to the beach twice a day, an effort that was greatly appreciated.[11] But both the unloading and the battle ashore were going painfully slowly.

More than 11,000 American soldiers were on Attu facing 2,400 Japanese soldiers, but the U.S. advance was slow. Calls for gunfire support were so frequent that all the battleships exhausted their supply of high-capacity ammunition. The force gunnery officer later observed that Army troops needed to be taught that naval gunfire was intended to neutralize, not destroy. Others felt more profitable results could have been realized from the battleships' heavy shells, but the age-old reluctance to risk the fire of shore batteries kept them at excessively long ranges. Air support was also less than perfect.

There was an air liaison party of one army officer, one naval officer, and two army radio men with each battalion, all of whom had worked with a marine observation squadron during training at Fort Ord. Unfortunately, the fliers from the *Nassau* were not properly trained in close support. Four of her fighters were lost in the terrible weather on 14 May, and on 16 May, her planes mistakenly bombed and strafed an advanced American unit, fortunately with only slight casualties. General Brown meanwhile told Rockwell that unless the reserve was committed to the battle, he doubted whether the Japanese could be subdued. These were not words the Navy wanted to hear. Both Rockwell and Kinkaid were getting restive about the slowness of the campaign and with good reason.

A Japanese torpedo fired by submarine I-33 nearly hit the *Pennsylvania* on 12 May, and a salvo of four more hissed through the transport area on 15 May without hitting anything. Rockwell and Kinkaid were thus eager for the campaign ashore to be wrapped up so their ships could clear the increasingly dangerous waters around Attu. Rockwell agreed to commit the reserve of 4,000 men, but Kinkaid decided a new hand was needed. Exercising the prerogatives of unity of command, he relieved General Brown on 16 May, replacing him with Maj. Gen. Eugene Landrum. Rockwell began sending the transports out of the area the same day and dispatched most of the covering force on 17 May. Those ships that remained escaped damage on 22 May when enemy torpedo bombers made a fruitless attack. The battle for Attu ended in the early morning hours of 29 May when the surviving enemy launched a screaming, human-wave attack on the American line. All the Japanese were either killed or died by their own hands, but they caused several-score American casualties.

Retaking Attu cost 549 American lives, making it a costly invasion in proportion to the forces involved. Insofar as the amphibious component went, the chief problems continued to be effective gunfire support, proper transport loading, and an adequate shore party. Attu was a fairly minor operation but did give the amphibious forces added experience in what was to be a busy year.

SOUTH PACIFIC: THE BIRTH OF CARTWHEEL

While the Joint Chiefs were struggling with questions of broad strategy through the fall of 1942, Admiral Halsey and General MacArthur were making plans for their respective theaters. Halsey believed the most productive course was continuing the drive toward Rabaul. MacArthur's ultimate interest in Rabaul was securing his flank on the road to the Philippines. Before he could get to either place, however, he had to clear the Japanese out of New Guinea. Halsey believed that plan would take too long and tie down too many ships and men. Halsey was under pressure from King to press the offensive but, with Nimitz, had warned King there were too few men and too small a logistical base to proceed.

Nonetheless, King's insistence was enough for Halsey to issue his first planning directive on 8 December; the next American operation in the Solomons began two months before the last Japanese soldier left Guadalcanal. Halsey envisioned a sequence of landings to establish airfields that could be used to cover the next leap forward in the offensive against Rabaul. The first major target was the Japanese airfield at Munda Point, 200 miles northwest of Guadalcanal on the southwest coast of New Georgia Island. There were no illusions among the Americans that an assault on Munda would be easy; the area in which the enemy airfield lay was almost inaccessible from the sea. The assault force would have to land elsewhere and make an overland attack.

Halsey was able to plan the next step because the war-driven output of American factories was finally beginning to make itself felt. A trickle of war-constructed LCTs and APDs was beginning to arrive in the South Pacific, providing some means to convert ideas into action. An intermediate step toward Munda was accomplished in February 1943, when American forces conducted an uncontested occupation of the Russell Islands, 30 miles north of Guadalcanal. Though illness and alcohol were assessing a toll on him, the ever-demanding Kelly Turner remained in command of the amphibious forces. The Russells operation was treated as a shore-to-shore movement, meaning the troops embarked in their landing craft at Guadalcanal and disembarked at the target. All movement took place at night; 16,000 men and 48,517 tons of supplies were landed between 21 February and 15 March. The operation was good practice, because the pace of the war was picking up.

Though MacArthur was confronted by a new Japanese offensive aimed at Wau in eastern New Guinea, he was simultaneously making plans for the reduction of the Japanese coastal positions at Lae and Salamaua. Despite their eagerness to go on the offensive, neither MacArthur nor Halsey could press ahead without approval from the Joint Chiefs.

The Casablance conference had shaped the broad outline of coalition strategy, but a strictly American meeting in Washington on 10 March 1943 began to fill in details of the South Pacific campaign. Rabaul remained the objective, but whether to put the locus of a drive along the coast of New Guinea or to island hop through the Solomons was the question. Representatives from both Halsey's and MacArthur's headquarters were on hand to argue for the competing demands of their respective areas. Typical of the attitude in MacArthur's headquarters was the insistence by his chief of staff that twice the planned resources be committed to the Southwest Pacific area. That there were two separate, competing headquarters highlighted the fact that hard decisions had to be made.

First was that continuing the drive through the Solomons toward Rabaul would necessarily enter the theater assigned to MacArthur. He fully expected to command that offensive, but King's refusal to subordinate major naval forces to him remained adamantly unchanged. Still, there was no avoiding the reality that the path to Rabaul lay in MacArthur's command jurisdiction. After some discussion, King yielded, but with conditions: MacArthur would have overall command with Halsey cooperating, but fleet units would remain under Nimitz's administrative control.[12]

King also used the conference to press for increased action in the Central Pacific. He suggested that if naval forces were not usefully employed in the south, they should be shifted to Nimitz for action against the Gilbert and Marshall Islands, a move the Joint Chiefs could not okay without British approval. That the compromise between competing South Pacific theaters would work at all can be attributed to the ability of one man to hold in check his personal ambition and to devote his energies to the common cause.

The institutional biases affecting King's relationship with the Army were equally a part of Halsey's professional life. In a letter to Nimitz, Halsey called MacArthur a "self-advertising Son of a Bitch."[13] Even so, he got along well with the general. After their first meeting, Halsey said, "I felt as if we were lifelong friends. I have seldom seen a man who makes a quicker, stronger, more favorable impression."

MacArthur returned the compliment, saying of Halsey, "the bugaboo of many sailors, the fear of losing ships, was completely alien to his conception of sea action. I liked him from the moment we met."[14] Halsey's willingness to work with MacArthur and his refusal to countenance any interservice rivalry in the South Pacific area kept a possibly crippling problem from ever developing. MacArthur's forces would clear the Japanese out of New Guinea while Halsey's would push them out of the Solomons. The issue of which command would go on the offensive first and which would receive priority of supplies was solved through compromise.

MacArthur naturally wanted the offensive to begin through New Guinea; Halsey argued that to do so would keep his burgeoning force uselessly idle. At Marshall's suggestion, both arms of the offensive were to be coordinated in a way that would keep the Japanese defenders off balance and not allow them to mass their forces. When the Japanese attempted to counter the operations of one command, the other would initiate action and vice versa. Resources were to be allocated on an equitable basis, making sure no assault was contemplated or planned that exceeded available means. Operation Cartwheel was the name given to the coordinated offensive, which was no small undertaking. The operational plan issued by MacArthur's headquarters on 26 April called for thirteen amphibious landings over a period of eight months. Furthermore, if the area of operations were overlaid on a map of the United States, it stretched from Washington state to the Mississippi River valley. The whole scheme was scheduled to kick off on 1 June.

CARTWHEEL: COMPLICATIONS AND PREPARATIONS, JANUARY–JUNE 1943

King was successful in his efforts to have control of fleet units remain with Nimitz, but efficient prosecution of the war dictated establishment of an amphibious command directly responsible to MacArthur. King assigned newly promoted Rear Adm. Daniel Barbey as commander of Amphibious Force, Southwest Pacific, established 10 December 1942. The personnel resources of this new command were thin; they consisted of Barbey and one other officer. Going in, Barbey had no way of knowing that over the next two and a half years his assignment would make him one of the more innovative and practiced amphibious commanders in history. He is almost unsung in the histories of the war, yet many Navy men consider him the best amphibious officer ever produced by the United States Navy.

Rear Adm. Raymond Tarbuck served on MacArthur's staff and made this observation about Barbey:

> There's no question in my mind . . . Vice Admiral Barbey will go down in history as the greatest amphibious commander, [although] the Central Pacific had some people senior to him and they did go into places like Tarawa and into Iwo Jima. But . . . wherever they went, they lost thousands of men . . . Barbey's losses were [about] two hundred and seventy-two men. It's amazing.[15]

Before reporting to Australia, Tarbuck was briefed in Washington, an experience he recounts: "A very strange thing happened to me when I was in Washington. . . . People tried to prejudice me against General MacArthur with their left hand and with their right hand they're issuing me orders to be a loyal member of his staff."[16]

The staff setup that confronted Tarbuck at MacArthur's headquarters was unlike anything he had ever experienced:

> there were forty-one naval officers all tucked away in various cubbyholes on this staff in GHQ. Here's one who is in a construction section; here's one who is in a war crimes investigation board. What I wanted to do was start a Navy section, put all these people under me, and then I

could answer any question they wanted to know. But this didn't fit in with this Army plan. These people were all segregated. This is part of the Bataan Club and part of the war between the Army and the Navy.[17]

Tarbuck's experiences in Washington and Australia were a microcosm of the always-simmering relationship between the corporate entity of the United States Navy and the self-proclaimed entity of Douglas MacArthur.

Tarbuck immediately became immersed in planning the New Guinea portion of Operation Cartwheel. He discovered he had to change his way of thinking:

> I . . . quickly learned how to make a staff study, Army style. The Army . . . Schools teach them how to make what they call staff studies. We don't use that term in the Navy. You make this complete study and at the bottom you recommend that they go in or they don't go in. If it's not complete, it isn't any good. I thought I was going to do all naval planning, but I wound up doing Army planning, too.[18]

Tarbuck had vivid memories of briefing MacArthur. Wrestling once with the problem of providing air cover for a landing, Tarbuck suggested the fighters be refueled in the air. MacArthur asked, "How?" a question to which Tarbuck could only say, "I don't know how. I'm not an aviator. But that's what should be done." The general's reply was cryptic. "If you don't know how, don't suggest it."[19] It was a politically charged and demanding atmosphere in which Dan Barbey had to work.

Barbey left Washington with decidedly mixed feelings. "In Navy Department circles, assignment to duty in the Southwest Pacific was not a cause for congratulations." Because of his stint on King's staff, he was "aware that Navy plans didn't include sending much to the South Pacific."[20] It is a measure of his professionalism that despite the many undercurrents, he chose to press ahead and attack the problem given to him by MacArthur. The general confidently outlined his plan for the advance on the Philippines and told Barbey, "Your job is to develop an amphibious force that can carry my troops in those campaigns."[21]

Barbey's task was threefold: create an amphibious force, train the crews of the landing craft that would soon be coming, then train the troops to use them. He had only six months before the ambitious schedule of landings envisioned by the Cartwheel planners began. He set to work at once.

Landing craft started to arrive in the Southwest Pacific in December 1942 and were assigned to an army training center. The Royal Australian Navy also maintained a separate center at which both Australian naval and military personnel trained. Barbey brought these facilities under a single administrative umbrella by establishing the Amphibious Training Command. The always-thin nature of amphibious resources in the Southwest Pacific Area is revealed in that Barbey's command had only one transport permanently assigned. The Australians contributed three LSIs but they were insignificant resources for the operations contemplated. Troop-lift assets did increase in April 1943 when both LCT Flotilla 7 and LST Flotilla 7 began to arrive. The first American unit to be assigned for training was the 1st Marine Division, which was coming off a period of rest after its Guadalcanal ordeal. The Marines were in Barbey's hands from the end of March through 15 May and got to experience some American innovation.

Barbey organized the training curriculum to teach officers how to control a regimental combat team or battalion landing team in an assault. There were also courses dedicated to individual specialties for all ranks. Forty LCVPs were available to the school but there were not nearly enough boats. Because no transports were available for training, LSTs had cargo nets slung over their sides for debarkation practice. To compensate for the shortage of ships, wooden mockups were built overhanging the water so troops could practice descending into landing craft. All hands understood it would not be long before the training would be put into practice.

In Paul Dull's opinion, the Japanese fought for Guadalcanal first by accident, then for pride, and finally out of desperation.[22] Whatever their reasons, it became clear that an American hold on the lower Solomons represented a significant threat to Rabaul and eventually to the Philippines. This perception that the Americans must be stopped at all costs caused Japanese troops to be fed into the Guadalcanal crucible from as far away as China. The problem for the Japanese became even greater as the Allies simultaneously pushed forward in New Guinea. Imperial General Headquarters reacted by ordering an "active defense" of the Solomons and an "aggressive offensive" in New Guinea.

Interservice rivalry was not confined to the American military. Japanese planning struggled with differing ideas between the Imperial Navy and the Imperial Army about how the task was to be accomplished. Unity of command was not a characteristic of Japanese military planning; no single officer had authority over the 25,000 troops defending the Solomons. There was a general agreement that the Navy would be responsible for defending the Solomons and the Army for New Guinea. Both services agreed the Americans should be made to pay the highest possible price for any gains. The slogan "A Hundred Years' War" became commonplace in Japanese military circles in 1943, reflecting the continuing belief that high losses would force the Americans to negotiate an end to the war that would be favorable to Japan. Navy Directive Number 213 of 25 March 1943 clearly voiced Japanese worries:

> Bringing the operations in the Southeast Area, especially New Guinea, to
> a successful end is a matter of vital importance to the national defense

of our Imperial homeland. Therefore, there are ample reasons to fear that poor planning or execution of the operation would lead to grave consequences. Furthermore, in order to maintain the impregnable strategic position of the Southeast Area at large, it is absolutely a minimum prerequisite to securely hold the present positions in New Guinea, Solomon Islands, and Bismarck Archipelago.[23]

The concern in Tokyo received added impetus from the bloody failure of one attempt to reinforce New Guinea. A convoy of eight transports covered by eight destroyers tried to land reinforcements at Wewak on the northwestern coast of New Guinea. Allied air patrols discovered the convoy, and after a four-day running battle, only four destroyers remained afloat. The battle was an object lesson to American planners on the folly of convoying troops without air cover.

The Japanese did reinforce the central Solomons, especially in air power. Adm. Isoroku Yamamoto sent two hundred carrier planes to Rabaul and increased the garrisons on the islands of Kolombangara, New Georgia, and Bougainville. Yamamoto's decision to view these preparations first-hand cost him his life. Information provided by U.S. Navy codebreakers allowed Army Air Force fighters to intercept Yamamoto's plane and send him spiraling to his death in the Bougainville jungle. Only a few weeks later, the American offensive Yamamoto was trying to counter got under way.

With several amphibious operations in the offing, it was fortunate that a partial settlement was reached in April 1943 of the long-running dispute over boat crew training. King and Marshall again proved their ability to work together when they reached a compromise over landing craft procurement and operation. The Army would continue to train and utilize engineer units in the Southwest Pacific; the Navy would be responsible for procurement in toto and for all training in the States. The theater commanders would decide which service was better suited to conduct boat-crew training within their particular areas.[24] Thus, one battle of the bureaucratic war ended just as a battle of the real shooting war was about to commence.

The first note in the MacArthur-Halsey amphibious symphony was somewhat muted, sounding with occupation of Woodlark and Kiriwina Islands off the southeast coast of New Guinea. They were wanted for airfields to support the planned invasion of Bougainville; because they weren't occupied, they would provide operational training for the more difficult operations to come. Halsey's newly numbered 3d Fleet provided ships to augment MacArthur's forces, but planning for Operation Chronicle took place entirely at MacArthur's headquarters. The operation was unique; after an initial scout of the two islands, two APDs landed an advance party whose job was to prepare the beaches for the landing force. When the main body arrived on 30 June, the troops went ashore without significant difficulties.

Simultaneously with Chronicle came a landing in Nassau Bay, New Guinea. A shore-to-shore movement was planned. More evidence of the scant resources available to Barbey is shown by the wide variety of craft used for troop lift; almost 1,000 men of the 162d Infantry Regiment embarked in three PT boats, twenty-nine LCVPs, a single LCM, and even in two captured Japanese landing barges. Departing from Morobe in the rain-swept dusk of 29 June, the motley flotilla proceeded in three waves for the forty-mile run to Nassau Bay.

The landing occurred with the usual mishaps: troops disembarked from the PT boats without loss, but seventeen LCVPs came to grief in the initial wave, the LCM broached on its second approach to the beach, and the third wave could not land at all. Rain and surf drowned all the radios carried by the assault force.

Fortunately, the Japanese in the vicinity chose not to contest the landing. Troops of the third wave eventually managed to get ashore and joined the advance inland. The Nassau Bay operation set the pattern for future South Pacific shore-to-shore movements, the very operation for which the Army's Engineering Amphibious Brigades were formed. Three of these units with an authorized strength of 1,380 LCVPs, 172 LCMs, and 30 LCTs went to MacArthur. They would soon begin to earn their keep.

Code-named Operation Toenails, Halsey's plan to capture Munda was moving ahead. The 43d Infantry Division would make the assault with the 37th Infantry Division in reserve. Two fleet carriers and three CVEs were allocated by Nimitz to augment land-based air support. In the same way Barbey was able to press forward, Halsey's offensive was possible because of the continuing arrival of new LCIs, LSTs, and LCTs. The first LCIs arrived in the South Pacific area in April and were soon followed by their larger cousins of LST Flotilla 5. Manned chiefly by reservists who had never been to sea, twelve LSTs arrived in Noumea on 14 May. Each carried an LCT on her main deck that was soon launched by the simple expedient of listing the LST and knocking the blocks from beneath the LCT. The slow-moving LSTs took sixty days to make the passage from the United States.

The official record of their passage is hardly the stuff of a bestseller, but by reading between the lines, one can visualize the transformation of green sailors and untried ships into a cohesive fighting unit. The flotilla departed New York harbor on a frigidly cold March day and headed south for Bermuda. From there, the course was to Panama, through the Canal, and thence to Bora Bora. Initial entries in the flotilla War Diary record a continuing battle with engine breakdowns, near collisions, missed flag or light signals, and ships falling out of formation. Human failings are noted in Panama, where a couple of sailors deserted. When Bora Bora rose over the horizon on 23 April, 6,655 miles of practice meant that formation keeping had become much better and the breakdowns greatly reduced.[25] What lay in the immediate future was the passage to Guadalcanal and the test of combat.

The arrival of these ships and those that quickly followed meant the amphibious war could be pressed. Fully realizing what faulty intelligence had meant to the Guadalcanal operation, the 1st Marine Raider Battalion got the job of gathering information on several proposed landing sites. Traveling by night and laying low by day, detachments landed on New Georgia, Kolombangara, and Rendova Islands during March and April. The Raiders scouted possible landing sites, enemy defenses, and overland approaches to objectives. The information they brought back was invaluable in ensuring that landings took place where Japanese defenses were weak or nonexistent. That information was vitally necessary, because Halsey intended not only to capture Munda, but to establish simultaneously three additional positions on New Georgia that could be used to stage ships and troops into Munda, as well as to secure Rendova Island, opposite Munda Point.

Other preparations also reflected recent experience. Close air support would be controlled from Turner's flagship while the fighter director was in one of the covering destroyers. All supporting aircraft, regardless of branch of service, received common frequencies on which they were to report to the controllers over the invasion area. As soon as the beachhead was firmly established, controllers would move ashore to stay in close contact with the troops. Even the transports were charged with providing gunfire support if the situation should warrant. The task of unloading the ships received even more attention.

Because every ship and landing craft would be worked to the limit to support the scope of Toenails, speed in unloading was essential. Fast unloading also reduced the time each vessel lay stationary at anchor or on the beach, where it was more vulnerable to air and submarine attack. Turner wanted all hatches worked from both sides and assigned large working parties to each vessel. Each transport received a hatch crew of 150, each LST 150, each LCT 50, and each LCI 25. Newly arrived Seabee units were assigned to augment Army shore parties in establishing supply dumps and getting materiel off the beaches. Turner was determined there would be no repeat of the logistics debacle that followed the landing on Guadalcanal. By mid-June, all was nearing readiness.

Meantime, in the Mediterranean, another, far more ambitious assault was in the preparatory stages.

THE MEDITERRANEAN: FEBRUARY–JULY 1943

Approval for the offensive that MacArthur and Halsey were preparing was a secondary effort squeezed from the British at Casablanca. The main Allied effort would be directed at Italy, aimed at knocking Mussolini out of the war. Though not a unanimous choice, Sicily was the target of the next amphibious assault. Eisenhower had not taken part in the discussions that led to Husky, but he did not share Marshall's distaste for operations in the Mediterranean. Eisenhower believed that not only should the Allies get some use out of the huge operating base they had developed at Algiers, but that the anti-British sentiment evident at Casablanca was detrimental to the common effort. Eisenhower's dedication to the alliance deceived many Americans; his detractors believed British ideas held too much sway over Ike's decisions. But behind Eisenhower's easy grin was unshakable determination, a quality he soon demonstrated.

Eisenhower understood very well that Alan Brooke's insistence on British deputy commanders for Husky was intended to put Eisenhower at a remove from operational decisions. He would have none of that and demanded of Marshall that unity of command must reside unequivocally in himself. Marshall demonstrated his concurrence by arranging for Eisenhower to be awarded the fourth star of a full general, making him equal in rank to his British subordinates. When Eisenhower's promotion arrived in February 1943, planning for Husky began simultaneously. Among the first business was command of the field forces. Patton again commanded the American 7th Army and Gen. Bernard Montgomery commanded the British 8th Army. Both reported to Alexander's 15th Army Group. On the naval side, Admiral Hewitt would reprise his Torch role, with responsibility for training falling to Rear Adm. John Hall. Hall got another hat when he was assigned with fellow Rear Admirals Richard Conolly and Alan Kirk as task force commanders of the three assault elements. With the objective known and commanders in place, shipping schedules and schemes of maneuver were soon being formulated in offices from Cairo to Rabat, Morocco.

As with every amphibious operation, Sicily presented the attackers with obstacles beyond those erected by the defenders. To begin with, the sprawl of Allied bases and planners across the North Africa rim was similar to the pre-Torch setup, though on a far grander scale. Patton's first headquarters was at Rabat, then Mostaganem, Algeria. The former was 555 miles from Hewitt's HQ in Algiers, the latter 165 miles away. Nor were Hewitt's task force commanders any closer to hand: Hall and Kirk were in Oran, 200 miles west, and Conolly eventually fetched up in Bizerte, 335 miles east. British efforts centered in Cairo, even farther east. Coordination and liaison required detailing officers to various headquarters and caused considerable travel for all involved.

Walter Ansel gives a hint of the work and confusion that inevitably attended the initial organization of an operation on the scale of Husky:

> When we got home [from Casablanca] I started the paper planning: which ports could be used, what they would need to become landing craft bases for vessels coming direct from the United States. There was the question of other forces that would come over to join us, where they would base, and what the division and organization of the command and staff channels would be. Even after Admiral Hewitt arrived with a small staff, there still was no staff planning and organization to get ahead with the job.[26]

Even though grand strategy once set in motion has a certain inexorability, Ansel's fears that too much was to happen too soon proved true. No comparable amphibious assault had ever been planned, much less put into motion. Three full months elapsed without a comprehensive or cohesive scheme of maneuver evolving. Part of the problem was that all the commanders were still intensely involved in the battle for Tunisia. There were also competing imperatives between the Allies and between the services. These problems came to a head in May. Meanwhile, the ultimate objective was known, allowing practical problems to be solved, at least.

Because of the Tunisia campaign, a complete troop list was unavailable to planners until after the German surrender, 12 May. Even then, it was certain that the in-theater units assigned to the Sicily assault would need amphibious refresher training. The eventual list of units scheduled for the assault included combat veterans and an untried division fresh from the States. The list included a combat command of the 2d Armored Division with another in reserve, the 1st, 3d, and 45th Infantry Divisions, with attached Ranger units. The first two infantry divisions were available in the theater but the 45th was coming from the States. Although sailing in combat-loaded ships, the 45th was also scheduled for amphibious refresher training once it arrived in North Africa. One combat command of the 2d Armored Division would land with the 3d Infantry Division with another held in reserve. The 1st Engineer Special Brigade, formerly the 1st Engineer Amphibious Brigade, had the job of unloading landing craft and keeping traffic flowing across the beaches. A naval shore party was detailed for service with the engineers to ensure proper coordination with the amphibians. Familiar problems of unit availability and scheduling plagued the Navy men.

An increasing stream of new landing craft and warships was beginning to flow into the Mediterranean, but the troop lift was no easier to forecast than availability of Army units. The biggest headache was the ever-present conflict between plans and the availability of transports to meet the demands of world-wide commitments. The only possible way to move these large numbers of men and their equipment was by sea. There were no C-5s that could position a division of soldiers half a world away in a week. Nor were there computers to rationalize the complex schedules of loading, sailing times, and convoy routes. It is little wonder that there were many furrowed brows on both sides of the Atlantic.

Eisenhower wanted more troops for North Africa, the Army Air Force wanted ships to support the bomber force buildup in England, and Ernie King refused to countenance any reduction in sailings to the Pacific. The brew was further stirred by a renewed German U-boat offensive that reached a crescendo in March. As happens when capable people invest all their energies, the problems were overcome.

Valorous sailors of the Allied navies, well served by Ultra, beat down the U-boats by late March: the German submariners would never again be capable of severing the trans-Atlantic route. By closely examining the number of ships available and by increasing the number of men and vehicles in each ship, the planners were able to show that enough troops and cargo could be provided to meet requirements. In April, both the British and the Americans contrived to find enough assault shipping to lift another regimental combat team each. All this was good news to the men assigned to direct the assault.

The paper battle fought by the planners was well matched by the physical obstacles. One characteristic common to many Sicilian beaches was a sandbar about 150 to 200 yards off the true beach. The landing craft could approach the sandbar without too much trouble, but the runnels between the bar and the beach were up to 10 feet deep, far too much to be forded by vehicles. Some sort of portable causeway would have to be provided. Another problem was that high summer in Sicily is very arid, making adequate provision of drinking water for an assault force of 85,000 men a serious concern. The solution was for the invaders to bring their water with them—twenty of the new LSTs were outfitted with enough tankage to hold 10,000 gallons of water. That source would provide a five-day supply, allowing the advance inland to bring local supplies under control.

The problem of reef-to-beach causeways was harder to solve. Before his assignment as a task force commander, Admiral Conolly was among the officers preparing the invasion plans, so he was aware of the need to bridge the runnels. Before leaving Washington for the Mediterranean, he inquired about possible solutions. None seemed too promising, but he was told about some small pontoon sections developed by the Bureau of Yards and Docks. After arriving in North Africa and discovering that no way had yet been devised to get vehicles from the LSTs across the runnels to the true beach, he remembered the pontoons. If enough of them could be put together, he thought, a portable causeway could be erected. He pulled strings to have a few pontoons assembled into a larger section that, although unwieldy, seemed adequate. Conolly immediately set about gathering enough pontoons from naval installations in North Africa and the States. He put Seabee units to work building causeway sections of 175×14 ft. The next component of the problem was how to transport completed sections to the invasion site.

Spurred on by Conolly, a British officer devised a system by which the causeway sections were carried alongside an LST. Special tackle was rigged, a ledge welded to the LST, the ship listed while being loaded, and the pontoon section hoisted aboard. One LST chosen to try the new rig was LST 386; Allen Pace remembers that the plan "involved using the ship's stern anchor engine and her 500 feet of heavy steel cable to hoist the causeway on its side. Elaborate rigging was required to hoist the causeway into . . . position, but the plan did work and once the procedure was established by the experts, the ship's crew could hoist the causeways."[27] Twelve were built in time for the invasion; they were unwieldy but proved to be invaluable.

Conolly also had to figure out how to use the LSTs in another way. He had to get the 3d Infantry Division ashore at Licata, but had no transports assigned to his task force. Expediency therefore pressed the thirty-eight LSTs he had been given into service as troop transports. Quick calculations showed each LST could accommodate a company of infantry. However, to provide the number of soldiers needed in each wave required an extra set of davits, giving each LST six LCVPs. Conolly made sure the necessary work was done to modify ships yet to leave the States. Thirty-six ships were fitted. According to Admiral Hewitt, they were instrumental in the success of the Sicily landing.

Pace notes that yet another use for the LST was tried out on his ship. A minirunway was installed over the main deck and an Army artillery spotter plane loaded aboard. Removing herself to a remote corner of Lake Bizerte, the ship turned into the wind and lumbered up to her best speed. The small plane cleared the deck with room to spare. As Pace recalls, another LST captain signaled, "I saw it but I still don't believe it."[28] An unfortunate sidelight to outfitting the ship as an "aircraft carrier" was that the white stripe painted down the center line of the deck served as an aiming point for a German strafing attack. Two of Pace's shipmates were killed and several others wounded.

The LSTs were not the only new landing vessels available to Hewitt. Cdr. Lorenzo Sabin had brought the ships of LCI Flotilla 2 to the Mediterranean earlier in the spring. He was the only regular officer in the flotilla and his reports clearly illustrate the challenge he had been given: "With regard to . . . officer personnel, this Flotilla Commander finds that the officers are woefully lacking in instruction in the following: Celestial navigation, communications, engineering, and naval customs"—in other words, every skill needed by a naval officer. Sabin was able to keep everything in perspective. "This situation is distressing but probably exists throughout the Navy."

Another personnel problem noted by Sabin reflects a Navy very different from today:

> One mess attendant has been received by each of 13 ships. Contrary to expectation of possible racial troubles incident to the presence of one negro [sic] on a small ship, no difficulty has been experienced so far. It is believed that the addition of a mess attendant will improve the general morale of officers and men because it will result in discontinuing the use of white enlisted men to wait on officers tables and take care of their quarters and [personal] belongings.

There were also a multitude of problems with the ships themselves. Chief among them were hulls so poorly welded that leaks were epidemic. Sabin noted that some compartments leaked badly, saturating all bedding. He called the shoddy work "inexcusable carelessness on the part of the shipbuilding concern." After considerable work and training, Sabin took his flotilla to sea bound for the Mediterranean. One can sense the hint of mystery inherent in "Secret Movement Order 6–43" that sent raw sailors and their roughly finished ships to war.

Heavy weather descended on the flotilla almost immediately after they entered the open ocean. Wind velocity reached 70 knots and waves of 25–40 feet towered over the small ships. Like their fellow sailors in LST Flotilla 5, Sabin's crews were considerably more experienced when the flotilla reached the Mediterranean.[29]

The problem of getting the boat groups assembled and the soldiers into the landing craft, something that had progressed with frustrating slowness during Torch, gave birth to another idea. One transport captain suggested lowering the boats with troops aboard, cutting down on assembly time and the need for the soldiers to cope with the boarding nets. Experimentally lowering loaded LCVPs from both davits and booms showed that it could work; Hewitt made the decision to load as much of the initial assault wave as possible at the rail. Another idea put into practice for Husky involved controlling naval gunfire. The usual provisions were made for naval personnel to go ashore with the soldiers, but this time, Army forward observers were also trained in controlling naval gunfire. A range was set up where the control parties learned the procedures and then directed firing from ships assigned to support duties.

Admiral Hall also gave Conolly responsibility for training boat crews. This job brought him into conflict with the Army, which had established its own school until directed to turn boat training over to the Navy. Conolly discovered the Army was insistent that initial assault troops be landed in rubber boats, supposedly to achieve surprise. Conolly scotched that idea, but it took Patton's personal intervention to settle the issue.

According to Conolly, as the Army took the floor to argue its case, Patton said, "Sit down! I'll settle this. Once and for all, the Navy is responsible for getting you ashore and they can put you ashore in any damned thing they want to."

These preparations made Conolly a busy man; "I never had so little time to prepare for a landing, and I was never so pressed as I was in the Sicily landings."[30] Connolly had ample company in feeling pressed; there were many other difficulties to be confronted.

Assembling the materiel resources for any amphibious landing is only part of the picture. Preparations for Husky included an elaborate attempt at deception, a continuation of the debate over surprise versus preassault bombardment, physical reconnaissance of the landing beaches, a serious lack of cooperation from the Army's own airmen in providing fighter cover and close support, and an almost last-minute change in plans.

It was evident to planners that once the North African campaign ended, the Axis would expect an Allied leap across the Mediterranean. The Navy men in particular believed Sicily was an obvious target. Thus a group of British naval officers hatched a scheme intended to divert German attention to Sardinia and the Balkans, the latter long a target publicly favored by Churchill. With the permission of his family, the body of a man who had died of pneumonia was dressed in the uniform of a major of the Royal Marines, provided with an elaborate set of personal props and official papers discussing upcoming operations, and put overboard from a submarine close off the coast of Spain. Since the air route from England to Gibraltar was heavily traveled, it was hoped that "Major Martin" would be taken to be the victim of a crash at sea. A Spanish fisherman retrieved the body and the spurious contents of a briefcase manacled to his wrist very quickly became known by the local Abwehr agent, as intended.

German records show an awareness that "Major Martin" might be a plant, but Hitler was taken in completely and ordered reinforcements sent to Sardinia, Corsica, and the Aegean coast of Greece. Despite the success of this scheme, Allied preparations for an assault were visible enough and Sicily clearly enough a threat that the capable German commander in Italy, Field Marshal Kesselring, began his defense preparations as early as mid-May.

Although nominally subordinate to Italian command, Kesselring was aware his allies felt they had no chance to repel the enemy. This bleak assessment by the Italian high command was a simple reflection that not only were the troops available in Sicily of mostly indifferent caliber, but the beach defenses were inadequate and in generally poor shape. A German assessment conceded that German troops would be needed to repel an invasion. Kesselring therefore tried to reinforce the Italian garrison barely three weeks before the landing. He sent the newly re-formed Hermann Goering Panzer Division to Sicily to reinforce the 15th Panzer Grenadier Division. Kesselring gave orders to attack any landing without waiting for orders from the Italians, thus ensuring that whether or not the Italians fought, and given that both German divisions were only partially trained, an invasion would not be a walkover.

The debate over prelanding bombardment versus surprise was an argument that had lasted for years. Army doctrine called for an invasion force to be put ashore at night to achieve tactical surprise, which the soldiers considered of the highest priority. Even after Torch, there was an institutional bias by the Army that Navy guns could not be counted on to knock out beach defenses; one evaluation of the landing problem stated that the Navy could not knock out the beach defenses because "naval gun power is not designed for land bombardment. . . ."[31]

Patton and his generals had little regard for the fighting qualities of the Italian soldiers who made up most of Sicily's defenders, but Ultra had forewarned them about German troops.

HUSKY: COMPLICATIONS, APRIL–JUNE 1943

With their recent experience in Tunisia fresh in their minds, Army commanders believed that getting ashore a large body of men before the Germans could concentrate was not only possible but paramount. Patton told Admiral Conolly that he believed achieving surprise was possible because of

> the advantage of the offensive against the defensive. Imagine sitting there on those defenses on the island of Sicily. Hell, they'd been there for four years. They can't keep alert all the time. We're going to land there and all of a sudden we'll be on their necks. That's the advantage. They don't know when we're coming.[32]

On the other hand, Navy and Marine doctrine held tactical surprise to be almost unachievable and preferred a heavy prelanding bombardment, both from the air and by supporting ships, followed by a dawn landing. Getting to the right beach and keeping units in contact was a lot easier in daylight. The delays and confusion experienced in the predawn darkness of Torch further confirmed the validity of this doctrine to the Navy men; Hewitt's Action Report contains a list of arguments, a few of which are cited, against the probability of achieving surprise that his staff brought to the planning process. None seem unreasonable:

> (d) The bombing by Allied aircraft of the RDF [radar] stations on the Southeastern portion of Sicily. This would obviously direct the attention of the enemy that we desired to render ineffectual his observation facilities in that local area.

*　　*　　*

> (h) The concentration of Allied landing craft in Tunisian ports.
> (i) The constant aerial reconnaissance maintained by enemy aircraft over Allied ports and contiguous waters.[33]

These were only some of the arguments rendered, but all went unheeded because both services accepted a basic premise of amphibious operations: unless physically impossible, it was the Navy's job to put the soldiers ashore where they wanted and when they wanted.

Timing the assault was further complicated by plans to drop two airborne divisions behind the invasion beaches just before the seaborne landings. The planned airborne landing was another component of the debate over the possibility of achieving surprise. The Army's position was that since naval guns could not be depended upon to destroy beach defenses, paratroops would do the job. The requirement for the paratroops to jump by moonlight narrowed the number of days in which the proper combination of light and darkness could be found to either 10 June or 10 July. As the Navy was quick to point out, moonlight for the paratroopers meant the seaborne forces would be brightly illuminated while approaching the transport areas. Furthermore, the sailors said, the airborne drop would bring defenses to full alert, making surprise impossible. The Navy arguments went for naught: the Army thought the paratroops were essential for softening the defenses.

High-level desires for a June landing notwithstanding, shipping schedules could only be juggled and training accelerated so far. On 13 April, the Combined Chiefs formally recognized that some things were simply beyond their control and approved 10 July as the target date for Husky. Darkness was essential to another preparatory component of the operation: unlike Torch, the beaches the Allied armies intended to go ashore across were ones about which they had some first-hand knowledge.

At both the Guadalcanal and North African landings, information about the landing beaches was gathered from secondary sources. Aerial and submarine photos are invaluable in providing a composite picture of fortifications and possible routes off the beach, but the best photos are no substitute for physical reconnaissance of the actual beaches. Phil Bucklew and his comrades were about to put into practice what they had been learning since the previous summer. The "amphibious commandos" for which they had volunteered were by then officially known as the Scouts and Raiders Battalion and their job was providing a first-hand peek at the proposed invasion beaches. In April 1943, a detachment went to Malta, where they joined forces with the British and began the dangerous assignment of stealthily examining the proposed landing beaches.

Debarking from a submarine, the men rowed ashore in a kayak. As Bucklew remarked, "operating from a kayak canoe is not the most secure method," but losses were light and considerable information was gathered. The scouts were able to sound many beaches, figure out the gradient, chart shoals, note changes in defenses, and bring back sand samples. Armed with their information, the amphibious forces generally knew where gunfire support would be most needed and whether the beaches would support the vehicles meant to cross them. From the viewpoint of both amphibious forces and the infantry, another component of preinvasion planning was less successful.

By summer 1943, Allied air forces had amassed in North Africa a combined strength of about 3,600 combat planes. Sicily was within reach of Allied fighters, though at a stretch, and well within the range of available bombers. Nonetheless, both British and American air commanders were extremely reluctant to commit themselves to providing fighter cover over the approaching invasion convoys or close support over the beaches. Hewitt's comments are direct:

> The weakest link in the joint planning of the U.S. forces was the almost complete lack of participation by the Air Force. . . . an Air Plan was promulgated but it was found to be completely unrelated to the Military Attack Plan and the Naval Attack Plan. [It] gave no specific information to the Naval and Military Commanders of what support might be expected during the assault or what, when, or where fighter cover would be provided. Up to the time of sailing neither the Naval nor Army Commander was informed of what bombing support, if any could be expected. The Air Plan did state, however, that after D-day, requests could be submitted with not less than 12 hours' notice to the Target Committee located in North Africa. Thus the Naval and Military Commanders sailed for the assault with almost no knowledge of what the Air Force would do in the initial assault or thereafter.[34]

The American airmen, in particular, were intent on proving that theirs was an independent, strategic force capable of isolating the battlefield. To that end, heavy bombing of enemy airfields and lines of communication in Sicily and on the Italian mainland began during the weeks preceding the landing. Further raids were set for the hours just before the landing, but close air support over the beaches was categorically unavailable. The airmen believed that to make specific commitments would rob their forces of the flexibility inherent in airpower. Unfortunately, no American aircraft carriers were available nor was King even remotely willing to hazard them within the confines of the Mediterranean.

The difficulties of planning air cover for Husky would not go away; they would reappear later in the summer when differing perceptions between ground and air commanders about the proper employment of air assets figured in plans for invading Italy. The intransigence of the airmen would combine with legitimate difficulties to make German air attacks a serious danger to the landing force. As difficult as all the problems were to those tasked with their solution, none were as daunting as the events of late May.

During preparations for Husky General Montgomery launched his tempestuous relationship with his American peers. As with Eisenhower, much has been made on both sides of the Atlantic about Montgomery's merits as a military commander. He was arrogant and vain, to be sure. He was tactless and never could seem to grasp the political realities of American preponderance in the alliance. Mirroring Alan Brooke, he was also unjustifiably contemptuous of Eisenhower. But he was also an extremely competent soldier. Montgomery was instrumental in delineating the scale and location of the assault on Sicily. The planners had first called for a phased series of landings at Catania on the east coast and near Palermo on the north coast. These landings were to be spread out over five days in an attempt to fragment the defense and to allow capture of several airfields.

Made aware of the location and that the assault was to be *en echelon,* Montgomery deemed the plan unacceptable. Not only would the attackers be operating at the limits of air cover, he warned, but most of the defenders would be operating along interior lines between the invaders and be capable of defeating them in detail. Montgomery was supported by an intelligence assessment that held the defenders capable of concentrating four divisions within three days. Montgomery also believed that previous experience with the Italians notwithstanding, both Germans and Italians would fight hard for Sicily. He demanded that the attack be made on a more concentrated front within reach of Allied fighters; among the immediate tactical goals of Montgomery's plan was seizing several existing airfields close behind the invasion front. An argument ensued among the British commanders that was finally settled when Eisenhower accepted Montgomery's plan. The American commander did voice his frustration to his chief of staff. "I have gotten so my chief ambition in this war is finally to get to a place where the next operation does not have to be amphibious, with all the inflexibility and delay that are characteristic of such operations."[35]

The days before Husky were trying for Eisenhower; he has been criticized for not exerting decisive leadership during the planning period for Husky, but he was still learning and his attention was largely absorbed by the battle for Tunisia. In any event, the original cast of Husky was cancelled on 23 April and the planners set to reshaping where the Americans would land. A new plan was ready by 3 May and accepted by the Combined Chiefs on the thirteenth.

Considering the skill with which the vastly outnumbered German garrison mounted its defense, it is clear that Montgomery's ideas were instrumental to Allied success. The scheme of maneuver that evolved from his demands called for simultaneous and adjacent landing of three American and four British divisions across a 100-mile-wide invasion front. The Americans would land on the British left flank along a 70-mile section of the southwest coast of Sicily.

Admiral Kirk's Task Force Cent would land the 45th Infantry Division at Scoglitti, Admiral Hall's Task Force Dime the 1st Infantry Division and Rangers at Gela, and Admiral Conolly's Task Force Joss the 3d Infantry and 2d Armored Divisions at Licata. Their combined objective would be to guard Montgomery's left, drive to the northwest toward Palermo, followed by a swing to the east toward Messina. The British would land on the southeast coast and push northward, also with Messina as the objective.

Patton was miffed at being assigned a supporting role, but upon being urged to protest, reportedly said, "I've been in this Army thirty years and when my superior gives me an order I say 'Yes Sir!' and then do my goddamnedest to carry it out."[36] He also reaffirmed his pre-Torch bravado by saying the Navy could land him on any beach they wanted and he would still be first to Messina.

Supplying the invaders presented a major logistical problem: if the advance went as planned, the British force would soon have port facilities at Syracuse through which supplies could be handled. Although the small ports of Licata and Scoglitti were expected to be available on D + 1, the Americans would have to be supported across essentially open beaches for a minimum of thirty days. This was worrisome to Hewitt and his planners because they did not initially believe sufficient supplies could be landed. Recasting the initial figures, however, seemed to show that it could be done. More important, Hewitt's men realized the job had to be done. As June brought summer to the Mediterranean, Husky passed from the hands of the planners to the soldiers and sailors who would put all the planning to the test. A great host of warships, transports, and landing craft bound for Scoglitti and Gela began to congregate at Oran and Algiers.

R. Samuel Dillon was executive officer of an LCI at Oran. He recalls an incident that took place just before leaving for Sicily. Then an ensign, he received orders to move his ship, LCI 235, to a different mooring just ahead of the British battleship *King George V*. As he relates the story, it proved to be not the simplest maneuver.

> The battleship had lowered two booms and a waterpolo match was taking place with some 1,200 seamen watching from the ship. I struggled as best as I could, but the near-empty 235, almost impossible to maneuver in high winds, took down the two booms to the cheers of hundreds of British tars. Luckily, the polo players were able to get out of my claws and were not injured. A few minutes later a British Navy lieutenant arrived . . . saying that the admiral wanted to see me on the battleship. Quickly, I put on a clean uniform, and trembling, took off for the *King George*. The admiral and several of his staff greeted me warmly. After offering me a whiskey, they praised my efforts and said that it had been a great performance for the crew. After some thirty minutes of conversation, mostly about LCIs, the admiral stood, put his arm around my shoulder and handed me a bottle of scotch. He said he knew the rules in our Navy . . . but believed that I deserved it.[37]

Farther east, the ships destined for Licata began gathering at Tunis, Sousse, and Bizerte. Axis efforts to interdict this seaborne traffic met with only slight reward: two LSTs were torpedoed enroute to Bizerte, damaged beyond repair. The Luftwaffe flew frequent air raids against the Tunisian ports, but Allied night fighters and heavy flak, much of it put up by the amphibs themselves, kept damage minimal. The ship's historian of LST 345 offers some recollections of these raids:

> The first German planes would drop flares . . . thus lighting up the whole area so effectively you could read a newspaper by it. Then the bombers would come in. Shell fragments from Allied guns peppered the deck every night. In addition, there was the threat of errant 20mm shells from our ships; they exploded only on impact, and woe be unto the vessel [which] provided the impact. Each morning one . . . job was to put a list on the ship so the masses of shell debris could be easily swept and hosed over the side.[38]

Enemy bombers were not the only nighttime intruders. While standing sentry watch one night, Raymond Dabate had the unnerving experience of seeing an Arab boatman stealthily approach the ship and begin to climb aboard. Dabate flipped the safety off his tommy gun, a weapon he had never before fired, and pulled the trigger. The muzzle jumped straight up into the air, the startled Arab fell backward into his boat and vanished into the night. Dabate had to explain to his suddenly awakened shipmates what had happened and also to request of the gunner's mate that somebody teach him how to shoot a tommy gun.[39]

Beginning on 22 June and continuing through 4 July, the assault units practiced embarking in their assigned ships that in turn practiced forming into their proper convoy assignments. Selected components of each regimental combat team loaded into their boats and practiced landing across a beach. Ansel remembered that since some beach approaches were known to be mined, coxswains learned to steer through the water of any mined boat on the theory that the blown craft had cleared the way. The units tasked with unloading the ships were also practicing and they had a new tool to help them in their labors. With the new assault craft was the recently developed amphibious truck (DUKW). The DUKW was developed to meet a 1942 Army requirement for an amphibious vehicle capable of carrying a useful payload directly from the landing ships to supply dumps ashore. General Motors came up with a design that incorporated the bed and chassis of the Army's standard 2½-ton truck into a boat hull with a screw for water propulsion. The result was a versatile, six-wheeled boat/truck that could carry a 5,000-lb. payload at 7 knots when afloat and 45 mph ashore. Sicily would be the first operational test of the new vehicles.

These practice maneuvers were not without risk; despite general lack of success, the enemy had shown his air force and submarines were active. Aerial reconnaissance and communications intelligence made the Axis aware that Allied operations were under way, so all training operations took place at night, heavily screened to prevent interference by Axis submarines or torpedo boats. The soldiers and amphibs were not the only ones practicing.

The support craft and boat salvage personnel also went through their paces. Hewitt's experiences during Torch led him to address specifically the latter problem in his op-order. "Ensure effective boat salvage operations." Even so, Hewitt later wrote that the rehearsal constituted no more than a " 'dry run' on a reduced scale." His biggest complaint was that "token rehearsals" did not tax the shore organization sufficiently to uncover problems.[40] In common with so many other commanders, Hewitt wanted more time to train but did not have it. Vehicles and boats in the practices had to be returned to staging areas, minor maintenance performed, and the complex loading and convoy plan put into motion. To the consternation of Navy men, there were a few last-minute attempts by some air force units to modify the carefully thought-out loading plan.

Ansel had to deal with one problem:

The worst laggards were the air people. At the last moment they came along and said they had to have high-octane gasoline available for such and such use. We asked where it was to be loaded. The answer was: on upper decks of the LSTs in five gallon cans. I had to be the bastard that said, "No." Mind you, the loading plans had been made weeks ago, the ships were loaded and these crackpots came along at the tail end. I found that that was a soldier characteristic. At the last moment they'd always want to double what they thought they needed, just in case. . . .

Loading progressed without the extra gasoline.[41]

A bigger problem facing an invader from the sea is that he must allow sufficient space and facilities in his fleet to care for wounded and injured. The Husky assault force was well prepared. Two American hospital ships were present and there were 166 doctors and 890 Navy corpsmen in the amphibious ships. The agreed-upon procedure was that the Navy would handle all casualties incurred in the boats or below the high water mark, and the Army all subsequent casualties. Naturally, before the Army was able to establish facilities ashore, all casualties were evacuated to the ships. Because casualties were lower than expected, these preparations proved more than adequate.

As the loading of men and equipment neared conclusion and the hour of departure neared, every ship's captain and troop commander was all too aware of one unequivocal sentence in the op-order: "The assault is to be pressed home with relentless vigor regardless of loss or difficulty."[42] In the *Florence Nightingale*, messages from Admirals Cunningham and Kirk were distributed to all hands. Typical of a less cynical and more trusting time, they were traditional exhortations to duty. From Cunningham came a more formal, British-style call to duty and from Kirk came words reminiscent of a coach's pregame pep talk:

> You have been trained for this job. You have been equipped. To the best of your ability your officers have made plans that will work. We are ready. We shall be opposed. The Italians are our enemies . . . they will be fighting on their home ground and they will have German help. We can expect a hard fight. The Army troops have a tough assignment . . . our job is to make it less tough for them. To do that we must also take care of ourselves. We shall be busy. We have bad news to deliver, but we are saving it for Benito Mussolini. GOOD LUCK![43]

Equally worth remembering are the words one sailor confided to his diary:

> Loaded Personal [sic] and anchored in outer Bizerta [sic] harbor. Destination is Sicily (Lacata) [sic] The nearer it gets the more afraid I am. I'll never see my wife again. I Love My wife more than anything in this world. If I do die or get killed it is comforting to know that She, My Brother Paul, Mother, Father and others may soon live once more as free Americans. God Love America and have Mercy on my Soul.[44]

The assault force destined for Sicily consisted of 594 ships and support craft. Admiral Hewitt and General Patton were embarked in the transport *Monrovia* while Admiral Hall and Maj. Gen. Terry Allen were embarked in the *Samuel Chase*. In contrast to the two transports pressed into service as force flagships were two new amphibious force flagships (AGCs) specifically outfitted for the purpose. Designed to fill the need of a headquarters ship well equipped with communications equipment, the *Ancon* and the *Biscayne* were pushed to completion in April and May, respectively. The *Ancon* flew the flag of Admiral Kirk and had Lt. Gen. Omar Bradley embarked. The *Biscayne* flew the flag of Admiral Conolly and had Major General Truscott aboard.

The development of these ships stemmed directly from communications difficulties experienced during Operations Watchtower and Torch as well as exposure to the Royal Navy's command ship HMS *Bulolo*. In contrast to the unsatisfactory, jury-rig arrangements previously crammed into a cruiser or transport, the AGCs had sufficient radio gear and staff working space to enable the embarked naval and military commanders to coordinate and control the diverse elements of the task force. The operation upon which they were embarking would provide a true test of the ships' capabilities.

The scheduling of convoys that saw this aggregation of amphibious power from its various ports in North Africa to the beaches of Sicily was masterful. Not only did the slower speeds of the LSTs and smaller landing vessels have to be factored into the desired rate of advance, but hundreds of ships of all types had to be formed into proper formation and shepherded through the vast minefield protecting Tunisian ports. As if the large number of ships present in North African ports wasn't problem enough, convoys bringing units from England also had to be fitted into the armada streaming toward Sicily. The tight confines of the Mediterranean and the proximity of Axis airfields made it impossible to conceal completely such a large-scale movement of ships. The Luftwaffe warned Kesselring that large Allied convoys were at sea and the Italian commander on Sicily predicted an invasion on the 10th. The commanding general of the Hermann Goering Division even placed his troops on alert as the unseen invasion fleet was approaching the island.

By 1300 on 9 July, the last of the ships assigned to Husky had cleared the North African coast into the teeth of a steadily rising wind. In common with so many other amphibious operations, the final stages of this complicated movement of ships and men had to be accomplished under the added strain of bad weather. As darkness fell, the task force was pounded by heavy seas and whipped by a 35-knot wind. The smaller landing ships were forced to slow down and the formations began to lose their cohesiveness. The thought began to intrude on more than one bridge that the landing was in jeopardy.

Before recounting the perils and successes of Hewitt's armada, let's return to the Southwest Pacific where Halsey and Kelly Turner had launched Operation Toenails. The route to the far side of a world at war must include a stop in Washington, D.C., where Roosevelt and Churchill had concluded another meeting.

TRIDENT: 12–25 MAY 1943

The agreements the Allies eked out so painfully in Casablanca had not committed the combined armies to any operations after Sicily. Operation Husky was still in the planning stages when Roosevelt and Churchill decided another meeting was needed to clarify strategy. Alan Brooke dreaded having to confront Ernie King so soon after Casablanca. On the other hand, Marshall and King thought another meeting was a good idea. The two American chiefs were eager to limit further operations in the Mediterranean. Marshall was particularly adamant that a commitment to invading France had to be wrung from the British and the buildup in England resumed. King was looking ahead, too. He wanted no further diversion of landing craft to the Mediterranean because he was already planning to launch the Navy's long-sought offensive in the Central Pacific. Looking ahead, his support of Marshall's desire for a firm commitment to a landing in France rested on his timetable for assaulting the Marianas, which King believed was the keystone of the Japanese defense perimeter.

On the political front, Marshall made it his chief priority to convince the president that a landing in France must be the number-one goal of the alliance for 1944. Roosevelt seemed amenable, but Marshall had continually to worry about Churchill's considerable influence on the president. Marshall also intended that the Americans would be fully prepared with staff studies and ready to press their ideas when the British arrived. On this note, the conference began.

A good omen was that the conference, which Churchill had dubbed Trident, began the same day the Germans surrendered in Tunisia. Over the next few days, it became clear that the Allies were as far apart as ever in strategic thinking. The atmosphere was rife with disagreement. Churchill led the British chiefs in resisting a landing in France. He warned that preparations for Overlord could not be completed unless Germany was near collapse by the spring of 1944. Instead, he wanted an invasion aimed at separating Italy from the Axis.

Churchill and his lieutenants held that if the Italians quit the war, German forces would have to garrison Italy. They could do so only at the expense of their forces on the eastern front and in France. Alan Brooke expressed his belief that invading the continent would not be possible until late 1945 or early 1946, a statement the Americans viewed with consternation. They quickly pointed out that if that were the case, the war in the Pacific would not end until 1947 or 1948, something the American public would not accept.

Roosevelt replied by unequivocally favoring an invasion of France in spring 1944. Marshall was quick to reinforce Roosevelt by firmly restating his conviction that France was the deciding battlefield. He pointed out that it would not serve the interests of either country if they were still talking while the Red Army advanced into Western Europe. The two sides were speaking a common language, but neither was hearing the other; the first day ended on a discordant note.

When the conference reconvened it quickly became a gentlemen's melee. The arguments became so direct and heated that at one point, Marshall ordered all the secretaries and other staff members out of the meeting room. King supported Marshall by bluntly telling the British that unless a landing in France was scheduled, he would have to begin sending shipping to the Pacific to support operations there. Marshall reciprocated by insisting that increased resources must go to the Pacific if favorable opportunities were to be exploited. Another heated session closed to all but the principals extracted provisional British acceptance of a 1 May 1944 assault on the continent; the next day the British presented a paper to Marshall suggesting that additional operations in the Mediterranean would deplete German strength enough to prevent their reinforcing France. Marshall therefore sought conciliation by accepting further operations after Sicily was secured, although with the proviso that they be approved by Eisenhower.

Despite any campaign then in progress, seven Allied divisions would have to be withdrawn from the Mediterranean and sent to England beginning in late fall 1943. The Americans also sought to soothe British worries by agreeing that the assault strength of the proposed invasion would be pegged to the number of landing craft that could be built by the following spring, rather than what the planners wanted.

Toward the end of the conference, King made sure the British understood his determination to wage war in the Pacific by calling for extended, "unremitting" pressure on the Japanese, expounding at length on the importance of the Marianas. He noted that if a date for the invasion of France could not be settled, then the landing craft under construction would have to be employed elsewhere. A paper prepared by the JCS titled "Strategic Plan for the Defeat of Japan" was also presented to the Combined Chiefs and accepted for "combined study and elaboration of future plans." The paper included seizing the Marshall and Caroline Islands as goals for 1943 and 1944. The combined import of King's words and the paper was clear to all: not only was the United States Navy irrevocably committed to a major offensive against the Japanese, but if the invasion of France was postponed again, all amphibious resources would be going to the Pacific.

When the Combined Chiefs at last presented themselves to their political masters, Churchill almost tipped the arduously built edifice of Allied unanimity back into chaos by insisting again on operations into the Balkans. He was prevailed upon to talk things over with Eisenhower, who had discretionary approval of all future operations in the Mediterranean. There were undoubtedly some suppressed groans when the strong-willed men who made up the Combined Chiefs agreed they would meet again in the late summer to review Allied progress. With that, Trident came to a close.

King flew to San Francisco after the conference to brief Nimitz and review plans for the summer and fall. He accepted Nimitz's proposal that Rear Adm. Raymond Spruance become commander of 5th Fleet with Kelly Turner as amphibious force commander. Nimitz also told King that he wanted Holland Smith to command the amphibious troops assigned to 5th Fleet, but had not yet asked the marine. When Nimitz returned to Pearl Harbor on 14 June after a tour of the South Pacific area, he had Holland Smith in tow and orders from the Joint Chiefs waiting on his desk. King's determination to bring the war to the Japanese was evident: Nimitz received orders to invade the Marshall Islands no later than 15 November. Both the 1st and 2d Marine Divisions were allocated to him, as were some naval units then assigned to the Southwest Pacific area. MacArthur's complaint was loud and immediate, but before this latest controversy could be settled, Halsey's men began their campaign to seize Munda.

5

CLEARING THE ROAD: AMPHIBIOUS ADVANCE

After a battle is over people talk a lot about how decisions were methodically reached, but actually there's always a hell of a lot of groping around.

VICE ADM. FRANK JACK FLETCHER

SOUTH PACIFIC: JUNE–AUGUST 1943

Halsey's long planned offensive to clear the Solomons was finalized on board Kelly Turner's flagship during the last two weeks of May 1943. Halsey issued the order for Operation Toenails on 3 June. First on the Munda timetable was a series of small-scale landings that were also scheduled to begin on 30 June.

The preliminary movements would be carried out by one task force while another would make the assault on Munda. These operations included securing an airfield site that would bring fighter cover closer to the scene, as well as establishing two other support bases. Air cover for the entire operation was to come from the Russells: the plan was to have at least thirty-two fighters overhead between 0700 and 1630 every day. Word that the Japanese had landed additional troops near the airfield site caused Turner to set Toenails into motion nine days early. Two companies of Marine Raiders landed from APDs at Segi Point, New Georgia, on 21 June. All other subsidiary landings were carried out by 30 June, but only the airfield at Segi Point proved of any value to future operations.

The success of Toenails depended on men who were as new to their work as their vessels were to the Navy. More than fifty years after the fact, their reminiscences are exuberant tales of work-filled days made all the more exhilarating by the knowledge that death and danger were constant companions. When a new skipper arrived to take over one LCT, his predecessor greeted the newcomer clad only in shorts, holding a beer in each hand. The new captain, freshly arrived from the States, was advised to take it easy and let the crew show him the ropes. The advice was willingly taken but had unexpected consequences: Very much aware that he knew little about conning the craft, the novice skipper had not been much more than a bystander upon returning from his first operation. His experienced crew made the landing smoothly and without incident; the captain was more than a little surprised when a messenger arrived from the flotilla commander requesting his presence. The green skipper was even more surprised when the boss suggested that he probably could tape over the pilot house portholes since his ship handling was so good! Needless to say, the novice made it his top priority to learn how to handle his vessel.[1]

The next objective was the island of Rendova, directly across Blanche Channel from Munda Point. The plan was to emplace artillery on Rendova that could support the Munda assault and to use the island as a staging area for a shore-to-shore movement. Turner began the move forward on 7 June when he shifted his headquarters from Noumea to Guadalcanal. Increased radio traffic forewarned the Japanese that something was up, so one force of transports and cargo ships remained at Efate to hide them from Japanese airmen. By late June, however, the entire assault force gathered in the Guadalcanal–Russell Island area. To further disguise the preparations, there was no dress rehearsal, though such a decision flew in the face of doctrine and previous practice.

Turner's men finished loading materiel for the assault on 22 June; on the twenty-ninth, the leading echelon of the sixty-five assembled ships and landing craft got under way and headed up the Slot. While the amphibs were steaming northward through driving rain and heavy seas, a cruiser-destroyer task force delivered a blistering bombardment to the Japanese air bases on Kolombangara and Bougainville Islands. The intention of the bombardment was to destroy aircraft that might be used against the landing craft and to interpose a covering force between the amphibs and any Japanese naval reaction.

The rain and rough seas provided additional cover but did not delay the approach to Rendova; by 0640 on 30 June, the first of 6,300 men in the landing force were getting into their boats. There was no opposition to the landing from the 120 surprised Japanese on the island, but shore batteries on Munda did open up and hit a screening destroyer. There were no appreciable difficulties getting the men ashore, but the heavy downpour caused other problems.

As noted, Turner had taken special pains to ensure that his men worked cargo most expeditiously. Increasing the size of the working parties had the desired effect: the *Libra* reported she unloaded her cargo in only four hours and twenty-four minutes, a performance matched by the other ships. However, the unrelenting rain soon turned the primitive roads behind the beaches into a quagmire. The Seabees who had the job of trucking the incoming supplies to the dumps quickly found their vehicles hopelessly bogged down. A familiar scene soon ensued with supplies piling up on the beaches faster than they could be moved. Even having to weigh anchor and maneuver due to an air alert did not delay unloading appreciably.

By late afternoon, cargo holds were empty and the task group was getting under way for the return to Guadalcanal. The transports and their escorts had no sooner shaken themselves into cruising disposition when a group of torpedo bombers from Rabaul attacked. Hot shrapnel falling on the *Libra* started a fire in a pile of cargo nets that was quickly extinguished. The amphibs, their screening destroyers, and the effectively managed CAP blasted most of the Japanese planes from the sky. Nonetheless, the survivors persisted, some planes closing to 500 yards before launching torpedoes.

The cost to the Japanese pilots for their bravery was high, but one did succeed in putting a torpedo into Turner's flagship. Turner shifted his flag to a destroyer and ordered the *Libra* to take the *McCawley* in tow. The task force beat off another air raid late in the afternoon, but two torpedoes mistakenly fired by a patrolling American PT boat later that night sent the *McCawley* to the bottom. Meanwhile, the follow-on echelons destined for Munda were enroute to Rendova. The amphibious forces gained considerable experience in the employment of LSTs during the Rendova operation. At one beach, the tight quarters in Rendova harbor would not permit the LSTs to ground with sufficient speed to reach the true beach. This experience led the task group commander to suggest that "the selection of beaches for use by LSTs from air reconnaissance only cannot be satisfactory. In planning future operations, every effort should be made to obtain reliable and actual information relative to beaches intended to be used by LSTs. Air photos are inadequate and even misleading thereby endangering the success of such an operation."[2]

Another slight setback occurred on 2 July, when an undetected air raid ripped into the piled-up supplies on Rendova's beaches. Sixty-four men died and a considerable amount of materiel went up in flames. Even with these difficulties, 28,748 men and 23,576 tons of supplies and ammunition were landed at Rendova over the next month. The men and supplies did not tarry long; the operation against Munda proper began on 2 July.

Two Army regiments landed six miles east of Munda that night in a shore-to-shore movement originating from Rendova. The troops were in LCMs, LCVPs, and LCP(R)s with PT boats protecting the movement. Six days' steady work landed the entire assault force; by 8 July, they were ready to initiate the attack.

While the Rendova to Munda movement was taking place, two battalions of Army troops and one of Marine Raiders landed on New Georgia, this time on the north coast, their main job to block Japanese reinforcements that might reach Munda from Kolombangara. They got across the beach, but not without some peril and in considerable confusion.

Japanese shore batteries opened up on the transport force, showering all the ships with shrapnel. The beach chosen for the landing was inadequate, so short that only four boats could touch down simultaneously. Japanese fire became more accurate as dawn lightened the sky. Fortunately, only 2 percent of the troops remained aboard ship when the task group commander made the decision to withdraw.

Though not in direct support of an amphibious landing, 3rd Fleet cruiser-destroyer task forces carried out four bombardments of Japanese defenses around Munda between 9 and 25 July. They fired many thousands of rounds into Japanese positions around Munda Point. Air spotting was used in only one bombardment; all the others were indirect, area-fire missions. After Munda finally fell, the Amphibious Force gunnery officer visited the scene to evaluate what had been accomplished. He was disappointed to discover that the answer was not much.

Very little damage of a lasting nature was inflicted on the airfield and deeply dug bunkers were little affected by high-capacity ammunition. Furthermore, he deemed the density of shells in any given area to be too low. His conclusions were several-fold: night area bombardments were too uncertain of results although they did serve to give new ships good practice. If used to support an advance in jungled terrain, naval gunfire should be delivered during daylight hours and in sufficient density to be effective. Unfortunately, the growing store of experience with both the capabilities and limitations of naval gunfire was not uniformly known throughout the amphibious community. Not fully understanding what naval gunfire could do and still not comprehending how incredibly well-built Japanese defenses could be would soon lead to near-catastrophe in the Central Pacific.

On the positive side, the sailors of III Amphibious Force continued to perfect their expertise with the new landing ships and boats. They moved 28,748 men to New Georgia and supported them with 30,471 tons of vehicles, supplies, and ammunition. Turner would have approved, but he was no longer with them, having turned over command to Rear Adm. Theodore Wilkinson on 15 July. Wilkinson would not have long to wait before he and his increasingly experienced command started the next step up the Solomons chain. Their comrades-in-arms in the Mediterranean had meanwhile made another contribution to the Navy's knowledge of amphibious operations with a successful landing on Sicily.

HUSKY: ASSAULT ON SICILY, JULY 1943

Throughout the day on 9 July, winds up to 40 mph buffeted the Husky task force. Unless the wind abated within the next few hours, the high seas would make a landing impossible. Eisenhower and Admiral Cunningham therefore began to consider the real possibility that the landing scheduled for the early hours of 10 July would have to be postponed, with all the attendant problems. As the task force drew nearer to Sicily, the wind fortunately began to abate and the island itself began to offer some lee protection to the approaching ships. With good navigation and some luck, the leading elements of the amphibious task force began to encounter the pre-positioned beacon submarines and marker ships late in the evening of 9 July. By 2330, the first ships started making their initial approaches to the transport areas.

Overhead could be heard the drone of transports carrying paratroopers toward their drop zones. The distant horizon was spiked by searchlight beams. In the *Samuel Chase*, General Allen sent one of his staff officers to Admiral Hall to ask why the Navy did not shoot out the searchlights. Hall had to disappoint the soldier by pointing out that the Navy did not have a gun that could shoot 60 miles![3]

As the task force approached the transport areas, firing could be heard from shore and many fires backlighted several beaches. Searchlights trying to locate the transport planes often swept across the approaching ships, causing a good deal of apprehension among soldiers and sailors alike. A searchlight illuminated Admiral Conolly's flagship for several tense minutes, but he ordered the ship's captain to hold fire and eventually the light went out. As the fire-support ships maneuvered to take up positions, the transports and LSTs with the assault troops embarked began to make their boats ready. The task was complicated by a heavy swell.

Off Scoglitti, attempts by some transports to place their landing craft at the rail before anchoring resulted in damage to many. The heavy swell imparted more motion to boats suspended from their davits than could be managed by steadying lines. The crew of one support boat being hoisted by swinging boom had a horrible experience:

> we were jerked into the air and our boat immediately crashed into the
> No. 2 tank lighter, bending our exhaust and damaging the flash hider on
> the tank lighter's .50-caliber machine gun. The steadying lines were too
> loose, if [they] held at all. Then we really started to swing, first across
> the port bow and then across the starboard bow . . . we started hitting
> both king posts, the boom itself, the blocks and falls, and anything else
> in the way. My first thought was one of anger at the deck crew for perhaps
> thinking that we were still back in Chesapeake Bay. I believed that we
> were going to be killed and expended without ever seeing action.[4]

The boat eventually made it into the water, but her experiences were repeated often before the transports reached their anchorages.

In many cases, the heavy swell caused abandonment of the plan to rail-load the troops. The soldiers then had to make their way down embarkation nets into landing craft bobbing violently enough to part 4-in. manila sea painters. The hazards of net loading in a heavy sea are recounted by Dell Ahlich, an engineer on one of the landing craft of the transport *Frederick Funston*:

> This was [a] chore as they had to climb down cargo nets on the side of the ship and drop into the landing barge when it was on the crest of a wave. This resulted in many injuries as they many times miscalculated their drop and fell some 12–16 feet to the bottom of the barge—also, many miscalculated, period, and took the deep six as they were all carrying maybe 70 pounds of combat gear, which you don't swim too well in! [sic][5]

Consequently, the loading schedule fell so far behind that all the planned waves were not ready when the moment arrived to start the boats for the beach. Hewitt granted a one-hour delay in the scheduled landing time for the nine Scoglitti beaches.

Under cover of a close-range bombardment from the fire-support destroyers and a rocket barrage from the support boats, the landing craft began to ground on the shallow gradient fifty to seventy-five yards offshore. The heavy surf quickly carried them farther in where the ramps went down, allowing the troops to wade ashore through two to three feet of water. Enemy resistance was sporadic, with some artillery and scattered rifle and machine gun fire directed at the soldiers as they disembarked. Two boats of one group came to grief on a cluster of rocks that were seen too late to be avoided: thirty soldiers drowned in the ensuing collision, struggling in the 12-foot surf. More threatening was the presence overhead of the Luftwaffe, which had reacted quickly to reports of the landings.

Parachute flares burst into glaring life with bombs quick to follow. A stick of bombs erupted off the bow of the destroyer *Tillman*, while the transport *Anthony* recorded two attacks that broke out the pilot house windows and scattered bomb fragments on her deck. As the morning progressed, artillery fire from shore increased. The *Philadelphia* was particularly busy firing counter-battery missions at several guns threatening the movement of the transports to their inshore anchorages. The fire-support destroyers, one assigned to each beach, spent the morning delivering call-fire and trolling along the beach line attempting to draw enemy fire. The destroyer *Champlain* silenced a battery the *Philadelphia* had bombarded without success.

Ahlich and his boat crew also had a memorable morning:

> We made another run with troops without mishap and then about midday we were carrying in a field howitzer and grounded on the first reef off

the beach. They hooked a line from a bulldozer on shore and pulled the gun thru the water to the beach—when it went off the ramp the bow went under water and the boat filled up with water and broached on the reef. There was no time to fart around so we dismounted the two machine guns and stripped off our coveralls and carried them ashore over our heads in neck-deep water. We dug foxholes in the dunes as German Stukas were dive bombing the convoy area and then strafing the beaches.[6]

Although the troops were getting ashore without too much difficulty, events that morning made it evident the amphibians were in for a strenuous day.

Sea conditions off the two Gela beaches were much the same as at Scoglitti. The first landing wave began to reach the beach there under sporadic-to-heavy fire that increased as the following waves arrived. The fire-support ships were busy putting out searchlights and dueling with shore batteries. Many landing craft broached in the heavy surf, but the LCIs of the following waves and the DUKWs that arrived on the scene in the LSTs were able to reach the beach. Though initial air attacks at Gela were fewer, the German fliers scored one telling blow when a dive bomber blasted the destroyer *Maddox* shortly before 0500. Two bombs demolished the ship's after section, sending her to the bottom in less than two minutes with heavy casualties. Retribution of a kind was exacted later that morning when the fire-support ships broke up an enemy armored assault that threatened the Gela beachhead.

Both the light cruisers *Savannah* and *Boise* had a full contingent of spotting planes in the air directing the fire of their ships. It was hazardous duty in the extreme, as German fighters were present in the area and quick to pounce on the slow biplanes; four of the spotters fell to enemy guns. One of the *Boise*'s planes was among the first to notice a cloud of dust advancing along an interior road toward the beachhead. A quick inspection showed the dust rising from a column of enemy armored vehicles that would wreak havoc, if allowed to reach the landing area.

Shore-control parties joined in directing the guns, but the absence of air superiority over the beachhead severely complicated the problem of keeping advancing enemy armored vehicles under fire. The cruisers were pressed even further by calls to suppress shore batteries directing accurate fire at the LSTs as they attempted to beach. The British monitor *Abercrombie* went from the Scoglitti area to Gela to reinforce the harried American cruisers. Reinforced by three destroyers, the hard-working naval gunners were able to pound the enemy tanks, reducing their numbers in one instance from twenty-five to six. Several tanks did make it into the village of Gela where the infantry eventually hunted them down and destroyed them.

The barrage the Navy gunners were able to put down also had its morale effect on one batch of Italian soldiers. As related by Carlo D'Este, some American paratroopers were preparing to assault a pillbox guarding a key road junction. Before making the assault, the Army captain in command prevailed upon an Italian POW to enter the pillbox and attempt to talk his countrymen into surrender:

> The Italian defenders were told the paratroopers controlled the naval gunfire and if they failed to surrender at once that fire would be directed their way. The prisoner was evidently an eloquent speaker for in a very few minutes after he entered the first pillbox, all occupants of the three pillboxes in the area came out with their hands up.[7]

In those cases where enemy artillery was not destroyed, the artillerymen were at least driven to cover. The LSTs meanwhile were coping not only with enemy shelling, but with difficult beach conditions.

The original landing plan called for early arrival of the LSTs, but at 0614, Admiral Hall directed that they hold off until more suitable beaching locations could be located. The problem was that the beach gradient was so slight the LSTs grounded too far offshore. Even using pontoons, the vehicles carried by the ships could not reach water shallow enough to allow disembarkation. When suitable spots for beaching were located around 0700, rigging the pontoons that had been developed for this very contingency proved more difficult than anticipated. Not only were they unwieldy, but the heavy swell often broke them loose from their beach anchors. Much hard work saw the two pontoons assigned to the Gela beaches finally in place around 0800 and LSTs queued for unloading.

First in line was the LST 338, which had brought a pontoon from North Africa. She was consistently straddled by enemy artillery fire, but still completed unloading and gave way to the next ship. Meanwhile, the German armored attack was increasing army anxieties enough that they asked Admiral Hall to hasten the unloading of tanks and artillery. Another pontoon arrived under the tow of a tug, but unloading continued at a slow pace. Hewitt switched several LCTs from Scoglitti to Gela around midday to help discharge those ships awaiting their turn at the pontoons. Late-afternoon raids by the Luftwaffe gave even more urgency to the unloading task.

Around 1835, a flight of enemy fighter-bombers swept in and sent a salvo of bombs crashing into one pontoon and LST 313. A fire erupted in her cargo of ammunition that quickly caused the ship to be abandoned. Unloading came to a halt as explosions from the burning LST scattered ammunition around the beach and prevented the damaged pontoons from being repaired and reassembled. The glare also illuminated efforts by a tug to haul broached LST 312 off the beach, an effort that met with success around 2400. Thus ended a busy day at Gela. At Licata, the third of the landing areas, events were equally busy.

The ships of the Licata landing force consisted entirely of LSTs, LCIs, and LCTs. Being slow, bluff bowed, and flat bottomed, they were more affected by the bad weather and arrived off Licata more strung out than the other task groups. As a result, many ships arrived late and anchored in the wrong positions. The usual delays in getting boats swung out and into the water disrupted the planned succession of landing waves. At one beach, the LCIs that were to follow the initial assault wave found themselves leading the assault. Resistance at each of the five Licata beaches varied from determined to nonexistent. The usual mishaps with boats broaching and swamping occurred, while enemy fire accounted for a few others.

Enemy fire raked several LCIs, especially LCI(L) 1. She was fired upon as she approached the beach, and according to the flotilla War Diary, the man at the engine-order telegraph was hit and slumped forward, jamming the lever to full speed ahead. At the same time, the helmsman was also hit and as he fell, the helm swung hard over to port. Going full speed ahead with her rudder hard over, the ship broached and found herself aground under the muzzles of a heavy machine gun battery. Although she fought back with her guns, she was thoroughly riddled by enemy fire. The infantrymen she brought to the island disembarked over her stern. One LCI met such heavy fire on her first approach that she backed off, made a second approach at another location, backed off there after the Army commander voiced his doubts about getting the men ashore alive, and finally made a successful landing at a third location.

The Luftwaffe was also active over Licata, though without as much effect as at the other two landing areas. Several ships experienced near misses, including LCI(L) 10, which reported that the blast of one bomb partially lifted the ship out of the water. As at Gela and Scoglitti, the fire-support ships were busy, too, though there was no armored assault to repulse. While going about her assigned duties, the destroyer *Buck* provided assistance in an unanticipated way. The LCI(L) 218 had grounded on a sandbar and struggled vainly for an hour to free herself. An enemy shore battery began to drop shells close aboard, bringing the *Buck* into the picture. As the destroyer maneuvered at 20 knots to bring the enemy battery under fire, her wash lifted the stranded LCI clear.

Immediately behind the infantry-bearing LCIs came the LCTs carrying the armored vehicles of the assault force. In one instance, enemy fire was heavy enough for the group commander to order the landing delayed while enemy shore batteries were suppressed. Admiral Conolly ordered the LCTs ashore despite the cost and directed two destroyers to lay a covering smoke screen. Fortunately, counterbattery fire neutralized the enemy guns. After the LCTs came the LSTs, and they experienced the same difficulties as at Gela. One impediment was the extremely fine beach sand, causing wheeled vehicles to bog down, but temporary, steel matting roadways eased that problem. Attempts to marry LCTs to the bow ramps of LSTs were hampered by the heavy swell, as were efforts to load the LCTs alongside. Unloading across the entire invasion front was far behind schedule as the clock slipped into 11 July. While some problems were directly attributable to weather and enemy action, an equal number again came from the Clausewitzian "friction" inherent in wartime operations.

Although the Army had increased the strength of its shore parties in response to the lessons of Operation Torch, there was no way to avoid at least some things going amiss when soldiers make an assault from the sea. Some engineer units landed in the wrong place; in their determination to find their assigned beaches, they wasted valuable time that could have been used building exits. Other engineers had first to act as combat soldiers to reduce the occasional pillbox attempting to retard the landing. In other cases, the chosen exits were densely mined, causing delays through blown-up vehicles and the need to clear the mines. There were other instances of friction as well.

Without the new DUKWs, the movement of supplies would have been hopelessly snarled. The drivers discovered that by letting some air out of the large tires, the DUKWs could traverse the beaches without undue difficulty. Using them as conventional trucks was, however, a case of robbing Peter to pay Paul. When the number of DUKWs returning to the ships for another load began to drastically decrease, the Navy found that the uniquely capable amphibious vehicles had been appropriated by the engineers to move cargo already stacked on the beaches to inland dumps. The soldiers provided Walter Ansel with a new experience:

> We had some alarming, almost comical, experiences with them at Sicily
> . . . soldiers when they get ready to land, at the last minute stuff their
> pockets and everything else full of things they might need as reserves,
> including personal pistols. They took everything they could find . . . and
> loaded themselves down. Our DUKWs were so overloaded the first three
> that went down the ramps kept right on going down to Davy Jones. The
> men were saved and the remaining DUKWs quickly lightened.[8]

Unfortunately, the organization for moving supplies was again tested and found wanting. A postinvasion narrative notes that at Scoglitti, "Much time was lost through lack of a central command. For a while the beach was under a naval beachmaster, the unloading was under an Army officer, and prisoners, who were available for unloading work, were under still another Army officer, all of whom had to be consulted before work could begin."[9]

Again, there was also the question of numbers: even with the increase in size of the engineer special brigades and the added help of the naval beach parties, there still weren't enough men assigned to the tasks of unloading the ships, attending to salvage, and moving cargo across the beach.

Finally, there was the quality of the men assigned to some engineer beach units. One division commander disgustedly labeled those in the Scoglitti sector as "rabble." These problems would become more urgent, for with the new day came an increased tempo of air attacks and a renewal of the armored assault at Gela.

As dawn approached on D + 1, enemy airmen intensified the pace of their attempts to destroy the invasion fleet. Air raids occurred across the entire breadth of the invasion front and were especially deadly to the ships off Gela. The veteran *Barnett* took a bomb close aboard her port bow that put a six-foot hole in her side and killed seven soldiers. More nerve-racking was a German armored counterattack that came near enough to the beach that the tanks were firing at landing ships. Though German tankers had participated in the D-day attack at Gela, that had been primarily an Italian effort. The attack that began around 0615 on 11 July included Italian units but was spearheaded by the Hermann Goering Panzer Division; although it was not the "crack" outfit portrayed in the American press of the time, it came very close to inflicting a serious defeat on the Americans. The two-pronged assault was stoutly resisted by a miscellany of Army units and heavy naval gunfire but continued to press forward.

Patton went ashore at Gela that morning and entered an observation point in time to see enemy tanks advancing toward the American lines. Noticing a naval officer nearby with a radio at hand, he made a typically Pattonesque request for the "Goddamn Navy" to drop some shell fire on the road. The *Boise* and two destroyers were quick to answer the call; their gunners began to rain a rapid-fire deluge of explosives on the advancing panzers. Admiral Hall ordered the gunfire-support ships as close to the beach as they could safely maneuver. Several tanks were soon burning and many others were too badly damaged to continue. Even under the punishment they were receiving, the German tankers pressed their assault.

David Donovan was another Navy man ashore that morning and he recalls that while standing near an Army AA gun, he could see some unfamiliar-looking tanks in the near distance. He turned to a soldier and remarked, "those are funny looking tanks . . . I never saw that kind before." The soldier's answer was disconcerting. "Well sir, they're German tanks." Dononvan immediately thought, "I don't belong here . . . I'm getting back on board ship where I belong."[10] Other Navy personnel on the beach found themselves suddenly cast as infantrymen and impressed into what appeared might be a last-ditch defensive line. The enemy assault was stopped before these makeshift naval "soldiers" were put to the test. So close did the panzers come that naval guns had to be temporarily silenced lest they hit American troops.

Though at least one American unit was overrun and others had to retreat, stout resistance by soldiers of the 82nd Airborne and 1st Infantry Divisions, plus the combination of fire directed at the Germans, eventually proved to be too much; by midafternoon they began to withdraw. In any event, the German assault raised the unpleasant specter of disaster implicit in the thought of a hostile armored force running amok among the service troops and thin-skinned landing ships. The assault also showed the importance of air support over the beachs. Events in Normandy would show that had American fighter-bombers been present overhead, the panzers would have been unable to threaten the beachhead.

The repulse of the panzer assault was not the end of the day's action at Gela. In a continuing example of the dearth of Allied fighters, another unopposed air attack struck late in the afternoon. The *Savannah* was able to maneuver out of harm's way, but an ammunition ship was hit and began to burn. She was soon abandoned and erupted in a colossal explosion soon after 1800. Flames pouring from the hulk served as a beacon to enemy bombers and cast an uncomfortable light across the transport area, but no more ships were hit. Casualties at the other two landing areas were slight: an air attack at Licata hit LST 158, which burned out after she had unloaded her cargo of tanks. There were no other losses at Scoglitti, but several ships were shaken by near hits. Allied air cover was again scarce to nonexistent. The Luftwaffe proved unable to repel the invasion fleet, but enemy air attacks contributed to a tragic disaster on the night of 11 July.

A regimental combat team of paratroopers was to be air dropped into the Gela beachhead on the night of D + 1. Despite the misgivings of some commanders, the operation proceeded. Both Army and Navy commanders made efforts to alert their units that friendly aircraft would be passing overhead, but as happens, not all hands got the news. Paratroop Gen. Matthew Ridgway visited six different AA positions on the afternoon of 11 July and found that none of the gunners knew of the pending operation. It was an omen that proved as bad as it seemed. The last enemy air raid had no sooner droned off into the night when the first paratroop-laden transports began to pass over the invasion fleet. The first few passed without incident, but catastrophe struck when despite repeated warnings from the fleet flag that no ship was to commence firing unless the flagship had done so, a blast of gunfire suddenly arced up from the ocean.

There is no way to identify which of the tired, nervous naval gunners opened up first. After a day of constant air attacks, the thunder of many planes overhead could only mean danger. His gun was quickly joined by dozens of others, filling the night sky with tracers and burning airplanes. Twenty-three transports went down, killing 141 men. The high cost of poor communications between the services as well as the folly of passing friendly aircraft at low altitude over a heavily armed and battle-weary fleet was tragically brought home. It was the culminating act of Husky for most of the Navy men; the next day, the amphibious forces began to clear the invasion area.

The material accomplishments of Hewitt's amphibious forces were considerable: 80,735 soldiers landed in the initial assault. By the end of July a total of 111,824 men, 21,512 vehicles, and 104,734 tons of supplies had been landed on Sicily. Naval forces continued to provide effective gunfire support as the Army advanced along the Sicilian coast. Capitalizing on control of the sea, the Americans made four more minor amphibious landings to outflank German defensive positions. The campaign came to a close on 17 August, when the last of 39,500-plus German soldiers made his escape across the Straits of Messina in a well-planned and superbly executed evacuation. Unknown to the Allied soldiers on Sicily, many of them would soon be participating in another amphibious operation within only a few weeks.

While the Army was slogging its dusty way across Sicily, the Navy was taking stock of the amphibious phase of Husky. Human casualties in the initial assault were unexpectedly light, though materiel losses in destroyed and damaged landing craft continued to be too high. Naval gunfire support proved particularly effective, especially given the lack of air support. Admiral Hall thought a prelanding bombardment would have kept casualties even lower, but as future events would show, the Army continued to believe that surprise was more important. With regard to loading, Hall believed the loading plan should be directed by a single officer and once agreed upon, no changes should be allowed. Because of problems stemming from naval beachmasters being overruled by Army engineer officers, Hall favored assigning to the beach parties naval officers equal in rank to their Army counterparts. Hall also wanted more LCTs added to the next operation, because those assigned to Husky had been badly overworked.

Hewitt suggested that davits be strengthened to handle heavily loaded boats, and that each LCT have twenty soldiers assigned to help unload. He also asked that Army-supplied hatch crews be substantially increased, even if that meant fewer troops in the assault wave.[11] Organizing boat pools for the assault troops again proved to be a stumbling block. Concentrating the troops in a few transports necessitated a complex boat assembly plan that inevitably became confused.

In light of his experience with Husky, Hewitt also had some suggestions for the Army about the age-old question of who commanded when. He believed the soldiers had a long way to go in learning who was in command during the amphibious portion of an operation. Hewitt's understanding of *Joint Action of the Army and Navy* was that he was in overall command of the operation until the Army was established ashore and had achieved a beachhead at least 10,000 yards deep. He discovered that the Army commanders assigned to Husky did not have the same ideas:

> military plans issued by various Army echelons set forth directives governing the disposition of navy craft and ship's boats . . . other Field Orders were issued controlling the opening of naval gunfire. On board ship, orders have been issued by Army Commanders controlling the admission of persons to the War Operations Room and other parts of the ship in which the military commander was embarked. Such false concepts of the authority . . . of military commanders can only come about through the belief that Army Commanders exercise extensive command functions when afloat.[12]

In sum, though the overall performance of soldiers and sailors alike was good, everyone realized that the landing phase of Husky had benefitted from not being confronted by more German troops. The prospect of the next landing being more difficult became a certainty as the Sicilian campaign ground to an end.

PLANNING AN AVALANCHE: MAY–SEPTEMBER 1943

Eisenhower did not waste any time carrying out the directive he had received from the Trident conference. Operation Husky had not yet been launched when Eisenhower directed planning to begin for four different operations, including possible landings aimed at seizing Corsica and Sardinia. He was also considering a landing in Italy once Sicily was secured, an idea he soon discovered was shared by Marshall. The chief of staff had modified his strongly voiced position against further Mediterranean operations for several reasons, among them the need for Allied amity and a fear of the British somehow entangling the Allies in a Balkans adventure.

In common with other senior officers, Marshall believed that if Italy collapsed, the Germans would at least withdraw to a defensive line in the north of that country. Allied forces would thus be needed in Italy to exploit the opportunity and to keep the Germans engaged. The chief of staff proposed to the Combined Chiefs that a landing be made near Naples as soon as practicable after Sicily was secured. On 18 July, the Combined Chiefs urgently directed Eisenhower to initiate planning for a landing on the Italian mainland, instructing him to land as far north as air cover would permit. Unfolding events gave additional impetus to Marshall's proposal.

Churchill's belief that Italy could be forced from the war by a successful landing in Sicily if not on the mainland itself gained credence on 25 July when Mussolini was deposed. Eisenhower, still expecting a speedy end to the Sicilian campaign, recognized that the moment was ripe for decisive action by the Allies. He was convinced that if they mounted a quick invasion of the mainland, the Italians could be coerced into switching sides. He also believed that with Italian cooperation, he could take Naples and be on to Rome before the Germans could react. Ike had no compunction about negotiating with the Italians if such a move would cause Italy's surrender.

Unfortunately, their experience with the French in North Africa made Roosevelt and Churchill leery of any "deals." They demanded unconditional surrender and forbade Eisenhower any leeway to open direct negotiations with the Italians. Valuable time was lost while Eisenhower sought some room to maneuver; his frustration grew daily as the fight for Sicily took longer than expected. Ultra meanwhile kept him informed of the steady reinforcement of German combat troops in Italy. The Nazis clearly were positioning themselves for what they believed was the inevitable defection of their ally. The delays imposed on Eisenhower while the Germans increased their strength in Italy cost the Allied armies dearly. As subsequent events would show, however, the crucial delays in launching the mainland invasion were caused by the skillful German defense of Sicily and by the subsequent shortage of Allied amphibious shipping.

The main political objective of an Allied landing in Italy was to reach Rome. The main military objective was to draw German forces away from both France and the Russian front. To achieve the latter, the Allies had to get an army into Italy close to a large port through which their forces could be supplied. Naples therefore became the ultimate target of the planned landings. Dieppe had convincingly shown the folly of a direct assault on a defended port, so attention focused both north and south of Naples. Some planners believed a landing to the north would cut off German troops in the south and put the Allied armies on the fast track to Rome. Despite Eisenhower's personal assessment that he needed to be more aggressive in his conduct of operations, he was afraid that the possibility of heavy German resistance precluded landing outside the range of land-based air cover. Even with more favorable terrain north of Naples, he made the final decision on 16 August to land to the south in the Gulf of Salerno.

Aerial photographs showed the Salerno area to have fewer fixed defenses, and the beaches appeared more favorable for landing craft. Though a ring of hills dominated the landing zone, Ike considered the risk acceptable. British troops would land at the northern edge of the gulf and American troops at the southern. The two sectors were split by the 8-mile-wide flood plain of the Rivers Sele and Calor, a factor that would figure prominently in the coming battle. From north to south, the invasion zone covered a span of about 20 miles. The planners hoped to ease the supply problem by having the small port of Salerno in operation within three days of the landing. George Dyer, then chief of staff to Admiral Conolly, remembered that his boss didn't agree with the decision:

> Admiral Conolly's position was that the Army Air Force had supplied so little air support at Sicily that it really didn't make any difference whether we had it or we didn't have it. And therefore, let us go into Gaeta [north of Naples] that had advantages from the point of view of being able to get to Naples more quickly. The determination against Gaeta was an Army determination.[13]

The 9 September target date for Operation Avalanche depended on availability of sufficient landing ships and transports, most of which were keeping the troops on Sicily supplied. Crews needed rest and the ships were well overdue for necessary upkeep. There were also the competing needs of the shore-to-shore movement to put Montgomery's men across the Straits of Messina into Calabria. By then, the most experienced commander of amphibious operations in the Navy, Admiral Hewitt, was the logical choice to lead the seaborne phase of Avalanche. He had to do the job without General Patton, still occupied with closing the Sicilian campaign. Gen. Sir Harold Alexander remained in overall command of Allied land forces, while Lt. Gen. Mark Clark commanded the assault under the banner of the newly designated Fifth Army. Subordinate to Clark were Maj. Gen. Ernest Dawley, the VI Corps commander, and British Lt. Gen. Sir Richard McCreary, the X Corps commander. Hewitt retained his two experienced task force commanders, Rear Admirals Richard Conolly and John Hall. Conolly would direct amphibious forces in the British sector, Hall in the American.

The immediacy of the planned landing caused serious concerns among the officers responsible for shaping and directing the operation. First, the landing had to take place long before the lessons of Husky could be completely assimilated. Second, some officers considered the scale of the assault inadequate. There were only three divisions in the assault landing, one American and two British, plus supporting units. The main weight of the American attack fell to the unblooded 36th Infantry Division, while the British contribution was the veteran 46th and 56th Infantry Divisions. Clark wanted two American divisions in the assault, but the number of ships available was insufficient to handle another division.

There *were* large numbers of troops and ships in the theater, but Marshall made it clear to Eisenhower that despite Avalanche, shipping and troops scheduled for Overlord must depart the Mediterranean for England as previously planned. George Dyer had this to say about getting Avalanche organized:

It was very difficult planning the operation for two reasons: One, there was a great difference of opinion regarding where the landing should be carried out. Second, there was a great difference of opinion about just how it should be carried out. I should really throw in a third, and that is we had less than four weeks to plan the Salerno operation from the date we left Sicily and returned to Bizerte and the date the landing craft had to sail for Salerno from Bizerte.[14]

Working under serious time constraints and having limited assets with which to make the assault, the planners set to work changing contingency plans into operational orders.

All the difficulties and administrative battles experienced in preparing for Husky were renewed. Coordination between the different headquarters was again complicated by the sprawl across the Mediterranean. The on-going employment of ships needed to supply the considerable army on Sicily made scheduling troop and logistical lifts a nightmare. The shipping situation was so tight that the number of ships available was still fluid as late as four days before the operation began. The planners somehow found space to embark two regimental combat teams of the 45th Infantry Division as a floating reserve for the American sector. None of these problems were made any easier by the Army Air Force, which again wanted too much space in the assault shipping.

Air cover was again a problem but this time the Allied air forces were somewhat more cooperative. They promised to keep at least thirty-six fighters over the beachhead throughout the day, but found themselves unable to tell Hewitt what coverage would be available over the troop convoys enroute to Salerno. Additional air cover would be available from seven Royal Navy aircraft carriers; fuel considerations would limit their stay to three days.

The unloading problem was addressed by assigning more men to the shore party; 5,700 soldiers would keep supplies moving across the beaches and 400 DUKWs were gathered to help them. There was no doubt in Navy minds that there would be considerable work in unloading the ships; Hewitt is unsparing in his criticism of Army loading practices. He thought the Army's transport quartermasters were working under several handicaps. His comments are cited in part:

Difficulties in this theater in combat-loading have been due to the following causes:

*   *   *

(c) Lack of knowledge by the Army of the principles and methods of combat-loading, and of its functions and effects in amphibious operations.

*   *   *

(f) Attempts by various special services of the Army, not connected with the assault divisions, to load their special-interest equipment and impedimenta in the combat-loaders.

(g) Failure of the Army properly to employ trained Transport Quartermasters in the loading of combat-loaders.

Hewitt cited some examples of what he meant:

[One] AKA reports that after loading had been completed and the hatches secured for sea, an attempt was made to place aboard this ship 35 tons of signal corps equipment. Since this ship was secured for sea, the further proposal was made that this cargo be carried on deck as loose cargo. When such ill-advised efforts were frustrated, attempts were made to circumvent the Navy Regulations by loading the ships by stealth. One ship reports the following incidents:

(a) One box marked "Signal Equipment" was inadvertently broken in stowing and found to contain shoes.

*   *   *

(e) A box of incendiary bombs was stowed in a troop officer's stateroom and was removed when discovered by ship's officers.[15]

While Army quartermasters were busy bedeviling Hewitt's sailors with unique loading schemes, the men of the 36th Infantry Division were also busy training at their camps in Algeria. As in the exercises conducted before Husky, all units moved at night to reduce exposure to enemy action. Hewitt was again unsatisfied with the artificialities of the exercise, but there was neither time nor shipping available for more comprehensive amphibious training. The experience of Husky was put to use; LSTs were again fitted as hospital ships and water carriers. Two were equipped with aircraft runways to launch Army artillery spotters and ten carried pontoon causeways. Two others carried Army radar equipment for controlling fighter cover over the beach.

Another improvement over Sicily was an increase in the number of salvage craft assigned to the landing force. Each transport had to outfit an LCM with a pump and hoses, extra cleats, and tow lines. The beach battalion also received six bulldozers to push stranded boats back into the water. At least one LCI was outfitted as a headquarters ship to lie off the beach as a command and control center. One area in which there was no improvement was the on-going dispute about prelanding bombardment.

Though the British planned a bombardment in their sector, the commander of the 36th Infantry Division steadfastly refused to consider one in his. He cited fears that the Navy might hit some of his men, and the loss of surprise. He later put another reason in his memoirs: "There are a few old emplacements back from the beaches, but there are no appropriate targets for navy gun fire, and I see no point to killing a lot of peaceful Italians and destroying their homes."[16] Hewitt not unexpectedly considered Army ideas about surprise to be hopelessly outmoded, but the soldiers still had their way. Aside from a few support craft accompanying the landing boats, there would be no bombardment.

Other problems bothering Hewitt and his officers included the uncertain rate of supply follow-up after D-day and the cloudy estimates of enemy resistance. As the day of departure drew nearer, options were steadily reduced to proceeding with the tools and information at hand. George Dyer was present at a conference called by General McCreary when that officer voiced his disquiet:

> he had a conference of all the senior officers of his corps. Admiral Conolly and I were invited to this conference. He got up on his feet with one of these little short whips that the British officers carry and whipped his legs. He said, "I have read the plan. I don't like it, but we are going to do it. It's too damn late to change it." And it was.[17]

While Hewitt and his men were working on Avalanche preparations, the global war was progressing on other fronts, militarily and politically.

ALEUTIAN SURPRISE: QUARRELS AT QUADRANT, AUGUST 1943

As the Husky assault force was wresting Sicily from the Axis grasp, another amphibious operation was making ready to brave again the rigors of the Aleutians. This time, the target was the island of Kiska, where a Japanese garrison had been isolated since the fall of Attu in May. The fierceness of Japanese resistance on Attu caused the Americans and their Canadian ally to plan for a substantially larger assault than previously anticipated. More than 34,000 troops were detailed for Operation Cottage, including 5,300 Canadians. The naval contingent under Rear Adm. Francis Rockwell included three battleships, eighteen destroyers, and more than thirty amphibious ships. The task force assembled on the West Coast and in Alaska.

Rigorous training that put the lessons of Attu into practice was conducted, including at least two weeks in the Aleutians for acclimatization. Holland Smith again directed some training exercises, this time from a base on Adak Island in the Aleutians. Naval and air units conducted a series of bombardments and air raids designed to soften the defenses and kill as many of the Japanese garrison as possible before the landing. Even after the expenditure of hundreds of tons of bombs and shells, it appeared that the assault would be the kind of fight the Americans had come to expect from the Japanese. Fliers continued to report that they were receiving ground fire even as the hour of the assault drew near. The on-scene commanders asked Nimitz for more softening up time but he turned them down. Therefore, the assault force left Adak on the morning of 13 August, as scheduled. Unknown to the thousands of soldiers who thought they were sailing into combat, the Japanese had already abandoned Kiska to the fog and the cold.

After the fall of Attu, the Japanese recognized that Kiska could not long stand. There was no way to reinforce the garrison nor would the sacrifice of their lives serve any useful purpose. Imperial Headquarters ordered an evacuation with the troops assigned to reinforce the Kuriles. Attempts were made to use submarines in the evacuation, but American ASW forces exacted too heavy a toll; a surface evacuation seemed the only way out. After one aborted try, a small task group of destroyers and cruisers crept into Kiska on the night of 28 July. In the short space of two hours, 5,183 men were ferried to the waiting ships and away into the Aleutian night. Only a few dogs were left behind. Incredibly, though they reported no visible activity on the ground, some American fliers insisted they were still being fired upon. Holland Smith asked for a reconnaissance party to land and snoop around, but he was overruled. The men who clambered into their landing boats on the morning of 15 August believed they were about to confront again the tenacity of the Japanese soldier on the defense.

Several thousand soldiers were ashore on Kiska by the end of the day. With no enemy fire to disrupt operations, the amphibians went about their assigned tasks routinely. However, all hands were disconcerted by the apparent absence of the enemy. As they probed through the swirling fog, troops keyed up for combat inevitably fired upon each other; twenty-five Americans were killed by fellow soldiers. After a week, it was finally clear that the enemy was long gone. The job of Rockwell's sailors then became one of transporting the soldiers away from Kiska and on their way to other battlefields. Stretching credulity somewhat, the landing could be said to have served a useful purpose in allowing some amphibious units of the Pacific fleet to conduct an operation under combat conditions. In reality, Cottage tied up valuable units for several months when all were needed elsewhere.

Both sides did gain some satisfaction. The Japanese were happy they had rescued their garrison from under the noses of their much stronger enemy. They also took no small delight in the American expenditure of so much effort against an abandoned island. For their part, the Americans were glad the expected cost in lives was so much lower and that the Japanese were gone from United States soil. The landing did have one small side effect: the momentary quiet that some Americans would experience as they approached other Japanese-held beaches would cause a quick flicker of hope that they were approaching another Kiska.

While the soldiers on Kiska were vainly searching for their vanished enemy, another battle of a different sort had been joined in Quebec, Canada. Roosevelt, Churchill, the Combined Chiefs, and an army of staff officers gathered for ten days of discussions. Marshall and Secretary of War Stimson had again used the weeks immediately preceding the meeting to stiffen Roosevelt's resolve favoring a landing in northern France.

Roosevelt became so enthusiastic for the project that he suggested to Stimson that if the British recanted, the United States would mount the operation alone. For their part, Marshall and King were both intolerant of further British resistance to their strategic designs. Marshall intended to get a firm committment to launching Overlord by 1 May; King's goal was to set into motion an offensive that would eventually assault the Marianas. Their determination was evident; King was especially blunt and Alan Brooke thought the Americans less flexible than ever.

The pattern that had evolved at previous meetings continued at Quadrant. Bit by bit, meeting by meeting, the outspoken men who directed the Allied war effort worked out their differences and agreed upon the campaigns of 1944. Marshall conceded an advance into northern Italy for firm British commitment to a May landing in France. The conferees also agreed that if any shortages developed, Overlord would have priority. The first day of meetings heard King announcing that not only would American troops land on Kiska the next day, but operations in the Gilbert Islands would commence 15 November. Alan Brooke's argument that a two-pronged offensive through both the South and Central Pacific was too expensive in resources was rejected by King. Marshall supported his naval colleague, effectively quelling Alan Brooke's complaint.

The meeting came to a close on 24 August, with the Americans at last feeling that their preconference agenda had been achieved. Most important, the British were tied to a specific date for invading the Continent and King's cherished Central Pacific offensive was on. The Combined Chiefs also agreed that the tentative plans drawn up for Overlord were satisfactory, that the landing in Italy could proceed, and that a landing would be made in southern France in support of Overlord.

Concerning the Pacific, they agreed Rabaul would be bypassed and that the alliance would strive to cause the defeat of Japan within twelve months of Germany's surrender. The agreements reached at Quebec promised to keep the amphibious forces in the eye of the storm; that promise would be upheld.

The Americans had to settle another matter after the conference was over: who would command Overlord? Roosevelt had insisted on an American and Churchill had to accede, since the United States would provide the bulk of the forces. Marshall was the president's first choice, but Roosevelt was unprepared for the outcry that arose when it became known that the chief of staff might be leaving Washington. Though he and Marshall were not close personal friends, King was a main cheerleader lobbying for Marshall's retention at home. King respected his Army counterpart and had come to rely on him for the soldier's selfless dedication to the larger problem of winning the war. The net result was that Roosevelt had to put the Overlord decision on hold. For the commanders in the field however, the war could not be put aside. In the South Pacific, both MacArthur's and Halsey's men were already taking the next steps on the road to the Philippines.

SOUTH PACIFIC: JULY–AUGUST 1943

Halsey had envisioned that after securing Munda the next logical step would be to seize the island of Kolombangara, eliminating its sizable Japanese garrison. In July however, Nimitz suggested that Kolombangara be bypassed and the smaller island of Vella Lavella be targeted next. There was no natural harbor there, but there also appeared to be no Japanese garrison and it did lay athwart the supply line between Kolombangara and Bougainville. Admiral Wilkinson immediately ordered planning to begin and scheduled the landing for 15 August. To provide up-to-date intelligence, a joint-service scouting party landed on Vella Lavella on the night of 21 July. They were on the island for a week without sighting any Japanese, information gladly received at headquarters. A landing force of 4,600 soldiers, marines, and Seabees would make the assault. As was customary throughout the South Pacific campaign, they would make the move in a grab-bag of amphibious craft.

Knowing the landing would be unopposed allowed guides to be put ashore on the nights of 12–13 and 13–14 August. Their task was to mark landing beaches and select bivouac areas for the incoming troops. The task force departed Guadalcanal throughout the day on 14 August and, despite being snooped at by Japanese patrol planes, was off Vella Lavella the next morning. The actual landing was accomplished without much difficulty. One of the beaches proved narrower than anticipated, delaying the unloading of the LCIs somewhat. Admiral Wilkinson supervised the operation from the destroyer *Cony*. All hands were grateful for the lack of opposition from the beach, although they did have to endure numerous air raids over the next few days. The amphibs did a creditable job against them: AA defenses on the LSTs had been beefed up by soldiers and marines mounting some of the automatic weapons or standing to the ships' guns.

The captain of the LST 395 expressed his gratitude in his Action Report:

Members of the 35th Combat Team who manned our extra guns are particularly to be commended. Although not experienced with 40mm guns they steadied well on the targets and behaved throughout as if they were fighting their own ship. After all unloading was completed they remained voluntarily at their gun stations on the ship until a few minutes before we retracted. As the ship was completely unloaded previous to the afternoon attack their action provided the ship with invaluable additional protection.[18]

Japanese fliers reported great successes, but no ship was hit and a score or more of the attackers were shot down. An internal explosion and fire destroyed one LST engaged in supplying the beachhead. On the plus side, Wilkinson's sailors transported 6,305 men and 8,626 tons of cargo to Vella Lavella.

Meanwhile, the Japanese had decided there was no point in remaining on Kolombangara. Despite American efforts at interdiction, a stream of skillfully directed barges and destroyers removed the garrison by the first week in October. Halsey's planners had by then turned toward Bougainville, which everyone knew would not be so easy. An estimated 98,000 enemy soldiers and naval infantrymen garrisoned Bougainville and some small neighboring islands. The situation was not easy for the Japanese either; their defensive problems were simultaneously being compounded to the west, where Dan Barbey's VII Phib had gathered enough naval and military strength to put into motion the other half of Cartwheel.

Barbey's target was the Japanese base at Lae, on the Huon Gulf in New Guinea. Lae was valued for its harbor and as a staging area for a following push onto the Huon peninsula. A combined assault of paratroops airdropped to the west and infantry landed across the beaches to the east was designed to squeeze the enemy garrison between a powerful pincer. The seaborne arm of the assault would put ashore two brigade groups of the Australian 9th Infantry Division just east of Lae on the morning of 4 September. The usual collection of APDs, LSTs, LCIs, and LCTs gathered the last week in August in Milne Bay and at Buna. They loaded out by 1 September and departed over the next two days, intending to be off the Lae beaches by 0600 on 4 September. In common with their compatriots in the Mediterranean, Barbey's sailors weren't totally sure of the cover they could expect from the Army Air Force.

Despite a consistent pattern of aggressive Japanese attacks on Allied shipping, MacArthur's air commander did not want to commit to continuous fighter cover over the task force. The airmen could only be induced to promise fighters standing by on ground alert despite Barbey's strenuous objections. The ensuing argument reached MacArthur and was settled when the air force promised fighter cover over the beachhead. Japanese planes shadowed the convoy every night while en route, but inflicted no losses. Barbey noticed that attacks seemed to develop only after the ships began firing their AA guns so he ordered fire held unless an attack seemed imminent. The landing was scheduled to begin at 0630, the earliest time at which navigational features could be discerned. Barbey and his staff were in the destroyer *Conyngham*, a far cry from Hewitt's *Ancon*. Charles Adair was one of Barbey's staff planners and he had a particular job that morning:

> The Admiral turned to me and said, "You've had a lot of experience around jungles, where do you think that assault beach is? Where is the beach we're looking for?" I'd been looking for some time, and I had made up my mind where I thought it was, and I said, "Right there, one point on the port bow is where we want to land." (And with more confidence than I really felt.) But it seemed to me that was it. So we went in, and it was the right beach.[19]

After a ten-minute barrage from the five-destroyer support section, the first wave of Aussie infantrymen pushed ashore in rubber assault boats. There was no opposition, allowing the second-wave LCIs to follow within minutes. As the boats approached the beach, a flight of Japanese bombers slipped in undetected and wrecked LCI 336 with a single bomb hit. The task force suffered more casualties in the early afternoon when a large formation of enemy aircraft pounced on a follow-up convoy of LSTs enroute to Lae. The attack was no surprise; a destroyer had been posted as a radar picket and had given warning, but some Japanese planes were able to get through the CAP. A coordinated assault of dive and torpedo bombers plastered LST 473 with bombs and hit LST 471 with a torpedo. Casualties were heavy but both ships were saved. It was the low point of a day that otherwise went almost as planned. By midafternoon, 7,800 troops and 1,500 tons of supplies had been landed, though not without some problems.

Again, there weren't enough men assigned to unloading and clearing the beaches. The 2d Engineer Special Brigade was assigned to support the landing, but, like its Mediterranean brethren, did not initially live up to expectations. Barbey was particularly unhappy with what he termed "unsatisfactory" preparation of exits from the beaches and roads to supply dumps. On the positive side, medical preparations benefitted from experience in other operations. One LST remained south of Lae at Morobe as a casualty clearing station; she was equipped as nearly as possible to a standard fifty-bed hospital. These preparations were no doubt well received, but aside from the survivors of the bombed ships, the work of the medical staff was kept mercifully to a minimum.

The Lae operation was successful, opposed only from the air, and it gave Barbey's VII Phib its first real experience of combat as well as a welcome boost of confidence. They had little time to rest because the purposefully choreographed Cartwheel timetable was picking up speed. Unwilling to give the Japanese the slightest respite, MacArthur's headquarters had already scheduled another landing at Finschhafen, 64 miles from Lae on the Huon peninsula. MacArthur's staff had done an outline plan and gave final approval on 17 September. Since the landing was slated for 22 September, Barbey's men had scant time to get everything organized. While they were hurriedly looking to their lists of available troops and shipping, Hewitt's sailors meanwhile had conducted their third major amphibious assault in a year. Unlike the somewhat easy landings at Vella Lavella and Lae, it had been a difficult battle fought under the specter of disaster.

INTO ITALY: BAYTOWN AND AVALANCHE, SEPTEMBER 1943

Italy was actually invaded six days before the landing at Salerno. The British Eighth Army crossed the Straits of Messina into Calabria on 3 September. Strong air and naval forces covered the movement as did artillery batteries emplaced on Sicily. The object of the operation was threefold: Allied troops in the toe of the Italian boot would mask Messina and allow free passage of Allied shipping through the straits. Second, whatever disposition the Germans had to evacuate southern Italy would be given impetus as Montgomery's men pushed northward. Third, any German forces opposing Avalanche would face being caught in the flank as the Eighth Army advanced. Although the crossing took place without difficulty, the British advance north was so slow it had no effect on the battle for Salerno.

The planners' need to simultaneously bring together more than 600 ships off Salerno resulted in sixteen different convoys. They came from as far away as Oran and as near as Sicily. There was the now-familiar division of slower landing craft plowing doggedly ahead while miles to the rear came the faster transports and cargo ships. Around the perimeters were the low, gray shapes of escorting destroyers and patrol craft. The truly allied nature of the expedition can be found in the intermingling of United States and Royal Navy ships under flag officers from both countries. Also included in the assault force were several civilian-manned cargo and hospital ships. Hewitt and General Clark were in the *Ancon* while Admiral Conolly was again in the *Biscayne*, with Admiral Hall in the *Samuel Chase*. Among Hewitt's worries as task force commander was the nagging thought that security had been compromised:

> [One officer] reports that various personnel of both the Army and Navy . . . were overheard making remarks indicating accurate knowledge of the time and place of the landing several days prior to departure.

> The CO of LST 369 reports that . . . several days prior to the receipt of the operation plans by that ship, the Executive Officer observed in the ship's radio room a map . . . on which the Gulf of Salerno had been prominently indicated by a heavy pencil mark. Upon interrogating the radioman, the latter volunteered . . . that Salerno was the site of the projected landing; that this information had been imported to him by another bluejacket attached to the Seabees.[20]

Whatever his thoughts as his task force approached Italy, Hewitt need not have worried about secrecy. The Germans were all too aware that while the entire Italian coastline south of Naples lay in an area exposed to Allied invasion, the logical choices for a landing included the Gulf of Salerno. Aerial reconnaissance flights revealed that Allied naval forces were engaged in large-scale movements toward Italy; air attacks on the approaching convoys damaged two ships. Field Marshal Kesselring and his field commanders had already prepared for a possible landing at Salerno.

The 16th Panzer Division was in the immediate area building strong points. At least three other divisions were within striking range. There was no threat from the British forces to the south; skillful German rearguard actions had slowed Montgomery's never-quick pace of advance to a crawl. Any invasion that came ashore at Salerno would have to face 17,000 well-equipped and experienced German soldiers.

Troops poised at the edge of battle are justifiably keyed up. The anticipation of action on the morrow gives them an edge that often is the difference between death and survival. Allied estimates of the defenses around Salerno were not totally accurate but did suggest that a hard fight might be in the offing, especially if German troops were present in large numbers. Unfortunately, politics intervened the night before the landing to blunt the fighting edge of the soldiers about to launch Avalanche.

Italian emissaries had been meeting secretly with the Allies to arrange the surrender of their country. An agreement was reached on 3 September but not revealed until Eisenhower made a public announcement at 1830 on 8 September. Troops clustered around radio speakers in the cramped confines of their transports and landing ships had but one reaction and that was to cheer. George Dyer had a more jaundiced view of the announcement:

> I would say that it [the announcement] had tremendous psychological repercussions on the troops. They could hardly go ashore determined to do or die when the enemy had just turned in his suit. The fact that the Germans hadn't turned in their suits was not readily apparent to the GI until somebody shot at him.[21]

It would be only a few hours before the high expectations brought to life by Eisenhower's announcement were violently dashed to pieces.

First off the beaches was a guide submarine. She had been in the area for several days and had provided confirmation that there were mines present. She surfaced late in the night of 8 September and began to display a green light to seaward. The oncoming invasion force picked up the light as planned and made its assigned anchorages without interference. The various scout, marker, and control boats began to move into position. Some landing boats loaded at the rail while in other ships the soldiers had to make the long climb down cargo nets. A calm sea allowed loading to go somewhat smoothly; the first wave was soon ready to form up and head for the shore. The boats were preceded by minesweepers whose job it was to clear lanes through the enemy mines moored off the beaches.

Reports had begun to filter into 16th Panzer headquarters that something was up, but not until the bombardment ships off the British sector opened up was it certain that some sort of Allied landing attempt was on. Farther to the south in the American sector, German artillery and infantry waited tensely behind their weapons, but no fire came from the dark sea.

The landing plan for the American beaches was for assault elements of two infantry regiments plus attached engineers to land abreast in the first wave. They were to be supported by a few rocket-armed landing craft with orders to hold their fire unless fired upon. Seven minutes later would come the reserve infantry companies plus more engineers and mine-clearing equipment. A third wave was scheduled eight minutes later carrying heavy weapons, medical personnel, headquarters units, and the Navy beach party. The fourth and fifth waves would bring bulldozers, self-propelled artillery, AA guns, and the reserve infantry battalions. Tanks, field artillery, and antitank guns were scheduled ashore two hours after the initial wave. Planners hoped that LSTs could begin beaching five or six hours after the initial assault. Much attention had also been devoted to establishing communications between the beaches and the invasion fleet.

Shore fire-control parties, various Army unit headquarters, Navy signal personnel, and the air support party were all to have their nets up and operating no later than two hours after the initial landings. As the first boats began to approach the beach in the early morning darkness, many men no doubt held out hope that all would go as planned. There were flashes and the low rumble of gunfire to the north where the British landings were under way, but all was silent in the American sector. That calm was transitory because the defenders were waiting.

The Germans allowed the first wave to reach the beach before they opened fire. They sent up flares to illuminate the landing craft and laced the beaches with a well-aimed barrage of machine gun and artillery fire. Plans so carefully drafted in the security of an office met with the sudden, brutal realities of war. The army history describes a common scene:

Landing craft struck by enemy fire burned near shore or drifted helplessly. Men swam for shore as boats sank under them. As a 60-mm mortar squad debarked, the gunner tripped on the ramp and dropped the piece into the water; machine gun fire scattered the men in the darkness; individuals joined whatever unit happened to be near them. An 81-mm mortar platoon came ashore intact but without ammunition; the boat carrying its shells had been sunk.[22]

A bitter fight followed with many individual acts of heroism as the soldiers clawed their way into the defenders' gun pits. Sgt. James Logan earned the Medal of Honor for single-handedly wiping out the crew of an enemy machine gun and then turning the weapon on its former owners. A few enemy guns were knocked out by the rocket-equipped support boats, but heavy naval gunfire support was still hours away. One LCT was almost at the beach with her cargo of tanks when a direct hit set the lead vehicle ablaze and killed the boat's skipper. The LCT backed off, upon which a second tank in line pushed the burning wreckage overboard.

After four hours of heavy fighting, the invaders had at best a tenuous toehold. Much the same situation existed in the British sector. Although not all the landings there were opposed on the same scale, fighting was fierce and costly to the assault troops. The northern attack began with Phil Bucklew and a shipmate just off the beach in a kayak, shining a light to seaward to guide the oncoming landing craft. From their spot low on the water, they witnessed a British support craft deliver a rocket barrage onto the beach.

> the rockets have a tremendous roar and they went overhead with a swish, swish, swish, and we didn't know what it was. The next experience there, I took a hit. I was hit in the chest—a good thump that took my wind away and I thought, "Well, that's it, it doesn't hurt too much but that's it." So I turned over my shoulder to my bo's'ns mate and said, "I think I took a hit, so you will have to take over." About that time, my life jacket began to smoke and smolder. I hadn't taken a hit, but I had taken a piece of rocket that was burning the kapok in my jacket. I was kind of embarrassed and my bo's'n let me hear about it quite a few times. He would say, "Boss, tell 'em about that hit you took."[23]

The British secured some initial objectives, but their hold was as tenuous as the Americans'.

Fortunately for the attackers, the overall situation could have been worse. There was no bad weather to contend with as there had been during Torch and Husky. Operational losses of landing boats were minimal, so a steady flow of supplies could come to the beaches once they were secured.

The enemy soldiers guarding the beaches had orders to delay the invaders only long enough for Kesselring to determine if the landing was an invasion, not merely a raid. Only then would tanks and infantry reinforcements be moved up. If German troops had been present in greater numbers, the initial beachhead could probably not have been established. By daylight, both sides had similar but competing imperatives: get enough men and firepower into the battle zone to thwart the enemy. If the Allies were to prevail, the issue depended upon the work of the Navy.

Several factors affected the Navy's ability to help the soldiers. First, of course, was the strong resistance from the beach. Intense fire kept dozens of landing boats and DUKWs circling offshore. Destroyers laid a smoke screen to shield the boats from enemy gunners, but the smoke also hid the beach from boat coxswains. The combination of enemy fire and obscured landing sites caused some boats to lay off up to six hours before they could beach. Once landed, many boat crews discovered that the Army shore party was nowhere to be found. The boat crews would hurriedly dump their cargoes at ramp's end and retract as quickly as possible. Supplies began to build up at the water's edge, effectively blocking other boats.

The offshore minefields were another problem. The transports anchored ten to twelve miles out to avoid the mines, making it a long haul for a boat. Although the minesweepers exploded or set adrift almost seventy mines, their presence invoked caution. Until the mines were swept in sufficient numbers, the transports could not get closer inshore nor could the gunfire-support ships get close enough to deliver effective fire. Help with the mine problem arrived from an unexpected source; a small boat flying a white flag approached the *Biscayne* shortly after first light on D-day. George Dyer met the boat, which carried five Italian officers.

> Up they came. The first thing that I told them was that I wanted the information on the mines that were in the area. A naval officer amongst them produced the chart, he had it right underneath his trousers. He pulled it out, and there was the chart with all the mines. If we'd just had a xerox system, it would have been just wonderful. I turned it over to the staff chief quartermaster and told him to make a couple of copies . . . right away quick and get one to Admiral Hewitt.[24]

This valuable intelligence caused mine-sweeping efforts to be extended farther southward; the minehunters discovered more than sixty additional mines.

Even so, the minefields exacted a toll; LST 386 struck one while approaching the beach. The explosion blew her pontoon causeway to bits and ripped a hole, estimated by Allen Pace to be 48 ft. long, in her side. With one engine out, the skipper ordered flank speed and rammed her onto the beach. Unfortunately, ruptured plates protruding beneath the hull brought her up short. Twelve feet of water at the ramp was too deep to unload without a causeway and the ship started to receive enemy artillery and machine gun fire. Her skipper ordered the crew to take cover while he attempted to get instructions. When he received no reply to any of his messages, he retracted his badly damaged ship from the beach. He finally did get orders to unload his cargo into LCTs, a task successfully completed.

The ability of the Navy to help with gunfire support was delayed because enemy fire had scattered and driven to ground the shore fire-control parties. Nor could targets near the beach be seen clearly; as suggested years earlier, the smoke that hid landing boats from enemy gunners also hid targets from offshore gun directors. Communication with all units ashore was so poor that Hewitt and the Army commanders had little idea what was going on, a situation Hewitt described somewhat laconically as an "extended nuisance." The need for gunfire support was so critical that Admiral Conolly even ordered the *Biscayne* closer to the beach to bring an enemy battery under fire.[25] Only at midmorning did the situation ashore begin to stabilize and Navy gunfire begin to make its expected contribution.

Between 1000 and 1200, the *Savannah* and *Philadelphia*, plus three destroyers, were able to take positions in the fire-support area. There was still only scant communication with any of the control parties ashore, but targets were designated through an ad hoc net of Army units calling for assistance, ship-launched air spotters, and several spotters provided by the air force. They had plenty of targets, because more German tanks had arrived in the battle area at dawn and were pressing hard against the embattled American infantry. Landings at one beach had to be suspended because a group of enemy tanks and supporting infantry had driven to within 80 yards of the water. Shipboard gunners quickly did their best to put the situation right, knocking out several tanks and putting others to flight. Spotters also directed naval gunfire with telling effect onto enemy artillery and machine gun positions. Soon, however, the gunfire ships themselves were in danger: as expected, the Luftwaffe came out in force to meet the invaders.

The planners believed the Germans had no fewer than 910 combat aircraft within range of the Salerno area. Some of them began to show up early in the morning of D-day. Although the combined CAP of Army Air Force and Royal Navy fighters was more successful than not in making interceptions, some inevitably got through. The German fliers strafed the beaches several times but managed to sink only a tug. One reason for the Luftwaffe's lack of success was the enemy fliers often couldn't see their targets. Smoke was used to the maximum extent possible to mask the transports, against which the Germans aimed the maximum weight of bombs. Destroyers and other patrol craft made funnel and chemical smoke;

even LCVPs with oil-fired smoke generators aboard were pressed into service. The smoke screen was so effective on one occasion that boat traffic almost came to a halt.

The strain imposed by constant air attacks was more than some men could bear. George Dyer, himself to become a casualty of an air raid, remembered one such man:

> I was on one side of the bridge . . . and I heard the Stukas coming in on the other side. In the narrow passageway . . . I met this great big gunner who should have been at his gun. Whenever afterwards we [would] have an air attack, I used to station myself right behind him and coach him. The German[s] . . . would fly very close to the ground . . . and then they'd come up and over the hills and bomb and strafe the ships. Our ships had roughly a minute or a minute and half to actually start shooting at them, before the planes . . . attacked. The general alarm went off and I rushed out to get behind the gunner. I was just going through the door of the chart house to get to my station . . . when zowie, I got hit in the left leg. My leg bone was somewhat shattered.[26]

German artillery was still pounding the landing areas by midday, but resistance in the immediate vicinity had been overcome. The LSTs were finally able to head for the beaches, where they also came under fire. The Salerno beaches proved to be a different problem from Sicily. The gradient was steep enough that some LSTs drove onto the beach at 8 knots and pumped ballast into the forward tanks to hold the ship on the sand. Pontoons again proved invaluable in bridging those places where LSTs were prevented from reaching the true beach. The wartime sobriquet "Large Slow Target" given to LSTs seemed well earned at Salerno. The LST 385 was hit three times while approaching the beach and twice more after grounding; struck by a dud aerial torpedo while en route to Salerno, LST 375 was hit twice by artillery and once by a bomb. Except for fifty killed in LST 375, casualties were incredibly light and all the ships were able to return to North Africa. As they had shown in the South Pacific, the LSTs were also capable of handing out some punishment; LST 355 brought her forward 40-mm guns into action against two German tanks, destroying one and driving the other out of range.

A definite sense of unease pervaded Hewitt's flagship:

> It was the lack of communications between shore and ship and the resulting absence of precise information for most of the day that made the higher echelons of command uneasy, and this contributed to shipboard impressions that the Salerno invasion was inordinately difficult. With the shore obscured first by darkness and later by smoke, rumors were rife.[27]

General Dawley found a situation that was being slowly sorted out as Army units pushed farther inland. Naval gunfire and an increasing weight of Army artillery continued to make itself felt while tanks were landing from the LSTs. The beaches remained congested with supplies, but efforts were underway to clear the jam. General Clark ordered the floating reserve to land late in the afternoon, a move that began before the day was out. Enemy air raids continued, but at a lower intensity than during the morning. A seven-mile gap remained between the British and American beachheads, but the feeling began to grow that the worst was over. Clark and his commanders focused on getting sufficient supplies, vehicles, artillery, and tanks off the ships and into the hands of the troops fighting to enlarge the beachhead. Several LCTs were shifted from the British beaches to help with unloading, and late in the day the transports moved closer inshore. The beachhead was far from secure by day's end, but all hands assumed the invaders were ashore to stay.

Unloading continued at an increasing rate on 10 September. By 2200, all embarked troops and vehicles were ashore. The shortage of labor troops on the beaches delayed the unloading of bulk cargo from the LSTs, but the first return convoys were preparing to leave the area to make room for the follow-up. To Hewitt's great disgust, his amphibious ships had again to send additional men ashore to help with unloading. From his perspective, "the Army had no established plan for beach operations."[28]

Army units continued to push inland, though progress was slow against determined resistance. German headquarters ordered four more divisions into the arena. The fighting of the first two days had convinced Kesselring and his field commanders that the invasion could be thrown back into the sea. That the fight was not remotely over became evident to the Navy on the morning of 11 September.

At midmorning, a radio-controlled bomb hit the *Savannah* directly atop her number 3 turret. The armor-piercing weapon sliced completely through the ship and exploded in the lower handling room. Casualties were heavy. The same day, air force headquarters advised Hewitt that the number of fighters over the beachhead would be reduced. The admiral responded emphatically in the negative but also asked the Royal Navy carrier task group commander if he couldn't keep his ships present for another day. That officer gallantly agreed, though by doing so he would have just enough fuel to reach Malta.

Ashore, the German buildup opposite the beachhead increased. Both British and American troops attempted to continue driving inland on 12 September, but resistance was heavy and German counterattacks swift and effective. Late in the day, reports of increased enemy strength began flowing in to General Clark, who had shifted his headquarters ashore from the

Ancon. He had done what he could to adjust his troop dispositions, including a seaborne shift of several battalions into the British sector to close the gap in the lines. The storm broke on 13 September, when a German counterattack began in strength, focused on the lightly held area between the Rivers Sele and Calor; heavy German attacks drove American units steadily back. Only the heaviest concentration of artillery and naval gunfire slowed the German assault. By the end of the day, as the enemy drew closer to the beaches, Clark came to the conclusion that he might have to evacuate the American sector. He directed Hewitt to be ready to move the 36th Infantry Division to the X Corps sector. The apparent grimness of the Allied position was punctuated that night when the Luftwaffe bombed and set ablaze a hospital ship despite her clearly illuminated markings.

It is amphibious warfare gospel that an orderly evacuation under fire and the pressure of an advancing enemy is almost impossible. Hewitt knew the inherent difficulties and argued with Clark that it could not be done successfully. He explained to the general that landing craft could back off a beach easily enough when unloaded but a loaded ship would probably be stuck. If each ship was to take a lesser load, there wouldn't be enough ships to get everybody off in time. Phil Bucklew had the same opinion.

> The power isn't there to withdraw. Under normal loading circumstances you can drive a ship in but you are offloading your troops, your cargo, which lightens your ship and you can withdraw. Well, it takes a little doing to ease the ship gradually off, it takes experience. And you don't really practice it . . . if we had such a withdrawal . . . it would also have been under heavy German fire, so your casualties, whether to the ships or the troops, would no doubt have been disastrous.[29]

Clark persisted. Hewitt therefore ordered unloading off the southern beaches to be stopped and plans drawn up for an evacuation. When Hewitt advised the British commander of the northern task force about Clark's proposed plan, that officer responded by saying that such an operation was simply "not on." Reinforcements were meanwhile on the way.

Clark had asked for the 82nd Airborne Division to be brought forward from Sicily. A drop of two battalions within American lines was hastily arranged for the night of 13 September. Memories of the disaster off Sicily were still fresh so both Clark and Hewitt issued strict orders that no AA fire would be permitted off Salerno after 2200. Six hundred men successfully parachuted into the beachhead, providing a lift in morale out of proportion to their numbers.

The Germans renewed their attack on 14 September and were again met with the heaviest possible volume of naval gunfire. Admiral Cunningham dispatched reinforcements to Hewitt in the form of two British light cruisers and two battleships. The *Philadelphia* fired so many support missions that she was in danger of exhausting her main-battery magazines. There was no supply of 6-inch readily at hand, so Hewitt sent a destroyer to Malta to clean out the damaged *Savannah*. General Alexander arrived at the beachhead on the same day and, after reviewing the situation, told Clark there would be no evacuation. He had already ordered the American 3d Infantry Division to be moved from Sicily to Salerno and promised Clark whatever reinforcements might be necessary. The defenses held that day, and that night 1,200 more paratroopers dropped successfully into the beachhead. When the two British battleships arrived off Salerno and joined the battle, they were engaging an enemy who had shot his bolt. Though Allied commanders did not yet realize it, the battle for the beaches was over.

Hewitt's amphibious forces remained busy long after the battle moved inland. The port of Salerno was so badly damaged as to be useless for more than two weeks after being taken by the British, so supplies continued to be landed across the beaches. By D+25, 225,000 men, 34,254 vehicles, and 117,572 tons of supplies had been put ashore at Salerno. More than 100 Allied ships and landing craft had been hit by enemy bombing or artillery fire. Opinions remained divided about the efficacy of naval gunfire; Hewitt believed the Army could not have maintained its position ashore without it. The Navy fired more than 11,000 tons of shells in support of the landing, but some Army officers still believed naval gunfire was limited in its usefulness;

> "The morale effect is, of course, terrific," one officer noted, "as the shell is large and the muzzle velocity astonishing." Though naval gunfire gave great psychological support to the Allied troops and adversely affected the Germans, the relatively flat trajectory of the shells limited their effectiveness in close support because of the large safety distance required between shellburst and friendly troop locations.[30]

These views were not shared by the artillery commander of the 36th Infantry Division nor by German Generaloberst Heinrich von Vietinghoff, who commanded the enemy forces opposing the landing. Late in the day of 9 September, Brig. Gen. John Lange sent the following message to be delivered to the fire-support ships: "Thank God for the fire of the bluebelly Navy ships. Probably could not [otherwise] have stuck out Blue and Yellow beaches. Brave fellows these; tell them so."[31] He was supported by von Vietinghoff, who later ascribed the failure of his counterattack to the quality of gunfire support the invaders received from the Navy:

> The attack this morning [14 September] pushed on into stiffened resistance, but above all the advancing troops had to endure the most severe heavy fire that had until now been experienced; the naval gunfire from at

least 16 to 18 battleships, cruisers and destroyers lying in the roadstead. With astonishing precision and freedom of maneuver, these ships shot at every recognized target with overwhelming effect.[32]

Even though they were proud of the job they had done, Hewitt and his men had recommendations for delivering even better support in the future. The commander of Cruiser Divison Eight wanted shore fire-control parties equipped with the portable radios then known as "walkie-talkies" to better communicate with the ships. Hewitt made several recommendations, including this one:

> During the planning and training period it should be impressed upon commands concerned that the effectiveness of Naval gunfire support depends largely upon the knowledge of its capabilities possessed by the Army artillery command, and the efficiency of ship to shore communications.[33]

Given the frustration again experienced in getting amphibious ships and landing craft unloaded, Hewitt devoted considerable time to the problem. He again asked that more Army troops be assigned to unloading, with hatch crews and on the beach. Hewitt said that with enough LCTs and LCMs, a combat-loaded transport should be unloaded in no more than 30 hours. He was particularly adamant about the Army's not dragooning the DUKWs once they had made their first trip to the beach:

> It seems that no matter what assurances may be given beforehand regarding the employment of DUKWs, circumstances will always arise which will prevent the Army command from ensuring that they are employed for the special tasks for which they were designed. The only solution for this seems to be that after they have landed their initial loads they and their drivers revert to direct naval control until the unloading is completed.[34]

Hewitt also made the point that bulk-loaded cargo should always be the last priority in unloading the LSTs because otherwise the pontoons were tied up too long. The skipper of one cargo ship suggested that a vessel specifically outfitted as a boat repair facility be provided to each assault force. By doing so, he thought the delays inherent in each ship's being responsible for repairing its own boats would be avoided and cargo handled at a faster rate.

Admiral Hall wanted a salvage unit established as a separate entity and properly equipped to deal with any contingency. One last after-action comment must be noted: Ironically, given Navy comments about Army loading practices, the Army was especially unhappy that not all the VI Corps staff had been embarked in the *Ancon*. After three major landings within ten months, the hard lessons of amphibious warfare were piling up. The accelerating pace of the attack on the Axis meant that there would be scant respite to absorb and put into practice the lessons learned. While those of Hewitt's amphibious ships not bound for England remained hard at work supplying the Allied buildup in Italy, the planners were soon to be equally hard at work drafting the next assault from the sea. In the Pacific, meanwhile, the accelerated pace continued. The Halsey–MacArthur pincer was closing around Rabaul and King's long-cherished Central Pacific offensive was about to begin.

CARTWHEEL KEEPS ROLLING: SEPTEMBER–NOVEMBER 1943

Finschhafen was no impulsive operation; its Japanese garrison had to be eliminated as part of MacArthur's plan to control the Vitiaz Strait between New Guinea and New Britain. A scouting party landed but had to lay low because Japanese were too near the proposed landing beach. Aerial photos revealed only a shoal that limited the beach to three LSTs at a time. Adair's planners had to work quickly:

> Admiral Barbey said to me, "You're going to have to go up to Lae and see General Wootten and plan this operation. We'll send you up in a PT boat leaving tonight. . . . You'll leave at dusk tonight from Buna. Plan the operation with General Wootten and then come back the next night." This doesn't give me much time when the 22d . . . is only four days away and our ships are still carrying supplies to Lae, which was assaulted on the [4th].[35]

Adair spent the day with the Australian general and returned to Buna the next night. His recounting of what happened after his return is vivid in its depiction of the vast differences between Dan Barbey's war and Kent Hewitt's war:

> Barbey said, "Well, you'd better get your breakfast and get started on that plan, because we've got to get that out in a hurry! We are going to have to make a distribution of that by daylight tomorrow morning!" So I gathered all *five* [Adair's emphasis] of our planners together on our small planning ship . . . and briefed them on . . . how the assault was going to be. Then I told the intelligence people what we were going to need from them for the plan. The planners were six, including myself. I was the one who was responsible for the organization of ships in the assault, the summary of the operation plan, the assignment of boats and ships to the direct assault waves, and the timing of the waves. Also, I drew up all the details of the resupply operations.

After working all day, the plan was ready for Barbey:

at 7 o'clock that night, I carried the mimeographed sheets over to him.
He flipped through the sheets taking a quick look at them and said,
"You know, I don't have time to read that plan, because you're going to
have to get to work and start printing it. Will it work?" I said, "Yes,"
and so he signed it gave it back to me, and said, "Go ahead. I am taking
all you planners with me on the assault. If the plan has to be changed,
we will do it there." So I went back to the planning ship, and we started
to run this off . . . with a hand-cranked mimeograph machine, and by
10 o'clock, I could see that we were not going to make it by daylight,
and we were going to need some help. I took a tour around . . . and
I found one cook who had not turned in and was available, so I asked
him if he would give us a hand. By 5 o'clock in the morning we had
[143 copies] of this plan assembled.

Next came the problem of distribution. The ships assigned to the assault
had been loaded without having the operation order available. Adair takes
up the story:

After loading they were due to be off the area where we were at midnight
that night (this now was the morning that we had finished the plan). So
we got PT boats and gave them copies of the plan, and they went out,
intercepted the ships enroute to the assault area, and put aboard these
plans . . . and the ships continued up the coast to the assault area.[36]

Adair had gathered a task force that included twenty-six small amphibians
and ten destroyers for escort and gunfire support. The Australian 20th
Infantry Brigade Group loaded at Buna and the assault force assembled in
the harbor of newly won Lae. Given the shortage of time, there was not
even the hint of a rehearsal. The task force departed on 21 September
under continuous fighter cover and was off Scarlet Beach, six miles north
of Finschhafen, as scheduled.

After a sharp bombardment from the destroyers, the first two waves
landed at 0445. They were slightly out of position, but resistance was so
slight no harm was done. The LCIs bringing in the third wave at the proper
location met stronger opposition, but the last Japanese was driven away
from the beach or killed by 0930. Anticipation of an enemy air raid caused
unloading to begin immediately. Putting his experience at Lae to work,
Barbey ordered 100 additional men assigned to each LST to speed up cargo
discharge. He also directed each ship to be more lightly loaded, reasoning
that the Japanese could not prevent follow-up echelons from arriving.

These preparations resulted in bulk cargo being unloaded at the rate
of 50 tons per hour, far faster than ever before. More than 850 tons of
supplies, 5,300 men, 180 vehicles, and 32 guns were ashore by the early
hours of 23 September. No casualties resulted from attacks by the few

Japanese planes that managed to slip through the fighter screen. The operation took place with such precision that by sunrise on the twenty-third, all the landing ships were enroute for Lae to begin the follow-up.

Despite a Japanese counterattack, Finschhafen fell on 2 October. The Japanese attempted a counterlanding on 16 October, but the assault force was annihilated. Two weeks later, the pendulum of the American onslaught swung to the east as Halsey's men launched an assault on Bougainville, the last Japanese stronghold in the Solomons.

Imperial Headquarters' plans for defending Rabaul depended heavily on maintaining control of Bougainville, the largest of the Solomon Islands. The Japanese had stationed a large garrison and built several airfields on Bougainville in expectation of an Allied invasion. Troop strength was concentrated in the southern end of the island, exactly where the Americans envisioned making their attack. An exhortation issued to the garrison is typical of the Japanese belief in their moral superiority:

> The battle plan is to resist the enemy's material strength with perseverance, while at the same time displaying our spiritual strength and conducting raids and furious attacks against the enemy flanks and rear. On this basis we will secure the key to victory within the dead spaces produced in enemy strength, and, losing no opportunities, we will exploit success and annihilate the enemy.[37]

The first assault plan worked up by Halsey's headquarters had to be abandoned when the Munda campaign took longer than expected. There were simply not enough troops available to overcome the 35,000 Japanese estimated to be defending Bougainville's airfields and beaches. Halsey's planners issued a revised plan on 22 September and alerted the I Marine Amphibious Corps for the operation. Rather than make a head-on assault, the planners decided to land just north of Cape Torokina on a relatively unguarded string of beaches midway along the western side of the island. No attempt would be made to seize the whole island; an enclave of sufficient depth would be carved out, airfields established to continue the assault on Rabaul, and a strong defensive perimeter built against which the inevitable Japanese counterattacks could dash themselves.

The Treasury Islands, 75 miles west of the landing area, would be seized five days before the main assault to clear the approaches and to serve as the site of an early warning radar. Because they were the only amphibiously trained American troops available, the 3d Marine Division under Maj. Gen. Allen Turnage got the job of assaulting Bougainville. The desert veterans of the 8th New Zealand Brigade Group got the Treasury job. The 2d Marine Parachute Battalion received the task of landing on the neighboring island of Choiseul to divert Japanese attention. Halsey issued an operation order on 1 October; Operation Goodtime, the Treasury landing, would take place on 27 October, with Operation Dipper, the Bougainville landing, 1 November.

The airmen began a concerted campaign of attacks against Rabaul and Bougainville to blast the enemy airfields out of commission and chew up his air strength. The Japanese fought back, but the combined assault of the 5th Air Force from new bases in New Guinea and Halsey's joint service, multinational air force was too much. Efforts to keep the Bougainville airfields intact slackened noticeably as D-day drew nearer. Despite the apparent success of the air campaign, however, prudence and harsh experience dictated to Wilkinson and his planners that they not consider the Japanese air threat defunct. Therefore, they set up a series of airfield bombardments to take place the night before the landing.

As had become practice by then, scouts landed on Bougainville to get a first-hand look at the terrain. They had to operate under the added threat of knowing most of the natives of Bougainville were friendly to the Japanese. They were able to determine that there were approximately 10,000 yards of beaches available and observed that the enemy patrolled the area regularly from the air. The submariners who brought the scouts to Bougainville also discovered that the vintage 1890s charts being used were more than seven miles out of position. The scouts were not the only ones experiencing difficulties.

Wilkinson's planning staff was feeling the pinch of the impending offensive in the Central Pacific as they tried to assemble the ships to transport the 3d Marine Division to the assault area and to bring in the 37th Infantry Division as follow-up. While the number of ships available to Turner and then Wilkinson had never been generous, and was certainly more than that available to Barbey, the diversion of amphibious lift to Nimitz meant there were only eight transports and four cargo ships left in the South Pacific Area. The requirement to move two divisions, their supporting units, and supplies meant that if any single transport or cargo ship was lost, the schedule could not be maintained. The planners took to calling the operation "Shoestring 2" in memory of the straitened circumstances at Guadalcanal.

Though intelligence knew the air campaign was costing the Japanese large numbers of combat planes, the proximity of Bougainville to the airfields of Rabaul dictated some changes to the typical landing scheme. The plan called for almost 1,000 troops to be landed the first day; unlike previous landings, nearly 40 percent of the total had the job of unloading supplies. The order called for landing the first boatloads of supplies immediately after the initial assault waves; 6,200 tons of ammunition, rations, heavy weapons, and other equipment were scheduled to be put ashore within six hours. A follow-up convoy of LSTs was scheduled to arrive on D + 5 and the 37th Infantry Division would be brought forward by D + 7.

The assault force managed some practice despite the shortage of time. As Wilkinson noted later, the mechanics of "rapid and efficient unloading" received particular attention. The destroyers assigned gunfire-support duties were able to conduct practice bombardments against defensive positions abandoned when the Japanese evacuated Kolombangara. The practice should have reinforced the necessity of getting as close as possible to the durable coconut log bunkers favored by the enemy, but it didn't. The assault units of the 3d Marine Division were also able to conduct practice exercises between 17 and 19 October. Much of the prelanding training took place on Guadalcanal and it was from there that a task force under Rear Adm. George Fort sailed for the Treasuries. Fort had thirty-one ships and a landing force of 6,300 New Zealand soldiers, American marines, soldiers, and Seabees. Once the fleet was in position off Mono and Stirling Islands, the accompanying destroyers opened up with a prelanding bombardment.

The Japanese garrisons defending the islands were fortunately small, because the poorly directed bombardment did virtually no damage. The troops landed against limited resistance, supported for the first time by a newcomer to the amphibious wars: two LCIs converted to close-support gunboats by increasing their firepower. Designated LCI(G), they were of shallow enough draft to follow the landing boats right up to the beach. Their purpose was to fill the gunfire-support gap that always occurred when the naval bombardment stopped to avoid hitting the landing boats. Their first test was hardly severe but was considered successful. Some mortar and sniper fire fell on the landing area, giving the crew of the LST 399 some experiences they would long remember. The ship beached on Mono Island and quickly received two hits from mortar fire, killing three men.

More shells continued to erupt around her as her bow doors opened, and the first three men off the ramp were shot. Careful scrutiny then discovered a well-concealed Japanese pillbox only eight yards from the port bow door. A volley of bullets sent whistling around the packed tank deck caused the bow ramp to be hastily raised. None of the ship's guns could be brought to bear nor were the soldiers already ashore having much luck in suppressing the enemy's fire. Some hardy soul mounted an embarked bulldozer, ordered the ramp lowered, and charged. "He then worked to the 'blind side' of the pillbox, lowered his blade, and plowed the pillbox and its seven occupants under the earth, 'tamping it down well all around, effectively silencing its fire.' "[38] The day's adventures were not yet over for the LST 399.

Near midday, enemy mortar fire again began to slam around the ship, and again she was hit. The same barrage hit an ammunition dump, which quickly erupted and began to shower flaming debris onto her forecastle. Her bow was soon enveloped in flames, causing the captain to flood the forward magazine. The fires were put out, but the ship's seeming magnetism for enemy fire caused the soldiers assigned as an unloading detail to drift steadily away. Efforts to keep the men at work proved unavailing; when she left the beach at 1943, she still had 20 tons of bulk cargo aboard. En route to Guadalcanal that night, a Japanese bomber slipped out of the darkness and dropped two bombs close enough aboard to shake her severely and put several more punctures in her skin. With that, her day was finally over. Attention in the South Pacific Area then turned to the impending assault on Bougainville.

Admiral Wilkinson was in command of the amphibious task force bound for Cape Torokina. He flew his flag in the Mediterranean veteran *George Clymer*. Although some of the separate elements were spotted by Japanese aircraft, the combined task force made its approach to the landing area without incident. The amphibious ships were approaching their anchorage when the destroyers opened the bombardment. They concentrated their fire in the immediate area of Cape Torokina, where intelligence photographs had revealed a few enemy emplacements. As the amphibians passed by Cape Torokina en route to the transport area, each of them let fly with its main battery guns to add to the weight of the bombardment.

Chester Eccleston was in the *Clymer*'s forward crow's nest, spotting for her guns, but as he says, "We used our forward three inch and didn't hit a thing." Nor did the bombarding destroyers. None of twenty-five bunkers behind the landing beaches were hit.[39] The amphibians meanwhile secured from their unfamiliar gunnery assignment and prepared to anchor.

The transports formed two lines 4,000 to 5,000 yards off the beach, with the cargo ships 500 yards to seaward. Each ship anchored off its assigned portion of the landing area, which was divided into northern and southern sectors. All first-wave assault troops quickly loaded at the rail; it took the experienced crew of the *Clymer* only thirty-seven minutes to get her troops into their boats. As the boats prepared to start for the beaches, waves of Marine fighters and bombers delivered a last-minute attack on the landing area. Like the gunfire of the destroyers, the bombs and strafing had no noticeable effect on the waiting Japanese. The first wave was approaching the beach when the failure of both bombardments was revealed. One bunker behind the southern beaches sheltered a 75-mm gun that was put into lethal play by the defenders. The leading boat group commander became one of the first casualties when his LCVP was blown to bits. The enemy gunners hit thirteen other boats, sinking three. The fire of this gun caused the first wave to become scrambled but did not stop the landing.

Although often put ashore out of place and separated from their units, the marines on the southern beaches immediately set about the business of cleaning out the defenders. Sgt. Robert Owens earned a posthumous Medal of Honor for his valor in silencing the gun causing such havoc among the landing boats. The Japanese fought with their usual bravery and tenacity, but by 1100 they were mostly dead or had retreated inland from the beachhead. Supplies were coming ashore in a flood and the situation seemed well in hand. Just a couple of miles to the northwest, however, things were not going so smoothly. There had been no resistance in the northernmost sector, but surf and beach conditions had severely disrupted the smooth flow envisioned by the planners. The inability of the landing boats to ground on the steep beaches was the biggest problem; with no purchase, they were almost immediately broached by heavy surf. The wrecked and damaged remains of eighty-six LCMs and LCVPs soon littered the three northernmost beaches. Wilkinson was determined that the amphibians would clear the landing area by nightfall, so he did not hesitate to alter the plan. He directed the five northernmost ships to land their supplies farther south; those transports shifted their beach parties accordingly.

As expected, a Japanese aerial counterattack was not long in arriving. The proximity of Bougainville to enemy airfields on Rabaul was reflected by the first air raid boring in while the initial landing waves were en route to the beach. A destroyer on radar picket duty provided sufficient warning for the amphibians to up anchor and get under way. Efficient fighter cover and heavy AA fire allowed the enemy fliers only a near-miss. A second raid that afternoon was again intercepted by the CAP and shot to pieces by shipboard gunners. Despite these interruptions, the added manpower devoted to unloading proved its worth; eight of the twelve amphibians were completely unloaded when Wilkinson ordered retirement at 1800. The four partially unloaded ships remained behind with orders to complete their task the following day. The caution implicit in the quick departure of the amphibians from the landing area was reinforced that night when the Japanese sent a force of cruisers and destroyers south to attack the invasion fleet.

Much progress had been made since the early days off Guadalcanal. The oncoming Japanese task group was properly scouted and reported to Admiral Merrill's covering force, allowing him to be in position to intercept. Merrill's task force fought the subsequent Battle of Empress Augusta Bay during the midwatch of 2 November; they sank one Japanese cruiser and one destroyer. American losses amounted to one cruiser hit by shellfire and one destroyer torpedoed but saved. Not only had the Imperial Navy been kept away from the beachhead, but stepped-up air raids against Rabaul thereafter caused them to withdraw their surface forces to Truk. The main threat to the Bougainville beachhead would be mounted by the Imperial Army.

There remained the job of landing the follow-up. More than 33,000 men and 22,127 tons of supplies arrived at the beachhead despite the lack of developed beach facilities. An attempt to solve the problem of unloading bulk cargo from LSTs got a limited tryout through the new technique of preloading it in trucks and trailers that could simply be driven off the ship. Another experiment involved the use of a pontoon trestle bridge, which was brought to Bougainville by LST 395. The ship beached at 0620 and by 0804, the ship's company and a detail of Army Engineers had put together the 45-foot-long structure. Unloading was completed by 1220, the bridge dismantled and stowed by 1330, and the ship ready to retract from the beach.

On the other hand, the *Libra* reported that organizational problems continued to hamper unloading. Her Action Report noted that her beach detail was "ordered to parts unknown by Army beach authorities," and that "beach conditions were congested and seemingly in turmoil."[40] All historical accounts are in agreement that the turmoil would have been far worse save for the presence of LVTs. Their tracked, amphibious capabilities were invaluable in moving supplies across the swampy terrain immediately behind the beaches.

Wilkinson's cautious feelings about the claimed reduction of Japanese air strength were well founded. The enemy carried out more than ninety air raids during November; one determined raid sank an APD, but good fighter cover and volumes of AA fire limited all other damage to single hits on two transports. One deterrent used to good effect was the employment of barrage balloons. The LST 354 reported that a Japanese torpedo bomber was shot down as it turned into the ship's gunfire while swerving to avoid the balloon cable.[41]

By mid-December, there were 44,000 Americans on Bougainville and the campaign in the Solomons was almost over. Plans to strike the few blows needed to complete the encirclement of Rabaul were already afoot. Now attention moved to the Central Pacific, where the bloodiest battle yet of the amphibious war took place late in November.

CENTRAL PACIFIC: SETTING THE STAGE, MAY–NOVEMBER 1943

Operation Galvanic was born of Pete Ellis's ideas and Ernie King's intense desire to launch what he thought would be the decisive thrust against the Japanese. While Watchtower and Cartwheel were vitally important in protecting Australia and wearing down Japanese strength, King did not believe them decisive. He thought the Japanese hold on the Mariana Islands was the linchpin of their defenses; by capturing them, the Americans could break the enemy grip on the Philippines, essential to safeguarding the route between Japan and the irreplaceable oil fields of Borneo. Capturing the Marianas would also bring the home islands within reach of the new B-29 bomber being developed by the Army Air Force. The

Imperial Navy had to fight for the Marianas; once defeated there, the road to Tokyo would be open. There were, however, some significant roadblocks on the route to the Marianas, chief among them the Marshall and Gilbert Islands.

Japan had controlled the Marshalls since the end of World War I and the Gilberts since the outbreak of the Pacific war. The Americans knew that both chains were fortified and heavily garrisoned. The Marshalls were on the most direct route to the Marianas, but any force approaching the Marshalls from the east would have to contend with Gilberts-based bombers on its flank. King proposed an assault on the Marshalls as early as February 1943, but Nimitz told him that there were neither enough amphibious forces available to mount an assault nor aircraft carriers to cover them. The latter point was particularly important, for the Marshalls were well beyond the range of any American land-based aircraft.

By June, enough new carriers were in commission for King again to bring his proposal to invade the Marshalls before the Joint Chiefs. Though he recognized the risk inherent in pushing ahead a plan not fully prepared, nonetheless he believed advantage should be taken of the difficulties Cartwheel was causing the Japanese in the South Pacific.

He urged action on his colleagues when he told them, "It appears to me urgent that we take the maximum advantage of this situation by mounting the operations in the Gilberts-Marshalls at the earliest convenient date practicable, even at the expense of not being completely ready."[42] When Nimitz returned from his inspection tour of the South Pacific, he found orders from the JCS directing him to assault the Marshalls no later than 15 November.

Nimitz's response was to suggest that securing the Gilberts should be considered a prerequisite. The threat posed to his southern flank by Japanese bombers based in the Gilberts had to be eliminated first. The JCS agreed and in July changed Nimitz's orders to take the Gilberts in November and the Marshalls in January 1944. Staff planners at Pearl Harbor immediately set to work. Assaulting the Gilberts was the first job for Vice Admiral Spruance, the newly appointed commander of the 5th Fleet.

Spruance was credited with having won the Battle of Midway and had subsequently served as Nimitz's chief of staff. He was a quiet-spoken but intense officer known for the strength of his intellect. His demonstrated talent for remaining coolly analytical while under pressure would allow him to remain distant from the inevitable conflicts between Kelly Turner and Holland Smith. Nimitz's choice of Spruance as commander of the 5th Fleet would prove to be inspired.

The scope of the coming offensive required the creation of an amphibious force command structure for the Central Pacific. Nimitz therefore established the 5th Amphibious Force under Kelly Turner late in August

1943. Sparks were destined to fly when the Fifth Amphibious Corps was also commissioned early in September under Holland Smith.[43] Turner and Smith together were a volatile mixture of single-minded personalities that might not have worked save for one thing: Raymond Spruance never allowed his subordinates' intensity to divert him from the task at hand. Spruance understood that both Turner and Smith were conscientious and capable officers. However much they might disagree, they would inevitably follow where he led.

Unlike the desperately lean days of June 1942, when he fought for Midway with a bare force of carriers and cruisers, Spruance was going to the Gilberts with a powerful striking force. American building yards had delivered scores of new warships in the ensuing months, including several new *Essex*-class carriers. No fewer than seventeen carriers of various classes were available to provide air cover and close support. The covering and gunfire-support forces had thirteen battleships, numerous cruisers, and more than two score destroyers. Sixteen transports, four cargo ships, and two of the new Landing Ships, Dock (LSD) were needed to lift the assault force. There were thirty-eight LSTs and eleven LCIs assigned to transport the LVTs and follow-up, as well as nine chartered merchant ships. The latter group was screened by another score of destroyers. The constant juggling of amphibious assets needed to fight the war is illustrated by the fact that six of the transports made the trek from the Mediterranean to get the troop lift up to the necessary strength.

A rendezvous at sea would bring the task force together from ports in New Zealand, Samoa, and Hawaii. Turner was directly in command of the task force headed for Makin, and Rear Adm. Harry Hill commanded the ships headed for Tarawa. Despite King's wishes to the contrary, there were several thousand soldiers embarked in the transports. He had originally wanted only marines to make the assault, but the demands of Cartwheel were such that MacArthur would not release the 1st Marine Division. Because Galvanic originally included a concurrent assault against Nauru Island, the job was beyond the capabilities of available Marine units. Marshall offered the Hawaii-based 27th Infantry Division, an offer King had no choice but to accept.

The 2d Marine Division therefore received orders to assault Betio Island in the Tarawa Atoll and, after a change in plan, the Army's 165th Infantry Regiment was assigned to take Butaritari Island in the Makin Atoll.[44] The command setup thus established contained not only a continuing dispute between Navy and Marine ideas but also the seeds of a bitter fight between the Army and the Marines.

Maj. Gen. Julian Smith, USMC, commanding the 2d Marine Division, and Maj. Gen. Ralph Smith, USA, commanding the 27th Infantry Division, answered to Holland Smith. Despite Marine ideas to the contrary,

Turner expected to retain control over the assault units even after they established themselves ashore. His op-order dictated that control would pass to the Marine commander only when Turner deemed it appropriate. Holland Smith arrived at Pearl Harbor the first week in September and wasted no time in making his presence known. He objected to Turner's ideas loudly enough for the argument to reach Spruance's ear. The unflappable fleet commander reputedly told his chief of staff, "Oh . . . don't worry about it. They know what I want to do, and they're not going to make any trouble. They'll do exactly what I want them to do. I know them both so well, and they know me, and they'll be all right."[45] For the moment, Spruance deferred to Turner.

The future problem lay in the fact that the Army was loath to put any of its divisions under the command of a Marine officer. The commanding general of Army forces in the Pacific, Lt. Gen. Robert Richardson, pointedly asked Nimitz if Army units assigned to Galvanic were expected to take tactical direction from Holland Smith. Nimitz replied succinctly that "the immediate superior combat commander of the commanding general, 27th Infantry Division . . . is Maj. Gen. Holland Smith, USMC."[46] There the matter lay for the moment.

Command disputes were not the only area in which Holland Smith made his ideas known. The JCS plan for the seizure of the Gilberts included a landing on Nauru Island. Neither Nimitz nor any of his naval commanders favored the operation. They believed that the distance between Tarawa and Nauru would put the naval forces too far apart for mutual support and that assaulting Nauru would take too many troops. They wanted to take Makin Atoll, another of the Gilberts group, instead of Nauru. Smith added his voice to their chorus. Faced with the united opposition of Nimitz, Spruance, Turner, and Smith, King approved the change when he visited Pearl Harbor in late September. Julian Smith then flew up from New Zealand to confer with Holland Smith, and an operation plan was issued to the assault units on 5 October. Both Marine generals recognized that Tarawa was a formidable task; Galvanic would be the first assault against a heavily fortified atoll and would put all the Corps' ideas about amphibious warfare to a true test of fire.[47]

There is bitter irony in the events that were about to take place; the defenses of Tarawa arose in part from the August 1942 raid on Makin. The Japanese had recognized the raid for what it was but, like the Germans along the Channel coast, were determined that it could never happen again. They decided to build an airfield on Betio from which bombers and patrol planes could sweep the surrounding seas. The 7th Special Naval Landing Force and portions of the 3d Special Base Force under the command of Rear Adm. Keiji Shibasaki provided the fighting strength of the garrison. There was also a sizable contingent of Korean laborers on the island

to build defensive positions. Once landed, the Japanese set to work with the energy characteristic of their nation. By the fall of 1943, Shibasaki was sufficiently satisfied with what had been accomplished that he supposedly said "a million men" could not take the island in "a hundred years." His boast would prove wrong, but the cost to the Americans would be high.

A carrier task force raided Tarawa in September and brought back clear aerial photos of the island. A submarine returning from patrol brought additional photos early in October. Photo interpreters carefully scanned the pictures and made what proved to be essentially accurate estimates of the defenses. They warned that there were approximately 3,500 enemy personnel on the 290-acre island with at least 110 guns emplaced. The guns were in solidly built bunkers supported by a comprehensive system of trenches and obstacles; concrete tetrahedrons were in place to channel landing boats into fire lanes, the approaches were spiked with barbed wire entanglements, the beaches were mined, and a coconut-log seawall blocked easy access to the interior of the island.

There was one other major obstacle confronting an invader, but it had been put in place by nature. Tarawa is encircled by an apron of coral reef 500 to 800 yards wide. Julian Smith and the planners knew the tidal flow across the reef was irregular, raising the distinct possibility that the water would be too shallow for landing boats to reach the beach.

Not only were published tide tables consulted, but an intensive effort was made to locate and interview former residents of the island. Estimates made by those who came forward varied from two to five feet of water over the reef. The former figure presaged trouble; a loaded LCVP needed at least 3½ ft. to clear. The locals also warned of the phenomenon known as a dodging tide, by which the normally anticipated water level would fail to occur. Most of those who were asked, however, were positive that there would be sufficient water to float the landing craft. One was not and it was his counsel that would move Julian Smith to warn his Marines that they might well face the unpleasant prospect of wading a considerable distance under fire. Turner was advised that the possibility of a low tide existed but chose to accept the risk.[48]

The LVT seemed an obvious solution to the problem, but two obstacles had to be overcome. First, there weren't enough of them available to land all the planned waves. Seventy-five well-used LVT-1s were gathered and refurbished while Holland Smith arranged for another 100 new model LVT-2s to be delivered from the States, fifty each for the Army and Marines. In the 2d Marine Division, twenty-five were reserved for logistic support, leaving 100 to carry assault troops. Only the first three waves could be embarked in the tractors; everyone else would have to ride LCVPs or LCMs. The second obstacle was Kelly Turner.

The additional tractors coming from the States were in LSTs. They were

supposed to rendezvous with the assault force at sea, but because of their slow speed, the "Ts" would have to depart before the transports. Turner was afraid they would be spotted by Japanese patrol planes and compromise the entire operation. In Holland Smith's account, he said he had to tell Turner that without the LVTs, there would be no assault. Turner's biographer paints the admiral as willing to accommodate Smith but constrained by Nimitz's instructions. The truth no doubt lies somewhere in the middle. Even with the additional tractors, Julian Smith was more than a little concerned.

He knew there were slightly fewer than 1,500 men in the initial assault waves and that the total assault force only outnumbered the defenders by a 2-to-1 margin instead of the accepted 3 to 1. He had been refused permission to emplace artillery on an unoccupied island nearby and the Navy had refused his request for a bombardment longer than the one planned. He had to make a frontal assault on a heavily defended island without support he deemed essential and with a clear lack of means to get his troops to the beach. He therefore told Holland Smith that he could not accept the responsibility without orders showing that the choice was not his. Holland Smith had the necessary orders issued, an action that would later haunt his reputation outside the Marine Corps.

There was no shortage of materiel or manpower assigned to the assault on Makin. The defenses there were insignificant compared to Tarawa; the Japanese garrison was less than 500 strong and many of them were Korean laborers. They had only a few machine guns and an equal number of defensive positions from which to fight. Arrayed against them was an assault force from the 165th Regimental Combat Team and 105th Infantry Battalion Landing Team numbering more than 6,000 soldiers. Because Makin was closer to the expected threat from the Japanese fleet, they were backed by no fewer than four battleships and four heavy cruisers. The only leavening factor was that the American soldiers were facing their first combat under leadership that would prove to be less than inspired.

Julian Smith's Marines trained with an emphasis on small-unit tactics and the need to keep the assault moving. They exercised in New Zealand until late October, when they boarded their ships and proceeded to Efate in the New Hebrides to conduct some practice landings. Security was very tight; save for a few officers, the men did not even realize they were leaving New Zealand. Two days of clambering in and out of landing boats ensued, followed by a short period of maintenance. With Admiral Hill and Julian Smith embarked in the battleship *Maryland*, the task force departed Efate on 16 November, destination unknown. An uncertain future holding the distinct prospect of action replaced fond memories of New Zealand.

The soldiers were meanwhile going through their training regimen. They conducted two practice landings, but Holland Smith considered them generally unsatisfactory because the Army made no attempt to land supplies. Gunfire support was only simulated and in a third and supposedly dress rehearsal exercise, the landing craft halted at the line of departure. What made the exercises particularly unsatisfactory to Smith was his belief that the Army officers did not measure up to Marine standards of performance. They had spent more than a year on garrison duty in Hawaii and, to Smith's eyes, were lax. His staff confirmed Smith's bad impression when they reported to him that officers of the 165th Infantry spent the night after the landing exercise in a hotel and then rejoined their troops in the morning. The Marine general's disquiet with the soldiers was more than matched by his outright anger when he discovered that Nimitz had given him no role in directing the assault.

As previously noted, Smith was unhappy about Turner's authority over the troops after they were ashore. He discovered late in October that there was no provision in the final operation order for his corps headquarters to accompany the assault. Smith was outraged:

> [With] the expedition ready to sail from Pearl Harbor for the Gilberts, I was amazed to discover that in the general directive from Nimitz, my name had been removed from command. Apparently, the Navy intended to . . . leave me, the Corps Commander, twiddling my thumbs at Pearl Harbor. Incredible as it may seem, there it was—or wasn't. Nimitz had appointed me . . . and when matters had reached the final stage I was to be left behind.[49]

He complained to Spruance and Turner, both of whom agreed that he should be included in the assault. Spruance had the plan changed, but Smith still had no tactical responsibilities. As his biographer noted, "the long argument left him bitter toward the Navy, and especially toward Nimitz's headquarters, which, in omitting his name from the operations order, had implied that high naval officers need no assistance from marine commanders in land fighting."[50] Even a last-minute modification to Turner's orders that passed control of the Marines to the troop commander after the latter officer was ashore didn't mollify Smith. The antipathy between Nimitz and Smith that resulted would continue to grow and would have its consequences several months later.

The assault and support elements of the Makin-bound task force left Pearl Harbor on 10 November. Spruance had his flag in the heavy cruiser *Indianapolis,* while Turner and Holland Smith were in the *Pennsylvania,* reprising her Aleutian role as an amphibious force flagship. Turner announced their destination the next day; being who he was, the next eight days were no rest cruise for the task force. The soldiers drilled constantly at debarkation and achieving their objectives once ashore. The ships' crews practiced making the landing craft ready and preparing to unload. The entire task force maneuvered regularly in formation turns and in repelling air attacks.

The situation was the same with the Marines in the transports beating their way northward from Efate. Officers broke out tabletop models of Tarawa for study and inspection on the morning of 14 November, finally revealing the intended target. Every element of the assault force drilled repeatedly in where it was to land and in what direction it was to attack. There was an unfortunate side effect to the briefings. Sufficient emphasis was placed on the prelanding bombardment for the wishful hope to grow among the assault troops that the enemy would be pulverized. There were many veterans of Guadalcanal present, so the fighting qualities of the Japanese were no mystery. But even the veterans would be stunned by what was about to occur.

However hard the battle might prove to be, the Marines had ample supplies. Despite being loaded to only 60 percent of capacity, holds were crammed with the means necessary to support the assault; among the thousands of tons of equipment were a ten-day supply of ammunition and rations for thirty days. The American mechanization of war is well illustrated: there were 732 vehicles embarked for Tarawa and 372 for Makin.[51] The largesse of American factories was no doubt reassuring to the men who had experienced the privation of Guadalcanal. They knew that at least they would not want for ammunition or rations.

Veterans and boots alike no doubt took comfort in what they also knew of other preparations. The medical plan was comprehensive, though unlike later operations, there were no hospital ships with the task force.[52] Particular attention had been paid to controlling naval gunfire support and fighter cover, and keeping in touch with the troops. Each assault battalion had an air liaison and shore fire-control party; two destroyers and each flagship had fighter-director teams assigned. No one could know then that all these preparations were about to be found wanting.[53]

6

TO THE OUTER GATE

Before the present war I had never heard of any landing craft except a
rubber boat. Now I think about little else.

GEN. GEORGE C. MARSHALL

ASSAULT INTO HELL: TARAWA, 20–23 NOVEMBER 1943

The opening shots of Galvanic were actually fired before the morning
of 20 November. Air Force B-24 bombers based at Funafuti in the Ellice
Islands made a few ineffectual raids. Aside from destroying many above-
ground structures and causing some casualties, the raids had no serious
effect on the defenses. A carrier task force attacked Tarawa in November
and succeeded in destroying or damaging a few gun emplacements. When
the planes were done, a task group of cruisers and destroyers left the carrier
screen to bombard Tarawa. The cruisers fired almost 2,000 rounds but
from too great a range to accomplish the pinpoint work of destroying
emplaced guns. None of these efforts had any substantive effect on the
ensuing battle.

Both the Tarawa and Makin attack forces approached their respective
targets early in the morning of 20 November. They remained undetected
throughout their voyage, in part due to the good work of the CAP that shot
down a Japanese patrol plane the day before. While the task force positioned itself in the moonlit darkness, all hands made their private peace or
struggled with their fears of what the coming day would bring. At Tarawa,
a murderous three days unlike any previously experienced by the Marine
Corps began with the *Maryland*'s launching one of her spotting planes.

The launch did not go unnoticed by the watchful Japanese: the plane
was barely off the rail when a shore battery took the battleship under fire.
The *Maryland* replied in kind, sending ten salvos of 16-inch shells into the
enemy position, ceasing fire at 0542 in anticipation of the first scheduled
airstrike against the island. The tightly wired schedule of the planners

immediately began to unravel. The fliers did not show until 0615; Hill could not call them in earlier because the first main battery salvo not only blasted the Japanese but also the *Maryland*'s communications. Other enemy gunners meanwhile used the respite to blaze away at the transports, forcing them to move out of range. The bombers finally arrived and delivered their attack, raising an impressive amount of smoke and flying debris. They zoomed clear at 0622 to be followed by a deliberate bombardment from the support group. Unknown to the thousands of watching marines, the impressive thunder and billows of fire from battleship and cruiser main batteries masked a terrible flaw in the plan of attack.

After reading estimates of Tarawa's defenses, Julian Smith asked for a three-day bombardment of the island instead of the four hours planned by Spruance's staff. As he put it in a 1953 story about the landing, "We Marines, all of whom had studied, and in some cases seen in actual combat, the effect of land artillery, ships' gunfire, and aerial bombardment, found naval officers unduly optimistic as to the results to be obtained from bombardment."[1] Smith attempted to give the Navy men the proper perspective; he told them, "Even though you Navy officers do come in to about 1,000 yards, I remind you that you have a little armor. I want you to know that Marines are crossing the beach with bayonets, and that the only armor they'll have is a khaki shirt."[2] The Navy had different ideas, however. With Savo Island still in mind, a commanding tenet of naval thought said that to keep a fleet tied to a geographical location invited disaster. Every naval officer from Nimitz on down firmly believed that the only safe course was to get in, land the troops and supplies, and get out to sea where the fleet could maneuver.

What Spruance did not want to do was bring in a bombardment force three days before the landing, then bring up the amphibians, and then have to wait still longer while the assault troops went about their task. He would therefore not agree to Julian Smith's request. He may well have also agreed with the comment made by Rear Adm. Howard Kingman, who commanded the bombardment force. Kingman said of the planned bombardment, "Gentlemen, we will not neutralize Betio. We will not destroy it. We will obliterate it!"[3]

Holland Smith, uncharacteristically, did not argue with the Navy's refusal of a three-day bombardment. Like his naval counterparts, his expectations may have been too high. The roaring, blazing barrage that was falling on Tarawa that morning gave the impression that nothing could survive. Trees flew into the air and great gouts of flame occasionally flared up as ammunition or fuel was touched off. The few Japanese who survived the battle admitted that the shellfire was terrifying but did little damage. In an era when smart bombs and other guided weapons seem able to thread the proverbial needle, the inability of massive amounts of heavy shellfire to destroy a pillbox or gun emplacement may seem inexplicable. Admiral Hill explains part of the reason:

> Pillboxes for automatic weapons and even riflemen had been scientifically constructed to withstand heavy bombardment. Around a concrete floor in a 3-to-5-foot excavation was built a 12-inch, reinforced concrete wall. Outboard of this were alternate layers of coral sand, coconut logs, and sand bags to the final thickness desired. Concrete, protected as described, will apparently require direct hits of heavy-caliber [armor-piercing] projectiles before penetration is made.[4]

For all the noise and apparent destruction, the density of heavy, armor-piercing shells falling on Tarawa was insufficient to blanket every possible target. A few troops in the open suffered, but most of the garrison huddled, however anxiously, in their reinforced positions and waited for the landing craft to approach the beach.

The landing craft were coming, but they were behind the schedule laid out so painstakingly in New Zealand. Moving the transports beyond the reach of shore batteries exacted the first delay. Then, the troops took longer than expected to transfer from their boats into the LVTs. Once underway, control officers discovered the older LVT-1s were only making 4 knots. They were still a considerable distance from the beach when the bombardment ended. Hill refused to reopen fire, fearing that the gunners could not safely judge the position of the attack waves because of the smoke and dust billowing out from Tarawa.[5] A last-minute strafing attack delivered by carrier fighters did little to keep the defenders from manning their guns. At 2,000 yards out, the marines began to receive the first smattering of enemy fire.

The first and second wave LVTs took some hits but crawled across the reef and delivered most of their men ashore by 0920. What happened after that was one of the most unrelenting maelstroms of violence and killing witnessed in World War II. Courage and valor were commonplace on both sides of the line; death was every man's companion, Japanese and American alike. Nowhere in the course of the Pacific war was the thin line between the success and failure of an amphibious assault more in evidence.

By the time the third wave got into range, the defenders had shaken off their concussion-induced befuddlement and unleashed a furious hail of machine gun and cannon fire. Some LVTs sank, leaving a few figures struggling to shuck their packs and weapons. Others blew up or staggered to a halt. Worse was immediately in store, for behind the LVTs came the LCVPs carrying succeeding waves. Eight hundred yards from the muzzles of the enemy's guns, they scraped to a halt; the gamble that the tide would be high enough had failed.

There was nothing for the embarked marines to do but consign themselves to the protection and mercy of their respective gods and plunge over the side. A horrified airborne observer watched the tiny figures below fall in droves. Those who made it across the bullet-swept reef found little respite on the narrow strip of beach abutting the coconut log seawall. Survivors later said that Japanese bullets were flying so thickly that if a man raised his hand, he would draw back nothing but a stump. Fortunately, from among the huddled knots of green-clad marines arose the few individuals for whom duty overcomes all fears. Among them was Staff Sgt. William Bordelon, who in a few violence-filled minutes, single-handedly blasted three Japanese pillboxes before falling at the aperture of a fourth. Bordelon received a posthumous Medal of Honor for his action, one of four awarded at Tarawa. By example and force of character, the few got the many over the wall and about their deadly business.

The day became a blur of worry for Julian Smith and Harry Hill. Communications with the landing force were spotty to nonexistent. Many of the radios carried by the marines failed or were destroyed. Ongoing problems with the *Maryland*'s radio equipment also contributed to the problem, truly leaving the task force and division commander in the "fog" of war.[6]

A reader today who sees electronic images and sound instantaneously transmitted from the Persian Gulf to the living room may wonder why radio communications were such a constant problem to World War II commanders. Although radio telephony wasn't exactly new, the radios still relied on tube-based technology. They were bulky, heavy, easily damaged by water, and not very shock resistant. Furthermore, they tended to drift off frequency easily, requiring skilled radiomen to keep them functioning properly. All those failings were obviously detrimental to effective communications in the water-soaked, jarring environment of an amphibious assault. Radio technology had continued to improve, but not in time to help the marines at Tarawa. Col. David Shoup, commanding the assault troops, had to rely often on runners to deliver orders to his battered command.

One exception to poor communications was the gunfire spotters, many of whom were able to establish communication with the support ships. Unfortunately, the conditions of the battle often served to reduce the effect of naval gunfire. Some targets could not be hit because the marines were either too close for safety or their positions were uncertain. Typical was the situation reported by the destroyer *Dashiell*:

> One rapid-fire gun . . . was spotted . . . firing into the boats and against advancing troops. Our visible troops on the north shoreline were close to this gun . . . this vessel could not open fire. The shore fire-control party was notified at 1229, but we were not allowed to open fire on this gun.

Two frustrating hours passed.

I then moved in as close to the beach as possible and at 1452 was convinced that we could get that gun without damage to our own troops. I so informed the [shore fire-control party] and was finally given permission to "get it." We opened purposely short waiting to see if there would be any "complaint." There was none so we spotted on and obliterated this position. The fire also unearthed a lot of Japs just east of the gun position so we opened on them.[7]

Naval gunfire support proved particularly effective in two regards: it kept the Japanese from moving freely and, most important, destroyed wire communications so effectively that the garrison commander was unable to coordinate the defense or launch a counterattack. For many observers, that latter handicap may well have shifted the balance in the battle to the marines.

While the marines ashore fought a desperate battle for survival, the amphibians were hastening to unload. One underlying assumption governing planning for Galvanic was the strong possibility that the Combined Fleet would contest the landing. The planners also accepted as a matter of course that air opposition would be heavy. Spruance's fleet was strong enough to preclude a repetition of the days off Guadalcanal when the transports had to make their unseemly exit, but neither he nor Turner wanted unloading to be delayed. Unfortunately, the tight schedule being followed by the amphibians did not follow the realities ashore.

The transport commander had exhorted his boat crews to keep the boats moving and get the marines their supplies. Until the tide rose, however, landing craft could not cross the reef. Loaded boats began to circle aimlessly just outside the lagoon awaiting direction while a few others approached the pier that bisected the reef. There they passed loads hand to hand to the beach. Despite a plan that cleared holds of the equipment required by any troops in the field, the only things marines ashore wanted were ammunition, their cannons and tanks, medical supplies, and water. Because the dwindling number of LVTs was being used to land additional troops, unloading began to lag.

The same problem of poor communications that hampered direction of the battle also affected the unloading plan. The transports were so out of touch with the beach that they did not know what the marines were asking for. Some loads that did make it ashore bore no relation to the needs of the moment, infuriating the hard-pressed troops. So desperate were the marines for their 75-mm howitzers that some guns were man-handled from stranded landing craft onto the beach. Only a few tanks made it ashore the first day; after debarking at reef's edge, several either drowned their engines or toppled into craters in the reef. The transport group commander sent a marine supply officer ashore for a first-hand report on the situation;

nonexistent communications also meant that after a night on the beach, the marine had to return in person to make his report. The inflexibility of the unloading plan as well as the general confusion and chaos were the subjects of considerable discussion.

The fragmentary nature of the information Harry Hill and Julian Smith were receiving from various sources, as well as being able to see that all was not going well, weighed heavily on them. At Smith's request and as required by Turner's operations order, Hill sent a message to Holland Smith requesting release of the corps reserve that ended with the gloomy assessment, "Issue in doubt." Their fears increased when a messenger from Colonel Shoup finally reached them around 1800, almost six hours after being dispatched. Shoup knew that his report of the tenuous situation ashore would be worrisome; taking a cue from Grant's report to Lincoln after the costly early summer battles of 1864, Shoup added some reassurance. "You tell the general and the admiral that we are going to stick and fight it out."[8] Shoup himself knew how to stick it out. As he said later, "Once ashore, I was never off my feet for over 50 hours, standing for the most time protected by an enemy pillbox with 26 live Japs therein."[9]

Caring for the wounded was particularly difficult on Tarawa. Basic to medical planning was the idea that wounded men had to be removed as quickly as possible from the presence of those engaged in the fighting. Not only did a wounded man need care, but his injuries might well unnerve his unhurt comrades. A casualty clearing station was set up in the shelter of a pier and a surgical team was sent ashore. More sophisticated care beyond the reach of further injury lay just offshore in the hospital wards of the transports. Because of the low tide, getting the wounded to the ships was another chore entirely; wounded men were rafted across the reef to waiting landing craft or loaded in LVTs for transfer at reef's edge. The course of the battle can be followed in microcosm by the casualty count recorded in the *Zeilin*. On D-day, she received 39 casualties aboard by 2000 and 64 by 2400. By 1800 on the twenty-first, she had taken 235 aboard and added 21 more by 2400. An entry made at 1100 on the twenty-first is a poignant reminder that those who fight and die at sea often leave no trace save a few numbers in a log and the silent, rolling sea:

The following named Marines having died of gunshot wounds were buried at sea this date at Lat 01° 24'N; Long 171° 53'E.
1st Lieut. C. N. Dunahoe, Jr. #266531, K Co. 3d Battalion 2d Mar.
H. ROE #812320 USMC
W. D. MCKIBBEN #311493 USMC
G. M. CONNOR #331500 USMC
J. F. DEMARCHE #394684 USMC
James O HARA #Unknown USMC[10]

Because Admiral Shibasaki could not communicate with all his men, no counterattack developed on the uneasy night of 20 November, much to the gratitude of the marines. The second day started out much as the day before; reinforcements landed that morning, again at great cost. Valorous Japanese machine gun teams had used the cover of darkness to slip into some of the countless wrecks that dotted the reef. They extracted a considerable price in blood before they could be wiped out, but their efforts only delayed what had become inevitable. Using flame throwers and demolition charges, and backed by every possible naval gun, the marines subdued their enemy.

Shoup sent a message at 1022 that said, "Situation ashore uncertain." Seven hours later he reported "Casualties many, percent of dead not known. Combat efficiency—we are winning."[11] One more day of carnage followed, with most of the casualties Japanese.

One last message from the Japanese to their headquarters signaled the end: "Our weapons have been destroyed and from now on everyone is attempting a final charge. May Japan exist for ten thousand years!"[12] Only 17 Japanese sailors were captured out of a garrison of 2,619 men. Of the 2,217 Korean laborers on the island, only 129 survived. The cost to the marines was 992 killed in action.

The Tarawa garrison had done its duty and held on for most of three days, but there was no help from the Combined Fleet. Submarines immediately departed the main base at Truk to attack the invasion fleet, but the campaign in the Solomons had drained the Imperial Navy of air strength and destroyers. Land-based torpedo bombers from the Marshalls did their best, but the CAP exacted a stiff price. The decisive fleet battle desired by admirals on both sides would have to wait.

The cost at Makin was much lower for the soldiers, but the Navy paid a heavy price. The assault at Makin was successful despite some of the same troubles with hydrography that plagued the Tarawa landings. An attempt to use rocket-firing LVTs failed due to technical difficulties and inexperience, but resistance at the water line consisted mainly of sniper fire. The real difficulties began after the soldiers were ashore; Holland Smith's worries about the quality of leadership in the 165th Infantry proved well founded. Estimates of enemy strength at Makin vary from 250 to 445, but there were 6,000 American troops in the assault force. The last Japanese did not fall until 23 November, the same day organized resistance at Tarawa ceased. The cost to the Navy was much higher.

A turret explosion ripped the battleship *Mississippi* on the morning of 20 November, killing forty-three men. She was engaged in bombardment duties when the accident occurred but continued with her mission. An air attack that same evening succeeded in hitting the light carrier *Independence* with a torpedo, killing seventeen more men. Worse occurred early in the morning of 24 November, when a Japanese submarine called up to attack the landing force scored. The CVE *Liscome Bay* was turning prior to launching aircraft when a torpedo from the I-175 gouged out her midships. Six hundred and forty-four men went with her; her loss confirmed to many Navy men the crying need for speed in conducting an amphibious assault. They believed the carrier's fate would have been avoided had she not been tied to supporting the slow-moving pace of operations on Makin. The Navy sorrowfully accepted the loss; Holland Smith's patent dissatisfaction with the 27th Infantry Division would come home to roost the following summer.

ROOM FOR IMPROVEMENT: AFTERMATH TO TARAWA

Spruance's chief of staff was among the many officers from the fleet who went ashore at Tarawa to view the aftermath of an amphibious assault at first hand. Carl Moore got a close look:

> I have never seen such a shambles—coconut logs everywhere, sheet iron, guns, ammunition, smashed tanks, equipment, shot-up cars, bicycles, carts. In fact, everything that goes with war was scattered all over— pillboxes, tanks, traps, slit trenches dug up through concrete strong points in such numbers they couldn't be counted. There were many Japs lying about . . . all in an advanced state of decomposition. I contented myself with smelling them and gave up the pleasure of closer examination. No one had an idea that the place was so thoroughly defended. Only battle-tested marines could have taken the place. They were wonderful.[13]

Holland Smith arrived at Tarawa on 24 November. The scene of destruction described by Moore alternately moved Smith to intense pride in his Marines and to bitterness toward the Navy. His biographer notes that one of Smith's aides "thought that the scenes at Tarawa affected him more than any other episode of the war." Because many of the dead were not yet buried, Smith was personally able to see the toll exacted by some of the Japanese positions. He inspected many enemy positions and noted with professional admiration, "Look at this defense in depth. The bastards were masters. No wonder they were sitting here laughing at us. You could take one redoubt, but every redoubt was covered by two others."[14]

Over the issue of naval gunfire support were sown the first seeds of future controversy. Holland Smith and his staff were instrumental in outlining and approving the fire-support plan. Even so, he bitterly exclaimed to Julian Smith that the Navy had not let the Marines run the show.[15] He was more circumspect at a press conference held at Pearl Harbor.

He told the assembled newsmen that the Navy had done "everything humanly possible" and noted in his Action Report that the landing succeeded largely on the strength of naval gunfire support. He was firm in his recommendation that future landings would require substantially longer bombardments to prepare the way, but after Tarawa his views were in the majority. Despite his public words of support, there was a sore spot festering within Smith that would only come out after all the guns had fallen silent.

Gunfire support was only one subject in the many hundreds of pages of recommendations that flowed in after the operation was over. Among the conclusions that came of Tarawa was that too much had been expected of air bombing. One carrier captain pointed out that hitting small targets like emplaced guns was beyond the capabilities of most bomber pilots. He suggested that such targets could be eliminated in the long term, but that prolonged naval bombardment would be more efficient. Admiral Hill seconded this recommendation, adding this comment: "Once gunfire has commenced, air bombardment against specific point targets such as guns, dugouts, bombproofs . . . will be impracticable, as the entire target area will be completely covered up by a cloud of dust and smoke."[16]

Concerning gunfire support, all hands from the flag to the bilges recognized that a longer prelanding bombardment was necessary. Examination of the Tarawa defenses also made it clear that a higher density of heavy caliber, armor-piercing shells was needed. To ensure penetration, Admiral Hill wanted the initial bombardment fired from a range sufficient to give a steeper angle of fall. His recommendation then called for the bombardment ships to close to almost point-blank range where they could fire slowly and deliberately. The impact of what had been experienced at Tarawa was such that Hill's recommendations, among others, were quickly implemented.

Communications difficulties came in for their share of criticism, too. Among the complaints were the complexity of the communication plan, the inadequacy of using converted battleships as amphibious force flagships, and the poor performance of Marine radios. Communication plans would remain complex as the scale of operations grew ever larger, but more attention would be paid to training operators and instilling circuit discipline. Amphibious command ships built for the job were also on the way. So were better radios; the Marines would begin replacing their bulky, too-fragile equipment with smaller, more durable models.

Comments about the unloading process included criticism and suggestions for change. Every Marine commander echoed Holland Smith's complaints about the unloading plan. The Marines believed the plan should fit the scheme of maneuver, not be driven by an overwhelming desire to get unloaded. Kelly Turner suggested that Army and Marine commands alike should reduce their allowances for equipment. It seemed obvious to him that an assault on an atoll called for only what the troops needed to make the attack. Like Hewitt, he wanted more LCTs to help unload and he also wanted DUKWs to supplement LVTs in crossing reefs.

Among his many comments about the LVTs was a recommendation that future models have a stern ramp so passengers could land under better cover. Turner also began to push for creation of underwater demolition teams to clear any obstacles that might keep landing craft from reaching the beach. One transport division commander suggested that each ship consider using balsa life rafts to carry supplies across reefs like the one at Tarawa. He reported that ships in his division conveyed loads as heavy as 75-mm guns across the reef on rafts. All transport commanders favored palletizing cargo as much as possible.

The Marines had their share of comments, too. Julian Smith told Holland Smith, "We made mistakes, but you can't know it all the first time."[17] Holland Smith was adamant that every division thereafter be given at least 300 LVTs. With good reason, he believed the Tarawa assault would have failed without the tractors and wanted never again to be caught short. Other Marine recommendations called for allotting one flame thrower to each platoon instead of one to a company. Flame throwers had proved indispensable in destroying pillboxes but there hadn't been enough of them.

Another recommendation was to dispense with light tanks and bring only mediums on future operations. The smaller tanks were too lightly gunned to overcome the bunkers encountered at Tarawa and there was no reason to believe those yet to be encountered would be any less stout. Finally, if at all possible, the Marines wanted artillery emplaced on surrounding islands before any future assault. They valued naval gunfire support, but field artillery fire could be brought in closer to friendly positions. The many hundreds of reports filed after Tarawa were still being read when another kind of storm broke over the commanders who had conducted the assault.

What is now called the "media" was in the pre-TV days of World War II limited mainly to magazine and newspaper correspondents. Journalistic coverage of military operations was subject to censorship, but unlike the controlled press of the Axis nations, American papers were still free to voice their opinions. Newspaper editors exercised that voice after the number of casualties suffered at Tarawa became known. Headlines like "Terrible Tarawa" and "Tarawa Fiasco" appeared and editors grumbled in print that the cost was too high. Part of the reason for the press reaction was that Nimitz's headquarters had initially issued a communiqué that said casualties were "light." Correspondent Robert Sherrod, who witnessed the battle firsthand, believed Americans had unrealistic expectations about the war:

I reasoned that many Americans had never been led to expect anything but an easy war. Through their own wishful thinking . . . they had really believed that this place or that place could be "bombed out of the war." The stories accompanying the communiqués gave the impression that any American could lick twenty Japs. The stories almost invariably came out liberally sprinkled with "smash" and "pound" and other "vivid" verbs. These "vivid" verbs . . . impressed the reading public which saw them in tall type. Whose fault was this? I had imagined that everybody, after two years, would realize the seriousness of the war and the necessity of working as hard as possible toward ending it. Justice Byrnes cautioned a group of newsmen that we might expect a half million casualties within a few months—and got an editorial spanking for it.[18]

Holland Smith's reply to the civilian critics was typically blunt:

Those who say that the casualties on Tarawa were too high and that such a thing must not happen again should realize that the Marines on Tarawa killed four Japs for each Marine that died. We lost approximately 1,000 Marines but the Japs lost everybody they had. . . . We've got the toughest and smartest fighting men in this world. But as long as the war lasts some of them somewhere will be getting killed. We have got to acknowledge that or else we might as well stay home.[19]

The same week that Smith's comments appeared in *Time*, Nimitz faced yet another controversy. This one, however, was carefully shielded from public scrutiny.

Lieutenant General Richardson, commanding all Army forces in the Central Pacific, shared the anti-Marine prejudices common to Army officers of his time. He did not believe that any Marine general, Holland Smith included, was qualified to command a corps. In a 27 December letter addressed to "(EYES OF ADMIRAL NIMITZ ALONE)," he stated his case for Army command of V Amphibious Corps.[20] Nimitz forwarded the letter to King, who shared it, in turn, with Marine Commandant Archer Vandegrift. Their joint reply was blunt and to the point: Marine officers were not only well educated in staff duties, but were far more experienced in amphibious warfare than their Army counterparts. They further noted that Holland Smith's staff was a smoothly functioning unit and his relationship with Kelly Turner was based on experience unmatched by Richardson's. It was their conclusion that Richardson's complaint was no more than a blatant attempt to usurp Holland Smith.[21] Nimitz let the matter die a quiet death, but Richardson had not had his final say.

However imperfectly carried out and bloody the cost, Galvanic was essential to the success of future amphibious operations. Doctrine is no more than words on paper until put to an operational test, and Tarawa was an especially arduous one. Turner can be faulted for gambling on the tide, but the defenses of Tarawa would have been no less difficult nor less stoutly manned. That the cost was so high moved change to occur at a faster rate than it might otherwise. Gunfire support, scales of equipment, communications, and unloading schemes were quickly rethought and re-tooled. The reality of Galvanic was harsh, but it did validate Marine ideas about amphibious assault. The operation was also a strategic success, advancing land-based air power 700 miles closer to the Marshall Islands and closing off the last avenue of threat to communications with Australia. Tactically speaking, the operation gave Spruance valuable experience in conducting an amphibious landing while simultaneously carrying out large-scale fleet operations. Particularly important was the experience gained in using the newly formed fast-carrier task groups to support amphibious operations.

The marines at Tarawa and the soldiers at Makin were nearing the end of their respective battles when another meeting of Allied leaders convened. Two conferences were scheduled, one between Roosevelt and Churchill, another that included Soviet leader Stalin. The first conference began in Cairo on 22 November.

OVERLORD FINALIZED: SEXTANT AND EUREKA, NOVEMBER–DECEMBER 1943

Almost three years of meetings with the British had taught the Americans well. The new battleship *Iowa* carried the president and his military chiefs to Cairo; among the other passengers were sixty staff planners. American goals for what was called the Sextant meeting were essentially straightforward: Marshall wanted to complete plans for Overlord and to avoid any further diversions to the Mediterranean. One of King's main goals was to keep Marshall in Washington; everyone at the conference knew Roosevelt could no longer tarry in naming a commander for Overlord and Marshall remained the favorite. During a preconference dinner attended by Eisenhower and Marshall, King voiced the opinion that Eisenhower was the perfect man for the job and that he intended to tell the president just that.

Two days of meetings with the British followed. Yet another unfettered argument developed, causing one American participant to note in his diary, "Brooke got nasty and King got good and sore. King almost climbed over the table at Brooke. God, was he mad. I wish he had socked him."[22] One session between the Americans and British heard Churchill again pushing for continued operations in the Mediterranean; as Marshall expected, the prime minister waxed eloquent about the "cheap prizes" available if only the Allies would commit the resources. He proposed keeping sixty-eight

England-bound LSTs in the Mediterranean for an extra month, a move Marshall could only view as a threat to Overlord. After much wrangling, Roosevelt consented to limited operations in the Mediterranean in exchange for a British commitment to operations in Burma. The president made no decision about command of Overlord before those assembled had to leave for Tehran and the meeting with Stalin.

After arriving in the Persian capital, King was soon summoned to a meeting with Roosevelt, Churchill, and Stalin. He spent most of the meeting listening, discovering that the Soviet leader had little interest in the diplomatic niceties. After twice being asked to make a few remarks, Stalin complied with a brief statement that ended with the brusque demand, "Now let's get down to business!" Then the Soviet leader listened to Roosevelt and Churchill espouse their competing strategies. When they had finished, the dictator came straight to the point: invading France was the only logical course. Anything else was a diversion that could not have any decisive impact.

At the second plenary session the following day, Stalin and his military commanders continued to press. The Soviets asked Alan Brooke point blank if he considered the invasion of France of primary importance. When he hedged, Stalin and his generals told him Overlord was paramount; other operations in the Mediterranean would be regarded only as auxiliary. The Soviets then wanted to know who was to command Overlord. When told no commander had been chosen, Stalin said, "Then nothing will come out of these operations." He was insistent that if the discussion could not be concluded then, it had to be finished within a week. He went on to lecture his guests about Soviet techniques in river crossings, clearly showing little understanding of amphibious warfare. Marshall was quick to reply.

> The difference between a river crossing . . . and a landing from the ocean is that the failure of a river crossing is a reverse, while the failure of a landing . . . is a catastrophe. Failure in the latter case means the almost utter destruction of the landing craft and the personnel involved. My military education and experience . . . has all been based on roads, rivers, and railroads. During the last two years, however, I have been acquiring an education based on oceans, and I have had to learn all over again. Prior to the present war I had never heard of any landing craft except a rubber boat. Now I think about little else.[23]

The next day the Allies told Stalin the invasion of France would be launched in May 1944, with supporting landings in southern France. Roosevelt promised a decision on the supreme commander within three to four days. Stalin responded by promising a Soviet offensive concurrent with Overlord that would keep the Germans from reinforcing either front. The die was cast; Overlord could be delayed only at the gravest risk to future relations with the Soviet Union. The conference broke up on a somber but promising note and the Americans returned to Cairo for more meetings with the British. There the two allies concluded that operations in the eastern Mediterranean could not take place if Overlord's needs were to be met.

King's Pacific strategy and Eisenhower were the main beneficiaries of the Cairo/Tehran conferences. King's never-wavering vision of Pacific strategy—the dual-pronged offensive—was formalized with the issuance of a Combined Chiefs' paper titled "Specific Operations for the Defeat of Japan." At long last, the admiral received formal approval for his anticipated assault on the Marianas, scheduled for 1 October 1944. In the shadow of the great pyramids Roosevelt also decided who would command the most important amphibious assault in modern warfare.

The president still wanted Marshall, but he first asked the general to express an opinion. Marshall wanted the coveted command, but his sense of duty overrode personal ambition. He told Roosevelt, "I wanted him to feel free to act in whatever way he felt was to the best interest of the country and to his satisfaction and not in any way to consider my feelings. I would cheerfully go whatever way he wanted me to go."[24] On 7 December, two years after the war began for the United States, Roosevelt remarked almost casually to Eisenhower, "Well, Ike, you are going to command Overlord." The general who, only five months previously, wanted to escape amphibious operations was suddenly in command of the largest and most complex landing ever conceived. In the Pacific, two landings of a far lesser scale completed what had been a busy year for the amphibians.

SOUTHWEST PACIFIC: DECEMBER 1943

Dan Barbey's VII Phib Force mounted two operations in December that made sure the Japanese in the South Pacific would not enjoy a happy new year. The landings at Arawe and Cape Gloucester on the island of New Britain continued Cartwheel's isolation of Rabaul. The first took place 15 December.

Arawe is on the southwest coast of New Britain and planners thought its harbor would be useful. In the style of operations in the Southwest Pacific, planning for Operation Director began only three weeks before the landing. The soldiers of the 112th Cavalry received ten days' training and rehearsal before they started out on 14 December. The small task force arrived off the target area on 15 December and aimed its first efforts at a small island covering the harbor entrance. One party landed without trouble, but a second landing at a nearby location was not so lucky; the Japanese were waiting and opened fire before the soldiers could get ashore. A gunfire-support destroyer was standing off the beach, but her gunners had to hold their fire for fear of hitting the troops. Twelve of fifteen boats were sunk before the ship could silence the enemy guns; sixteen men died. The Americans quickly killed the few Japanese on the island and attention turned to the main landing.

Preparatory fire laid down by subchasers and two rocket-armed DUKWs proved more than adequate. Further support came from a squadron of B-25s that delivered a last-minute bomb and strafing attack. The Marine-manned LVTs of the 1st Amphibian Tractor Battalion had meanwhile floated out of the one LSD present and embarked their loads of troops. The LVT drivers had some difficulties forming up and keeping the waves co-ordinated, but managed to get the cavalrymen ashore without loss. Bar-bey's plan emphasized speed, so the first supply echelon of LCMs and LCTs arrived that afternoon. They received a warm welcome from Japanese fliers, who scattered bombs around without effect. No air cover was present the second day, an absence that allowed the enemy to attack with better suc-cess. One small transport was sunk and more than forty Americans were killed. Arawe proved of little substantive value to the campaign. At the very least, it was another psychological blow to Japanese hopes that the American advance could be stopped.

Another landing took place on New Britain only eleven days later. Bar-bey's smoothly running amphibians put the 1st Marine Division ashore at Cape Gloucester the day after Christmas. Code-named Operation Back-hander, it was a mirror image of Arawe, but on a larger scale. Barbey did not want to hazard his few transports in waters so close to Rabaul so the landing force again embarked in a collection of APDs and LCIs. The marines of the 1st Division had not participated in a landing since Guadalcanal so they had to be given extra training to familiarize them with the new land-ing ships and landing craft.

Rather than bring the marines to rear-area training facilities, Barbey instigated a mobile training unit that brought schooling to the marines. To Charles Adair, it was a waste of time:

> They got very little training, but it wasn't necessary. We'd send in some of these small ships, and they would have a chance to get aboard, and we'd run them into the nearest beach and let them see how they get off the ship, for about one day, that's all. But to me, such training is very much a waste of time. We picked up troops, we put the bow on the beach, opened the ramp and they walked off—how can they go wrong? I am sure "The Book" says train, train and train. But that is for crawling over the side of an APA ten miles out, and that is not the way to run an assault.[25]

The division's attached pioneer battalion also exercised until its unloading time for a LST dropped from more than four hours to less than one. Adair no doubt heard that news with some satisfaction; he had lost an argument about the number of LSTs to be landed the first day of the assault. The Marines wanted fourteen LST loads put ashore on D-day, far more than Adair thought prudent:

> There are too many ships on the beach, it takes too long to get them unloaded. . . . I could see that if we put in [14], we were going to be late in getting out with the ships. They would make a fine target. But General Rupertus was adamant on needing all these stores on D-day. He said, "I went into Guadalcanal, they unloaded part of my stores there, the Japanese came over . . . the transports ran off and left me. It was a long time before they got back."

Adair assured the general that supply would be adequate, but the Marine would not be swayed. If the Navy couldn't put fourteen LSTs in on D-day, the assault could not be made. Adair recognized what he was up against:

> So I said okay. I knew that there was no use in my telling him "no." Here I am a commander and he's a major general in the Marine Corps. If we go back and it's a knock heads situation, why naturally I won't get support. He's the assault general and he knows what he has to have. So I said, "Okay, we'll do it the way you want it."[26]

Fire-support duties fell to a task group of Australian and American cruisers. Six destroyers would screen the amphibious task force as it moved across the Vitiaz Strait from New Guinea. War knows no holidays; the assault force embarked on Christmas Eve and got underway Christmas Day.

The day after Christmas, the assault force approached Cape Gloucester on the northwest coast of New Britain. The air force had done its part by dropping more than 3,200 tons of bombs into the assault area during the preceding three weeks. The bombardment force added to the softening-up process with more than an hour of shelling. The airmen made a final contribution with a carpet of white phosphorus bombs that sent a blanket of smoke rolling across the beaches. The first LCMs grounded at 0748 and except for some resistance on the left flank, all went according to schedule. Unloading commenced immediately, greatly simplified by the new practice of having supplies already loaded in trucks that drove off the LSTs straight to a designated supply dump. More than 500 trucks were employed, some of which experienced difficulties with inexperienced drivers, but the scheme was considered a success anyway.

Most rewarding was the performance of the Marine shore party. They were able to keep bulk supplies flowing smoothly into the dumps despite the narrow, constricted beach. They were also ably supported by a naval beach party that had trained with them in the weeks before the landing.

The division commander would later commend the beach and shore parties.

As usual, an enemy air raid was not long in developing. Unlike many others, it was very effective. One destroyer took two bombs and sank with 108 of her men. Another survived several very near hits that riddled her with bomb fragments and sent her limping back to base. It was a small victory for the defense but, again, could not undo the landing. More than 13,000 troops were ashore by day's end, along with 7,600 tons of supplies. Admiral Tarbuck later called the operation a "masterpiece" for Barbey. It was a fitting end to a year that had seen landings from Sicily to Kiska to Tarawa to Cape Gloucester. A corps of capable amphibious commanders had gained unparalleled experience in polishing doctrine and in developing tactics and equipment. The coming year would see increased demands on their expertise.

STALEMATE AT ANZIO: JANUARY 1944

Among Allies and Axis alike, New Year's Day 1944 brought with it the sure knowledge that the growing abilities and might of Allied amphibious forces would decide the issue that year. The Germans anticipated an invasion of France sometime during the spring, while the Japanese were making hasty preparations to defend their vital Central Pacific bastions. Airborne over the Atlantic, Dwight Eisenhower had only recently assumed the Overlord mantle; at Pearl Harbor, Chester Nimitz and his commanders were deeply engrossed in planning an assault on the Marshall Islands; in Naples, Mark Clark and Frank Lowry were setting up an amphibious assault on Anzio; in the South Pacific, Dan Barbey and Ted Wilkinson were busy preparing the last steps to isolate Rabaul while looking ahead to the Philippines. Barbey was first off the mark with another of his patented, quick strikes along the New Guinea coast.

The Japanese base at Saidor, on the northwest coast of New Guinea, was the target. Taking and holding Saidor and its airfield would allow a large Japanese garrison farther to the southeast to be bypassed. Adair and his staff spent Christmas Eve planning for a landing on 2 January. Barbey accompanied the force in the *Conyngham*, with a screen of eight destroyers. The unopposed landing began at 0700, and by 1600 that afternoon the fast-moving amphibians had discharged 2,400 troops and all the embarked supplies, and were safely away from the beaches. A belated Japanese air raid blew in and found nothing to attack. The Philippines were a step closer and the Japanese had the choice of evacuating their garrison at Sio or watch it perish from starvation. Accustomed as they were to working with fewer resources than their comrades in the Central Pacific, Barbey's planners probably would have sympathized with other planners in the Mediterranean.

In late fall 1943, the situation in Italy seemed to offer no further opportunity for an amphibious assault. Though Clark established an Amphibious Operations Section on his 5th Army staff, the demands of Overlord dictated that most amphibious craft available in the Mediterranean would be withdrawn to England. Those remaining were tied up with the logistics demands of the Allied armies attempting to break through the German defenses, or supporting the strategic bomber force assembling in southern Italy. This shortage of amphibious lift overshadowed strategy when the ground commanders began to assess how to break the defensive stalemate the Germans had imposed on the Italian front.

Kesselring's strategy was to pin the Allies south of Rome as long as possible; Clark's goal was to reach Rome as quickly as he could without suffering crippling casualties. Thirty miles south of Rome on the Mediterranean coast, Anzio was astride the German lines of communication to the fighting front farther south. If a sizable-enough assault force could be put ashore, the Germans would have to withdraw or their forces in southern Italy would be cut off. A landing at Anzio was first mooted to Eisenhower during the first week of November, receiving his tentative approval pending two important conditions: 1) the Combined Chiefs had to grant permission to retain enough LSTs in the Mediterranean, and 2) the assault could not be launched until the 5th Army had advanced within not less than 50 miles of Rome, thus within reach of joining up with the beachhead.

Memories of Salerno were fresh enough for Eisenhower not to want another isolated beachhead facing annihilation. He received permission to keep sixty-eight LSTs in the theater until 5 January 1944, but his second condition seemed out of reach. Despite valiant efforts, 5th Army could not make headway against the resolute German defenders making the best use of mountainous terrain. On 18 December, Clark advised Eisenhower the amphibious assault planned for Anzio should be canceled. Only a week later, the dogged determination of Churchill to continue offensive operations in the Mediterranean brought the plan back to life.

After his meetings with Roosevelt in Cairo, Churchill met with Eisenhower and his commanders to ponder the future course of the war in the Mediterranean. He was firm in expressing his sentiment that the offensive in Italy had to be maintained; to do otherwise was to accept defeat. Though Eisenhower was against the Anzio operation because it had every possibility of interfering with Overlord, Churchill was not easily diverted: Anzio was reinstated. The size of the assault was upgraded from one to two divisions because Churchill wanted to throw a "wildcat" ashore in the German rear. He believed that if a sufficiently large assault force landed simultaneously with a renewed offensive on the main front, the Germans would not be able to contain both and would have to withdraw north of Rome. As happens, the soldiers and sailors who had to turn those words into action had a lot to do. Even Churchill could not ignore the fact that the LSTs for Anzio had to leave the Mediterranean by 25 January or Overlord would be thrown off schedule.

Fortunately, planners had been working in Naples to set up the assault. The original naval plan was actually finished on 22 December but had to be recast to add another division. The main problem was that there were enough ships to make the initial lift, but almost none available for a follow-up echelon. Reconnaissance showed there were only two marginally suitable beaches and a small port. Seizing the port intact was vital because if the weather kicked up, resupply across the poor beaches would be impossible. The prospect of bad weather also dictated that all supplies had to be off-loaded within forty-eight hours of the landing. To lighten the LSTs sufficiently to allow the closest possible approach to the beach, DUKWs were preloaded and positioned to leave the ships before beaching. To hasten unloading, the planners insisted on no bulk loading. The revised plans were finished in the nick of time, for the Navy required twenty-days' notice to assemble the necessary ships in Naples and load them. Rear Adm. Frank Lowry commanded the naval forces and Maj. Gen. John Lucas's VI Corps the military forces.

The 3d Infantry Division, making its second amphibious landing of the Italian campaign, and the veteran British 1st Infantry Division made up the assault force. These two divisions, their supporting units, and the amphibious ships began to gather in Naples early in January. As in previous operations, Operation Shingle was a combined effort of the U.S. and Royal navies. Royal Navy gunfire ships would support the American beach; shore fire-control parties would direct ships from either navy. Loading was without undue difficulty despite many ships having to anchor at a considerable distance from the loading points: the accumulated experience of 1943 was being felt. On the other hand, the rehearsal held off Naples on 17–18 January was labeled a "fiasco" by General Lucas.

Only ships that would make the landing before sunrise took part in the rehearsal. Not only was there considerable confusion, but forty DUKWs sank in choppy seas along with several artillery pieces. These losses had to be made up in a hurry because the invasion force was alerted on 20 January that the landing would take place two days later. The assault force, including 140 landing ships, left Naples early on 21 January. Admiral Lowry and General Lucas embarked in the *Biscayne*, by now a veteran amphibious flagship. The task force steered a series of diversionary courses to mislead any German watchers. Lowry's ships arrived off Anzio just after midnight on 22 January.

Led inshore by the ever-present van of minesweepers and aided by a reference ship anchored at midpoint of each landing beach, the amphibians immediately began their work of landing the 40,000 embarked soldiers. Because of the poor beach gradient, more than half the troops carried in LCIs had to be off-loaded into LCVPs to reach the beach. The smattering of enemy fire caused only a few casualties. One early bonus was that Army Rangers leading the assault captured a party of German engineers who were supposed to demolish the Anzio port facilities. Surprise was complete even though the prospect of an Allied amphibious landing had long figured in German plans.

Through Ultra, Clark knew the Germans were expecting a landing behind the main front no later than 15 January. Anzio was one logical site, but there had been no particular beefing up of its defenses. Kesselring's own intelligence service had provided him with an accurate appraisal of the forces available to the Allies in Italy, just as Clark knew what units Kesselring had available to resist Shingle. (Kesselring was the same commander who had directed the forces opposing the landings in Sicily and came close to wiping out the Salerno beachhead.) When the first reports of the Anzio landing reached Kesselring, he immediately set panzer and infantry units into motion to seal the beachhead. He was too good a soldier not to recognize the threat posed to his main front, which even then was absorbing the blows of a renewed Allied offensive. His quick action, along with a confused sense of purpose among the Allied high command, soon had a telling effect on the beachhead.

Off the Anzio beaches, the amphibians were going about their business with dispatch. The beaches had such a gently sloping gradient that beaching a landing craft became more difficult by orders of magnitude. The LSTs had to lighten their loads by disembarking laden DUKWs first, but also had to ballast forward, a reversal of their usual practice. Pontoons were essential, some even put to use as barges when they proved too short to reach the true beach. The beach assigned to the British 1st Infantry Division was worse than the American beach, but even there landing ships had to hunt for a good place to ground. The problem would have been far worse but for the light and sporadic German artillery fire and air raids.

Resistance on the ground was minimal because there were few German troops in the vicinity. Luftwaffe raids developed quickly, but an effective CAP provided by the air force kept most of the raiders away. The assault force was able to push steadily inland and by 24 January had a beachhead 10 miles deep. Army Engineers were quickly on the job in the port of Anzio, where the first LCTs and LCIs were able to unload on D-day. The engineers worked so quickly and efficiently that by D + 4, the port could accommodate five unloading LSTs at once. The urgency to unload was not misplaced; the Germans were very quickly building a perimeter around the beachhead.

On D + 2 a furious storm struck the landing area. The gale that howled off the Mediterranean broached one LST, seven LCTs, and three causeway sections. The Luftwaffe took advantage of the weather, hitting one destroyer badly enough to send her back to Naples. Another destroyer hit a mine the same day and had to withdraw. Those casualties among the gunfire-support ships were the most action they had seen. An initial lack of targets and the subsequent establishment of a front line beyond the reach of their guns had largely idled naval gunners. They would soon see some action in support of the troops.

All the ships lying off Anzio and those engaged in bringing up supplies had first to cope with the cold, ugly weather. Another storm slammed ashore on D + 4, this time broaching twelve LCTs and all the remaining pontoon causeways. Poorly coordinated salvage efforts caused some dissension between Army and Navy officers. One after-action summary noted that after the second storm, only the port saved the beachhead.

By 29 January, the amphibians had delivered 68,886 men, 508 guns, and 27,250 tons of supplies in support of Shingle. The amount of work done by individual ships is shown in the record of LCT 224. She made twelve trips to Naples and back, and thirty-four trips between the transport area and the beach unloading Liberty ships. Another expedient was for the larger ships to embark a crew of stevedores in Naples, take them to Anzio where they served as hatch crews, then return them to Naples. These efforts were only just enough, because the rapid German buildup was about to be felt. The fleet paid an additional toll for the first week ashore when air raids sank a British cruiser and a Liberty ship. German airmen also bombed three hospital ships despite their being well marked and illuminated.

The confusion of purpose and command difficulties that engulfed Shingle in the ensuing weeks are beyond the scope of this narrative, but suffice it to say that Churchill's "wildcat" became, in his view, "a beached whale." The beachhead was effectively sealed by a rush of German reinforcements. Like the landing at Salerno, Shingle would soon face the possibility of defeat. Although the German counterattack was eventually repulsed, it would take almost five months for the troops to break out. The logistical and gunfire support provided by the Allied fleet was essential to the survival of the forces landed at Anzio and to the success of their eventual breakout. R. Samuel Dillon, by then far removed from the green ship handler who had cleared the boat booms off a British battleship, remembered the long period of supporting the stalemated beachhead:

> In early February, as we were maneuvering off Anzio, Commander
> Gregor came alongside to say that we were to stay there as a command

ship in charge of unloading . . . cargo ships. For the next four weeks we operated twenty-four hours a day supervising the discharge of cargo for the beachhead. And the weather was horrible . . . it was cold with sleet, hail, and lots of plain cold rain. Some of the skippers of the cargo ships would up anchor . . . and head out to sea. Unless they had cargo which the beach wanted badly we made them suffer and sit and wait. It was one of the most exciting, exhilarating times of my entire life.[27]

That the operation did not achieve the goal originally envisioned was through no fault in execution of the amphibious component. The speed with which the operation was planned and carried out showed a level of expertise and a scale of material resources that had not existed a year earlier. There were, of course, recommendations for improving future operations, among them a desire to see LCI gunboats employed, for salvage operations to be coordinated through a single commander, and for a radio circuit to be assigned solely to salvage forces. Admiral Lowry suggested that unloading would be expedited if no ship beached until sufficient men were available to unload her. He also wanted more refrigerator space, because the Navy had to supply the beachhead with rations.

Lowry was particularly annoyed by the behavior of Army troops when embarked in his transports: "The high incidence of sudden seasickness and unrestrained habits of hard-bitten infantry all contribute to deplorable conditions of filth in troops' compartments unless their officers are made to enforce restraining or remedial action."[28] These and other recommendations would sit on the shelf for a while, because the next opportunity for the amphibians of the 8th Fleet to exercise their skills would not come until August. Meanwhile, their countrymen in the Pacific were bringing the amphibious war to the Japanese with unnerving speed.

ISOLATING RABAUL

The ongoing conflict between Douglas MacArthur and the Navy was affecting amphibious operations. The Combined Chiefs' formal approval of the Central Pacific offensive had not set well with the general. In mid-January, he sent a statement to the secretary of war labeling the assault on Tarawa as a tragedy and asking that he be given direction of the war in the Pacific. Included in MacArthur's proposed plan was a call for Halsey to mount an assault on the Japanese base at Kavieng on 1 March, while MacArthur's own forces attacked the Admiralty Islands the same date. There were problems with that plan.

To carry out MacArthur's scheme, carriers and amphibious resources would have to be diverted from the Central Pacific, an impossibility given the upcoming assault on the Marshalls. MacArthur suggested that the

Joint Chiefs control the allocation of naval assets, thereby removing control of the fleet from Nimitz. MacArthur also wanted the South Pacific theater to come under his command when the dual offensive converged in the Bismarcks. There could be no immediate diversion of naval forces from the Central Pacific, so the Chiefs told MacArthur to delay his assaults until 1 April, when carriers and amphibious ships would be sent south. Command issues would have to await further study.

After the landing at Cape Gloucester, it appeared there would be a lull in Halsey's South Pacific area. Since an assault on the major Japanese base at Kavieng on New Ireland wasn't possible until carrier and amphibious resources were available from the Central Pacific, Nimitz agreed to make the loan but not until Operation Flintlock was completed successfully. Halsey was unwilling to give the enemy a respite until April, when the carriers would be available. He therefore settled on the Green Islands, a small atoll off the southern end of New Ireland. An air base there would further tighten the air cordon around Rabaul. Plans were set late in December for an assault no later than 15 February.

The men of III Phib were by now as adept at the quick organization of an amphibious assault as Barbey's sailors. Troops of the 3d New Zealand Division, present in the Treasury Islands and on Vella Lavella, were assigned to this landing. A task group of APDs, LSTs, and LCIs assembled to carry the assault force. Each LST was loaded with no more than 500 tons of supplies to enable rapid discharge and quick release from the beach. Halsey assigned a covering force of cruisers should the Imperial Navy decide to contest the landing. Scouting parties discovered that the designated beaches were perfect and the Japanese garrison numbered no more than 100. The natives seemed friendly to the Allies and the enemy garrison was so small that the scouting party recommended no prelanding bombardment.

Despite the unending Allied air campaign that cost the Japanese hundreds of planes, enemy fliers from Rabaul kept up a constant harassment of the task force as it approached the Green Islands. They hit a cruiser but no amphibians. The landing took place on schedule with the APDs putting the assault troops ashore followed by a second echelon of LCIs and a third of LSTs bringing up supplies. An enemy air attack occurred as the landing craft were approaching the beach but was successfully intercepted by Marine fighters. Practice and training showed when the task group took only three hours to unload. On the downside, the bulk-loaded trailers proved disappointing: thirteen of the twenty-nine embarked suffered mechanical breakdowns that somewhat negated their value. The atoll was declared secure on 20 February.

Logs and War Diaries paint a picture of constant activity and much hard work for South Pacific amphibians. By the spring of 1944, bases stretched from Guadalcanal through the Russells to the Treasuries, Bougainville, and the Green Islands. Supplies had to be brought forward, units transferred, casualties evacuated, and equipment shifted where it was needed most. Daily life in the LSTs was a steady routine of loading, transit forward, unloading, reloading, and returning to base. In between were periods of upkeep, training, modifications to the ships such as the addition of ever more antiaircraft guns, and occasional periods of liberty in Noumea or Australia. Inevitably, the day came when familiar signs that another assault was in the offing punctured this tedium. In the Central Pacific, the new year brought such a moment.

FLINTLOCK: THE PERFECT ASSAULT, JANUARY–MARCH 1944

Late in January, Nimitz convened a conference of senior officers at Pearl Harbor that further aggravated the problems of command and strategy confronting the Joint Chiefs. The group, including MacArthur's chief of staff and air force commander, gathered to discuss the course of the war in the Pacific. After listening to MacArthur's men make their presentation for a concentrated line of advance through the South Pacific and hearing his own chief of staff suggest that an attack on the Marianas would be too costly, Nimitz sent a representative to Washington supporting the Army plan.

MacArthur's elation at the prospect of having the striking power of the carriers and V Amphibious Corps under his command was short-lived; King would have none of it. In a typically blunt letter to Nimitz, he noted that he had read Nimitz's comments with "indignant dismay" and concluded that MacArthur's plan was "absurd." Furthermore, as King reminded his subordinate, the Army plan was "not in accordance with the decisions of the Joint Chiefs of Staff."[29] Meanwhile, the Central Pacific offensive had taken a large step closer to the Marianas.

The Marshall Islands were the original target proposed for opening the Central Pacific offensive. The Gilberts, and Tarawa, were substituted and provided U.S. armed forces with a bloody eye-opener about amphibious assaults against a defended atoll. The Marshalls remained a target after Tarawa, but the planners now had a new appreciation of the risks. Nimitz and his operational commanders were determined to avoid the high cost in lives; their staffs had to assimilate quickly the lessons learned at Tarawa, incorporating them into preparations for what was being called Operation Flintlock.

Because the Japanese had controlled the Marshalls from the end of World War I, tightly restricting Western access, the true extent of their defenses was largely a matter of speculation. Given the dearth of information and the experience of Galvanic, Kelly Turner was not alone in his stated opinion that the Marshalls would be as heavily defended as Tarawa. Nimitz, distraught about the human cost and resultant criticism of Galvanic, responded to the problem in several ways. He ordered replicas of the Japanese defenses at Tarawa reconstructed and bombarded until the right combination of destructive munitions could be found. More important, he began to consider whether Wotje and Maloelap, the easternmost enemy bases in the Marshalls, couldn't be bypassed. Nimitz believed the enemy defensive scheme would be unbalanced if the amphibians leaped farther west to seize Kwajalein, the islands' administrative center.

Once Kwajalein was in hand, Spruance wanted to jump at once on Eniwetok atoll, another westward leap that would put American bombers within range of the huge Japanese naval base at Truk. Nimitz was well aware that scheduled offenses in the South Pacific called for him to lend much of his carrier striking power and amphibious resources to MacArthur and Halsey. So, he had to break the Japanese hold on the Marshalls, and quickly; bypassing Wotje and Maloelap seemed a giant step in that direction. On 14 December he gathered Spruance, Turner, and Holland Smith for a final discussion of this proposal. The meeting was a solid demonstration of Nimitz's ability to command.

Holland Smith would say later that he supported Nimitz, but in reality he joined with Spruance and Turner, trying to argue the fleet commander out of his choice. All three of Nimitz's subordinates believed that bypassing Wotje and Maloelap left enemy bases dangerously astride the fleet's line of communication. On his part, Nimitz believed his carriers could keep Japanese land-based air power sufficiently beaten down to avoid any threat to the amphibious assault force. He listened patiently to his commanders' arguments, then announced Kwajalein *was* the objective. Ignoring their protests, he said quietly, "This is it. If you don't want to do it, the department will find someone else to do it. Do you want to do it or not?"[30] They all came on board, newly reminded that their Texan boss was a determined commander.

The Marshall Islands are comprised of thirty-two separate island groups: Kwajalein, the largest island in an atoll bearing that name, lies 2,100 miles southwest of Pearl Harbor and only 980 miles from Truk, then the primary Japanese fleet anchorage in the central Pacific. An American fleet staging from the Marshalls could clearly threaten Truk. More important, it would be perfectly poised to launch an assault on the Marianas, which the Japanese considered indispensable to their defensive perimeter. After the fall of Tarawa, the enemy realized the Marshalls were probably the next American objective and began trying to beef up defenses there.

Although American submarines took a heavy toll of shipping bound for the Marshalls, some building materials and reinforcements got through. However, most of the defensive preparations centered on Wotje and Maloelap, which the Japanese, like Kelly Turner and Holland Smith, considered the likeliest targets. As Spruance's planners rushed to fill the gaps in their knowledge of the kinds of defenses awaiting the assault force, the increased Japanese work soon came under the scrutiny of American photo planes flying from the Gilberts. The planners also received a series of periscope photos taken late in December.

Far to the northeast, what the Japanese anticipated was taking shape. Originally, the assault had been mandated for 1 January 1944, but Spruance told Nimitz that deadline was impossible. On 18 December, therefore, the fleet commander notified King that Flintlock would occur 31 January. Two other islands in the Kwajalein atoll, Roi and Namur, would also be invaded. The Eniwetok assault would take place 1 May.

Gathering the necessary ships for mounting the assault was a formidable task. The newly constituted 4th Marine Division and the veteran 7th Infantry Division would make the Kwajalein assault: with air cover, the logistics load, gunfire support, and escorts figured in, the task force totaled 375 ships.

Its amphibious component alone included seventy-three transports and cargo ships. Eleven carriers of various classes provided close air support, with seventy-five destroyers for screening and gunfire-support duties. The gunfire-support force included seven battleships, eight heavy cruisers, and four light cruisers. Turner remained in overall command of the amphibious forces, with Mediterranean veteran Rear Admiral Conolly assigned to seize the connected islands of Roi and Namur. Turner himself was in charge at Kwajalein. Turner and Conolly worked from the new AGCs *Rocky Mount* and *Appalachian*, respectively. Maj. Gen. Charles Corlett commanded the 7th Infantry Division and Maj. Gen. Harry Schmidt the 4th Marine Division. Spruance would accompany the fleet in the *Indianapolis*; he planned to stick close to the fast carriers.

Preparations for the assault incorporated what had been learned so painfully at Tarawa. Carrier task forces began raiding the Marshalls in December; a concentrated program of bombing that targeted all Japanese airfields in the Marshalls would begin two days before the assault on Kwajalein. Holland Smith recommended that Marine squadrons be based on the carriers to provide close air support. King chose not to act on that recommendation, which hadn't been well received by the naval aviators. Instead, Navy fliers went through a more specialized course that improved greatly their accuracy in attacking smaller targets like pillboxes and gun emplacements. The carriers were backed by bombers flying from bases in the Gilberts; before the landing, Army planes would drop more than 1,000 tons of bombs on Marshall targets. More softening up would be achieved with a prelanding bombardment far heavier than at Tarawa.

The fire-support groups would open the bombardment on 30 January.

They would be the first ships to put into effect what they had learned at the new gunnery range on Kahoolawe Island. Ruthven Libby played a major part in establishing the training course. After arriving at Pearl with a squadron of new destroyers, he was assigned to a staff job to develop shore bombardment doctrine:

> [It] sounds like a very simple thing for a ship to steam offshore or lie to offshore and shoot at the beach. But it's not that simple, because you're shooting at a fixed target . . . from a moving platform, and you've got to compensate for your own motion and the current. The genesis of this field that I had to develop had hitherto just been a rather hit-or-miss job. We'd just go shoot at something without any sure idea of how accurate we were, so I got them to lay out a firing range over there with triangulated targets so we knew exactly what their latitude and longitude were. Then I took the ships over . . . they really learned something about close gunfire support. It paid dividends, because from then on you could send any ship to close gunfire support—he'd been through the school and knew what to do.[31]

Every known enemy position in the Marshalls would be hit with a mixture of long-range, plunging fire and point-blank, direct fire. Harassing fire would be maintained throughout the night of 31 January–1 February, and full-scale neutralization fire reopened at first light. Twenty-five minutes before the landing craft hit the beach, the gunfire-support ships would blanket the beach area with a concentrated hurricane of high explosives. The heavy cruisers wouldn't cease fire until the boats were within 1,000 yards of the beach, the destroyers at 500 yards, and the newly converted LCI gunboats only when they could no longer avoid endangering the assault waves. Additional firepower would be available from Army and Marine artillery units scheduled to be landed on four adjoining islands on 31 January. Finally, the bombardment was not tied to the clock; if the landing craft were late getting to the beach, gunfire support would be extended.

Choosing the landing beaches came in for considerable attention. Enemy defenses seemed heaviest on the seaward side of each island, but that wasn't the only factor. A study of the prevailing winds and typical sea conditions suggested an assault from the lagoon or lee side of each island. An attack from the lagoon also sheltered the transports and landing ships from submarine attack. An examination of charts and photos showing sufficient beach to land enough assault troops simultaneously made the decision easy. Communications and obtaining adequate supplies of amphibious tractors were two other closely scrutinized topics. The Joint Chiefs had ordered establishment of a specialized communications unit trained and equipped to support amphibious operations. The Joint Assault

Signal Company, or JASCO, resulted. The Marshalls would be the unit's first test.

In keeping with post-Tarawa recommendations, the Marines had increased the number of amphibious tractors to 325 per division. There were now enough troop-carrying tractors to carry all the assault waves. They were more heavily armored and would be accompanied by the new LVT(A), armed with a 37-mm cannon and additional machine guns, intended to provide fire support right across the beach. The drawback to the rapid increase in tractors was a shortage of trained drivers. The 7th Infantry Division had some success with that problem by transferring a few organic antitank units to LVTs. The Marines would experience considerable difficulties with their inexperienced drivers, but all hands were grateful for the tractors. The Army also had 100 DUKWs available for hauling supplies.

Deciding upon the volume of supplies for the assault force brought to Nimitz's attention another difference between Army and Marine doctrine. The Army wanted to bring ten units of fire, or ten days' supply, for its weapons, reflecting an Army preference for a slower, more methodical attack that attempted to subdue the enemy through firepower. Nimitz's opplan had called for five units of fire, a requirement reflecting the Marine preference for a slashing, fast-moving attack that emphasized speed and maneuver. After a discussion with his commanders, Nimitz raised the requirement to eight. Much of this ammunition was palletized for quick handling across the beaches, another outgrowth of past experience. Another important ammunition requirement was how to resupply the gunfire-support ships. The increased scale of bombardment required replenishing depleted magazines a long way from any ammunition depot. Four thousand rounds of 5-in. ammunition were parceled out among several LSTs, while another 1,350 rounds of 8-in. were stowed in the holds of three cargo ships.[32]

Handling supplies, always a problem and often a major weakness on previous landings, got special attention from Kelly Turner. First, he assigned an officer from his staff to concentrate solely on organizing beach and shore parties, directing that each beach and shore party would train together and be transported to the landing area in the same ship. The first members of each party would accompany the fourth wave to the beach.

Training naturally occupied available time between the decision to mount the assault and the date when the task force would head to sea. Holland Smith wanted at least seventy-five days to prepare; he didn't get it. The 4th Marine Division at Camp Pendleton had even less time than the soldiers, who were already in Hawaii. Conolly's experience planning Operation Husky, with staffs spread out all over North Africa, caused him to establish his headquarters at Camp Pendleton. Nevertheless, he still found his patience tested as he did his best to give his sailors and the new

Marine division a better sense of what they were about to do. His primary problem was that most of the transports and their crews were as new to their jobs as the marines were. Practice landings took place 2–3 January at San Clemente Island and revealed there was much left to do.

Tractor and boat waves were ragged and disorganized; transferring troops between boats and landing craft was hopelessly slow. Never having worked together before, there was no teamwork between the marines and the sailors manning the transports and LSTs. The LVTs embarked in LSTs, which in turn were responsible for fueling and provisioning the tractors. Amid the confusion of this first full-dress exercise, Marine LVT drivers were incredulous to discover that unless they returned to their parent ship, the sailors on other LSTs would not refuel their gas-hungry tractors.[33] Even worse, some LSTs were unwilling to allow a "stranger" aboard even when the LVT crew reported mechanical troubles. One can only speculate about Marine opinions of the Navy.

Two days after the exercise, the LSTs carrying the LVTs had to depart for Pearl Harbor. The next three weeks would see scores of ships on the move from San Diego, Pearl Harbor, and Samoa as the elements of the assault force began to converge on Kwajalein. Some units received copies of the operation order only days before departure, others had theirs delivered at sea. Holland Smith, who was instrumental in putting together the operation order, was himself a late addition to the passenger list. Nimitz's chief of staff had once again excluded Smith, but the Marine general wasted no time in demanding of Spruance that he be included. Impossible to refuse, Smith was with Turner in the *Rocky Mount*, officially in command of the assault troops once they were established ashore.

No more than the usual number of submarine alarms and false air contacts marked the transit to the Marshalls. The War Diary of LST 41, carrying the men and guns of the 31st Field Artillery, has an entry for 29 January that reads, "The CO reported that the morale of the ship's company and troops was good, bordering on enthusiasm."[34]

The bombardment was already in full swing when the first portion of the amphibious plan began. Four islands bordering Roi, Namur, and Kwajalein were wrested from their small bands of defenders on 31 January. As usual, the Japanese either chose to die resisting the Americans or by their own hand when defeat or capture seemed imminent. By the end of that day, Marine and Army artillery was landed, sited, and registered on the landing beaches. Getting the tubes ashore and set up so quickly represented a minor triumph of ingenuity for the artillerymen. Most guns went ashore in DUKWs slightly modified for the task. Floorboards were lowered to make the craft more stable with a gun aboard; the wider standard wheels of the gun carriages were exchanged for truck wheels enabling them to fit in a DUKW's cargo box. An A-frame fitted to four DUKWs in each company swung the guns and their ammunition over the side. It all worked exceedingly well.

A new Navy underwater demolition team, created in response to Turner's post-Tarawa recommendations, conducted a survey of the beaches at Kwajalein. Under cover of heavy gunfire, they approached to within 300 yards of the surf line and found no mines, wire, or other underwater obstacles. They also laid buoys marking the boat lanes that would be needed the next day. Under cover of darkness, the swimmers carried out a similar reconnaissance of Roi and Namur, with the same findings. But the lack of obstacles meant the team could not provide any new ideas about clearing beach approaches under combat conditions.

There was no rest for the Japanese that night; they knew what the morning would bring. One enemy soldier recorded in his diary, "When the last moment comes, I shall die bravely and honorably."[35] Neither was there any rest for the Americans; all the LVTs and landing craft had to be refueled and their mechanical defects corrected. In the transports, boat crews went over their assignments one last time, while in the troop compartments, soldiers and marines gave their weapons a final cleaning and waited for the morning.

Dawn of 1 February promised both rain and the prospect of imminent peril for many thousands of men. Soldiers and marines began the arduous process of disembarking from their transports into LCVPs, from the bobbing landing craft up scrambling nets onto LSTs laden with LVTs, thence into the tractors and back into the water where the assault waves began to form up. According to Isely and Crowl, many marines were as ready to get into the boats as the sailors were glad to see them go:

> There was a certain amount of animosity between the navy personnel and the marines . . . aboard some of the larger amphibious shipping. Both the navy and the marines were to blame. At least a few of the sailors and their officers had not been indoctrinated in the basic fact that an amphibious lift has but one reason for being, namely to transport troops to the target. On the other hand, there is evidence that some of the marines were not very pleasant passengers, destroying shipboard property and failing in certain essential housekeeping duties.[36]

While they were loading their passengers into the landing craft, the men of the transport *Wayne* got a hint of what the marines faced once ashore. A lookout spotted what proved to be a Japanese life raft drifting just off the port side. As a boat closed to investigate, three Japanese aviators arose from the bottom of the raft and graphically showed the no-quarter way they fought. One opened fire on the boat with a pistol, another threw a grenade, and the third detonated a second grenade that killed himself and his comrades.[37]

Moving the tractors loaded on the weather deck to the bow doors on the tank deck proved difficult on more than one LST. Not only were the LVTs a ton-and-a-half heavier than the rated capacity of the LST elevators, but they were too long. An inclined ramp had been devised that allowed them to be positioned on the elevator in a way that barely allowed their passage. Even so, one LST had to station a crew with a cutting torch to remove splash guards before the tractors would pass through.[38] In the LST 226, a mechanical failure caused both bow doors to swing freely, preventing the bow ramp from being lowered. Hurried preparations were made to burn through the door hinges with a torch, but the deck gang quickly rigged wire restraining straps. With the bow ramp down, LST 226's log records seventeen LVTs launched in eight minutes.[39] The LST's men managed all that to the background thunder of the continuing bombardment amid the overhead drone of carrier bombers adding their weight of explosives to the assault.

Admiral Conolly ordered the LSTs off Roi and Namur to enter the lagoon before discharging their LVTs. Even with that added protection, they had considerable difficulty in forming the assault waves. Problems with current and wind, most stemming from inexperienced drivers, caused most of the confusion. Another issue was that the control destroyer was also assigned as a gunfire-support unit. Before the assault waves formed, she had to leave her control station to take up bombardment duties, throwing the already lagging process into further disarray. Only hard work by the alternate control ship and boats at Roi and Namur sorted out the confusion so the marines could head toward the beach.[40] The more advanced level of training among the Army LVT crews showed at Kwajalein, where their landing took place on schedule. The khaki-clad "sailors" made the beach on time and in good order but slightly out of position.

As the landing craft approached the beach, a string of flares dropped from an orbiting carrier bomber signaled the artillerymen and shipboard gunners to shift their fire inland. At Kwajalein, a tragic accident showed the danger artillery and naval shells posed to aviators. Artillery fire hit a Navy spotting plane, sending it down in flames. At one point, Turner directed the *Mississippi* and *Pennsylvania* to close within 2,000 yards of the beach to deliver fire support. The success of the gunfire support plan was clearly manifested in that all the assault troops got ashore with only minor resistance from the enemy.

The Marines needed only one day to annihilate the surviving Japanese defenders of Roi and another to secure Namur. The ferocity of the bombardment left enemy troops dazed and their physical ability to resist greatly reduced by the destruction of their defensive works. One after-battle assessment held that 50 to 75 percent of the defenders were killed by the bombardment.[41] Most Marine casualties occurred when someone unknowingly flung a demolition charge into a Japanese munitions bunker; the ensuing explosion killed and wounded more than 100 Americans. The battle for Kwajalein was a different story: although almost 12,000 troops landed by nightfall on 1 February, a larger enemy garrison and the Army's more cautious offensive philosophy caused the fight to last for four days. To Holland Smith, that was two days too long.

Smith's views about Army tactics were no secret, having been voiced more than once. Unlike at Makin, however, the corps commander chose to remain aboard Turner's flagship. Samuel Eliot Morison has stated that Smith kept a low profile at Kwajalein because General Corlett threatened to arrest the Marine officer if he stepped ashore. Documentary evidence shows that Smith was annoyed by what he saw as inexcusably slow progress. In his autobiography, Smith makes no comment and his biographer says no proof of Morison's allegation has been found.[42] What is known is that Smith remained in the *Rocky Mount* until the fight was over: his culminating confrontation with the Army would wait until summer.

In any event, nowhere could this battle be compared to Tarawa. The Japanese were unprepared for the speed of the American advance; the short time since Galvanic caught them with their defensive works neither as numerous nor as well built as at Tarawa. Instead of dozens of sturdy bunkers and pillboxes, the Japanese in the Marshalls fought mainly from trenches and skillfully concealed fighting holes. Those positions that survived the bombardment quickly felt the heat when the attacking American infantry called for support. Still, the enemy soldiers who survived the bombardment fought with predictable stubbornness.

During the planning, considerable attention was paid to directing gunfire and air support more effectively. Since good communications were essential, each air and gunfire-control party had enough radios to continue its task if one or two pieces of equipment became damaged by seawater, enemy action, or the rigors of the field. Reducing the number of control frequencies also ensured simplicity; each infantry unit received several fluorescent ground panels to mark its position, and a radar control site was quickly established on an adjoining island. An air observer patrolled overhead in a bomber to keep track of the battle line and to help coordinate air strikes. The forward observers who directed the artillery so successfully emplaced on 31 January were trained artillerymen. As part of that training, they learned that Marine and Army gunners used different methods to correct fire.

In common with Tarawa, all the Marshall Islands were so flat that ships firing from one side of an island had to be careful not to endanger ships on the opposite side with overs. Another concern was that shells delivered from close range could ricochet: one heavy cruiser was hit that way but damage was slight. Admiral Conolly solidified his position with the Marines when he ordered the *Maryland* to "close in" while delivering gunfire support.[43]

Both artillerymen and naval gunners kept up a steady nighttime bombardment, including copious use of star shells to disrupt the well-known Japanese nocturnal infiltration tactics. Ship searchlights were tried once at Kwajalein, but drew such heavy enemy fire the experiment was quickly halted. In all, Roi, Namur, and Kwajalein were bombarded with some 6,000 tons of munitions. Although some reports suggested later that even better results could have been had for the expenditure, none of the infantrymen present had any complaints. Nor could the commanders upon whom lay the responsibility for sending their men into mortal peril complain too loudly: taking Roi, Namur, and Kwajalein cost the lives of 313 marines and 173 soldiers, a far lower toll than anticipated and vastly lower than what was soon to come. Japanese casualties were on the same gruesome scale as in previous fights: of the approximately 8,000 defenders and their Korean laborers, only 265 were captured.

The battle ashore was winding down on 3 February when the hospital ship *Solace* arrived at Kwajalein, and the *Relief* at Roi. They stayed long enough to load a combined total of 951 wounded before returning to Pearl Harbor the next day. Unloading the vast armada of cargo brought to the Marshalls was also moving as quickly as possible. The initial hours of the assault on Kwajalein brought the first use of what the Army called the "hot cargo" system. General Corlett's quartermasters preloaded forty DUKWs with supplies most likely to be needed by an infantry unit engaged in an assault. This system worked very well at keeping the soldiers supplied with ammunition and water, the two items most in demand.

Attention then turned to everything else. Landing craft and DUKWs scuttled steadily back and forth between the anchored ships and the shore, while sweating shore parties directed the tide of cartons, crates, boxes, and barrels into dumps. With no warehouse space ashore and the rubble of battle remaining to be cleared, one expedient for storing thousands of barrels of fuel was to "corral" them with cargo nets in shallow water. Another solution was to detail an LST as a floating warehouse.[44] The usual desire to get supplies off-loaded as quickly as possible was matched in the Marshall operation by the need to get more than 200 LVTs reloaded and headed for the South Pacific area, where the final isolation of Rabaul was about to take place.

By 15 February, most of the transports, cargo, and amphibious ships were riding high in the water and ready to depart for Pearl Harbor. Others were staying behind to conduct the suddenly speeded-up next move forward. The success of Flintlock was so clear that on 2 February, Turner recommended to Nimitz that the assault on Eniwetok be undertaken immediately with the resources at hand. His enthusiasm was buoyed by information gleaned from captured enemy documents that showed Japanese strength to be less than expected. Nimitz flew out to Kwajalein on 5 February and, after meeting with Turner and Holland Smith, ordered the attack to take place by 17 February. Smith claimed after the war that he had prepared a plan to seize Eniwetok before leaving Pearl Harbor, but Harry Hill said later that the credit was Kelly Turner's.

Once the fighting on Kwajalein ended, Turner quickly cobbled together an ad hoc task group organization. He remained in overall command but assigned the amphibious task group to Harry Hill. Command of the assault force went to Marine Maj. Gen. Thomas Watson; his Tactical Group 1 consisted of a mixed force of 6,000 marines and 4,000 soldiers, all lifted in an amphibious task group of nineteen ships. A substantial gunfire-support group that included three battleships went along to cover the landings; no time was allocated for rehearsals.

There are three islands in Eniwetok Atoll: Parry, Engebi, and Eniwetok. Japanese reinforcements arrived six weeks before the Americans; their defenses were similar to those at Kwajalein. The assault began on 17 February with the same pattern followed at Kwajalein. Outlying islands were seized to set up fire bases for the artillery while the targeted island received a heavy bombardment from the gunfire-support group. Engebi was first and received a heavy pounding: almost 7,000 shells poured into the tiny island. The landing began on schedule against automatic weapons fire. Among the few American casualties was the crew of a tank that went down with the LCM in which it was loaded when the bow ramp was opened too soon. Although the surviving enemy defenders fought desperately, it took the two Marine assault battalions and their supporting units only until 1500 to secure the island. By 1900, the assault troops and their LVTs were being reembarked in the transports and landing ships. Only nineteen Japanese survived out of a garrison of 1,200.

The soldiers of the 106th Infantry were assigned to the landing on Eniwetok itself, an operation that began on the morning of 19 February. This assault didn't go as smoothly as the day before: there was no artillery support and the naval bombardment wasn't as destructive, the LVTs weren't able to get the soldiers as far off the beach as planned, the beaches became congested with soldiers, and the enemy sprang an ambush that inflicted serious casualties. Nor, in General Watson's eyes, was the Army commander competent. The Marine watched the problems ashore build up as long as he could stand it before he angrily ordered the Army man to join his men on the beach. A battalion of Marines landed to add weight to the assault, but it still took until the twenty-first for the island to be secured. Only Parry Island and its 2,462 defenders remained.

American casualties had been relatively light, but Admiral Hill and General Watson recognized that the pace of operations was wearing the men down. Captured documents had warned them the garrison on Parry was bigger than anticipated and would attempt to defend the island at the surf line.[45] Hill and Watson therefore decided the island would receive an extra day's saturation with artillery and naval gunfire.

When the LVTs neared the beach, they sailed into such heavy clouds of dust and smoke that visibility was obscured and the troops landed slightly out of position. The reduced visibility also exacted another price: one destroyer was firing her assigned support mission under radar control when she inadvertently raked three LCI(G)s accompanying the assault waves. Thirteen sailors died and another forty-three were wounded, but the gunboats stuck gamely with their missions.

The weight of supporting fire caused heavy Japanese casualties, but hard fighting again greeted the invaders. Not only was the garrison bigger, but their positions were the best prepared of the three islands. Three battalions, two Marine and one Army, supported by tanks and artillery fought through the day and into the next morning before the last Japanese was killed or subdued.

The always difficult problem of knowing the precise relationship of friendly positions to those of the enemy was again reinforced on Parry. A Marine battalion called for naval gunfire support but misidentified its location. The naval gunners fired where directed, but their shells landed among the marines they were trying to support. Several marines were wounded before the guns could be called off. Almost 4,500 Japanese servicemen and Korean laborers died defending the three islands; only 66 were captured. The Americans lost 348 soldiers and marines killed. Though undoubtedly of small consolation to their survivors, it was a small price in blood for such a significant advance.

The major tasks of Flintlock and Catchpole were accomplished by the end of February. From 8 March through 5 April, the Marines carried out twenty-nine more landings as they swept clear of their few Japanese the smaller islands around the new bases. The four remaining enemy bases in the Marshalls were effectively cut off; they did not surrender until the war ended. The ability of the amphibious forces to strike at a place of their choosing had removed thousands of Japanese soldiers from the war as effectively as any assault and at a far cheaper cost. Spruance and his commanders were justifiably satisfied with the accomplishments of Flintlock as they returned to Pearl Harbor. Their next task was to evaluate what could be improved and consider that their next task would be an assault on the Marianas.

Events that followed the successful completion of Operation Flintlock were of more than passing importance to the amphibious forces. King's advocacy of constant offensive pressure seemed validated by the low casualties and relative ease with which the Marshalls fell. Also validated was the ability of the Central Pacific offensive to make huge leaps westward while bypassing significant numbers of Japanese. Early in March, the Joint Chiefs therefore issued updated instructions to the two principal commanders in the Pacific.

Because a diversion of naval resources from the Central Pacific was not possible if the landings in the Marianas were to take place, MacArthur received orders to drop the previously planned assault on Kavieng. His orders also directed him to accelerate the movement into the Admiralty Islands, the last gap in the encirclement of Rabaul. Nimitz received orders to isolate rather than assault Truk, to move the assault on the Marianas up to June, and to be prepared to invade the Palau Islands in support of MacArthur by 15 September. With his flank thus secured, the Chiefs directed MacArthur's long-wanted return to the Philippines to begin no later than 15 November. Both MacArthur and Nimitz were to be ready for a combined assault on Formosa no later than 15 February 1945.

At the operational level, Flintlock came in not only for considerable praise but also an honest evaluation of those areas needing improvements. Every level of command voiced the oft-repeated complaint that more time was needed for preparatory training. All hands agreed it would be helpful to have aerial photos at least ninety days in advance. Another report revealed that after two full years of war and several major amphibious assaults, coordinating the logistics load-out remained a problem. Comments by the commanding officer of the *Calvert* showed that the loading difficulties recorded by Admiral Hewitt were not confined to the Mediterranean.

The *Calvert*'s skipper noted that planning between ships' officers and the troop quartermaster took six days. Even so, cargo still arrived dockside not in order of priority. The next day, the divisional quartermaster added another eighty-three tons of low-priority rations to the agreed-upon load. Another day later came forty-five pallets of ammunition, eleven trucks, and instructions to remove five LVTs from the loading plan. The third day of loading brought 525 more tons of ammunition with no information about its unloading priority. The *Calvert* commander's recommendation was that once established, everyone involved should stick to the agreed-upon loading plan. Second, he wanted no more cargo put aboard than could be unloaded in twelve hours.[46]

Amphibious tractors and DUKWs again figured in postoperation remarks. General Schmidt wanted the tractor battalions established as organic components of each division, not assigned on temporary duty. Difficulties in getting the LVTs over some obstructions on Kwajalein showed their limitations as armored fighting vehicles. Though army DUKWs again proved invaluable, the wear and tear of constant operations steadily reduced the numbers of vehicles available. One recommendation was to set up a repair station ashore as soon as physically possible. Even though supplies moved across the beaches expeditiously, another recommendation was to increase from fifteen to thirty per division the number of tracked cranes for unloading landing craft. Communications between ship and shore had been generally good; the only apparent flaw in the plan was too few radiomen to adequately monitor the assigned nets.

After several visits ashore, the sights and smells of war's costs were images that returned to Pearl Harbor with Nimitz and his commanders. Though they were neither bloodthirsty nor inhumane men, they would spend the next few months incorporating the lessons of Flintlock into a plan that would make the Japanese pay the heavier cost when the Marianas were invaded. First among the many orders of business was for Kelly Turner and Holland Smith to pin on a third star. Unfortunately, how the promotions were handled further affected Smith's relationship with Nimitz and ultimately the Marine general's position with the amphibious forces.

Nimitz had recommended both Spruance and Turner for promotion but had ignored Smith. The Marine general, who saw Nimitz's action as a typical Navy slight and who justifiably believed that his position as V Amphibious Corps commander rated the third star of a lieutenant general, took his case to the Marine Commandant. King could not ignore the truth of the matter and prevailed upon Nimitz to recommend Smith's promotion. Kelly Turner's biographer states that King nonetheless held Smith's promotion until after Turner's, thus ensuring that the admiral would remain senior. Smith's relationship with Nimitz had never been particularly warm and thereafter was less so. There would be consequences later in the summer. On the other hand, Smith's distrust of naval officers ameliorated somewhat in his relationship with Kelly Turner. The two men had often argued, but after Flintlock, the Marine sent his naval comrade an appreciative letter that said that V Amphibious Corps "would storm the very gates of Hell" for Turner.[47]

CARTWHEEL COMPLETED: ADVANCE IN NEW GUINEA, FEBRUARY–JUNE 1944

Turner's men were finishing in the Marshalls when VII Phib made its next move forward. The landing took place on Los Negros Island in the Admiralties and came about because of MacArthur's willingness to strike as circumstances dictated. An Army Air Force bomber flew at low level over Los Negros on 23 February without drawing fire, leading to MacArthur's decision to put a landing force ashore as a reconnaissance in force. Plans already in motion were accelerated; Adair remembered that "a meeting was held immediately. We stopped issuing the other plan, which had been completed, and attended a meeting . . . about this particular landing. None of us had heard anything particular about this landing in this location, so it was somewhat new to us." Adair was nonetheless ready for the questions that came his way.

When the discussion about the proposed landing site made its way around the room, the Army and Air Force staff people had no objections. At Barbey's turn, he turned to Adair:

> "Charley, what do you think of that assault?" And I stood up and said
> "I don't like it. I have looked at photographs of that area and it is going
> to be very difficult to get troops ashore. Then behind it is a jungle, and
> I can't see anything particular in there, but I just don't think it's safe to
> land in there. I would suggest instead . . . that we land up in Hyane
> Harbor." It's a small harbor in which you go in through this very narrow
> entrance . . . but I didn't think there was anybody around that area. "I
> want to land there [and] I want to take more troops." Admiral Barbey
> said, "I like it." And so did the rest.[48]

But the matter wasn't settled so easily, as Adair soon found out. The Army commander simply would not agree to the additional troops. Adair wasted no time arguing.

Under Adair's guidance, a landing force of 1,026 soldiers was loaded into three APDs and eight destroyers. Air support for the landing was arranged and extra gunfire support delegated to the light cruisers *Phoenix* and *Nashville*. General MacArthur chose to accompany the task force in the *Phoenix* to observe the assault at first hand.

The assault force arrived off Hyane Harbor on 29 February. While en route from New Guinea, a six-man reconnaissance party went ashore and discovered the area was "lousy with Japs," but their report did not reach the approaching task group. The fire-support ships immediately began their bombardment while the APDs made ready to land the first wave. With only twelve landing craft available, it took only minutes to form up and head for the beach. Since there weren't sufficient gunfire-support ships to maintain a constant barrage, the Japanese quickly opened fire whenever the bombardment lifted. They didn't stop the landing, though they did manage to hit several landing craft, as reported by the APD *Brooks*:

> All boats were under fire all the way out of the harbor and it was very
> strong from both sides of [the] harbor entrance. Our guns poured out an
> incessant stream of fire all the way. When out of range a survey was
> made of damage done. Boat No. 3 had taken two or three 20mm shells
> in the ramp . . . No. 1 had taken a 20mm shell in the engine and the fuel
> line had been cut. It had already lost three fourths of its fuel. No
> personnel had been injured.[49]

In response, the destroyers closed to within 2,000 yards of the beach to bring accurate fire on Japanese positions. The gunfire-support problem was made more difficult by the geography of the landing area but was still good enough to impress MacArthur.[50]

Low clouds and rain made air support impossible as the morning passed but it also shielded the amphibians from Japanese eyes. Fortunately, the enemy was unaware just how small the landing force was. MacArthur went ashore for an hour to talk with the troops; he left instructions to hold the beachhead at all costs. The landing force had to withstand heavy enemy attacks that were beaten off only with the help of naval gunfire. Reinforcements arrived in six LSTs, but heavy fighting persisted until 4 March when the Japanese withdrew.

The rest of the Bismarck Islands were secured by 3 April. Seeadler Harbor, one of the goals in seizing the Bismarcks, remained in use for the rest of the war and served its intended purpose as a jumping-off place for the Philippines invasion. Only the seizure of Emirau Island remained to complete the total isolation of Rabaul. That task was completed on 20 March when III Phib put ashore two battalions of the 4th Marines against no opposition. Rabaul and its garrison of 98,000 soldiers was effectively out of the war. The amphibious pendulum next swung toward New Guinea, where the advance toward the Philippines continued.

The enemy's defensive perimeter had been pushed back considerably since the gloomy days of 1942, but he still had considerable forces in New Guinea. If the goal of assaulting the Philippines in the fall was to be realized, they would have to be destroyed or bypassed as soon as possible. Planning for the next advance was therefore going on at MacArthur's HQ even while operations in the Bismarcks were under way. The never-ceasing need for air bases dictated the next target, as it had in previous operations. Operations Persecution and Reckless would advance Allied air power 500 miles closer to the Philippines by seizing Japanese air fields in an area of northwest New Guinea known as Hollandia. Three landings employing 50,000 troops would be carried out, at Aitape, Tanahmerah Bay, and Humboldt Bay.

All three proposed landing sites were beyond the range of land-based fighters, so when Nimitz visited MacArthur's Australian headquarters on 25 and 26 March, the loan of 5th Fleet carriers was one of the first items discussed. MacArthur wanted the carriers to remain in the invasion area for eight days, but Nimitz could not agree. He knew the carriers would be needed to support the upcoming attack in the Marianas so he could only consent to three days. He did allow eight CVEs to remain for a longer period, but under no circumstances would he allow the carriers to come under MacArthur's operational control. Several amphibious ships also would be forthcoming from the Central Pacific, but they too would have to be returned immediately to 5th Fleet.

Prelanding preparations included raids by Nimitz's carriers on Japanese bases in the Carolines and the Palaus. The naval airmen destroyed hundreds of enemy aircraft and caused Imperial Navy fleet units to be withdrawn farther westward. Land-based bombers of the Allied air forces raided every Japanese air base within range, including one spectacular attack that destroyed more than 100 enemy planes inexplicably lined up wingtip to wingtip. The destruction of so many Japanese aircraft in the South Pacific illustrates the mutually supporting character of the dual American advance. Not only were the planes unavailable for the defense of New Guinea, they were also unavailable for transfer to the Central Pacific.

All three landings occurred on 22 April. Admiral Barbey had to stretch his staff thin to cover three landings; he gave the Aitape job to his chief of staff, Capt. Al Noble. A single regimental combat team got the task of making the assault, but Noble also had to contend with a heavy load of construction equipment. The plan was to quickly repair the existing Japanese airfield, allowing Allied fighters to move in and replace the soon-to-depart carrier fighters. Noble did have the "luxury" of two AKAs, but the load-out was still accomplished only through extreme effort by all hands. Army planners wanted additional landing craft to be loaded aboard the larger ships or towed to Aitape, but Barbey said no. He did detail three LSDs to make a quick turnaround and return with the additional boats requested by the Army.

The assault force rendezvoused at newly won Seeadler Harbor before proceeding to each objective. At Aitape, a lack of gunfire-support ships meant that even the guns on the amphibians had bombardment roles. Navy planes arrived at the proper time and delivered a last-minute carpet of bombs. Intelligence estimates placed 3,500 Japanese soldiers in the vicinity, but the bombardment and aerial attack drove the few present into the jungle. Army Engineer Special Brigade coxswains put the assault force ashore against only scattered small arms fire. Unloading proceeded expeditiously despite all cargo's being bulk loaded. At Tanahmerah Bay, Barbey was having mixed success with Operation Persecution.

Scouts went to Tanahmerah Bay to assess the terrain behind the proposed landing beaches, but unfriendly natives betrayed them to the Japanese and they had to go to ground. Barbey and the soldiers he brought to the landing zone soon found themselves wishing the scouts had not been foiled. The bombardment took place as planned, but the lack of return fire and no signs of life caused Barbey to call off softening-up air strikes. Once ashore, the troops found an impassable swamp immediately behind one of the two beaches, which caused a tremendous traffic jam as supplies and vehicles began piling up on the small beach. Stacks of ammunition and rations grew to heights of 8 feet or more as the shore party struggled to unload. It was obvious to Barbey and the Army commanders that the landing site was unable to support planned operations. After a late afternoon meeting, they made a joint decision to shift unloading to the more passable beach but to direct the follow-up to Humboldt Bay, where the landing was going as planned.

The other component of Persecution took place with the smoothness that had come to mark VII Phib operations. The bombardment raised the usual hubbub but no resistance. Rear Adm. William Fechtler was in command of the task force, which got the troops ashore without casualties. As was true during this operation, logistics problems replaced the lack of enemy resistance. An enemy supply dump near the beach had been blown up during the bombardment. Scant effort was made to extinguish the fire and American supplies began to pile up in the vicinity.

There were no doubt many who wished more effort had been made to put out the fire. On the night of 23 April, a Japanese bombardier guided on the fire and put a bomb into the stacks of supplies. Ammunition, fuel, clothing, food, all went up in a spectacular blaze that destroyed an estimated 60 percent of the supplies landed. Twenty-four Americans died, and the infantry at the front were put on half rations until the losses could be replaced. Ships already loaded with vehicles and construction equipment had to be hurriedly reloaded with rations and ammunition. This task was accomplished only by round-the-clock effort, but the follow-up convoy left on schedule anyway.

Adair had visited the destroyed dump just the day before and scrounged some Japanese supplies:

> there were boxes that looked about four feet square and inside those boxes . . . were what appeared to be little paper sacks that looked like they might have been about six inches square. So, being curious . . . I decided to walk over there and take a closer look. And I found out it was tea, Japanese tea. . . . I grabbed all I could get. I took it back with me . . . it's the best tea I've ever had—strong, black and green Japanese army tea. And I've always wanted to get some more, but not under those conditions![51]

Although the Japanese didn't fight for the Hollandia beaches, they did fight for the airfields. Even so, the land battle did not slow the planners, who were already contemplating the next amphibious leap. The target was Wakde Island, 325 miles northwest of Hollandia. An estimated 11,000 Japanese troops were in the area, but Wakde seemed a good site for yet more airfields.

The original schedule called for Operation Tornado to be launched on 15 May, slightly more than three weeks after Hollandia, but Barbey asked for a delay. There was so much congestion at Tanahmerah Bay and Aitape that he didn't believe there was enough time to clear away the materiel being unloaded and still gather the separate load needed for Wakde. Perhaps it is a measure of MacArthur's faith in the oft-demonstrated ability of Barbey and his sailors that the admiral got only two days' delay; the operation was scheduled for 17 May. Furthermore, an assault on Biak Island was to be mounted only ten days later. Nimitz had asked for land-based air support for the Marianas operation and Biak seemed a good place to locate the long-range bombers.

Adair explained how he and the other officers on Barbey's staff coped with the rapid pace of operations:

> We always took a look at what the requirements were and where the troops were to be loaded. And while we were drawing up the details of the planning and the assault, [another planner] would take the information that we generated . . . and they would rout out the ships necessary to haul the troops and get them moving. And that really is the only way we were able to make these dates. . . . We would start the ships moving almost immediately . . . even before the plan was out. Get them going, load the troops, and then they could read the plan enroute to the assault operation.[52]

Adair believed that the short plans he and his fellow planners wrote were also beneficial:

> The plan is just worthless if you don't have good initiative on the ships to go with it. When I read about plans in other areas where [they] turned out a 303-page plan . . . and it finally got down to the poor ship handler who's going to . . . carry the troops in . . . I don't think they read them at all. They probably get somebody to skim through it and tell them what they were supposed to be doing and when, and let the rest of it go.[53]

The 163rd Regimental Combat Team, the same troops landed at Aitape, got the Wakde job. With supporting units, the assault force comprised 7,000 men loaded into twenty-two ships. Captain Noble again commanded the task force, which included five cruisers and twenty destroyers for fire support and escort. The 800 Japanese on the island resisted to the best of their ability, showering the landing craft with heavy machine gun and small arms fire. Enemy gunners badly riddled two LCIs as they delivered close-in gunfire support. The weight of the assault was too much, however, as was the supporting fire available to the Americans. It took a little more than a day for the Japanese to be killed, though they took forty-three Americans with them. There was no respite for the enemy high command because the landing on Biak took place as scheduled only six days after Wakde fell.

Biak is one of the Schouten Islands, lying 180 miles farther northwest from Wakde. The veteran 41st Infantry Division, less one regimental combat team, drew the assignment. They were to land across four beaches, supported by heavy bombing and naval gunfire. The landing was expected to be somewhat difficult owing to the heavy coral reef surrounding the island. The airmen therefore had orders not to crater the reef, so passage for the LVTs and DUKWs would be easier. There was no evasive routing but the task force arrived undetected off Biak.

The approach to the beach was marred only by one battalion's landing 3,000 yards out of position; smoke created by the bombardment had obscured the coxswains' landmarks. The mix-up did delay deployment of troops toward their initial objectives, but the lack of Japanese resistance allowed the problem to be overcome without loss. Unknown to the troops, there were far more Japanese on the island than expected. Intelligence estimates placed 2,000 enemy soldiers on Biak but the garrison numbered closer to 12,000. Fortunately, with so much recent practice under their belts the amphibians unloaded quickly. Twelve thousand Americans with their guns, tanks, and 3,000 tons of supplies were on Biak by 1700. An air raid scored a hit on the LST 456 late in the afternoon, but the real battle ashore didn't begin until the next day.

Naval gunfire support and the boats of the Engineer Special Brigade proved essential to the Biak campaign. Japanese resistance was heavy and skillfully led. One battalion of infantry was cut off at one point and saved only by seaborne evacuation. Naval gunfire was heavily employed though the terrain often limited its effectiveness. The enemy did manage to barge in 1,200 reinforcements, and a small naval action was fought off Biak as another reinforcement convoy was turned away. The job of securing the island took until early August, far longer than expected. None of the airfields were ready to support the invasion of the Marianas, which took place as scheduled in mid-June. When the battle ended, 6,127 Japanese and 400 Americans were dead. Another 220 Japanese were prisoners, a much higher proportion than usual.

The amphibious successes of the spring also brought some change to the American command structure in the South Pacific. It was the swan song for Halsey's South Pacific area, which was soon to be folded into MacArthur's command. Some ships that had served with Halsey found themselves headed for the Central Pacific while others moved to the 7th Fleet. The two-year-old goal of neutralizing Rabaul had been realized largely through the skillful practice of amphibious warfare. The Japanese had done their best, but they were outmaneuvered by the ability of the amphibians to strike where they were not expected. No assault can succeed if the infantry isn't well trained and well led, but equal credit must go to the sailors who put the soldiers and marines ashore. The sailors of Barbey's VII Phib and Wilkinson's III Phib learned their tasks well and made do with the tools they had. The proof of their expertise lies in their success.

Admiral Barbey and Charles Adair also got a breather from the war. Barbey had to go to the States and took Adair with him. They stopped in Pearl Harbor, where Adair had some interesting experiences. Barbey asked him to confer with the planners at Nimitz's headquarters to see what he might pick up about the way amphibious warfare was conducted in the Central Pacific. Adair wasn't prepared for the formality of staff headquarters in Pearl and had some difficulty gaining admittance to the planning section. Once there, however, he found things to be far different from "home" in the Southwest Pacific. After asking many questions and getting no satisfactory answer, he gave up in disgust:

> I wanted to discuss those things with these people. They'd been doing it for some time, and everybody shied away. They'd say, "Well, I don't know anything about communications" . . . or "I don't know anything about amphibious boats." . . . I could not find a single person I could talk to, or who would answer any of my questions. And I finally had to give up . . . I finally had to go back to Admiral Barbey and say, "I'm sorry. I can't find anybody over there that seems to know how to run an operation."[54]

As the summer of 1944 approached, American amphibious forces were about to embark on two operations whose scope would have been unimaginable only two years before. In the Pacific, Nimitz's men were preparing to make an assault more than 2,000 miles from their main base. In Europe, Eisenhower's men were about to launch an army of two million men across the much narrower span of the English Channel. The amphibians in both theaters were poised to deliver a mortal blow to the Axis.

7

PIERCING THE WALLS

"O.K., let's go."

GEN. DWIGHT EISENHOWER

OVERLORD: THE PLAN

The winter of 1943–44 would be stamped with indelible clarity in the minds of the men who directed Overlord. Almost four years after the fearful days of Dunkirk, the Allies were coiling for the assault into occupied France. When Eisenhower arrived in London on 4 January 1944, the question was no longer if or when, but in what numbers and how fast could they be reinforced. Organizing the means to do the task and reconciling the competing demands for men and equipment was a monumental job occupying the full attention of many thousands of staff officers. They took their direction from the general who probably knew more about the problems and risks inherent in an amphibious assault than any officer in the U.S. Army. Eisenhower's long journey from Torch through Husky and Avalanche had given him the tools he needed to do the job.

With the late December appointment of General Montgomery to direct the landing force, the high command for Overlord was in place. Eisenhower was supreme commander with Air Chief Marshal Arthur Tedder his deputy commander. Operational commanders were Montgomery directing 21st Army Group, Air Chief Marshal Trafford Leigh-Mallory the tactical air forces, and Adm. Sir Bertram Ramsay, RN, the naval forces.[1] Subordinated to Montgomery for the immediate period of the assault but in command of the American 1st Army was Lt. Gen. Omar Bradley. The American naval commander was another Mediterranean veteran, Rear Adm. Alan G. Kirk.[2] Kirk had enjoyed a good relationship with Bradley while in the Mediterranean and was glad to renew the association. None of the officers were strangers to the process of planning an amphibious assault, but immediately upon Eisenhower's arrival in London they found their experience and abilities pushed even harder than before.

Even prior to being named supreme commander, Eisenhower had seen the outline prepared by COSSAC, the planning staff for Overlord previously established by the Combined Chiefs. Ike and his chief of staff had immediately determined that the projected three-division assault was too modest and recommended an increase to five divisions. When General Montgomery became operational commander of the landing force, he too took up the five-division cudgel. There was some discussion, but with both top commanders in agreement the strength of the assault became five divisions.

The American assault contingent would be the 1st and 4th Infantry Divisions. The 115th and 116th Regimental Combat Teams were temporarily assigned to the 1st Division to beef up its assault, with the 29th Infantry Division in reserve. Eisenhower also agreed to reinforce the single airborne division scheduled to drop in advance of the landings with two more. The immediate problem for the naval planners was assembling enough landing craft.

The number of landing craft Overlord needed had been a consistently elusive target for the planners. An intense debate extending across the entire spectrum of command tried to nail down the numbers. Some Americans thought early British estimates were unrealistic and proof the British did not want to attempt the landing. As experience grew and it seemed there couldn't be too many landing craft available for any operation, Overlord's needs conflicted more and more with other theaters.

King was particularly stingy; with planning for the Marshalls and Marianas operations in full swing, he was unwilling to loosen his hold on any landing craft headed for the Pacific. To counter arguments that shipbuilding schedules be modified in favor of landing craft, King insisted that previous attempts to accelerate production had caused too much disruption to other needed classes of ships. On the other hand, King was a professional naval officer who understood what was at stake; in September 1943, he ordered a 35-percent increase in production. Despite the additions, when a five-division assault began to be contemplated, it was clear there still wouldn't be enough landing craft.

Marshall made sure the Army understood the gravity of the situation in a December cable to all commands: "The landing craft situation is critical and will continue to be so for some time to come. You are directed to make every landing ship and craft available for and apply them to the maximum battle effort." He did have his doubts about Navy claims; his biographer notes that the general thought King was deliberately underestimating the availability of landing craft. Marshall wrote to Eisenhower that "staff planners estimated there were in Europe more than enough vessels to mount a seven-division Overlord and a simultaneous two-division Anvil.''[3]

But there *weren't* enough landing craft to go around. A significant factor in the shortage was Eisenhower's insistence on a continuation of planning for Anvil, projected simultaneously for southern France. The shortage of landing craft proved insurmountable, so Eisenhower eventually had to give way; he issued orders on 21 March postponing Anvil.[4] Adding the increased production to vessels released from the Mediterranean provided the necessary margin, but barely. Every landing ship and craft would have to be loaded to its utmost safe limit. To meet the lift requirement, serviceability among the vessels assigned to the American sector would have to exceed 95 percent.

There are considerable differences posed to amphibious planners when making an assault on a defended island as compared with a continental landmass. The main element is that the defender is not cut off from further reinforcement and supply. Therefore, the invader must have a plan incorporating two simple ideas: first, he must strike at the chosen spot with enough violence to guarantee a beachhead; second, the invader must be able to reinforce faster than the defenders can deliver reserves from rear areas to mount a large-scale counterattack. The raid on Dieppe and experience in Italy had amply proven the validity of these truths. The planners recognized German propaganda about the Atlantic Wall for what it was, but they knew Overlord was a frontal assault against a prepared position. As such, it ran significant risks.

The scheme of maneuver for the American sector alone entailed an assault force of two reinforced divisions with the goal of having twelve divisions ashore in eight days, with eighteen available by D + 14. Previous experience with the natural want of Army quartermasters to burden each ship to its maximum and beyond caused the Navy to review loading plans with increased scrutiny. In one case, Army quartermasters gave one LST a full load of vehicles *and* 600 soldiers, when safety dictated the personnel load to be 400. The importance of the post–D-day buildup is underscored by Montgomery's projection of a major German counterattack no later than D + 5 or 6. Another intelligence summary held the Germans capable of putting twenty-eight divisions on the invasion front by D + 14.

Where the invaders would land was endlessly argued by the Germans and was the subject of considerable debate among the Allies as well. Dieppe notwithstanding, quick seizure of major harbor facilities was essential to the buildup. All commanders accepted that supply would have to be conducted over the beaches until a port could be rehabilitated, estimated at not less than three months. Therefore, the assault beaches had to be not the most heavily defended, firm enough to handle heavy vehicle traffic, and be within reach of an existing road network. Several areas were examined and rejected, including Pas de Calais, the French port closest to England. Calais was unsuitable because it was too obvious a target and breaking through the well-developed defenses would be too costly. Attention finally settled on Normandy. The beaches were adequate, the defenses ranged from heavy to weak, and the port of Cherbourg was within reach. With the major issues settled, there remained the task of preparing the assault force and the follow-up.

Admiral Kirk was deeply involved in the planning process. He later admitted he had a strained relationship with Admiral Ramsay, largely because of differences between Royal Navy and U.S. Navy methods of preparing an operation order. Ramsay's staff prepared a document of more than 1,000 pages, detailing responsibilities to the smallest detail. Kirk believed in the American philosophy: providing an outline plan for his subordinates and letting them get on with the job. Kirk and General Bradley were quick to seal an agreement that they would cooperate fully in all joint aspects of their preparations.

Philip Bucklew was also in England from the Mediterranean. He again found himself in a small boat off a darkened, hostile shore:

> The purpose of our reconnaissance was to obtain sand samples from the Normandy beaches. Our equipment on the beach looked like a rack of test tubes, a specially built rack. They were set up in a prearranged fashion—one to use at one depth and the next at another. On the beach itself we had to come back with a bucket of sand. On one occasion I was in the boat with two British Navy men . . . all of a sudden everything cut loose—flares from the beach etc. . . . the rocket flares in this case told us it was time to get out. In another half hour we ran into our MTB. As the Britishers put it, "a jolly good evening."[5]

Another group was not so lucky and was captured off Pas de Calais in mid-May. The information provided by Bucklew and his comrades confirmed that the Normandy beaches were firm enough to permit passage of both tracked and wheeled vehicles.

Kirk's Western Naval Task Force would put the American assault ashore on two separate stretches of beach. Rear Adm. Don Moon's Force U would land the 4th Infantry Division across a 3,500-yard stretch of shoreline known as Utah Beach. The 1st Infantry Division plus the attached 115th and 116th Regimental Combat Teams had a 7,500-yard sector known as Omaha Beach; Rear Admiral Hall's Force O would get them there. Naval fire support delivered at close range and in proximity to the assault troops would be essential to the success of the landing. Kirk and all the other American officers involved in preparing the fire support studied reports forwarded from Tarawa. They knew from aerial photographs and other intelligence reports that German positions would be no less tough to crack.

Kirk reported later that some German gun emplacements were protected by 6–7-ft-thick, reinforced concrete walls with 12-ft-thick ceilings overlaying steel plates. He also listed the gun defenses encountered on Omaha beach, in part: "9 guns 75mm or larger—35 pillboxes with a gun of 75mm or less—18 antitank guns of 37–75mm—85 machine gun positions—38 rocket launchers."[6] Since it was clearly impossible to destroy all the enemy positions, the gunfire plan concentrated on neutralizing fire. Because the need for surprise precluded a lengthy bombardment, the support groups would open up at first light and force the defenders to keep their heads down long enough for the assault waves to land. Gunfire would continue until it endangered the troops rather than being controlled by the clock. There were nine Shore Fire Control Parties with each assault division and twenty-three support boats would accompany the landing craft.

After the strength of the assault was increased to five divisions, a shortage of gunfire-support ships became evident. Original plans called for the Royal Navy to provide all gunfire support. Ramsay wasted no time telling his American subordinates that the R.N. ships simply weren't available. Admiral Hall later said that he made well known his displeasure about the shortage of gunfire support: "I banged my fist on the table and said, 'It's a crime to send me on the biggest amphibious attack in history with such inadequate gunfire support.' Finally, Admiral Cooke said, 'Hall, you've got no right to talk that way.' I said, 'Who had a better right to talk that way? All I'm asking you to do is detach a couple of squadrons of destroyers.' " Kirk's account of the matter is not so dramatic. He said he had a discussion with King's chief of staff about the gunfire problem when that officer visited London during the spring.[7] The upshot of differing accounts is that three American battleships, three heavy cruisers, and thirty-one destroyers participated in Overlord.

Intelligence is of considerable concern before any amphibious landing. Even though the Allies had a priceless advantage in Ultra, they didn't know everything about German preparations. Kirk noted that air photos were so important that the demand for prints often outstripped the ability of the labs to provide them quickly enough. Air photos were the principal means for determining the beach gradients. Recon planes flew over the beaches at different known heights of tide to photograph the water line; photo comparisons provided the necessary data. The airmen rephotographed the entire target area during April to assess the effect of recent winter storms. Photos also revealed the steadily thickening array of beach obstacles being installed by the Germans.

The appointment of Field Marshal Rommel to command the coast defenses put a different cast on German preparations. The so-called Atlantic Wall had been under construction during most of the occupation, but the resulting effort had not created the unbroken barrier of fortifications featured by German propaganda. Rommel knew that the troops available to defend against an invasion were not of the same caliber as in years gone by. Compared with the blood-soaked eastern front, France had long been a quiet backwater. Worn-out divisions refitted in France while the Channel garrison was mostly static, second-class infantry divisions. A considerable panzer reserve existed behind the coast, but they were under Hitler's personal operational control. Rommel and his superior, Field Marshal Gerd von Runstedt, also had philosophical differences about the best strategy for countering the invasion. Von Runstedt wanted to hold back a significant reserve then launch a massive counterattack that would drive the invaders back into the sea. Rommel asserted that Allied air supremacy made any such scheme problematical. He believed the only hope lay in defeating the invasion at the waterline.

Rommel put the troops along the coast hard at work building beach obstacles and planting extensive minefields. They placed row upon row of concrete tetrahedrons, steel hedgehogs, and stout ramp stakes to ensnare and block landing craft. They ran thick entanglements of wire among the beach obstacles and mined them to demolish any landing craft that might come into contact. The natural exits from each beach were similarly prepared and covered by the fire of several guns. They flooded the low-lying areas directly behind Utah beach, channeling all traffic onto only a few roads. A fortunate but unintended benefit to the Allies was that the troops were so busy working on defenses that they had little time to drill.

Training to successfully overcome the German defenses was a top priority of the Allied armies. However, there were so many soldiers encamped and so much materiel stockpiled in the English countryside that precious little space was left to conduct live-fire exercises. The British solved that problem for American forces by moving all civilians out of a 30,000-acre area of southwestern England in the winter of 1943. Thus, a space was made available where naval gunfire could be brought to bear on shore targets and landing craft could be grounded on beaches similar to Normandy's. A series of exercises began in March to refresh soldiers and sailors alike in amphibious techniques and to let them practice against replicas of German fortifications. The exercises began with battalion-strength landings, eventually working up to full divisions.

Thirty-two Naval Combat Demolition Units practiced clearing beach obstacles. Improvements in communications technology had all twenty-seven of the shore fire-control parties equipped with a new FM radio set that was more durable and transmitted a clearer signal. Control parties consisted of both U.S. and Royal Navy personnel. Many air spotters would also be employed, with pilots from the Royal Navy, the U.S. Navy, and the Army Air Force. Beach parties also went through strenuous maneuvers. The Army assigned three full Engineer Special Brigades and three Beach Battalions as the shore party. Among the sailors practicing so hard were Bud Farmer and Harry Heckman.

Both had arrived in England late in the winter. Farmer drew an LCT transferred from the Royal Navy in a sort of reverse Lend Lease. Heckman was at the U.S. Navy depot at Deptford, where his LCT was assembled. He remembers that four or five petty officers were assigned to help in the assembly, which was completed by English workmen. Both moved to the south of England during the spring in voyages that took place in darkness. Heckman's flotilla was assigned to Utah Beach, Farmer's to Omaha. Once established on the south coast, both agreed that they trained incessantly. Not all the exercises went smoothly. Exercise Tiger, in April, ended in disaster.

The main live-fire area for American forces was Slapton Sands, near Plymouth. The landing exercise that began on 27 April was supposed to test the lessons learned in previous exercises and to give newly arrived amphibious units some practice. The eight LSTs in follow-up convoy T–4, scheduled to arrive at Slapton Sands the morning of 28 April, were a case in point. They were newcomers to the theater and had never worked together as a unit. As they approached the exercise area in the early morning hours of 28 April, they carried heavy loads of Army vehicles and personnel. Two escorts had been assigned, but a mix-up in orders by British naval authorities left only a single corvette guarding the straggling flock of LSTs. Unfortunately, there were several German wolves circling in the darkness.

German naval strength in the Channel consisted of a force of destroyers and torpedo boats vastly outnumbered and outgunned by the Royal Navy. Nevertheless, the German sailors remained a persistent danger to coastal traffic with their opportunistic raids and mine-laying expeditions. The specter of an enemy warship loose among amphibians heavily laden with troops and munitions had long been a planner's nightmare. With the buildup for Overlord, patrols were intensified off German bases, but on the night of 27–28 April, a small group of seven torpedo boats, commonly known as E-boats, slipped through this cordon. Just into the midwatch of 28 April, their course brought them into contact with convoy T–4.

In the LSTs, the first sign of something close at hand in the darkness was the sound of engines. The notion they were aircraft engines disappeared when a fast-moving E-boat materialized out of the night close aboard LST 507. She opened fire, but only an instant later, a torpedo ripped into her, setting the ship ablaze. At the distant head of the American column, lookouts heard the gunfire and saw the glare of the burning ship, but did not recognize the reason for the commotion. The convoy commander gave no orders to increase speed or to change course nor did the single escort investigate. Several ships reported unidentified radar contacts, but the convoy plodded on, an opportunity the Germans did not ignore. Shortly after 0200, torpedoes hit two more LSTs. Wild gunfire erupted as the German boats roared through the now-scattering convoy. The escorting corvette scurried back from the head of the column but made no contact with the raiders.

Two of the three ships hit suffered fatal damage. More than 700 men died and the already-tight lift capability was made even more so by the loss. Fears that the invasion had been compromised were great; medical units treating the wounded received orders not to mention the incident upon certain court martial. Naval authorities launched an investigation to figure out why the escort was so shorthanded; other than the deeply expressed regret of the British naval commander, no punitive action resulted. Documents captured after the war revealed that the Germans had rescued some survivors and made them prisoners, but had drawn no conclusions about the impending invasion. Painfully reinforced was the absolute necessity to protect the amphibians from a determined and skillful enemy.

Getting the men safely across the Channel was one problem. When to land them was another. The Navy won the argument for daylight in Normandy, holding that the success of the infantry assault depended upon enough light for the bombardment ships to see their targets. There was also the question of tides; the Army wanted the engineers landed below the obstacles where they could blow lanes for the follow-up waves. Finally, the American landings had to come in time proximity with the British sector lest the enemy have too much opportunity to react. Once preparations seemed complete, the right combination of light and tide would determine the date.

LOGISTICS AND OTHER PROBLEMS: JANUARY–MAY 1944

Logistics was always a concern to amphibious planners and Overlord was no exception. Field experience proved that one American division consumed 600 to 700 tons of supplies daily. Kirk and Bradley addressed one initial requirement by preloading thirteen barges with 1,000 tons of ammunition each and including them in the assault convoy. Once the initial beachhead was established, these vessels would be beached and unloaded into trucks at low tide. So many ships were in the follow-up that one officer would direct inbound convoys and another outbound. The risk of having to depend upon supplies coming across beaches exposed to the vagaries of Channel weather caused a novel but expensive solution.

The often unique needs of waging war lend themselves to the invention of strange machines. One of them was what became known as the Mulberry artificial harbor. If no port was available on the French coast, why not build one and bring it with the invasion force? A massive engineering effort began that developed and built a complicated system of caissons to act as a breakwater and floating pier heads over which the ships could unload. Two copies of the apparatus, known as a Mulberry, were built in sections that would be towed to Normandy. One would be positioned in the American sector and one in the British. Both Admirals Ramsay and Hall were dubious about the supposed utility of the Mulberries. Hall's retelling of his comments to Ramsay is little short of contemptuous, but as events showed, both proponents and detractors of the scheme would believe their ideas had been vindicated.

The need to increase firepower in the assault waves saw some LCTs modified with a special platform that allowed two Army tanks to fire over the bow ramp during the approach to the beach. The same imperative engendered the design of a flotation system for a medium tank. The plan was for the tanks to swim ashore immediately behind the infantry. Another expedient was for Army artillery pieces to fire from LCTs as they approached the beach. Admiral Hall was against all three of the former proposals. He believed the tanks would be unlikely to make the shore, and without a stabilized aiming system, neither the tanks nor the artillery could hit anything from a pitching landing craft. Events would prove Hall's doubts correct, but plans went ahead over his objections.

Other preparations saw several Liberty ships equipped with plotting rooms and radar to serve as fighter direction ships. Acquiring yet another job, several LSTs had railroad tracks fitted to carry rolling stock across the Channel. Several were equipped as hospital ships in a continuation of prior practice.[8] A designated salvage and firefighting task group was formed and given LCMs, LCTs, and a couple of LCIs specially equipped for towing and other salvage jobs. Recognizing that Overlord embodied the hopes of millions of people who would want first-hand reports, Eisenhower's headquarters issued specific guidelines for public relations. Fifty war correspondents received permission to accompany the landing with courier boats allocated to carry their dispatches from the French coast back to England. Two Navy photo units with a complement of thirty-four Navy and Coast Guard photographer's mates were also on hand.

The month of May saw the last, urgent preparations completed. Admiral Hall was engrossed in making sure that all the required landing ships and landing craft were available. Boat and shipbuilding yards throughout England strained to finish last-minute repairs and modifications. Hall's efforts resulted in 99.5 percent availability of the vessels allotted to the American assault. Also ready were seventy-five Rhinos, large vehicle ferries made up of pontoon sections welded together and outfitted with outboard motors.[9]

The problem of securing air support continued up to the last moment. Eisenhower wanted the strategic bomber forces subordinated to him in support of Overlord. He had to endure many old arguments from the air-men about not sacrificing their flexibility in support of a tactical land battle. Eisenhower eventually got what he wanted, but only after considerable grumbling by the bomber chiefs. Coordinating tactical air support was more easily done, but there were battles there also. The tactical air forces carried out a successful interdiction campaign against German lines of communication and air cover scheduled for the invasion convoys was more than adequate. Not so well done were arrangements for close support of the assault force. Requests for close support had to be relayed from Normandy to tactical air force HQ in England, which would then issue the orders to squadrons. The final air plan was not available until 4 June, just as the fleet was ready to sail. Fortunately, the more than 4,000 aircraft available to the Allied tactical air forces so vastly outnumbered the Luft-waffe that enemy interference was only a limited possibility.

FINAL DECISIONS

The single item of information most wanted by the Germans—when the invasion would come—was the subject of considerable discussion, but ultimately was the decision of one man. The planners originally chose 1 May as the target date to avoid the worst of the spring storms in the Channel and to have the whole summer in which to campaign. The choice of May also stemmed from an unsettling accumulation of news about powerful new German weapons that might make the invasion impossible. Because the need to gather more landing craft had eliminated May, attention turned to tide tables and weather data for June. The latter issue was important not only for the day of the assault, but for the weeks afterward. If historical data showed a pattern of bad weather in June, supply across the beaches would be in jeopardy. The proper combination of moonlight for the paratroopers, daylight for the naval gunners, and tide for the land-ing craft came on 4, 5, and 6 June. Research showed no undue pattern of bad storms, so the buildup didn't seem jeopardized. On 8 May, Dwight Eisenhower made the decision: Overlord would take place Monday, 5 June.

The Allied high command held a final meeting on 15 May at St. Paul's School, which also served as Montgomery's headquarters in London. The entire command structure of Overlord was present, as were King George VI and Churchill. It may be appropriate that given the nature of their gathering, the assembled host of admirals and generals sat on the hard wooden benches of the school auditorium. At the front of the assembly was a single row of armchairs reserved for the king, Churchill, and a few oth-ers. Montgomery gave one of his crisp, trademark briefings that imbued his listeners with a clear sense of confidence. His tone was well received by Eisenhower, who even at that late date remained unconvinced that his allies believed in the operation. He related in his memoirs that Churchill had told him more than once, "General, if by the coming winter you have established yourself with your thirty-six Allied divisions firmly on the Continent and have the Cherbourg and Brittany peninsulas in your grasp, I will proclaim this operation to the world as one of the most successful of the war."[10]

Fears of a German repulse were not limited to Churchill and his British colleagues. Many memoirs mention a heavy sense of dread hanging over the entire Allied camp. Everyone knew that if Overlord failed, another attempt might not be possible. One component of the dread was that security might be breached, forewarning the Germans. Extraordinary measures were put in hand to preserve secrecy: on 1 April, all visitors were banned from the assembly areas in southern England and on 17 April, all diplomatic travel from England was stopped. The Army implemented an elaborate program of false radio traffic and dummy assembly areas full of canvas tanks and wooden artillery pieces to create the illusion of an invasion army massing opposite Pas de Calais. German uncertainties aided these efforts.

By this time, the Luftwaffe could rarely penetrate British air defenses, but the few photos they did get gave the Germans a good idea about where the invasion force was concentrating. What they didn't know was when it would arrive. The German field forces practiced defending different sections of the coast, Normandy included, but their intelligence was only a stab in the dark. The relationship between good weather and an amphibious landing is obvious, but the Germans had no way to chart atmospheric systems far out in the Atlantic, where Channel weather began. The last intelligence analysis von Runstedt received before the attack stated no landing would come before 12 June.

OVERLORD: THE ASSAULT

The pent-up sense of waiting so pervasive among the two million men of the Allied Expeditionary Force began to find some relief on 25 May. Unit commanders opened the operation order that day, putting an end to the inevitable speculation that more training was in the offing. Within a week, thousands of vehicles and hundreds of thousands of men were clogging the narrow English roads. All over the south of England, the assault troops began to file aboard the waiting amphibians. Bud Farmer and Harry Heckman had mixed emotions as they watched the soldiers and their vehicles arrive—the invasion was clearly imminent. To Heckman, there "was no secret about that." Farmer said, "When you put those tanks on, you knew something was coming—it's not a pleasant thought." From the perspective of fifty years later, Farmer remembers, "Nobody was smilin'."

With Force O spread out over nine separate ports and Force U five more, loading lasted until 3 June. Then came a final, heavy pause. No one could leave his ship, nor were any visitors permitted. Then the sky filled with clouds and the wind began to rise. Farmer quietly noted that the wait and the worsening weather "did grind your nerves."[11]

Rising seas or no, those convoys based in the westernmost ports had to get under way if they were to reach the assault area at the appointed time. On the afternoon of 4 June, the ships of Admiral Moon's Force U shoved off from Plymouth into a steadily rising sea. At Eisenhower's forward headquarters near Portsmouth, the already high level of tension was increasing steadily.

Weather had played its part in Torch and had threatened Husky, but the stakes involved in Overlord were vastly higher. More than 1,000 men-of-war and almost 5,000 other vessels were participating in the assault. Scheduling their diverse routes to Normandy was an immense task not easily modified. Eisenhower was particularly concerned that the Air Force would not be able to play its part in covering the fleet and providing ground support if the weather were too bad. The staff weatherman, RAF Group Capt. J. M. Stagg, was direct in his assessment of the worsening weather: the storm could very well threaten the success of the invasion. Early on the fourth, Eisenhower ordered a recall of the ships already at sea. The paramount urgency of the moment was such that the recall message, "POST M ONE," was broadcast in the clear. Only one group of ships missed the message, but they were overhauled by a destroyer sent racing after them.

To Harry Heckman, it was his worst moment. He had been able to concentrate on the notion that "You got a job to do—we'll read about it in the *Stars and Stripes* later." When the convoy turned around, then was the moment he says he got scared. It seemed inconceivable to him that the convoy had gone unnoticed by the Germans and that the entire German army would not be waiting when the invasion force returned. Gunners Mate Heckman, self-described as a kid with no brains, was not the only one feeling anxiety.[12] During the next few hours, Dwight Eisenhower would show that he lacked nothing in the courage department.

Throughout the day on the fourth, Stagg pored over his weather data from Admiralty and Air Force reporting stations. As the rain slashed, day lengthened toward evening, and he concluded that enough of a lull would exist over the invasion area on the morning of the sixth to warrant going ahead. Stagg shared the information with Eisenhower and his principal commanders at a late evening conference. The Supreme Commander thanked the meteorologist, then polled his commanders for their views.

Montgomery and Ramsay said "go"; Tedder thought the attack was "chancy." Eisenhower stared out the window at rain driving almost horizontally across his view. At 2145, he turned to his subordinates. "I am quite positive that the order must be given."[13] Ramsay left the room to set in motion the naval machinery. His tensely expected order soon had the multitude of convoys again on their way. With an assigned speed of advance of only 5 knots, the landing craft were the first to leave. They were followed a little later by the faster fire-support ships, many coming from ports farther north.

Meanwhile, Eisenhower and his lieutenants agreed they would reconvene at 0400 to make the final decision. A gray dawn brought a short discussion during which the same opinions of the night before were voiced. Outside, the rain was lessening as all eyes turned again to Ike. At that moment, the entire weight of the enterprise rested solely on him. If he was wrong, a military disaster of epic proportions was a clear possibility. In his typical self-effacing fashion, his account offers only a spare assessment of his thoughts. But boldness, however quietly presented, and good fortune were his companions. In a quiet but firm voice, Eisenhower said, "O.K., let's go."[14]

Kirk and his commanders were already at sea. Admiral Moon and the commanding general of the 4th Infantry Division, Maj. Gen. Raymond O. Barton, were in the transport *Bayfield*. Also aboard were four war correspondents and Lt. Gen. Lawton Collins, the corps commander. Admiral Hall and Maj. Gen. Clarence Huebner, commanding the 1st Infantry Division, were in the *Ancon*. Commodore C. D. Edgar commanded the follow-up force loaded with the 29th Infantry Division plus three more infantry and an armored division. Kirk and General Bradley were in the *Augusta*, again pressed into service as an amphibious force flagship. Kirk sailed from Plymouth at midday on 5 June knowing among other things that he and General Bradley would miss a promised social appointment. On Sunday, the two officers had been guests at a luncheon during which they were asked to appear at a parade a week hence. Security could not be breached so both men accepted the invitation, knowing they would be otherwise engaged.

The convoy assembly area was near the Isle of Wight, an area scheduled so heavily with invasion traffic it was nicknamed Picadilly Circus. Traffic divided into five lanes, two headed for the American beaches. All went well despite the heavy weather. Good planning had its part, but Kirk suggested that much of the success was due to the forge-ahead spirit of the reservists manning the amphibious ships. One reservist whose confidence was returning was Heckman. His attack of nerves was assuaged by the Morse Vs flashed by the paratroopers as they passed over the invasion fleet. He felt even more confident as faint daylight began to reveal the immense armada all around his ship. He thought there was "no way they were gonna stop us."[15]

The assault force was bearing down on an enemy who was sure they *were* coming, just not then. One enemy intelligence officer had warned that enigmatic messages broadcast on the BBC presaged an invasion, but German naval weathermen said conditions in the Channel precluded a landing. Rommel had taken the weather report to heart and left his headquarters on the fifth for a trip to Germany. Other generals were away from their divisions en route to a war game during which they were to practice defending against the invasion. No warning of the invasion convoys came from coastal radar stations, which the Allies jammed, spoofed, or heavily bombed. Meanwhile, Allied paratroopers were dropping into the invasion zone. Though badly scattered, this disruption of their plans served to confuse the Germans more; something was up, but the defenders weren't sure what. Dawn brought the answer.

More than 200 mine sweepers led the way, laying buoys and marking lanes through the large offshore minefields. In their wake came the transports and landing ships moving into their assigned areas; fears of German coastal artillery stopped the transports eleven miles offshore, which meant a long, rough ride for the infantry. The amphibs immediately began lowering their boats; the tension of the moment is evident in a notation made by Admiral Moon that the troops loaded into the boats in almost complete silence. Also through the cleared lanes passed the bombardment ships as they closed in to take up their fire-support stations. Air Force heavy bombers were to deliver a last-minute carpet of bombs across the beach defenses but caution brought on by the thick overcast negated that plan. Not wanting to hit the ships massed below, the bombers delayed their release so much they scattered their loads harmlessly behind the beach areas. The bombardment ships took up the assault at 0536. As at Tarawa, their efforts would prove less than adequate.

Naval gunfire did exact a toll from the many emplacements guarding the beach, but there weren't enough bombardment ships and they did not have enough time to do the kind of job done in the Marshalls.[16] Many enemy guns were in low-lying emplacements set back enough to be hardly visible from the sea. A blast wall hiding the aperture from view further protected the German guns. Coastal defense guns also proved hard to silence. Kirk noted that not a single protected battery suffered serious damage from the prelanding bombardment. The bombardment did detonate many land mines seeding the beach. The approaching infantry would soon begin to pay the price extracted by the many undamaged gun positions, especially at Omaha Beach.

One unpleasant surprise awaiting the assault force at Omaha Beach was the unexpected presence of the veteran 352nd Infantry Division. Intelligence knew the enemy unit was in the invasion area, but its move to the Normandy front was not communicated to the assault troops. The veterans of the 1st Infantry Division were about to collide head-on with enemy soldiers whose experience matched their own. Many American soldiers were also miserably seasick. The gale of the day before had abated but the stiff wind was still kicking up a choppy sea, making an 11-mile ride in a small landing craft an uncomfortable, wet experience. The German soldiers hunkered in their positions on the high bluffs that dominated Omaha Beach and waited for the landing craft to ground. Bullets were ringing against the oncoming boats but the real storm started after the ramps began to drop.

The weight of German fire falling on the beach was so heavy the infantry could only seek what small shelter it could find among the dunes. The combat engineers who followed immediately behind the infantry were so badly decimated they could blow open only a few of the planned lanes through the tangle of obstacles. Admiral Hall's fears about the amphibious tanks became fact when the rough seas collapsed their flotation screens, sending most of them plunging to the bottom. The few tanks that did reach the shore by any means, including LCTs, were quickly put out of action by antitank guns. German mortars and artillery were well registered and deadly accurate. Shore fire-control parties suffered heavy casualties, which left the destroyers hovering offshore uncertain about where and at what to shoot.

A muddle of landing craft and DUKWs began to pile up off the beach, their way mostly blocked and such small passage as there was always in immediate peril. Farmer was among the men for whom unpleasant reality replaced unknown fears. His job as coxswain was to put his LCT onto the beach, hold it there long enough for the embarked tanks to get off, and get out. His ordeal began before reaching the beach when a shell burst near his station, wounding him in five places. He stayed at his post despite his wounds and drove the LCT onto the beach. In the few minutes it took for the three embarked tanks to get off, the craft took fifteen more hits. Farmer then backed the LCT off the beach, spun around and headed out of the maelstrom. A seventeenth and final hit destroyed the rudder, leaving Farmer without a job. His LCT didn't sink, but she and Bud Farmer were definitely out of the battle.[17]

Offshore in the *Augusta*, little could be discerned about the progress of the battle. What could be seen wasn't heartening, but the battle was beyond the commanders' immediate control. What got the assault moving was the same sort of individual example that moved the marines off the beach at Tarawa. One naval officer commanding a shore fire-control party was thwarted in his attempts to get his men ashore so he stationed his badly riddled LCVP a short distance offshore. From there he managed to establish radio contact and begin directing naval gunfire onto enemy positions that were firing on his section of the beach. Badly holed or sunken boats stranded more than one landing craft crew on the beach. Many of them turned to getting the wounded under shelter and administering first aid.

Several destroyer captains took the initiative of firing on those enemy positions they could see despite not being under the control of a shore party. One shore party called for such a heavy volume of fire that the soldiers had to be warned they were exhausting the ship's magazines. The destroyermen were told to keep up the good work and keep firing. Destroyers also paid the highest price among the men-of-war. Three destroyers and one destroyer escort were all fatally mined off Utah Beach. One problem for all ships off the beaches was the heavy congestion and the need to avoid sunken wreckage. With the wrecked landing craft also came many men floating in the rough water. The skipper of one patrol craft later reported that his attention was fully taken up trying to pull exhausted men from the water.

The deputy assault group commander closed inshore and began reorganizing the milling mass of landing craft into waves. They were then sent ashore to add their weight to the assault. Follow-up waves began to arrive from the transport area around midmorning and after that the assault began to make progress. Individual soldiers led the way, blasting German positions into silence one by one. The infantrymen got point-blank gunfire support from several destroyers that closed to within 800 yards of the beach. As defensive fire began to slacken, engineers could begin clearing lanes in the obstacles, allowing more men and tanks ashore. By midafternoon, though the foothold on Omaha Beach was tentative at best, the cohesiveness of the German front had been broken. Beach and shore parties struggled to bring some order into the scene of wartime chaos.

The landing at Utah Beach went much more smoothly, though more as a quirk of war than by design. The approach mirrored the one at Omaha, with all transports in position without undue difficulties. Loading the assault waves went smoothly despite desultory fire from enemy coastal artillery. The bombardment also went as scheduled, led by the old battleships *Arkansas* and *Texas*. The plan began to go fortuitously awry when artillery fire struck the primary control ship. She quickly went to the bottom, depriving the oncoming landing craft of direction. The leading waves were unknowingly being set off-course by the current and the dust raised by the bombardment obscured navigational checkpoints. Therefore, the first waves set down 1,000 yards west of their designated point, but away from the teeth of the enemy defense, as well.

The assault troops did take some fire, but the bombardment had been more effective; some Army officers later said all that remained was debris and clouds of dust. The enemy soldiers at Utah Beach were not of the same caliber as at Omaha. The men of the 4th Infantry were soon across the beach and forging inland. Their attack was proceeding so well that General Barton established his command post ashore at 1400. The beachhead at Utah was the largest gained on the invasion front, but the Allies were by no means securely ashore.

The BBC announced the invasion to the world at midday on 6 June. That Eisenhower did not know for hours of the difficulties experienced on Omaha Beach was fortunate, for among his many worries was the fear that the landing might be repulsed. He had prepared a message for such an eventuality that ended, "The troops, the air, and the Navy did all that bravery and devotion to duty could do. If any blame or fault attaches to the attempt it is mine alone."[18] His immediate fears of disaster were no doubt lessened by day's end on 6 June, but he also knew that all depended upon the follow-up.

THE BUILDUP

German attempts to disrupt the buildup were necessarily limited. Both the Luftwaffe and the Kriegsmarine were so vastly outnumbered that their efforts, however bravely attempted, amounted mainly to harassment. No U-boat could penetrate the Allied ASW screen and no E-boat got close to a transport. German air raids scored scattered hits and seeded mines that claimed an occasional victim. The bridge of ships carrying the Allied armies and their material strength from England was never disrupted by enemy action. German counterefforts were greatly impaired by the lack of unity among the high command and uncertainty as to whether the Normandy landing was the main Allied effort. The lack of trust between Hitler and his generals was no match for the unity of command Eisenhower demanded. The major threats to the buildup were the magnitude of the job and Channel weather, not enemy action.

With so many ships supporting the landing, confusion became inevitable. The Army contributed to one backlog by insisting that ships lying off the beaches unload according to their cargo priority. Unfortunately, loading manifests had been misrouted to the British sector. The Navy officer in charge of unloading had to go from ship to ship by small boat seeking information about cargoes. He made the decision to unload without regard to priority. Ramsay concurred, saying that expeditious unloading would sort out priorities.

The need to get so much materiel ashore led to the practice of drying out LSTs; they beached at high tide and their loads of vehicles drove directly onto dry land. The wide, flat beaches of Normandy lent themselves to the practice but there were risks; any ship so beached was absolutely stationary until the next high tide, making it a ready target for German artillery. Enemy gunners hit several while they were high and dry. Another problem was hull damage stemming from uneven stress; hull plates could be sprung and machinery thrown out of alignment.

Work on the artificial harbors began as soon as a beachhead was secured. A row of old ships was sunk to seaward to form a breakwater after which all the apparatus of the Mulberry was carefully positioned. The first vehicles rolled ashore across the causeways on 16 June. Though the Mulberries were shown to be more than an implausible idea, they were only one avenue for supplies. Civilian-manned, chartered merchant ships were another part of the logistics pipeline as they hauled many thousands of tons across the Channel. Kirk did record that their sense of fire discipline was so bad they eventually had to be forbidden to open up unless an air attack came directly at their ship.

Far more disruptive to the buildup was the gale that blasted the invasion front on 19 June, destroying the Mulberry in the American sector and driving ashore hundreds of landing craft. The influx of supplies dropped to a trickle as the salvage group worked desperately to refloat and repair the beached LCMs and LCTs. The Mulberry in the British sector survived and became the focal point for unloading until enough landing craft could be put back in service.

Naval gunfire support continued to be vitally important to the invaders for days after the fighting moved off the beaches. The *Nevada*, which had fired 337 rounds from her main battery and 2,696 rounds from her 5-in. battery on D-day, remained hard at it. Among her many fire missions was one against a concentration of enemy tanks that she delivered from 27,000 yards on 8 June. She fired another mission from such a distance that her report notes that "we had to depress the elevation stops to reach the target."[19] The battleships and cruisers were being called upon to such an extent that Admiral Ramsay had to send a message warning that the stock of heavy-caliber ammunition in England was close to exhaustion.

Medical planning bore fruit as the thousands of casualties returning from the front lines were evacuated in orderly fashion. The transports also served as casualty collecting points; fifty crewmen showed up at the *Bayfield*'s sickbay after an appeal for blood donors. Ninety-five LSTs would eventually carry wounded to England. One of those transported was Bud Farmer. After his LCT was finally disabled, he made his way to a hospital LST where he received treatment for his wounds. Eventually, he ended up in an army hospital in England and from there was shipped back to the States. Naturally, concern for the wounded extended to ships not formally part of the evacuation process, as an event recorded in the War Diary of LST 288 illustrates.

The ship was returning to England when she overtook the British

LCI 525. The deck of the British ship was crowded with casualties, many in serious condition. The British captain finally agreed to come alongside despite a choppy sea and twenty-two wounded were transferred to the American ship. Medical personnel also transferred to the British vessel to help out:

> Of the 22 survivors brought aboard, 15 were in deep shock. It was the opinion of the doctors aboard that if transfer had not been made and plasma and blood immediately administered, the majority of these cases would not have survived. Ship's supply of blood was exhausted and direct transfusions given until . . . arrival in Weymouth.[20]

Though progress ashore was slower than planned, General Bradley went ashore on 10 June to assume command of the American effort. The heavy brass arrived in the invasion area on 12 June. Eisenhower, Kirk, Marshall, and King all toured the assault beaches and conferred with Bradley about the progress of the battle. Admiral Ramsay's 17 June announcement that the assault phase was over recognized that the lodgment in France was permanent. The Navy remained heavily involved in supporting the invasion front but the amphibians were already looking ahead to other jobs. The recapitulation that naturally followed was extensive but there were no profound recommendations for change.

Kirk restressed the need for good organization and an overwhelming bombardment. He had considerable praise for all who were involved in planning the operation, especially for General Bradley. Kirk made the following comments:

> A firm tradition of mutual trust and confidence now exists, but this record could easily be marred in special instances by the personal incompatibility of two commanders of different services. There is no effective guarantee of success—it takes one to command and two to cooperate; and the existence at a remotely high level of a supreme commander cannot ensure cooperation against the will of subordinates.[21]

The conclusions to be drawn about Overlord's success are several. However large and complex, an amphibious operation always has some element of surprise in its favor. Allied weaponry was not innately superior to German weaponry nor were Allied soldiers any braver than their enemies. The Germans were vastly outnumbered in men and materiel at the point of attack, however, an advantage derived from the ability of amphibious forces to strike anywhere. The Germans were also confronted by an Allied force that despite its numbers of untried soldiers had a heavy leavening of veterans of amphibious warfare across the breadth of the Mediterranean. Both the supporting Allied navies were determined to prevent the invasion from being driven off the beach. Most important, the Allied command was unified in purpose, however much it disagreed in private. Much the same conditions applied in the Pacific, where the largest invasion of that war began late in June.

FORAGER: INTO THE MARIANAS, APRIL–MAY 1944

The Marianas are a group of large islands lying approximately 3,500 miles west of Pearl Harbor. Conversely, they lie only 1,400 miles southeast of Tokyo, well within range of the new B-29 bombers entering service. Since the Japanese considered the Marianas essential to the defense of the homeland, the islands figured prominently in their defensive plans. The Marianas also were central to Admiral King's strategic vision. Not only would the enemy supply line to the Carolines be cut off, but King and his admirals also thought the Japanese fleet would likely seek battle and thus court destruction. King received support from Air Force commander Gen. Henry H. "Hap" Arnold, who wanted to get his B-29s into action against the Japanese homeland as soon as possible. MacArthur did not share King's ideas nor was Nimitz fully convinced. But King was not to be denied; the 12 March dictum from the Joint Chiefs ordered Nimitz to proceed against the Marianas not later than 15 June. When the units assigned to Flintlock returned to Pearl, planning was well underway.

The same triumvirate of commanders who had been so successful in the Marshalls not unexpectedly found themselves responsible for an even more complex invasion. Spruance was again fleet commander, Kelly Turner would direct the amphibious forces, and Holland Smith had overall command of the landing force. Operation Forager differed from any previous amphibious operation in the Central Pacific for several reasons. Unlike the small, flat atolls assaulted in the Gilberts and Marshalls, the three target islands in the Marianas ranged from 38 to 206 square miles in area. Second, the garrisons of the three islands, Saipan, Guam, and Tinian, were larger than any previously encountered, so the landing force and its associated amphibious lift would have to be larger than yet attempted in the Pacific. Supplies would have to be transported across greater distances than ever and all ships assigned to the assault would be tied up for at least three months. Finally, Holland Smith would be commanding troops in corps strength for the first time.

The complexity of Forager kept the planners who were shaping the operation working long days. Spruance followed his custom of staying at a remove, allowing his mind to remain free of details better handled by his subordinates. Turner, on the other hand, immersed himself in the smallest details, driving himself to the point of exhaustion. His biographer notes that he was drinking heavily, but without apparent effect on the quality of his work. Holland Smith also delegated but always with a careful eye for the well-being of his marines.

Four-and-a-half divisions would make the assault: the 2d and 4th Marine Divisions under Maj. Gens. Thomas Watson and Harry Schmidt respectively would land on Saipan. They would mount in Hawaii and make the journey in the ships of Turner's task force. The 3d Marine Division under Maj. Gen. Allen Turnage plus the 1st Provisional Marine Brigade under Brig. Gen. Lemuel Shepherd would load in Guadalcanal and be lifted to Guam in the ships of Admiral Conolly's task force. The Army's 27th Infantry Division under Maj. Gen. Ralph Smith would be the floating reserve at Saipan; the division had the additional job of assaulting Guam. The 77th Infantry Division was alerted for possible movement to the Marianas should it be needed. Planning initially called for Saipan to be assaulted on 15 June, Guam on 18 June, and Tinian on 15 July. However, the Japanese soon upset that timetable. The Saipan assault force numbered more than 127,000 troops, including 85,680 marines and 41,891 soldiers. A garrison force of 38,000 more troops stretched Nimitz's amphibious lift capabilities to their limit.

There were 535 ships in the various task forces, far different from the 71 that had appeared off Guadalcanal only two years previously. The fringing reef that surrounded the islands to be assaulted also demanded almost 1,000 LVT and LVT(A)s. The need for shipping was so great twenty-one chartered merchantmen were included in the assault. Even with the huge increase, however, almost every ship not needed for routine maintenance of existing bases was required for the initial lift. With few available to provide a quick follow-up load of supplies, there were hard choices to be made in the loading plans. The planners understood that the demand for ammunition and other consumables would be heavy. Given the distance and transit time from Hawaiian or South Pacific supply depots, the landing force would have to carry not only what it needed for the immediate assault but enough to sustain the attack for a prolonged period.

As in Flintlock, one significant component of the load was ammunition for the gunfire-support ships; the holds of the assault force held almost 36,000 rounds of 8 in. and 5 in. Another component was 150,000 gallons of aviation fuel and ammunition for planes that would be flying from newly captured airfields. Still another was the amount of ammunition needed to support the thirteen battalions of artillery in the assault force. The guns were preloaded in DUKWs and LVTs. Tanks were also preloaded in LCMs.

Since there weren't enough transports to lift the large number of assault troops, LSTs would double as troop carriers. The latter task was not a new idea, but it had never been done over such a long distance, so the planning staffs did a careful study of space, messing, and sanitation requirements.

The plans added 300 men to the load of each LST, even stipulating that 80 men could be berthed under the LCTs stowed on the main deck.

Despite the imperative to make sure there was enough of everything, habits born of painfully learned wartime experience are hard to shake; the usual quickness with which the Japanese sent air attacks against landings in the South Pacific affected loading for Forager. As in the Solomons and elsewhere, quartermasters followed the practice of packing each transport only with what could be unloaded within eight to twelve hours. Each ship was crammed with troops, but not loaded with cargo to its maximum capacity. On the other hand, Admiral Conolly noted that because of the heavy loads carried by the cargo ships, extra efforts to get the cargo ashore quickly had to be taken. Twenty-five additional tracked cranes joined the load as well as pontoon barges. Someone had the idea to station a few of the barges off the fringing reef with a crane aboard. The crane could swing netted loads of supplies from landing craft onto LVTs and DUKWs, materially speeding up the process. Choosing what to take and what to leave continued to be a bother.

Holland Smith's staff looked at every ship's loading plan and tried to weed out everything they deemed inessential. Even so, taking some things meant others had to be left; there were adequate rations, but all the divisions had to give up half their vehicles. With so many new vessels coming into the theater, Smith's men often could not draw up a loading plan until the ship arrived at Pearl. They would then go aboard and measure her holds so they could figure out what she could carry and in what quantities. One feature of the loading plan was that only "emergency" supplies of water, ammunition, and medical supplies would be in the initial off-loads onto the beach. In total, Turner's ships would be carrying 320,000 tons of supplies to the Marianas.[22] Difficulties would develop in Hawaii; Admiral Conolly noted that in his area at least, the loading plan that evolved managed to escape the usual last-minute changes that tended to pile extra equipment on a load already carefully stowed.

Improving communications between the shore fire-control parties and the supporting ships was again at the top of the list. The landing force was beefed up with more officers and radiomen. Gunfire-support specialists worked out a flexible system that coordinated the many calls for fire with the true position of the requesting troops and the available ships. All the ships assigned to support duties had to visit the range at Kahoolawe. Gunfire planners thought two days of heavy bombardment would be sufficient to destroy most of Saipan's known defensive emplacements. Destroyers would keep the beach area under main battery fire until the assault waves were within 300 yards of landing.

Twenty-five of the popular LCI(G)s would then take over and lead the assault waves to the beach where they would remain on hand for close-in support. More than 100 LVT(A)s were to accompany the troop-carrying tractors, acting as seagoing tanks. General Watson protested against the idea, believing the LVT(A) unsuitable for such a job. He received permission to change the plan in his area of responsibility; events proved him right. Each assault battalion had a destroyer assigned for fire support. Even more fire could be called down from the sky.

Twenty-six aircraft carriers of various classes participated in Forager, including eleven CVEs assigned directly to the assault force. Aircraft therefore got a considerable portion of prelanding bombardment duties. Once the final bombardment began, the firing ships were limited to a band only 1,000 yards deep. The bombers would attack everything inland from that point. Maximum ordinates of naval gunfire, the highest level reached by shells fired into the beach area, were carefully coordinated with air strike plans.[23] Land-based bombers from the Marshalls and Bismarcks were supposed to add their weight to the softening up.

There were flaws in the plan, despite the attention paid to lessons already learned. The expected heavy demands on gunfire support and the known quantity of ammunition available for immediate resupply made conservation a priority. The Japanese penchant for nighttime movement and attack was to be countered by almost constant star shell illumination; finite magazine space meant a ration on how many star shells could be fired per gun per day.

Other lessons learned were apparent, too. The difficulties of controlling and directing a mass of landing craft had not been eliminated although there had been considerable progress. The planners had only to remember what happened at Roi and Namur. The scale of resistance expected at Saipan made it imperative that there be no delays in getting a large number of troops to the beach in good order and in timely fashion. Turner's staff devoted some effort to seeing that there was no repeat of old difficulties.

There was a force control officer as well as a control officer with each assault division. Twenty-four control communications teams were formed, each with an officer, radiomen, and signalmen. Additional support craft were allocated to oversee marshaling the LVTs and landing craft at the line of departure. Others would keep boat lanes properly marked. Still others would control the transfer line where secondary wave troops shifted from LCVPs into LVTs. All control personnel worked closely with troop commanders to make sure everyone understood the plan. One crucial job was for two sizable underwater demolition teams to clear any obstacles or mines. The UDT men would do their work during daylight, though under the close covering fire of several ships. As usual, key elements of the planning were training and rehearsals.

Drawing upon his success before the Marshalls when he set up shop at Camp Pendleton, Admiral Conolly moved his headquarters to Guadal-canal to be near the marines his amphibians would haul into combat. The marines would be taking the most tanks they had ever used in an assault so they paid considerable attention to training tank/infantry teams. A similar scenario played out in Hawaii, where Harry Hill was overseeing amphibious training for Turner. One device used by the marines on Maui was to chalk out a scale outline of the Saipan beaches and then do a walk through. They then held a large-scale rehearsal complete with naval gunfire support and beach landings from 17 through 19 May. The Army did likewise 18 through 24 May. Hill was unimpressed with the first Marine rehearsal. Part of the problem was that many veteran amphibious captains were transferring to shore duty with their places taken by officers new to the game.

One evolution being practiced was loading LVTs from the open sea into LSTs. As Gene Watts remembered, not the easiest task: Each LVT would approach bow on to the LST's ramp. Steadying lines would be rigged to the LVT's bow and the tractor started up the ramp. As the tractor climbed the ramp, it would rise at a steep angle until reaching the balance point. With tracks braked, it would pitch forward with a loud clatter of steel on steel, sending the line handlers scurrying. Once brought to a halt, the tractor would spin on one track and back into position.[24]

Tragedy marred these exercises when two deck-loaded LCTs especially configured for gunfire-support sank after they broke their lashings and crashed overboard from their parent LSTs. Nineteen marines drowned and part of the gunfire-support plan was disrupted.

Even more disheartening and potentially disrupting to Forager was a disaster in Pearl Harbor on 21 May. Late that afternoon soldiers were unloading ammunition from the LST 353, one of eight nested together in Pearl's West Loch. All were heavily loaded with tightly packed vehicles, ammunition, and drummed gasoline. No one close to the blast lived to tell what happened, but a sudden explosion in the 353 sent flaming debris cascading across the nest. Gallant efforts to fight the ensuing fires amid the blasts of exploding fuel drums and ammunition were accompanied by panic and ill-disciplined flight. Turner showed the part of his nature that could not delegate by boarding a fireboat and plunging headlong into the center of the firefighting effort. Holland Smith also sped to the scene and had a command post set up. His goal was to find out the exact toll of loss and how soon it could be replaced. Six LSTs were a total loss, 163 men were killed and another 396 injured.

Holland Smith's hard-working supply officer got the necessary supplies from the depots. Turner's staff found five replacements for the burned-out ships among the few uncommitted vessels available. There was little time for any of the replacements, soldiers or ships, to become better integrated with their units; the various task groups began heading west only three days after the fire. All would rendezvous at Kwajalein and Eniwetok.

The LSTs of Flotilla 5, newly transferred from the South Pacific, were among the ships in passage. The flat-bottomed landing ships were not an easy ride, a characteristic that had its effect on some marines; the flotilla War Diary has an entry for 2 June that reads, "many of the Marine passengers aboard LSTs found the rail a comfortable and convenient place to stay." Four days later, the diarist noted, "The ships . . . descended upon the port of Kwajalein like a band of raiding Comanche Indians."[25] In the *Doyen*, casualty handling procedures received considerable attention. "Daily instruction was held for the hospital corpsmen in surgical techniques, advanced first aid, x ray, and nursing." It was the aim of her medical officer "to have every corpsman capable of carrying out any function or duty assigned to him."[26]

The records of the *Callaway* reveal the precise boat-handling and loading skills needed by a transport assigned to an amphibious assault in the summer of 1944:

> (1) To boat the reserve battalion of the 23rd Regiment's Combat Team immediately upon arrival at the Transport Area

> *   *   *

> (3) To furnish guide boats and guide boat officers to lead the . . . troops from the *Belle Grove*, where they were transferred to LVTs to the line of departure.

> *   *   *

> (6) To furnish two (2) balanced-loaded boats containing ammunition, rations, and medical stores to the line of departure.

> *   *   *

> (8) To furnish two (2) LCM(3)s to the U.S.S. *Storm King* for boating tanks.[27]

How heavily some of these responsibilities must have weighed on the young men assigned to carry them out.

Mirroring what had happened only a few days earlier in the crowded ports of southern England, there was a brief pause before the storm. Along with transferring assault troops from their transports to the LSTs before the final passage to Saipan, another benefit of the stop in the Marshalls was to absorb any last-minute intelligence about the defenses. Aerial photos played the primary role in determining Japanese strength. Ultra intercepts and documents captured during Operation Flintlock were also available. Carrier planes brought back the first pictures after raids in February, but photo coverage was ongoing. A submarine also made a complete mosaic of the Marianas beaches during April.

Aerial photos taken over Saipan on 29 May were compared to others taken on 18 April and revealed an increase of eighty-seven gun positions. For all the information available to the assault planners, there was a significant gap in what they knew; estimates of enemy troop strength were far too low. The planners thought there were 17,000 Japanese on the island, but the enemy numbered over 32,000. Estimates of Japanese troop strength on Guam and Tinian were similarly too low. Fortunately, flaws in their defensive preparations and unrealistic expectations would again offset the tenacious valor of Japanese soldiers and naval infantry.

The loss of the Marshalls, and the speed with which they had gone, was an especially ominous tocsin for the Imperial Army and Navy. The Marianas had to be next, but their defenses were anything but complete. Although defeating the Americans at the waterline remained a goal, an overall defense in depth was to be prepared. The invaders might get ashore, but they would be contained long enough for the Imperial Navy to drive off their covering force and allow the garrison to destroy the landing force.

Thousands of reinforcements embarked for the islands but they had to run the increasingly dangerous gauntlet of American submarines intent on stopping them. Some did get through; many others drowned when their transports sunk. Many troops that did make it to the Marianas arrived as unarmed survivors plucked from the sea. Their lost ships took more with them than the soldiers' guns and ammunition. Badly needed supplies of concrete and steel for the construction of pillboxes and bunkers also went down. A Japanese report captured after the fall of Saipan noted that the rescued soldiers were not only unarmed, but "without hats and shoes and are in confusion."[28] There were naval infantry troops on Saipan, but the Imperial Army was in charge.

The Imperial Navy intended to make itself felt through Operation A-Go; upon receiving word that the Americans had attacked, the fleet would sortie en masse. Aircraft based in the Marianas would attack the American battle fleet, reducing its numbers. After the airmen had whittled down the invaders, Japanese carrier planes would finish the job, leaving the amphibians helpless. With the American fleet destroyed or scattered, those troops already landed would be annihilated. Typical of Japanese plans, A-Go placed great dependence upon the martial spirit of their servicemen to overcome material inferiority. There was also a fatal, concomitant belief that the same spirit would overcome American countermeasures. Unfortunately for the Japanese, the legion of gray ships advancing on the Marianas was not only well armed, but possessed of a martial spirit all its own. Raymond Spruance and Holland Smith knew the coming fight would be hard; Spruance left Pearl Harbor with the expectation that a fleet action was probable. Nimitz's orders directed him to exercise every opportunity to destroy the enemy fleet, but not at the risk of uncovering the amphibians. Spruance knew that a victory was anything but automatic.

THE BATTLE BEGINS: JUNE 1944

Several Japanese snoopers fell before the guns of the CAP, allowing the invasion force to reach the Marianas unmolested and apparently unreported. Japanese hopes that their land-based bombers could cut into American strength began to dim on 11 June. Four carrier task groups sent a cloud of fighters to scythe its way across Japanese air fields. By the end of the day, enemy air strength was a few scattered planes capable only of harassment. Spruance then detached the battleships that normally screened the carriers to begin bombarding. Unfortunately, the newer battlewagons had not trained on the range in Hawaii. Firing from long range, they delivered a bombardment that gave the visual impression of wreaking great havoc but causing little substantive damage. The better-trained support force moved in on 14 June; the experienced bombardment group closed the range considerably and set to work.

Historian and teacher Samuel Eliot Morison was again participating in history as it occurred. Aboard the light cruiser *Honolulu* as she took part in the bombardment, he wrote in his diary at 0540 on 14 June, "Flashes of return fire. 'The nerve of 'em' says a bluejacket. I feel trembly at the knees with excitement." Another entry made three hours later reveals the writer within: "The fire from a far-off cruiser and [battleship] is like the swift thrust of a snake's tongue." We also learn that in the *Honolulu* at least, Forager didn't begin on empty stomachs. "Had a swell breakfast of canned orange, grapefruit, ham & eggs and shaved while were servicing planes."[29] For all the real and apparent destruction, the bombardment didn't hit the large numbers of Japanese artillery pieces lying concealed behind the beach areas. It did wreck some pillboxes and hit several known battery positions. But enemy camouflage was skillful, his artillery positions carefully sited, and casualties were light. Any impression that might have suggested total destruction would soon be forgotten.

While the bombardment group was raining explosives on Saipan, the UDT teams were swimming right up to the muzzles of the enemy's guns. Destroyers and LCI(G)s gave the swimmers close cover, but the job still required the UDT men to come within 75 yards of the beaches. They discovered no obstacles or mines while reaffirming that LVTs would be needed to get the troops ashore. Draper Kauffman commanded the demolition teams. He and his men were doing something so new they had to figure out their tactics as they went. To measure distances, they devised a system of fish line knotted at precise intervals. Gauging water depth was a problem solved with a little ingenuity and paint:

> I'd been complaining because people would come back from a rehearsal and say, "The water is knee-deep," or "It comes up to my chin." So I made everybody stand up against [a] turret . . . which we duly measured and marked, and we took some ship's black paint and painted a solid black line around each man every foot of his height above the deck and a dash halfway around every half foot. We did the same thing up the arms from the fingertips. The black paint must have been a special kind because it was forever before we got the darned stuff off.[30]

The UDT casualties at Saipan were incredibly light considering their task: only four killed and several wounded. Kauffman and his men spent the night preparing a report to be delivered to Kelly Turner and the assault force commander.

Harassing fire continued throughout the night, providing a backdrop for the approach of the landing force. Turner and Holland Smith were in the *Rocky Mount*, which, with the rest of the amphibians, arrived off Saipan in the early darkness of 15 June. Kauffman dispatched his officers to Turner's and Hill's flagships with the results of their reconnaissance. Unexpectedly, Kauffman found himself assigned to lead some tanks ashore when he pointed out that their previously planned route was unusable.

The scheme of maneuver called for landing on an eight-battalion front across a span of 4 miles. The first step was to get the LVTs into the water; LSTs disgorged them like so many crocodiles plopping into the water. Assembling the hundreds of LVTs took place on schedule, a clear indication that the extra attention paid to controlling the forming up of assault waves had paid off. Under fair skies and a curtain of shell fire, the troop-laden tractors headed for the beach around 0830. The gunfire-support groups kept up their fire until air-dropped flares signaled that the landing waves were within 300 yards of the beach.

Ninety-six LVTs of the first wave were preceded by LCI(G)s that began to saturate the beaches with 4.5-in. rockets and 40- and 20-mm fire. The gunboats advanced to the reef line before turning on a course parallel to the beach and moving out to the flanks of the landing zone. Additional suppressive fire came from the 37- and 75-mm cannons of sixty-eight LVT(A)s interspersed with the troop carriers.

The avalanche of men and firepower inexorably drawing up to the beaches of Saipan did not approach unanswered by the defenders. They had endured four days of what one Japanese diarist called "brazen" aerial bombing and naval shell fire and were eager to finally reply in kind.

When the first wave was approximately 1,000 yards off the beach,

Japanese artillery and mortars began to take them under fire. Although they also had to contend with a heavy swell that capsized a few of the LVTs, the first wave got ashore with light casualties. The assault plan then began to go awry. The LVT(A)s were supposed to proceed up to 1,500 yards inland to give the beachhead some depth. A combination of rough terrain and enemy fire that quickly began to take a heavy toll thwarted that effort. The hoped-for momentum of the attack stalled immediately and troop-carrying tractors began to pile up on the beach. Enemy fire continued to grow in volume and accuracy, knocking out dozens of LVTs and causing heavy casualties. Some drivers refused to proceed any farther than the waterline while others wandered aimlessly along the beach. The mass of Japanese artillery that had gone undiscovered was exacting a stiff price for too brief an American bombardment.

All the problems faced by the soldiers on Omaha Beach were encountered by their Marine brethren on Saipan. One battalion landed out of position as the LVTs veered off to avoid enemy fire. A gap thus appeared between neighboring units. Heavy casualties and disabled radios among the shore fire-control parties hobbled gunfire support. Tanks began coming ashore, but many drowned out crossing the reef. Artillery couldn't be landed until there was room for the guns to set up. As at Omaha, individuals began to move the assault forward. Bit by bit, radiomen established communications with the waiting gunfire-support ships, bringing down fire on Japanese positions. The well-managed control apparatus kept feeding troops into the beachhead, enemy fire notwithstanding, so that 8,000 troops landed in twenty minutes. Artillerymen began getting their guns ashore; despite rapid and accurate enemy counterbattery fire, they added some needed weight to the assault.

To reduce beach congestion, the "emergency supplies"-only system was again in effect. One effort that suffered a breakdown was evacuating casualties. Two LSTs stood off the beaches as casualty clearing stations with a third standing by in reserve. After taking aboard about 100 casualties, each LST was to move them to a designated transport for further treatment. Unfortunately, the number of casualties pouring off the Saipan beaches overwhelmed this system. One hospital LST mistakenly left the area while the others became swamped with wounded marines.

Turner's report gives an idea of the number of wounded:

Between 1040 and 1500 on D-day, [711] casualties were received aboard the transports. During the next twenty-four hours [1,715] were received aboard the transports. The following day an additional [1,744] were evacuated to the transports. By this time several APA's had over [200] casualties on board, and were forced to use other than medical department personnel to handle the casualty load.[31]

Getting the mass of injured parceled out to the transports required considerable effort; two transports received orders to close the beaches and bear a hand. Unfortunately, many casualties had to endure transfers from an LVT to an LCVP, then spend hours lying in the bobbing landing craft before reaching medical care.[32]

The pressing need to get boats closer to the beach led to Kauffman and his UDT men getting the job of blasting a channel through the reef. He had the unique experience of trying to find the beachmaster while clad only in swimming trunks and a face mask, all the while under fire. Kauffman and his swimmers would use the approaching night to cover their work; so would the Japanese, though with less success.

The enemy wasted no time organizing and mounting a counterattack; their preparations were revealed by the harsh light of star shells put up by support ships. The battleship *California* answered one call for support with over thirty rounds of main battery fire, blasting a group of enemy soldiers into oblivion. The heaviest portion of the Japanese attack, which included a sizable force of tanks, came in the early hours of 17 June. The Marines beat back the enemy, though at heavy cost. Illumination and gunfire support provided by the fleet were crucial to the Marines and set a pattern for the coming days. Not only were there more Japanese defenders than expected, but they were ably supported by artillery. The Marines often measured their advance in yards and then only after heavy expenditure of artillery and naval shells. The second day of the battle also saw most of the gunfire-support ships pulled out to join Spruance's carriers. The Japanese fleet had emerged to do battle and was bearing down on Saipan.

American submarines had reported the sortie of the Japanese fleet, causing Spruance to put his battle plan into effect. He told Turner on the morning of 16 June that most unloading would have to be suspended on the evening of the seventeenth. Turner was to take his amphibians away to the east, out of the immediate danger zone, while Spruance fought the impending fleet action. Only enough ships to keep the Marines supplied with ammunition, medical care, and provisions were to remain off the beaches. After those unloaded, others were to be rotated in. Unlike the situation on Guadalcanal, when the amphibians began to clear Saipan on 18 June, they had not left the Marines short of supplies. More than 33,000 tons had been landed and many more were just over the horizon. Adequate fire support was a greater problem, with only one heavy cruiser and six destroyers remaining behind to answer calls.

Holland Smith was also ashore on the seventeenth. By then he was aware the battle was going to be harder than anyone thought. Casualties during the first two days had been twice the number expected and there was no replacement pool of marines available. Smith therefore wasted no time asking Turner to commit the 27th Infantry Division immediately.

With the Japanese fleet approaching, Spruance had already canceled the attack on Guam, but Turner still hesitated to release the Army division. Smith was insistent in his unique way, so the soldiers began going ashore on 18 June into line alongside the marines, joining a slugging match that lasted another twenty-three days.

While the marines and soldiers inched forward, Spruance's carriers fought the Battle of the Philippine Sea. His need to protect the amphibians thwarted the wishes of his carrier admirals for more offensive action, but Spruance would not be diverted from his responsibility to cover the amphibious force. Japanese naval air power went to its destruction in what the Americans labeled the Marianas Turkey Shoot. An airstrike launched at the limit of flying range inflicted some damage on the retreating Japanese fleet but the hoped-for destruction of the enemy task force did not occur. Nonetheless, the Imperial Navy was essentially toothless in the new era of carrier-based naval warfare. Consequently, Turner's amphibians could bend themselves to unloading without fear of enemy interference.

What interfered more was the nightly retirement to seaward to reduce supply ship exposure to air or submarine attack; the transports spent each night cruising the open sea. Ruthven Libby's destroyers were screening the transports, which brought him under Turner's scrutiny;

> One of my boys one night distinguished himself. We had just gotten formed up and just gotten well on our way out to sea . . . and Kelly Turner called me up on voice radio and said, "There's a hole in your screen." He had a better radar than I . . . and had spotted that there was a hole in the screen. [It was] pitch dark . . . you couldn't see anything. I called the guy who was supposed to be in the screen and I said, "Your station is thus and so." He came back indignantly, "I am in station thus and so." Still the hole persisted. So after half an hour of argument . . . he rather shame facedly called over and said, "Okay, I'm in the wrong formation." But then he came home.[33]

The screening destroyers did sink one Japanese submarine, but a greater nuisance were the constant air raids from the Carolines and enemy bases on Iwo Jima. Fortunately, the Japanese airmen got little more than an occasional hit. Smoke was employed on a large scale for the first time in the Pacific to screen the transport areas.

Kauffman's "frogmen," meanwhile, had blasted the wanted channel through the reef. They planted more than 5,000 charges, strung them together with primer cord, and fired them in one prolonged blast. The water column drenched Hill's flagship, causing the admiral to send for his demolition man. "I can remember going into Admiral Hill's cabin and dripping water all over his fine rug. Admiral Hill and I discussed the advisability of letting the task force commander know the next time I was going to fire a shot like that!"[34] Though LSTs could use the channel to beach, LVTs and DUKWs still did most of the unloading.

There was some confusion when the 27th Infantry Division landed but their immediate needs were met from Marine supply dumps ashore. Despite often being under small arms and artillery fire, beach and shore parties worked as planned, their organization greatly speeding the flow of materiel to front-line units. There were situations that never appeared in the press reports of the invasion. Many boats and their crews were left behind when Turner took away the amphibians to the east on 18 June. Their crews seemed to believe they had somehow become spectators to a grand show, as related by the captain of the cargo ship *Alcyone*:

> When this ship anchored off Saipan on 19 June for general unloading, dozens of empty idle boats were observed laying all over the anchorage. These boats were tied up in groups of two to six or more. Some were anchored, some drifting. The crews were swimming or bathing. Some few were seen to be cleaning their boats. Practically all of these boats were attached to ships not in port. During the afternoon this ship ran out of boats. Requests for additional boats brought no response. Therefore we rounded up several of these idle boats and put them to work.[35]

How hard they worked is evident in tonnage unloaded. According to a report filed by Holland Smith, Turner's men unloaded an average of 4,683 tons of supplies daily from 15 June until 20 July.[36]

Crucial to American success was the heavy volume of naval gunfire available. From 28 June through 2 July, the gunfire-support groups fired more than 1,165 tons of shells per day. One Japanese report lamented the problems caused by naval gunfire: "The practical experience of the defense forces of Saipan in this battle lasting over half a month lay in the power of the enemy naval bombardment. If there were just no naval gunfire, we feel we could fight it out with the enemy in a decisive battle." A prisoner of war stated that naval gunfire was the greatest single factor in the American success. Asked how he knew the difference between artillery and naval gunfire, he said, "it was not difficult when one was on the receiving end."[37]

Ammunition supply remained a constant problem for the support ships. They quickly used the extra supply brought with the assault force, forcing reliance on other expedients. Ships leaving the area transferred all but a small remainder of their ammunition to whatever ship was replacing them on the gun line. An ammunition ship arrived on 21 June, temporarily alleviating the situation. Five other shiploads left directly from the States, but before they arrived, the availability of naval and artillery ammunition had bordered on critical. Turner told the gunfire ships on 6 July that no reserves remained and the corps artillerymen heard on 7 July that no 105-mm ammunition remained in the dumps. All captains had strict orders not to waste any ammunition. Another gunfire-related problem was keeping the firing ships updated on the position of American units. The system of regimental and battalion liaison officers worked out ahead of time worked well, but naval gunfire hit American units on at least two occasions. One system that *didn't* work too well was close air support.

As noted, Holland Smith and every other Marine officer wanted Marine squadrons put aboard the carriers assigned to close air support. They had not yet been successful, but Saipan bolstered their argument. The complex system of liaison between the airmen and the infantry that was in place for Forager proved totally inadequate for delivering timely support. Requests from frontline units had to work their way back through battalions to regiments to division to the amphibious command ship lying offshore to the carriers providing support. An hour might pass before planes would appear to carry out the assigned mission only to discover a completely changed tactical situation. Nor did the marines on the ground consider the air support adequate when it was delivered. They contended that Navy fliers simply did not understand close air support nor had they been trained properly to assess the ground situation from the air. Aircraft rockets and napalm were first used in close support on Saipan with favorable results, but the Marines wanted more and better.

Holland Smith's ire with the Army finally overflowed during this campaign. His perceptions of the soldiers had not been good since he observed the performance of the 27th Infantry on Makin. Smith and the Marine Corps had also taken a severe public relations beating after Tarawa, when the press suggested that Army tactics were more sparing of American lives than those of the Marines. He had further to endure General Richardson's efforts to remove him from command of V Amphibious Corps, including before Forager began.

So it is no surprise that Smith believed the performance of the 27th Infantry Division was unsatisfactory. The Marine general made his displeasure known to the Army division commander, who agreed that his units were not performing well. There is no doubt the soldiers had poor leadership, but they also had to contend with heavy resistance and rough terrain. Nonetheless, when they could not keep up with the advance of the flanking Marine divisions, Holland Smith used the pretext of some conflicting orders issued by himself and Ralph Smith to relieve the Army man from his post.

A typhoon of accusations and counteraccusations blew across every level of command in the Pacific and back to Washington. This controversy was encouraged by the press, some of whom repeated the canard that Smith and his Marine tactics were wasteful of American lives.[38] Smith had the support of Spruance and was within his prerogatives as commander of a joint operation. Naturally, his detractors within the Army did not see the issue the same way and tried to show again that the Marines were not properly trained to command such a large expeditionary force. General Richardson stoked those fires by castigating Smith to his face and having a terrible row with Turner.

Nimitz, responsible for interservice relations in a huge theater of war, did his best to smooth things over. He refused to take sides and would not allow any derogatory remarks about the performance of the 27th Infantry Division to appear in any official report. Both King and Marshall stood by their respective commanders, but they also made it known to their subordinates that such a controversy should not have been allowed to develop.[39] However valuable he was, Holland Smith's cool relationship with Nimitz numbered his days as a combat commander.

On Saipan, the end came as it had before in other places and would in the future. The defenders were pushed steadily back, suffering grievous losses while inflicting severe casualties on the Americans. By 7 July, the enemy held only a small area; cohesion and control were fast slipping away from their garrison commander. He gave instructions for a suicide charge by every available man, with the aim of taking at least seven American lives for every Japanese. The screaming mass of about 3,000 doomed men smashed into Army lines early in the morning of 7 July. Before the soldiers contained the attack and annihilated the survivors, 451 more Americans were dead. Accounts differ, but the final toll for Saipan was more than 3,000 Americans killed in action and more than 11,000 wounded. Accounts again differ about Japanese casualties, but about 25,000 enemy soldiers were buried and thousands more entombed in caves blasted and sealed off. A picture was beginning to emerge of the probable cost to invade the Japanese homeland. More immediately, there were some changes in the Pacific command structure and there remained the problem of Tinian and Guam.

The first change had occurred before the troops landed on Saipan. With the Solomons conquest complete, Admiral Halsey was out of work. He was too experienced to languish in a backwater, so Nimitz decided to alternate him with Spruance in command of Central Pacific naval forces. While Spruance was on an operation, his forces were designated 5th Fleet. Then, Halsey and his staff would remain in Pearl Harbor planning the next operation. When Spruance finished his task, he would be relieved by Halsey and the task force renamed 3d Fleet.[40] Spruance and his staff would return to Pearl and begin the planning process all over. The other change involved Holland Smith.

The controversy engendered by his relief of an Army general remained an explosive issue that Nimitz correctly feared would resurface. To keep Smith's expertise at hand but remove him from the firing line, Nimitz named the Marine general commander of the Fleet Marine Force effective

12 July. Harry Schmidt took Smith's place as commander of V Phib Corps. Smith would participate in another assault but would thereafter be concerned mainly with training marines, kept away from any possible flash point with the Army. Smith's talent was manifest but his outspokenness and tenuous relationship with Nimitz had exacted a price.

FORAGER CONTINUED: JULY–AUGUST 1944

Both the approach of the Japanese fleet and heavy resistance on Saipan dictated postponement of the Guam invasion. The men of the 3d Marine Division and the 1st Marine Provisional Brigade were removed therefore from harm's way and returned to Eniwetok to await developments. They would spend a few days involved in rehearsals, but would essentially be confined to their ships for almost fifty days before going ashore on Guam. War diaries of the transports have the same entry, "at anchor," for seventeen days from 1 through 16 July. These troops endured a monotonous routine of head cleaning and mess duty, all carried out as the ships swung slowly at the hook under a blazing equatorial sun. Hot, slow days were followed by sweltering nights in the tightly packed living spaces.

Part of the delay was the time needed to bring forward the 77th Infantry Division from Hawaii. Spruance told Nimitz on 3 July that the Army unit would be necessary for the assault on Guam. Nimitz did not want to wait, warning Spruance that delaying would let the Japanese regain some of their balance. The 5th Fleet commander told Nimitz it was his prerogative to override recommendations from the field, but the Army unit was still needed for the assault to succeed. One of Nimitz's great strengths was to listen to his subordinates; he committed the 77th Infantry Division to the campaign, but he did move up the assault from 25 to 21 July.

The familiar sequence of softening up the Guam defenders began with air raids on 8 July. The airmen directed their efforts at the steady increase in fieldworks and pillboxes revealed by aerial photos. Photo interpreters did a daily damage assessment and recommended repeated strikes on a single position if necessary. Naval bombardment began the same day and continued for the next two weeks. The long-suffering troops from Eniwetok began their second run on 11 July, sure that this time they would see action. Admiral Conolly was the task force commander, flying his flag in the AGC *Appalachian*.

Since a fringing reef again blocked the beach approaches, large numbers of LVTs were needed to put the troops ashore. Kauffman's UDT men smoothed the path by blowing up more than 900 obstacles and planting flags designating cleared lanes to the beach. The landing began on the morning of 21 July across two sets of beaches. The enemy had anticipated that the beaches chosen were likely landing sites so they had sited strong defenses covering them. There was a well-developed system of infantry fighting positions protected by pillboxes and bunkers. The bombardment had taken out many of them but other enemy guns hidden in caves appeared and brought some beaches under fire. An inverted V of LCI(G)s led the landing craft to the beach. Even with this close-range suppressing fire, a few stout-hearted defenders continued to man their machine guns and began exacting a blood toll for possession of Guam.

Fortunately for the Americans, the volume of Japanese artillery fire was minuscule compared to what had fallen on the Saipan beaches. Not that enemy guns weren't in action: one battery was smashed by a destroyer that closed to "rock throwing" range. Enemy shells dropped desultorily and without the pinpoint accuracy previously experienced. The Marines would later gratefully acknowledge that the Japanese seemed unable to mass their field guns in the way preferred by the Americans. Mortar fire was much heavier and often deadly; several LVTs took hits and stopped right on the beach. The conduct of the *Wayne*'s doctor while under this fire was lauded by the beachmaster from another ship:

> The amount of mortar fire was terrific . . . there were [540] shells dropped on our beach between "H" hour and noon of "D" plus 1. Of these . . . over [300] landed within a radius of 300 yards of . . . where we were dug in. During this period the wounded came in a steady stream to Lieut. Kerman's evacuation station . . . while the rest of us sought the shelter of our foxholes, Lieut. Kerman, seemingly oblivious to his danger, continued his work on casualties in the open.[41]

The weight of the assault could not be denied; almost 55,000 marines and soldiers landed quickly, followed by thousands of tons of materiel. There was no rest for the amphibians that first night, as Conolly ordered unloading to continue nonstop. As at Saipan, a contingent of tracked cranes sat astride the reef to swing cargo loads into LVTs and DUKWs. The former vehicles proved especially valuable because the amphibious trucks were able to reach only one beach due to the large number of coral heads, potholes in the reef, and a heavy accumulation of silt that bogged them down.

The 22–24 July War Diary of the *Zeilin*, long a veteran of the amphibious wars, shows a three-day span of hard work beginning early in the morning and ceasing late in the evening. Other ships came alongside at regular intervals to transfer casualties aboard, receive fuel, pick up equipment, replenish water supplies, and discharge ammunition. The *Zeilin* and her sisters unloaded 20,000 tons of supplies during the first four days of the operation.[42] The steady movement of so much materiel across the beaches was helped in no small part by the three assault units with a combined total of 9,681 men in their respective shore parties. One lesson of the amphibious war had momentarily been taken to heart.

The fight for Guam lasted almost three weeks. Difficulties with close air support persisted, including slow response time and accidental bombing of friendly troops. On the other hand, naval gunfire support was managed smoothly, with quick response and accurate fire. Star shells were in such short supply that the destroyers assigned to fire support had authority to illuminate with searchlights. After-action reports show that supplies were available to the Marines in adequate quantities; there was never a shortage of small arms ammunition. The Japanese fought desperately but the amount of firepower arrayed against them was overwhelming. Bitter memories of 1941 were partly assuaged by a flag-raising on the former site of the Marine barracks; colors sounded on a captured Japanese bugle made the ceremony complete.

American casualties came to 1,744 killed and 5,648 wounded. Almost 11,000 Japanese were buried and hundreds more killed after the island was declared "secure" on 11 August. The LCI gunboats stayed busy for weeks afterward, patrolling the shoreline and assisting the Marines as they tracked down the many bands of Japanese stragglers roaming the island. The War Diary of LCI(G) 466 has an entry for 3 September that from the vantage point of fifty years later is a sad vignette of the war. The ship embarked four Marine officers and set out for her patrol area off the northern tip of Guam:

> At 1640 sighted single naked Jap soldier on reef. He remained fixed in his tracks and seemed very frightened. After futile attempts to get him to surrender, the order from the Marines was to attempt to kill him. We fired a few shots around the Jap hoping he would surrender. This action caused him to make a dash for a nearby cave. He was killed by our starboard 20-mm gun at the close range of 200 yards. The body washed to seaward the next day.[43]

Cultural differences and a bitterly fought war would not allow a man to surrender even when confronted by a heavily armed enemy ship only 200 yards away.

The fight for Guam was well under way when the last element of Forager swung into motion. Tinian lay only 3 miles off the south coast of Saipan; planners wanted its flat expanse for bomber bases. They envisioned the attack as a shore-to-shore movement, launched from Saipan. Preparations began shortly after the landing on Saipan; some American artillery employed there began lobbing shells into Tinian on 21 June. As more resources became available, the volume of fire grew correspondingly. Army fighter-bombers based on Saipan made their contribution to the bombardment, as did the Navy from offshore. There weren't as many Japanese on Tinian nor were they as heavily armed with artillery as the defenders of Saipan. Nevertheless, Turner was determined that the first two days of Saipan would not be repeated on Tinian. One big decision facing the Americans was the choice of landing beaches.

Area view of reconnaissance photos showed only two places considered adequate. One was so obvious that the bulk of the enemy's defenses was concentrated there. Holland Smith favored the second, but it was so narrow Turner didn't believe the job could be done. A tremendous argument followed between Turner and Smith during a visit by the admiral to Smith's HQ on Saipan. According to a witness, Turner told the Marine he would not land the troops on the narrow beaches. Smith's reply was to the point: "Oh yes you will . . . you'll land me any goddamned place I tell you to. All you have to do is tell me whether or not you can put my troops ashore there." The argument continued, with Turner insisting the beaches were inadequate and Smith insisting they were fine. Since the dispute was being conducted over an open bottle, it grew more heated as it went along.

Turner attempted to downplay the value of a planned reconnaissance by a team of Marines and Navy UDT personnel. "They don't know what to look for. They're just a bunch of Marines. People will laugh at you, Holland, if you keep on talking about this idea. They'll think you're just a stupid old bastard." To which Smith replied in kind, "These recon people are better at this than anything you've got. They've had plenty of experience and they've proved themselves before. You don't want them to go over there because you're afraid I'll be right." Turner attempted to close the argument by saying he had had enough and would not land on the beaches of Smith's choosing. The Marine would not be deterred:

> You ought to know by now that you can't bluff me Kelly. You've tried it plenty of times before and you've never succeeded yet. . . . You know goddamned well that it's my business and none of yours to say where we'll land. If you say you won't put us ashore I'll fight you all the way . . . I'll take it up with Spruance, and if necessary with Nimitz. Now just put that down in your goddamned book.[44]

Turner stormed back to the *Rocky Mount*, but soon after that announced the landing would be across the beaches chosen by Smith.

The reconnaissance had shown that a landing would be at risk because of the beaches' narrowness and some overlooking high ground favorable to the defenders. However, the beaches were weakly defended and a properly managed landing would undoubtedly catch the enemy off guard. After Saipan was finally secured, preparations went ahead at a faster pace though both Marine divisions had to reorganize and refit. The assault force needed thirty-seven LSTs to lift the troops and their LVTs. There were more than

100 DUKWs in support and another ninety-plus LCMs that would bring tanks and artillery to Tinian. The troops themselves were to travel light, unburdened with packs. There were to be no beach dumps that might cause congestion and the shore party's main job was to keep traffic flowing across the beach. Throughout the preparations, artillery, air, and naval guns kept Tinian under constant fire. Veteran amphibious commander Harry Hill had everything ready by 24 July.

The day began with a fake, diversionary landing staged off the beaches favored by Turner. With a gunfire-support group providing a backdrop, landing craft approached the beach close enough to draw Japanese mortar fire before retiring. The defenders were wrong in thinking they had "repulsed" a landing, but they were not wrong in thinking they had struck some heavy blows against the gunfire-support force. A carefully concealed 6-in. battery opened up suddenly and ripped the battleship *Colorado* with twenty-two hits, causing heavy casualties. The real landing force was meanwhile approaching the two beaches, one 60 yards wide and the other 160, chosen by Holland Smith.

Unlike the landing on Saipan, nearly everything went according to plan. Resistance was slight; more casualties came from exploding mines than gunfire. The landing force pushed off the beaches as planned, quickly followed by tanks and artillery-laden DUKWs. A specially designed ramp mounted on several LVTs proved instrumental in getting wheeled vehicles over the terrace that skirted the beaches. More than 15,000 marines landed with all the supplies and ammunition to fight the battle. Shore fire-control parties also benefited from their experience at Saipan; coordination with the gunfire-support ships was much better, resulting in quicker responses to calls for fire.

Bad weather flared up on 28 July, closing the beaches to landing craft. A squadron of Army C-47 transports came up from Eniwetok in case an airlift of supplies was needed, but the weather abated soon enough. More Marine tanks were employed on Tinian than in any previous operation, which helped keep casualties low. The Marines declared the island secure on 1 August, at the cost of 328 Americans and 5,000 Japanese.

The amphibians had brought the war to the Japanese castle wall; War Minister Tojo resigned in shame after the Marianas fell. Many in the political hierarchy were thereafter convinced that the war itself was irretrievably lost. Unfortunately, Japanese military men were stuck in the cultural trap of being unable to consider surrender. The amphibians' war would go on.

The assessment of what had worked and what hadn't began before Forager was over. Volumes of reports followed, containing more than a few suggestions for improvements. Harry Hill recommended establishing a team to decide whether air, naval guns, or artillery should take on a particular target. The skipper of the *Calvert* suggested one way of keeping boat crews from "getting beyond the reach of discipline" was for them to tie up to any available LST or LCT when unloading secured for the night. The *Alcyone*'s skipper suggested that a boat control officer be designated, responsible for rounding up unoccupied boats and assigning them to ships in need.

Control of gunfire support came in for some comments from the battleship *California*. Her captain suggested that "Shore Fire-Control Parties still do not appreciate fire-control problems of fire-support ships nor the fact that [the] amount of ammunition carried by one ship is limited." His ship had answered a call for "full salvos as rapidly as possible" with 1,399 rounds of 5-in. fire. His objection was that the fire control party had provided no spots nor information about the effectiveness of the fire. The mission was, he believed, "an unwarranted expenditure of ammunition."[45] The number of Japanese defensive positions that survived the bombardment inevitably led to calls for a longer period of shelling. The report of the 1st Provisional Brigade suggested that 10,000 rounds of shellfire spread out over thirty days probably would be more effective than the same amount of fire delivered in two days.[46] More than one marine suggested seven to ten days. They wanted not only more days, but a higher proportion of high-capacity ammunition to blast away enemy camouflage.

Political battles are revealed in Marine calls for better close air support. The Marines suggested that Army pilots were superior to Navy fighter bombers in delivering support because they understood the ground problem better than the naval fliers. The familiar plaint about poor radios was heard again with the usual call for better waterproofing. The Marines also wanted more replacement flame throwers provided because the equipment was easily damaged. Maps of the landing beaches were held to be inaccurate, forcing the troops to depend on Japanese maps when they had them.

Loading drew attention in requests for each major unit to establish a command post at dockside to monitor loading. All Marine reports were unanimous in complaining that the number of vehicles brought along was totally inadequate. One also suggested that more spare tires be provided for the DUKWs, with a greater allowance for repair equipment for the LVTs. The relative merits of palletizing were discussed; the captain of the *Harris* believing the need to stack pallets made loading more difficult unless there was adequate room for a forklift. A possible unloading expedient was suggested by the *Sumter*'s captain when he requested that hoisting straps be left in place on vehicles after they were stowed in the holds. Given the frontline experience of his men on Saipan, he also wanted the beach and shore parties to have more infantry training.[47]

The large number of casualties experienced at Saipan strained medical facilities and caused concern among medical personnel. One writer thought the portion of medical supplies allocated to "emergency" loads was insufficient. Another report noted that the large number of casualties lying on the beach unnerved survivors and contributed to the straggler problem. The *Wayne*'s chaplain suggested that boats carrying wounded from the beach should be provided with tarpaulins to protect them from rain and spray. Psychological problems also cropped up. Some veterans felt they had been asked to do more than their share and in one group of twenty-seven slightly injured men brought to the *Harris*, only two volunteered to return to their units.[48]

Not all the after-battle comments involved changes or problems of such gravity; the eternal war of fighting men against paperwork was voiced by the captain of the *Sumter*: "It may be frankly stated that reports caused this command far more worry, nerve strain, and trouble than enemy air attacks or unloading problems."[49]

All these suggestions received their share of attention, especially the need for better close air support. In September, King would finally give way to the steadfast advocacy of the Marines for their own air support and agree to the assignment of Marine squadrons to four escort carriers. The need for changes had to be balanced against the fact that offensive pressure against the Japanese had to be maintained. Operation Forager had reinforced the need not to allow the enemy time to thicken defenses of the islands still under his control. At the same time, the high cost of the landings in the Central Pacific again brought to center stage Douglas MacArthur and the question of strategy.

A MATTER OF COST

While Central Pacific forces were getting most of the headlines during the summer of 1944, MacArthur's amphibious forces were making two more of their unspectacular but efficient advances. The first took place in July when Admiral Barbey's VII Phib quietly seized Noemfoor Island, 75 miles farther up the New Guinea coast from Biak. Planes based at Noemfoor could interdict the supply route to Biak, where the fight for that island was taking longer than expected. A small assault force built around the 158th Regimental Combat Team assembled and, after several delays, made ready to land on 2 July. As usual, the infantry rode in LSTs and LCIs. There was no naval air cover available, but there were enough Army fighters. Despite the ever-increasing disparity between Japanese and Allied air strength, logistic planning derived from the need to keep supply loads in the assault shipping small enough to be unloaded in one day. The 6th Infantry Division was tapped to provide 800 men, 100 per LST, for unloading details. There was some difficulty getting everything coordinated, but the Operation Cyclone assault force drew up off Noemfoor on the morning of 2 July.

There were fewer than 2,000 Japanese on the island, but they were the recipients of as heavy a bombardment as three cruisers and ten destroyers could deliver. The Air Force also contributed a healthy dose of bombs before the landing craft pushed off. The landing occurred on the beaches expected by the Japanese, but the bombardment had done its job; resistance was nonexistent, allowing the LVTs to deliver the infantry in good order. Artillery quickly went ashore by the now-familiar method of specially equipped DUKWs, while causeways just as quickly bridged the reef. Practice and organization got 8,000 men and all their supplies ashore before the day was over. The garrison held out until 10 July, but when the guns stopped, another 1,730 Japanese and only 63 American servicemen were dead. The planners were already preparing the next move.

This target was the Sansapor area of the Vogelkop peninsula; bombers from its airfields could reach Mindanao, the planned entry point for MacArthur's return to the Philippines. Planning for Operation Typhoon began 8 July with a projected landing date of 30 July. Loading out the assault force, drawn from the 6th Infantry Division, was complicated by the amount of engineer equipment needed to build the desired airfields. Heavy rains were an impediment as was the need for the assault troops to load supplies. The assault force met the departure schedule despite these problems and 7,300 infantrymen landed against no opposition. Unloading was delayed somewhat by the Army's insistence on pallet loading the LSTs, a practice Barbey's men had warned against.[50] The engineers quickly began working on the airfields while the planners looked at their charts and contemplated the last two small islands lying on the route to Mindanao.

Before it could be decided where the next landing would be, Marshall summoned MacArthur to Pearl Harbor to discuss strategy. MacArthur had always been loath to leave his headquarters, preferring to send subordinates or to have conferees come to him. Nor would he willingly have gone to Pearl that summer of 1944 save for Marshall's direct order. The difference then was that Franklin Roosevelt was calling the conference.

In an election year, Roosevelt wanted to be seen as an active commander in chief. But he was also reacting to MacArthur's continuing insistence that an offensive through the Philippines represented the best way to defeat Japan. The general had again raised the issue in early July, only to be refuted by Nimitz. Hewing to King's favorite line, Nimitz agreed Mindanao should be seized, but argued that the remainder of the Philippines could be bypassed while the main effort focused on Formosa and the Chinese coast. The president thought the best way for the argument to be settled was for all parties to meet in Pearl late in July to make their respective cases. King flew out to the Pacific earlier in the month, visited Saipan and Guam with Nimitz, made sure he and his subordinate were of the same mind, and returned to Washington before the president arrived.

Despite a theatrical entrance by MacArthur, all present were forced to admit that he was eloquent in his presentation of the need to seize the Philippines in their entirety. He not only insisted the honor and future prestige of the United States in the Pacific was at stake, but insinuated that the Central Pacific offensive had been the result of outdated thinking that needlessly wasted of American lives. Seizing the Philippines would be decisive and less costly. Furthermore, MacArthur held that even as powerful as American forces had become, there was no way both avenues could be followed. The president issued no orders nor did he express a preference. MacArthur nonetheless flew back to Australia convinced he had won his case and thereby direction of the war in the Pacific.

In reality, Roosevelt left the decision up to the Joint Chiefs. Marshall took MacArthur's side while King remained adamant enough about the value of Formosa to order Nimitz to begin preparing for operations. The JCS could not come to a definitive decision so they prepared a tentative timetable that gave them leeway to choose later. They did accept enough of what MacArthur said to schedule a landing on Leyte for 20 December. When Nimitz asked Spruance for an opinion, he said he preferred taking Iwo Jima and Okinawa. Two operations that would cost the amphibious forces and the fleet that protected them dearly were unknowingly given their genesis.

As the summer of 1944 lengthened, the amphibians' war continued unabated. The battles in the Marianas were winding down, but several others were in various planning stages. In the South Pacific, Barbey's sailors were about to take an Army assault force to Morotai Island. In the Central Pacific, Wilkinson's III Phib was figuring out the final details of an assault on the islands of Peleliu and Angaur. In the not-too-distant background lay the upcoming move to Mindanao and the likelihood of another fleet action. In the Mediterranean, the final act of the amphibious war was being played out on the beaches of southern France, where a hotly argued operation took place 15 August.

8

THE AMPHIBIANS ASCENDANT

"It took me only 30 or 40 long strides to reach dry land, but that was one of the most meaningful walks I ever took."

GEN. DOUGLAS MACARTHUR

DRAGOON: DECEMBER 1943–AUGUST 1944

The landing that eventually became known as Dragoon began life as Operation Anvil. Eisenhower originally conceived the plan as a good way to use Allied forces in the Mediterranean. An assault on southern France would necessarily draw German attention from the English Channel, forcing them to split available forces. British resistance to the landing was palpable but Marshall agreed with his subordinate. The Combined Chiefs instructed Eisenhower to begin planning in December 1943; his headquarters issued the first directive on the 28th. Eisenhower subsequently moved to England to take over the helm of Overlord, but the problems associated with Anvil could not be left behind. The primary and overriding problem was too little shipping. As the scale of Overlord increased from a three- to a five-division assault, the ships for carrying these additional troops had to come mostly from the Mediterranean. Eisenhower was forced to admit that Anvil could not be carried out simultaneously. Shipping was not his only headache.

Churchill, and especially Alan Brooke, did not favor the landing. The prime minister fervently wanted operations in the Balkans, believing them far more profitable than another landing in France. Because the assault troops needed for Anvil would have to be removed from the Italian front, he was even less in favor of the operation. Led by Marshall, the Americans refused even to contemplate operations in the Balkans, insisting Anvil was essential to secure additional ports through which the armies could be supplied. Try as he might, Churchill could not sway his allies from the concept, something he would try to do as late as a week before the scheduled landing. According to legend, he ordered the operation renamed Dragoon in honor of his unwilling acceptance.

While the politicians and strategists fought their battles, the operating forces did what they had to to finalize the plan. British commanders had replaced Americans at the top in the Mediterranean, but Kent Hewitt remained and was the logical choice for naval commander. Initial planning took place in Algiers during the late winter and early spring of 1944. The planning effort had an added dimension: American and British ships would lift the assault force, but the operation also included French units for the first time. American infantry would make the assault but six to seven French divisions would follow up. Who would land first was a sensitive issue with which Hewitt had to deal:

> The French—and you couldn't blame them—were very, very anxious to be the first to land on their own soil. General Delan was very strong for that. I had to convince him . . . that it was hard enough to get soldiers and sailors working together in the same boat in the first place, but with the language barrier it would be absolutely impossible. Fortunately, I had my friend Admiral Lemonnier to back me up on that.[1]

American troops would land first with the French divisions in the immediate follow-up. French ships would also share in bombardment and gunfire-support duties. First thoughts were to form gunfire-support groups by nationality so each could be comfortable with common operating doctrine. The need to parcel out available ships to bring sufficient fire against the defenses caused that plan to be scrapped. Another difficulty was assembling and training the assault troops.

Three American infantry divisions, the 3d, 36th, and 45th, were picked to make the assault. They had to be removed from the Italian battle front, brought south to the Naples/Salerno area, refitted, rested, and given refresher training in amphibious warfare. There was the ever-present problem of collecting enough ships to meet the lift requirements; the success of Overlord fortunately released both transports and gunfire-support units to Dragoon.[2] They were joined throughout the summer by reinforcements from the States; in June alone, forty-seven LSTs and LCIs arrived in the theater. Headquarters moved to Naples in July to be near the training area established at Salerno.

Hewitt had by then assembled his three task force commanders, Rear Admirals Lowry, Moon, and Bertram Rodgers. Rodgers was a newcomer to amphibious warfare but not to combat. His skill at the conn of the heavy cruiser *Salt Lake City* saved the day for an American task force at the Battle of the Komandorski Islands in March 1943. Admirals Lowry and Moon had done Anzio and Utah Beach, respectively. What the three officers were being asked to do was make an assault into an area where the enemy expected just such an attack.

German strength in southern France was no secret thanks to Ultra. But they had been occupying the area since November 1942 and had taken the time to add to defenses built earlier by the French. There was a minimal tidal range that made beach obstacles more difficult to clear. Intelligence knew minefields existed in profusion and that many gun positions overlooked the beaches. Because the Germans built more emplacements than they occupied, careful study was done of aerial photos to decide which posed the greatest threat. An arbitrary scale was conceived that weighted each position according to its potential danger to the landing zone. This weighted score determined the number of fire-support ships assigned.

The planners worried because the ammunition available for bombardment was limited. Hewitt prevailed upon the Army to accept a daylight landing so the bombardment could be delivered with maximum effect. A new device, an LCVP loaded with 8,000 lb of explosives and remotely controlled, was devised to destroy obstacles. Known as Apex boats, they would precede the landing craft and blow lanes through the minefields and obstacles.

For the first time in the Mediterranean, there was an abundance of air cover and close support available. The Air Force and the Navy were singularly and together to contribute air support. Seven CVEs, five British and two American, were available to provide the naval air contingent. The Army ground commanders argued against bombing in the invasion zone, saying it would alert the Germans to the attack. Hewitt's planners countered that old argument by pointing out surprise would be impossible to achieve, even in the face of cursory observation by the enemy. Together with the Air Force, they worked out a comprehensive program of pre-landing bombing aimed at softening up the defenses and isolating the battlefield from reinforcements. Air Force officers participated in the planning and were included in Hewitt's shipboard staff. Two LSTs had GCI radar mounted to guide fighters over the task force and a fighter direction tender would keep the air picture under control. In a reversal of his comments after Husky, Hewitt would later praise the airmen's performance.

Ground troop training began in earnest in July and continued throughout the month. One training device was rubber topographical models of each landing area. A shop had been established in the Navy Department that could put any requested model into the hands of the troops within two weeks of the request. Assault and service troops from all three divisions participated in comprehensive exercises. Beach and shore parties functioned as they were intended. New radios made naval gunfire control far easier than two years previously and experienced coxswains landed and retracted their landing craft with an ease born of practice and experience. The large body of accumulated experience bore fruit, because nowhere in the records is there mention of a "fiasco" or similar language.

The amphibious task force that headed north from Naples in mid-August had already suffered one casualty. Admiral Moon had commanded the assault force at Utah Beach; he then transferred to the Mediterranean, where he threw himself into preparations for Dragoon. After his experience off Normandy, he firmly believed the operation should not be launched until every possible contingency had been covered. He therefore asked Hewitt for a postponement, a request Hewitt denied. The strain of overwork and the worry that his men might suffer as badly as those at Omaha Beach proved too much; Moon committed suicide in his cabin aboard the *Bayfield* on 5 August. Hewitt replaced him with his own chief of staff, Rear Adm. Spencer Lewis. Like the engine of war it was, Dragoon plowed on inexorably.

The six different task forces of the invasion fleet proceeded toward southern France from ports and locations as widely spread as Algiers and Corsica. Scheduling, no less complex for having been done before, was arranged well enough for all the different groups to be in their proper positions before sunrise the morning of 15 August. Hewitt and the Army commander, Maj. Gen. Alexander Patch, were in the AGC *Catoctin*. Another reason for the AGC is illustrated by the roll of staff officers; there were 438 Navy, Army, and Allied staff personnel on her.

A multitude of minesweepers, some even converted to use German gear, moved inshore to clear the way. Several commando-type operations took place to seize German batteries, one of which proved to be so-called Quaker guns. A small German convoy had the misfortune to encounter some destroyers of the screen and paid the price. The sound and fury of the day began at 0550 when the first waves of bombers swept in to deposit their loads on defenses. A naval bombardment followed at 0606, some of which was spotted by planes launched from the battleships and cruisers.

Of three separate landing areas, resistance at two was minimal. The combination of air bombing, naval gunfire, and low-grade troops manning the surviving defenses allowed the assault waves to get ashore without much trouble. Some naval gunfire was directed by control officers lying just offshore in LCCs, but shore fire-control parties quickly set up and established contact with the support ships. Machine gun and artillery fire impeded progress in the third area, but in no event was the resistance anywhere near the scale of Normandy. One holdup was that all of the explosive-laden Apex boats didn't work as planned. One detonated inadvertently close aboard a control ship, causing severe damage. Another circled, out of control, in front of an oncoming wave of landing craft. The boats had to be held at the line of departure until the errant drone could be brought under fire and detonated. Difficulties in placing the others where needed limited their usefulness.

The Luftwaffe tried to disrupt the landing, but the fighter direction tender handled the CAP efficiently. Smoke was also employed, as was the budding area of electronics countermeasures. A watch was established on the known frequencies of German radio-controlled bombs when enemy aircraft were in the area. As soon as an aircraft bomb-directing transmitter came up, several ships began transmitting a jamming signal. Only one ship was hit, and she was a total loss. Hewitt had also insisted on strict rules governing the use of AA fire—the tragedy of Husky was not forgotten. As he noted in his Action Report, however, "The education of 40mm and 20mm gunners is not yet completed."[3] Gunners in the smaller ships tended to open up despite the established safety height and often far beyond effective range. The *Charles Carroll* was hit by several 20-mm shells during one fusillade loosed by "uneducated" gunners, but suffered no serious damage.

Unloading was carried out efficiently and quickly. The *Carroll* had her load of soldiers and vehicles ashore by 2010 with the aid of two British LCTs. Beach parties also worked efficiently, as did the engineers in clearing exits from the beaches. The *Carroll* was ready to leave the invasion area by 0130 on 16 August, in company with all the other transports that had finished unloading.[4] A similar scene was played out with the gunfire-support ships over the next few days; the need for gunfire support declined rapidly as the Army advanced inland. In the nine days immediately after the assault, the amphibs landed 172,569 men and 98,328 tons of supplies. Follow-up supplies continued to land across the beaches for several weeks. The amphibious war in the Mediterranean closed with a stunning success.

The Navy remained active in supporting the war against Germany— LCTs would unload millions of tons of supplies in captured ports. Navy landing craft also would carry troops across the Rhine the following spring. Operation Dragoon was the final effort of the European amphibious war that began off Casablanca in November 1942. The experienced sailors who had fought the war across the Mediterranean were soon to be transferred to the Pacific, where their expertise could be put to good use. It was also the last battle for Kent Hewitt, who had gone from training landing craft crewmen to one of the most accomplished amphibious commanders of the Navy. This winding up of one facet of the war was matched in a way by the high-level conference that convened in Quebec early in September.

OCTAGON TO STALEMATE: SEPTEMBER 1944

The meeting in Canada between Roosevelt and Churchill that began 11 September differed from other summits in that there were no far-reaching strategic problems pressing for resolution. Political issues filled most of the agenda, but King continued to ruffle British feathers. Churchill offered to send the British battle fleet to the Pacific, an idea in which King had no interest. Roosevelt accepted, much to King's dismay. That same evening, a series of messages arrived that directly affected the amphibious war in the Pacific.

Halsey's fast carriers had been raiding Japanese bases in the Carolines, Palaus, and Philippines in support of upcoming landings. When far lighter opposition than expected met the air raids, Halsey advised Nimitz that Mindanao should be bypassed and the landing on Leyte advanced. He was confident the carriers could provide necessary air support. Nimitz immediately made an offer to MacArthur of an amphibious task force then preparing to seize Yap Island in the Carolines. MacArthur was at sea enroute to Morotai Island but his chief of staff quickly accepted the offer and the Joint Chiefs were so informed. The message arrived during a formal dinner from which the Chiefs excused themselves. After a brief period to mull over the proposal, they sent their Pacific commanders a new set of directives that decided the final course of the war. The landing on Yap was canceled, as was the one on Mindanao. Leyte was to be attacked no later than 20 October. With Leyte in hand, Luzon was the logical next target and one that obviated any need to seize Formosa. The idea that the Chinese would prove to be important in the final defeat of Japan also gave its last wan flicker. Before operations against the Philippines could begin, however, there remained the landings on Morotai, Peleliu, and Angaur.

Part of the Molucca Islands, Halmahera and Morotai lie approximately midway on the 650-mile line from the northwestern tip of New Guinea to the southeastern tip of Mindanao. MacArthur's planners wanted to eliminate the Japanese air bases there to protect lines of communication to the Philippines and to base their own planes supporting the upcoming invasion. Halmahera had originally been targeted, but when Nimitz told MacArthur that fewer amphibious ships would be available than originally thought, Morotai became the substitute. It had a smaller garrison, would take fewer troops to seize and thus have a lesser chance of delaying the assault on Mindanao.

To assault an estimated garrison of 500 Japanese, Barbey's VII Phib got the job of lifting 28,000 combat troops from the 31st Infantry Division and 126th Regimental Combat Team. The assault troops would be followed by another 40,200 service troops whose job it would be to quickly prepare the necessary airfields. Barbey again had no transports but did have an armada of smaller landing ships. Four cruisers and ten destroyers provided fire support with air support from six CVEs. The troops rehearsed during the first week in September and started out on the eighth. Despite the greatly weakened state of Japanese air power and the knowledge that the garrison was very small, the task force steered a roundabout course to arrive unexpected at the target. The precautions seem somewhat out of place given that there was neither a prelanding bombardment nor air bombing. Nonetheless, the troops landed on 15 September without casualties. The last of the Japanese garrison managed to survive until the first week in October, but the issue was never in doubt. Far more costly was the assault on the Palau Islands of Peleliu and Angaur.

The Palaus are the westernmost of the huge Caroline chain. MacArthur and Nimitz believed the islands must be seized to prevent Japanese aircraft based there from attacking the right flank of MacArthur's sea lanes into the Philippines. American aircraft based in the Palaus could support operations in the Philippines and would further prevent the Japanese from sending air reinforcements to their bypassed bases in the Carolines. Halsey disagreed with Nimitz's assessment, holding that the cost of seizing the islands would far outweigh any possible benefit. Furthermore, Japanese strength had been so reduced and the American ability to keep their bases pounded down so expanded that the enemy airfields in the Palaus were no real threat. Nimitz didn't agree; in July he issued orders for the seizure of Peleliu and Angaur, the two southernmost islands of the Palaus. The assault had the name Operation Stalemate.[5]

The Japanese had controlled the Palaus since the end of World War I. Like the Marshalls, little was known about their defenses. They had long been in the backwater of the war, but the Japanese began sending reinforcements early in 1944 as the American advance gathered headway. Most preparations centered on the islands of Babelthuap and Koror, where the Japanese thought the Americans were most likely to land. Fortunately for the Americans, there were competing Imperial Navy and Army commanders in the Palaus. They proved unable to put aside their service differences and competed for building materials, slowing down defensive preparations. Nonetheless, two veteran regiments moved from Babelthuap to beef up the defenses of Peleliu and Angaur. The soldiers arrived in April 1944, whereupon the Army garrison commander put them to work on an intensive construction program. Japanese defensive strategy underwent a change in July, when Imperial General Headquarters decided to concentrate the heaviest defenses away from the beach. Breaking up the landing at the waterline remained a goal, but denying the Americans use of the island and tying up large numbers of their troops became paramount.

The Americans planning the assault did not yet know about these changes in Japanese tactics. Through a windfall of documents captured in the Marianas, though, they did have an accurate picture of enemy strength in the Palaus. Peleliu and Angaur were known to have garrisons of 10,500 and 1,400 men, respectively. The 1st Marine Division under Maj. Gen. William Rupertus would take Peleliu and the 81st Infantry Division under Maj. Gen. Paul Mueller got the Angaur job.

Julian Smith pressed for a change in the original plan, which scheduled the Angaur landing first, with Peleliu following once Angaur seemed in hand. Smith argued that since reinforcements could be funneled from Babelthuap down through Peleliu, the latter island should be seized first, effectively cutting off Angaur. His argument won out; the assault on Peleliu would take place first. The Army division would be held in reserve off Peleliu until General Rupertus thought the situation ashore was under control. The soldiers would then be released to carry out their assault on Angaur. Admiral Wilkinson's III Phib got the task of landing both divisions; Wilkinson would direct the landing on Angaur while Rear Adm. George Fort would handle Peleliu.

Planning the Peleliu attack was difficult for several reasons. Julian Smith and his staff did the initial planning, but the corps commander assigned to control the landings was Maj. Gen. Roy Geiger. Geiger and his staff were still busy on Guam so more responsibility than usual fell on Rupertus's divisional staff. Uncertainties about the availability of shipping kept loading plans in constant flux; Halsey notified all commands that each ship would be expected to carry its maximum authorized load. Training also brought out its share of problems.

The 1st Marine Division had fought two hard campaigns, the first on Guadalcanal, the second on Bougainville. Many marines believed they deserved a long rest. Instead, they got an influx of replacements and a primitive camp on Pavuvu Island in the Solomons, into which, to make it habitable, they had to devote considerable backbreaking work. The island was not big enough for a division-sized encampment plus adequate training areas so exercises were severely restricted. Shortages of equipment were many, including arrival of some small arms ammunition that was badly corroded. One LVT battalion trained with vehicles carrying a 37-mm gun only to have them replaced just before embarkation with models carrying a 75-mm gun.

Much of the preparation had become commonplace through previous practice but some new wrinkles were added for Operation Stalemate. The Marines would be taking the first flame-throwing LVTs into action as well as an experimental model of a flame-throwing tank. The almost total lack of infantry replacements on Saipan led to the creation of two provisional rifle companies that would start out as part of the shore party. These men would be detailed to line companies as need arose. A field depot would take over management of all supply dumps, centralizing control over supplies. Twenty-four barges were in the shipping load, several to serve as floating supply dumps just off the reef. Two would be floating service stations for LVTs and DUKWs, marked with a conspicuous sign saying "GAS." Others were to be loaded with essential supplies and have large markings that told LVT drivers what was aboard.

Air support was available in adequate strength—plans were put into motion to keep the islands under steady aerial bombardment by land-based planes and fast carriers. Other carriers were available to provide close air support and a Marine air wing was scheduled to arrive once the airfield on Peleliu was operational. Naval bombardment would be carried out by a task force consisting of five battleships, eight cruisers, and fourteen destroyers. The planners scheduled only two days of firing, which quickly brought complaints. In view of what had just happened in the Marianas, General Rupertus believed the bombardment was too short and made his dissatisfaction known. He wanted four days of bombardment; he got the original two day's allotment of ammunition spread out over three.

Navy confidence that a two-day bombardment was adequate stemmed from what proved to be a faulty premise. Air and submarine photos were available in profusion. Practiced photo interpreters picked out the installations they could discern and drew up a target list that seemed consistent with a two-day bombardment. What they didn't know or suspect was the scale of defenses they could not detect. Peleliu was heavily wooded with very rough terrain. The Japanese had skillfully used natural cover and terrain to construct a warren of interlocking positions, most of which were invisible from the air. All would provide unpleasant surprises to the Marines.

Administrative and logistical difficulties were sorted out as well as they would be by the end of August. The 81st Infantry Division went south from Hawaii to Guadalcanal to join the task force gathering in the Solomons. The combined assault force included the AGCs *Mount Olympus* and *Mount McKinley*. The task groups of the assault force rendezvoused at sea on 14 September as they began to approach Peleliu. The bombardment group meanwhile had preceded the amphibians and done what it could to blast an entry. The defenders chose not to fire on the bombardment ships. On the other hand, they did their best with small arms and machine gun fire to kill the UDT teams clearing the many mines and obstacles obstructing the beaches. The demolition men were successful; the bombardment ships were not. Because the Japanese refrained from exposing their hidden gun positions, the bombardment group ceased fire early in the mistaken belief that there were no more targets worthy of attention.

The assault on Peleliu began as scheduled on 15 September. Some defenders died under the bombardment, some were stunned. Most of the rest left the safety of their bombproof caves and shelters to man their well-sited guns. As the assault waves neared the beach, they began to take an increasing volume of fire. A scene already played out at Tarawa and Saipan was repeated; there were too many assault craft to stop all of them, but many were blasted and torn by Japanese shells. Marines got ashore on both sets of landing beaches, though at a heavy cost.

The fire aimed at the assault troops did more than kill and wound men. Beaches began to clutter with disabled tractors and men trying to dig in lower than their buttons. The beach party from the *Wayne* got ashore and immediately dug foxholes. They stayed in their holes for most of the first day because the beachhead was only 150 yards deep. The ship's Action Report notes that one enemy battery delivered sixteen four-gun salvos per hour onto the beachhead for twenty-two hours before being knocked out.[6]

Another hazard to movement was the large number of mines on the beaches, including some made of aircraft bombs buried fuse up. The metronome-like schedule meanwhile kept depositing more men and equipment on the beaches until the only option for the assault troops was to move forward. Tanks arrived in the fourth wave, following an LVT that scouted the way across the reef to prevent any of the armored vehicles from being drowned in shell holes. Artillery tubes began arriving as the morning progressed, but the smallness of the beachhead limited the number of guns that could be landed.

The Peleliu beaches severely tested the invader's medical services. Some casualties were enroute to help within an hour of being hit, but many had to wait much longer as the medical services struggled to keep up. The *Wayne* stationed an LCVP just off the beach with a medical section aboard to screen casualties, administer aid, and direct the outgoing boats to the appropriate receiving ship; the corpsmen assigned to the boat directed the evacuation of 700 casualties in three days. There were so many casualties that the flow of supplies was interrupted by more LVTs and DUKWs than expected being used to evacuate wounded.[7] Communications were hit hard because so many radiomen were killed and radios lost. General Rupertus knew troops were ashore, but for many hours he did not know which way the battle was going. The beachhead that existed by late afternoon was smaller than planned and was about to receive a counterattack.

The counterattack, including thirteen Japanese tanks, developed late in the afternoon of D-day and rushed headlong at Marine lines. The thinly armored Japanese vehicles suffered badly under Marine fire, but at least two of them penetrated forward positions and approached the beach area before being destroyed. Although the accompanying enemy infantry was slain in vast numbers, the whole incident was a scary reminder of just how tenuous the beachhead was. Not all the artillery was ashore, naval gunfire was severely circumscribed by the close quarters of the beachhead, and communications were extremely spotty. All observers agreed that had the

Japanese possessed heavier tanks, the situation could well have become critical. The first night ashore held the terrors common to every assault of the Pacific war. Gunfire-support ships kept the night filled with star shells while stretcher bearers evacuated wounded and working parties brought badly needed supplies to the front lines.

Supplying enough ammunition and medical supplies became critical because of congestion on the beaches and because so many tractors were lost. The captain of the *Wayne* thought the shore parties showed a "lack of interest" in unloading, hardly surprising given the smallness of the beachhead and the intensity of enemy fire. The second day nonetheless saw Marine positions consolidated and an increasing volume of supplies delivered ashore. Providing water to the troops became another serious problem when much of the water brought in drums proved contaminated. This problem disappeared when distilling gear was brought ashore and enough wells were sunk inside Marine lines. Another serious shortage was ammunition and parts for tanks. They fired off so many rounds in support of the infantry that the only way they kept going for the first few days was to cannibalize what they needed from disabled tanks.

General Rupertus went ashore on D + 1 to assume control of the troops, despite having suffered a broken ankle in a training accident. The foremost problem confronting him was the volume of casualties his division had suffered. He had told his men just before the landing that he expected a hard fight, but one that would last no more than four days. Rupertus naturally had the utmost confidence in his marines, so even in the face of what had taken place on D-day, he apparently still held on to the idea of a short campaign. When he made no mention of needing reinforcements to General Geiger or Admiral Fort by midday on the sixteenth, they released the 81st Infantry Division for the assault on Angaur.

The landing on Angaur went as planned on 17 September. A diversion took place off one area while the soldiers of two regimental combat teams landed in another against only sporadic resistance. The landing was made easier because there was no reef and the Japanese commander had concentrated his men away from the beaches he knew he could not defend. Terrain similar to Peleliu caused the American advance to be slow and methodical with a heavy reliance on fire power. Even so, the cost on Angaur was 264 American and 1,300 Japanese lives. The heaviest fighting lasted three days, fortunate because the battle on Peleliu wasn't going well.

Japanese resistance had slowed the Marines' advance to insignificant gains. Worse yet, heavy casualties had substantially reduced the combat effectiveness of some units. General Geiger went ashore on 21 September to assess the situation and didn't like what he saw. Geiger could see that despite Rupertus's confidence in his division, reinforcements were needed. The corps commander asked General Mueller to provide one regimental combat team for immediate movement to Peleliu. The soldiers loaded out the same night on Angaur and arrived on Peleliu the next day. They immediately moved into the line, where they fought with distinction for the remainder of the campaign. What Rupertus thought would be a four-day battle lasted until November. The Japanese fought with unusual skill and discipline, determined to make the Americans pay for every inch of the island. They succeeded in no small part due to the rugged terrain.

Naval gunfire proved incapable of reducing defenses that were based mainly in caves. Ruthven Libby's destroyer squadron was doing its best to help:

> We had some white phosphorus shells . . . as I remember. This . . . shell is very useful . . . for incendiary purposes and also for spotting. . . . because we were close in to shore . . . we had to fire them just about straight up, almost vertical. We also had to fire reduced charges, because the thing weighed practically nothing . . . if you put a full powder charge it would overshoot the target. We found, to our consternation, that with a reduced powder charge there wasn't sufficient setback to arm the projectile, and nothing would happen.[8]

Artillery fire was better and close air support, including Marine aircraft after 28 September, did its share. The bulk of the battle still had to be fought by tank-infantry teams closing with the enemy and sealing him in or burning him out of his defenses. Naval forces played other roles in the campaign, including intercepting Japanese barges attempting to bring in reinforcements from Babelthuap. Several LVT(A)s joined in the same task and even sank some enemy barges. The enemy did manage to land 600 more men on Peleliu, but they could not affect the outcome.

The unexpected length of the campaign meant ships were tied up supplying the marines longer than anticipated. Bad weather complicated the problem by making the beaches unusable for small landing craft and thrusting most of the work onto a group of six LSTs. Cargo ships would anchor and their loads be transferred to LSTs, which moved the supplies onto the beach. Not only were the "T"'s badly overworked, but having to work alongside another ship in heavy seas brought its own troubles. One former LST captain wrote of his experiences off Peleliu after the war:

> It was not easy duty. The ships were not constructed for it. They were so high-sided that when they lay alongside another vessel they caved in their sides, crumpled the bridge wings, and turned their boat davits into masses of twisted steel. They loaded out in the open sea, the ships secured together moving slowly up and down parallel to the island as they worked. The surging vessels snapped lines and brushed off fenders. Each

commanding officer watched his straining crew and battered, shapeless ship, wondering when it would be its turn to be washed up on the beach with the others.[9]

When the work and the fight finally ended, 1,512 marines and soldiers were dead, as were almost 11,000 Japanese soldiers and sailors. As in the aftermath of Tarawa, a public debate raised questions about the usefulness of the islands versus their cost.[10]

The airfields in the Palaus got only minimal use in support of operations in the Philippines, but the Japanese garrisons of Koror and Babelthuap were trapped for the rest of the war. The official Marine Corps history points out that the concept of amphibious assault against a well-defended target was again validated, but one must ask if the idea hadn't already been proven. More to the point is the assertion that Nimitz and his commanders were doing what they thought best with the information available. Ruthven Libby believed King's and Nimitz's choice of targets "amounted to nothing short of genius." Halsey reaffirmed his opposition after the war, a sentiment echoed by the gunfire-support group commander a few years later: "if military leaders were gifted with the same accuracy of foresight that they are with hindsight, undoubtedly the assault and capture of the Palaus would never have been attempted."

Admiral Fort believed that Stalemate was the "most difficult amphibious operation of the Pacific War." He thought what happened later at Iwo Jima overshadowed the operation. "The only difference between Iwo Jima and Peleliu was that at Iwo Jima there were twice as many Japs on an island twice as large, and they had three Marine Divisions to take it while we had one Marine Division to take Peleliu."[11]

On a lower level of involvement were the comments made by the captain of the *Wayne*. He forcefully reminded superiors that despite the eventual success of the operation, some things were not done correctly and others needed improvement. He wanted a chief pharmacist mate sent to the beach aid station, not a doctor. His argument was that the doctor's skills were essentially wasted on the beach, where most treatment was in the realm of first aid; the doctor would be better utilized aboard the ship once casualties began to come aboard. He also noted that one problem in dealing with a large influx of casualties was the number of loaded weapons and hand grenades that had to be collected and safeguarded or disposed of. Lastly, he didn't believe it proper for the ships to send their beach parties hot food twice a day while the troops were eating C rations if they were eating at all.[12]

Even while the fight for Peleliu continued, the immediate goal for which Stalemate and so many other landings had been launched was realized; American soldiers waded ashore in the Philippines on 20 October.

AMPHIBIOUS RETURN: THE PHILIPPINES, OCTOBER–NOVEMBER 1944

The American relationship with the Philippines needs no retelling here. MacArthur had persuasively framed their recapture not only in strategic terms but as a matter of national and personal honor. In a typically florid message to the Joint Chiefs, MacArthur warned that if the United States chose to bypass the Philippines, "We would admit the truth of Japanese propaganda to the effect that we had abandoned the Filipinos and would not shed American blood to redeem them." The consequences would be "such loss of prestige among all peoples of the Far East that it would adversely affect the United States for many years."[13]

The revised plans evolving in the fall of 1944 for invading the Philippines drew upon the combined strength of the 3d and the 7th Fleets. Most of the Navy's Pacific combat strength was allocated, including both III and VII Phib. Crucial to success was the air support provided by Kinkaid's meager force of CVEs and Halsey's fast-carrier task forces. The operation would be the largest landing yet carried out in the Pacific. Operation King II would put four Army divisions ashore with the supplies they needed to mount the campaign.

As was the case for some time, Charles Adair was at the center of planning:

> a meeting was called by General MacArthur . . . for the discussion of the Leyte Gulf operation. Of course, Com7th Fleet was there, General MacArthur and all his staff, the Army commanders were there. There was Admiral Wilkinson . . . along with some of the other Central Pacific Amphibious Force commanders, and then Admiral Barbey and his planners. That was the three of us. But the hall they had the meeting in was filled. I don't know how in the world they could find so many people that weren't working. I felt that with all the people there, we had almost enough to make an assault, and that Admiral Barbey and his three planners could have roughed out an assault plan by the time it took to get the people out of the hall![14]

Adair and his colleagues set to work with the practiced ease of veterans. That the invasion was to take place in only one month was no extraordinary problem to men who had fleshed out other landings in the course of a day. They were doing what they had numerous times before, except on a far grander scale.

The Japanese tried to prepare for the impending American threat to the Philippines; they rushed Army reinforcements to the islands throughout the summer of 1944, while naval planners prepared for a decisive battle with the American fleet. If the Americans took the Philippines, the oil fields of Borneo would be cut off and the Imperial Navy starved of fuel.

The realization that defeating a landing at the waterline was unlikely led the Japanese to continue the strategy first put into practice on Peleliu. They would defend the islands in depth with the aim of inflicting a heavy defeat on the invasion forces. A secondary goal was to deny the Americans those areas that would support airfields; the Japanese had long recognized that air cover was integral to each American advance. One perceived advantage was that the main islands were big enough for defenses to be established beyond the range of naval gunfire. Signal intelligence and sightings of shipping on the move alerted the Japanese to some pending action; all commands in the Philippines were ordered to be alert in the latter part of October. Leyte seemed a likely target.

The plan Adair and his colleagues were drawing up would land 145,000 assault troops on Leyte, followed by another 55,000 in the second echelon. Lt. Gen. Walter Krueger was in command of the sixth Army, which controlled the campaign. Admiral Wilkinson's III Phib, which the change in plans had diverted from an assault on Yap, would comprise one attack force lifting the 7th and 96th Infantry Divisions. Admiral Barbey's force would lift the 1st Cavalry and 24th Infantry Divisions to Leyte. The 77th Infantry Division would again start a campaign in reserve. No Marine infantry units were assigned but Marine fliers and artillerymen would participate. Ships were meanwhile gathering all over the South Pacific to collect the assault troops.

The logistical problem for King II was immense. Sixth Army planners estimated that 400,000 tons of ammunition and supplies would be needed immediately by the assault force with another 332,000 tons required every thirty days after that. There was also the need for considerable construction equipment to build airfields. Confronted as they were with an infinite load and a finite amount of space in which to stow it, transport quartermasters resorted to the much-maligned practice of a 50-percent reduction in divisional vehicles. The soldiers would get their bullets and beans, but they would have to walk until more trucks could be brought in by the follow-up. Additional backup was provided by four ammo ships positioned at Hollandia and another twenty-two vessels programmed to arrive from San Francisco. To ensure that enough ships would remain available, MacArthur insisted none would be returned to the Central Pacific without his approval.

Rehearsals took place in Hawaii and Hollandia; new replacements got their first sense of a great adventure while veterans of Attu, Kwajalein, Los Negros, and Guam were reminded that they were once again about to venture into harm's way. Some of the more superstitious passengers no doubt felt a chill when the convoy gathering at Hollandia departed on Friday the thirteenth. With its powerful phalanx of battleships and other fire-support ships in the van, the fleet began its approach to Leyte. The largest assault force gathered in the Pacific included among its orderly columns 5 AGCs, 40 APAs, 151 LSTs, 79 LCIs, and a multitude of other landing ships.

The twelve ships of LSM Group Four, the newest landing ship design, were making their combat debut. The Landing Ship Medium (LSM) was designed to fill the gap between the LCT and the LST. It was a 203-ft., seagoing ship, but had a shallower draft and was faster than the LST. With a normal crew of four officers and fifty-five enlisted men, approximately 500 of these ships were commissioned before war's end.

Halsey's aviators meanwhile worked over Japanese airfields on Formosa trying to prevent any transfer of enemy aircraft to the Philippines. Closer to hand, the minesweepers and bombardment groups arrived at the entrance to Leyte Gulf on the seventeenth. First into action were the minesweepers and they had plenty to do. Two small islands flanked the entrance to the gulf and a large minefield lay between them. It had to be cleared and the islands seized before the assault force could approach its landing areas. Army Rangers landed on the seventeenth and eighteenth to rid these islands of Japanese, a task accomplished with few casualties. After the minesweepers cleared more than 200 mines, the bombardment group moved in and took the southern section of the assault area under fire on the afternoon of the eighteenth. The UDT teams meanwhile moved inshore to reconnoiter.

The Japanese aimed heavy fire at the swimmers, hitting several of their boats, but could not stop them from completing their task. There were no obstacles in the water and the beaches were clearly suitable for landing craft. The northern beaches, 14 miles away, received the same treatment the next morning with the same results. Air strikes from Rear Adm. Thomas Sprague's force of CVEs added to Japanese woes, bombing and strafing every enemy airfield within range. With their path smoothed, the landing force approached the assault areas on the morning of 20 October. Because so many mines had been swept, the transports received orders to stream paravanes.

The heavy thunder of battleship main-battery fire opened the final bombardment at 0600. There was no thickly sown defensive system of bunkers and pillboxes, so the bombardment fell in areas immediately behind and next to the beaches. The troops began to go ashore around 1000 against varying levels of resistance. In a tableau reminiscent of the landings on Sicily, some units were held up until they could put a pillbox out of action while others landed unopposed. Japanese artillery fire hit a few LCVPs and a few LSTs later in the morning. In the cold mathematics of war, the loss of fifty-four soldiers to successfully storm the beaches of Leyte was a small price.

Getting supplies ashore proved far harder than getting the soldiers landed. The LSTs quickly discovered they could not get close enough to all the beaches to unload. Since moving bulk supplies efficiently depended upon the trucks loaded in the LSTs, the whole logistics plan was immediately thrown off. Wilkinson's force had pontoon causeways, Barbey's did not. There hadn't been time to obtain them, leaving Barbey with a serious problem. He asked Wilkinson to send some pontoons up from the southern beaches, but they could not arrive before dark. Barbey compensated somewhat by shifting more LSTs to the areas where they could beach, but the result was a mountain of supplies in one area, instead of even distribution.

At this late date in the amphibious war, there is a certain measure of surprise to read in the official U.S. Army history that with one exception, there weren't enough men available to the shore parties. The logistical plan called for supplies to begin landing one hour after the assault troops, so the effort to get supplies across the beach and into dumps began in the hole. It was fortunate that there were no air raids the first day because the badly congested beaches presented a target that would have been hard to miss. One bright spot was the performance of the 7th Infantry Division's shore party. They not only handled the first wave of essential supplies, but had their dumps established and ready to issue all needed supplies within six hours. What came ashore the first day was not efficiently handled nor properly dispersed, but there was a lot of it; 107,450 tons were landed, no small accomplishment.

One soldier who was glad to get ashore that first day was Douglas MacArthur. He had accompanied the assault force in the *Nashville*. Once the northern beachhead was secured, he wasted no time in fulfilling his promise to return. MacArthur waded ashore from a landing craft in the company of the Philippine president and made a passionate appeal to the Filipinos to "rise and strike! For your homes and hearths, strike! In the name of your sacred dead, strike!" It was the Japanese who attempted to strike first, though in a sense different from that envisioned by MacArthur. News from the invasion area that the Americans were landing on Leyte put into effect the previously drawn up Sho plans. The remaining strength of the Imperial Navy sortied from Borneo and Japan to engage the invasion fleet in what the Japanese admirals hoped would be a decisive battle. All available aircraft within range launched attacks on the American fleet in an attempt to wear it down and even the odds. The approaching Japanese fleet did not go undetected, causing Halsey to put his counterplan into effect. His eagerness to destroy the enemy fleet almost cost the amphibians.

The Japanese divided their fleet into three task forces. The northern force included four aircraft carriers stripped of most of their aircraft.

Knowing Halsey's propensity for attacking carriers, they were to decoy the Third Fleet away from Leyte Gulf, allowing the center and southern forces to demolish the amphibians that remained there. The ploy worked and Halsey headed north. Largely because of the peculiar command arrangement whereby Halsey reported to Nimitz and Kinkaid reported to Mac-Arthur, nobody blocked the path of the powerful Japanese center force. On the morning of October 25, this fleet stumbled into a much weaker task force that included six American escort carriers. The melee was won by the Americans through the aggressiveness and bravery of the escort carriers, their destroyer escorts, and destroyers, which lost several of their number.

During the previous night the Japanese southern force had attempted to enter Leyte Gulf from the south. Their route was blocked by a Seventh Fleet task force that included five battleships salvaged from the Pearl Harbor disaster. It was an uneven match and all the Japanese except one heavy cruiser and one destroyer were sunk. Only one American destroyer suffered a few casualties.

These three actions, when combined, were the largest naval battle in history. They were also the last serious threat by the Japanese fleet. Although the bulk of the American invasion force had already left Leyte Gulf, and thus the Japanese could not have turned the tide, a Japanese attack on the remaining ships could have taken the lives of many amphibians.

The amphibians worked hard supporting the land battle on Leyte. They hauled in supplies by the thousands of tons and mounted two more assaults in December. Japanese reinforcements had been arriving on Leyte through the port of Ormoc, on the island's west coast. General Krueger asked that a division be landed near Ormoc to cut off that avenue and to squeeze the retreating Japanese between two fronts. MacArthur wanted to hit Mindoro next so he had to be talked into the operation. Krueger got support from Admiral Kinkaid and General Kenney, the air commander, so Mac-Arthur consented to putting off the Mindoro operation until 15 December. A task force that included twelve of the new LSMs brought the 77th Infantry Divison to Ormoc the morning of 7 December. There was no resistance, so all the troops landed without difficulties. All supplies were preloaded in vehicles to speed unloading; once they rolled off the bow ramps, the amphibians were on their way.

Unfortunately, they could not get away fast enough. Conventional air attacks were accomplishing so little that the Japanese had turned to a stratagem of deliberately crashing into American ships. The suicide attackers were formally known to the Japanese as Special Attack Groups. They became commonly known as "kamikazes" (Divine Wind), after a typhoon that had once saved Japan from invasion. By the time of the Ormoc landing, there had already been several kamikaze attacks, so the events of 7

December didn't come as a total surprise. Fighting their way through a CAP of Army fighters and as much flak as the ships could put up, several attackers smashed into three destroyers, an APD, and one LSM. Two of the destroyers went to the bottom, as did the LSM. It was a hellish preview of what the fleet would endure off Okinawa only a few months later.

The third assault in MacArthur's Philippines campaign came only ten days after Ormoc with a landing on the island of Mindoro. The goal was again sites for airfields, this time needed to support the upcoming attack on Luzon. The assault force consisted of 12,000 soldiers plus another 1,200 for the shore party. Rear Adm. Arthur Struble commanded the naval task force. En route to Mindoro, a kamikaze hit his flagship, causing heavy casualties, among them Struble's chief of staff and much of the Army staff. Struble transferred to a destroyer and continued to the objective, where the unopposed landings took place as scheduled on 15 December.

The landing on Mindoro successfully closed the amphibious war of 1944. The techniques learned in 1943 were honed and refined into a formidable weapon. Nineteen forty-four had been a year of hard fought battles matched by incredible growth in the knowledge and strength of the amphibious forces. In Europe, the amphibians had broken through the Atlantic Wall and put ashore the armies that would eventually destroy the Third Reich. In the Pacific, the amphibians had pushed the Japanese defensive line back thousands of miles at a rate not even theorists had thought possible. There had been mistakes in both theaters and great loss of life. There had also been well-directed and well-executed landings that confounded the Axis and unhinged their defensive strategy. The idea that the war was unwinnable was at the outer walls of the Japanese castle, largely through the efforts and sacrifices of the amphibians. Unfortunately, Japanese inability to conceive of surrender meant the amphibians would have to scale that outer wall in 1945.

LUZON: JANUARY 1945

The last year of World War II witnessed the armed forces of the United States carrying out a series of amphibious assaults that brought the offensive begun at Guadalcanal to a successful conclusion. First off the mark was the assault on Luzon, the largest of the Philippine Islands. The landing was originally scheduled for December, but delays in building airfields and the depredations of kamikazes forced a reluctant postponement on MacArthur.[15]

The landing, rescheduled from 20 December to 9 January, would take place north of Manila in Lingayen Gulf. Three Army divisions were to be lifted, the 25th, 37th, and 43d Infantries. Old hands Dan Barbey and Ted Wilkinson drew the assignment; both had already returned with their staffs to New Guinea to direct the planning. The considerable polish of the planners is amply demonstrated by the fact that the three divisions were coming from New Caledonia in the New Hebrides, Bougainville in the Solomons, and Aitape, New Guinea. Between 17 and 30 December, both landing forces completed rehearsals, made their respective rendezvous, and headed for the entrance to Lingayen Gulf, where they and their supporting forces were to assemble.

There was no hope of concealing the approaching force from the Japanese; kamikazes began assailing the bombardment ships and escort carriers on 4 January. The threat they posed to massed amphibious shipping was made frighteningly clear by their success against the far more heavily armed bombardment ships. Enemy planes fell as blazing comets, fell in fragments as shipboard gunners blasted them into bits, and fell with dead pilots slumped over the controls. Enough still got through the CAP, avoiding the flak barrage or slipping in unnoticed against the backdrop of nearby islands, to blast several ships. One hit a CVE, setting her ablaze so badly she had to be abandoned. The attacks continued over the next five days, each successive wave exacting its toll. Another suicider smashed into the battleship *New Mexico*, killing more than a score. The support force commander warned that unless the kamikazes could be stopped, the invasion was in danger of being repulsed.

The CVEs assigned to the task force were doing their best, as were the Army fliers assigned to air cover. Halsey's carriers were providing distant support by working over enemy airfields on Formosa; on 7 January, he brought them into Philippine waters in an attempt to kill some would-be kamikazes while they were on the ground. When his fliers claimed seventy-five planes destroyed on their fields the level of attacks on the invasion fleet fell dramatically. The carriers then returned to Formosa to prevent replacements from being flown in.

Despite the threat from the sky, the bombardment force also had to tend to its main task. Firing on scarce targets began on 7 January, as did the now-standard reconnaissance of the beaches by underwater demolition teams. Resistance was nonexistent and the UDT men found no obstacles. The sailors of the bombardment force got a poignant reminder that they were returning to what had long been considered American territory. A spotting plane reported that despite the danger, a large crowd of people waving an American flag was gathered on one landing beach. Firing ceased and a plane scattered leaflets warning the Filipinos off the beaches.

Smooth seas and clear weather greeted the dawn of 9 January. Among the transports was the veteran *Doyen*. The accumulated experience of the amphibious war is given voice in her report, which states that eleven LCVPs arrived from the transport *Sheridan* so expeditiously that "all assault waves were boated and formed within 26 minutes after arrival in Transport Area 'Charlie.' "[16] There was slight resistance at one of eight landing beaches, but the troops otherwise poured ashore and inland so fast their first-day advance exceeded expectations. A kamikaze hit the transport *Callaway* while she lay off the beach, killing twenty of her men but sparing her load of soldiers. With the troops ashore, attention turned very quickly to unloading. Ships from the Central Pacific found something new in Charles Adair's loading plans:

> We had told these transports that we wanted them to load . . . only in the amount that could be unloaded on D-day . . . because we wanted them to leave the area by 5 o'clock on the afternoon of the assault day. Well they said they couldn't load that way, that it would be impossible to unload. We said, "It doesn't make any difference what you've been doing in the past. In this operation . . . you're going to leave on D-day in the afternoon at 5 o'clock. So, load them for that departure time."[17]

Adair had the last laugh:

> Well, at 5 o'clock in the afternoon, they were all unloaded. . . . That unloading was something different—ships and the people on those APAs had never done this before in their lives, and they were waving and shouting and laughing and everything else. They thought that was the best thing they had happen to them—to get out of there and get away on D-day.[18]

The *Doyen*'s captain also commented on two suicide attacks that he witnessed; his observations offered an ominous portent for the future:

> Despite the most intense AA fire from every ship that could possibly bear, neither plane appeared to be affected by the fire, indicating that (1) the planes were heavily armored or (2) the pilots were extremely fortunate or (3) the shooting was poor or (4) a combination of all the first three.[19]

The *Sumter*'s captain addressed the need to stop the kamikazes by suggesting the 20-mm gun was inadequate to meet the new threat. The fleet would soon see the truth of all these comments while off Okinawa.

Though many transports left the invasion area during the late afternoon of 9 January, the ships that remained faced another form of suicide attack that evening. A Special Attack unit of the Imperial Navy brought its explosives-packed motorboats out of concealment under the cover of darkness and made its run on the invasion fleet. Gunfire from the screen shattered most of the boats but the suicide boats did hit two LCIs, which eventually sank. The bad weather that kicked up the next day caused more disruption by breaking up pontoon causeways and delaying the onshore flow of supplies. The unexpectedly deep advance of the troops caused another problem by tying up motor transport longer than expected. Supplies began to build up on the beaches.

These difficulties notwithstanding, organization and experience were in place to overcome logistical problems, leaving planners ready to confront the next leap forward. Though the Philippines were by no means liberated from Japanese control, the locus of the American offensive was about to return to the Central Pacific. There were clashes at the top; as had often been the case in the past, MacArthur had ideas of his own.

9

CRESCENDO AND DIMINUENDO

"Almost every weapon the Japs have got can reach us on the beaches. We have to take high casualties on the beaches—maybe 40 percent of the assault troops. We have taken such losses before."

LT. GEN. HOLLAND SMITH

DETACHMENT: PREPARING FOR IWO JIMA, NOVEMBER 1944–JANUARY 1945

Iwo Jima is one of the Bonin Islands, which had been Japanese possessions since the nineteenth century. Midway between Tokyo and Guam, it covers only eight square miles, five miles across at its widest. Born of a volcano, Iwo is covered with ash, reeks of sulfur, and has no natural source of water. Although inhospitable in the extreme, the island drew American attention in the spring of 1944 because it lay beneath the projected route of the B-29s flying from the Marianas to bomb Tokyo.

American interest was threefold: on the one hand, Japanese planes based on Iwo could threaten B-29 airfields in the Marianas. On the other, the island represented a natural haven for damaged B-29s returning from Japan. Finally, American fighters based on Iwo could escort the bombers to their targets, something they could not do from the Marianas. In May 1944, the Joint War Plans Committee therefore targeted the island, recommending a three-division assault.

Admiral King had no interest in Iwo Jima; his goal was to invade Formosa, then blockade the Japanese into submission. Spruance did not share King's ideas, and despite being told by Nimitz after Operation Forager that Formosa was next, told his staff not to waste any time on planning. Spruance had come to believe that Iwo, then Okinawa were the next natural targets and told Nimitz as much. Nimitz made Spruance's views known to King, who had the foresight to order preparatory planning.

When King summoned Nimitz to San Francisco in September for meetings, he invited Spruance, too. Nimitz's chief of staff made Spruance's case for Iwo by showing convincingly that there weren't enough troops available to assault an island as large and as strongly held as Formosa. The upshot was that Nimitz told Holland Smith to keep two or three divisions available for an assault on Iwo Jima. The Joint Chiefs followed with a directive to Nimitz ordering him to seize Iwo Jima on 20 January and Okinawa on 1 March. Nimitz and his commanders now knew where they were going, but many decisions remained.

The command setup for Operation Detachment reflected both recent changes in organization and the increased number of experienced amphibious commanders. Kelly Turner and Holland Smith had formal overall responsibility, but operational control of the landing force lay with V Amphibious Corps commander Maj. Gen. Harry Schmidt; Turner turned over similar responsibility for the naval component to Rear Adm. Harry Hill.

Three Marine divisions, the 3d, 4th, and 5th, would make the assault. Schmidt wanted to land all three in the initial assault but was vetoed by Holland Smith. The 4th, under Maj. Gen. Clifton B. Cates, and the newly constituted 5th, under Maj. Gen. Keller Rockey, were to make the landing, while the veteran 3d under Maj. Gen. Graves Erskine would be in reserve. The 3d Division was on Guam recuperating from the rigors of Forager, while the 4th and 5th were training on Maui. Chief among the issues facing Schmidt and his planners was how much preliminary bombardment would be needed. Their concern was well founded because the Japanese were fortifying the island at a furious rate.

The Japanese knew Iwo Jima would eventually have to be defended against an American assault. Lt. Gen. Tadamichi Kuribayashi was sent to the island and told to make it impregnable. Imperial General Headquarters held no illusions that a landing could be stopped, but Japanese military men continued in their conviction that an assault force could be bled dry. Kuribayashi based his defensive plan on digging the garrison deeply into the island in a complex maze of interlocking bunkers, caves, tunnels, and pillboxes. Kuribayashi's orders were to dig, and that is what his soldiers and the naval infantry on the island did.

American planners had plenty of photos. Carrier task forces and Army bombers flying from the Marianas raided the island regularly after the fall of the Marianas. The pictures they brought back gave clear evidence of extensive Japanese preparations to receive an assault. Though skillful camouflage prevented detection of many emplacements, photo interpreters noted an increase in covered artillery positions from thirty-nine to sixty-seven between 3 December and 10 February. The Iwo Jima garrison was extremely well armed. Among their arsenal: 630 cannons and antitank guns. Given what occurred, it was fortunate for the Americans that at least some weapons and supplies destined for Iwo Jima were sent to the bottom by U.S. submarines and air action. General Schmidt didn't know the full extent of what awaited his men, but he knew he wanted a ten-day bombardment to pave the way into what was clearly a tough target.

Determining what constituted an adequate bombardment had been an elusive goal throughout the course of the amphibious war; Iwo Jima was no exception. Turner's response to Schmidt's request was that three days were enough. Schmidt countered by asking for nine, which Turner also denied. The Marine then asked for four days at the very minimum, a request Turner again turned down. Not yet willing to concede, Schmidt asked that the full three days of bombardment be concentrated near the landing beaches rather than throughout the island. That request was bucked up to Spruance, who supported Turner's original plan.

Spruance made the point that the heavy volume of supporting fire needed on D-day and the lack of immediately available replenishment ammunition precluded longer bombardment. The fleet commander did authorize a fourth day if it seemed necessary. He apologized to the Marines for upsetting their plans but added that he knew they could do the job. Previous experience would seem to have given weight to the Marines' request, but a complex dynamic of interlocking events was at play.

One component of both Spruance and Turner's decision-making process was tactical, another strategic, a third logistical. As distant support to Detachment, Spruance was taking the fast carriers to Tokyo to bomb aircraft factories. The raids would take place on 16 and 17 February, giving them time enough to get back to Iwo Jima, where the carriers could cover the invasion fleet. He needed the fast battleships, two of which had been included by the gunfire-support planners in the bombardment program, to protect the carriers. Spruance therefore ordered the two ships to accompany the fleet to Tokyo, decreasing the number of big guns available for bombardment. There were also the competing demands of the Philippines campaign on ships. Much of Spruance's gunfire strength had been seconded to MacArthur's area with the proviso that the ships had to be released in time to participate in Detachment. Not only had the delay in assaulting Luzon set back their release, but the unexpectedly heavy casualties inflicted on the fleet by kamikazes had made inroads on the number of ships available. Finally, there was a logistical problem.

As Turner pointed out to his Marine comrades, there simply weren't enough ships or ammunition available to conduct a ten-day bombardment. A request by the Marines to stockpile ammunition on Saipan and shuttle ships back and forth was turned down by Turner as impracticable.[1] Turner's response to concentrating all three days of bombardment on the beach areas was twofold. He said the defenses of the whole island had to be reduced sufficiently to allow close-range fire and to permit observation planes to get low enough for accurate spotting. Conspicuously absent throughout this debate was the forceful presence of Holland Smith.

Smith was titular commander of the Marine forces engaged in Detachment. As such, he reviewed all of General Schmidt's plans before endorsing them and forwarding them to Turner. Smith had strongly endorsed all of Schmidt's requests for a longer bombardment. Nowhere is there a record of a "Howlin' Mad" argument when Turner denied each one. Smith's apparent passivity seems at odds with the preinvasion apprehension he recounted in his memoir. "I could not forget the sight of Marines floating in the lagoon or lying on the beaches of Tarawa, men who had died assaulting defenses that should have been taken out by naval gunfire."[2]

During the planning process, Smith had projected that at least 20 percent of the landing force would be casualties. Even in the face of continued naval resistance to a longer bombardment, he remained uncharacteristically passive. There seems little doubt that the strains of the previous year, including the Saipan controversy and his uncertain relationship with Nimitz, had lessened his influence.[3] Harry Schmidt was therefore in an unenviable position; he did not doubt that he needed a longer bombardment, but he did not have Holland Smith's forceful personality. However reluctantly Smith accepted the Navy plan, Schmidt was not the man to buck the tide.

Another issue that had to be decided at a high level was the return of Central Pacific ships from the Philippines. After years of making do with assets vastly fewer than those assigned to the Central Pacific, MacArthur and his naval commanders were loath to return their "borrowed" ships. A gentlemanly argument ensued in January among MacArthur, Kinkaid, and Nimitz about the need to retain ships in the Philippines. Nimitz was sympathetic but knew he needed the ships as soon as possible if operations against Iwo Jima and Okinawa were to be carried out on schedule. The delay from December to January in attacking Luzon had already pushed Iwo Jima and Okinawa back into February and April, but Nimitz knew he could wait no longer.

The issue was compounded by the large number of ships that received kamikaze damage in the Philippines. Some could be repaired at Ulithi but others had to return to Pearl Harbor. Until they could be returned to duty, Nimitz had no margin with which to work. Fortunately, Japanese naval losses in the October battles buttressed his argument for recalling ships from the Philippines. With no enemy surface threat, there was no rationale for keeping the gunfire ships in the area. What happened was that the number of ships Kinkaid managed to hang on to, combined with those put out of action by the kamikazes, still left Nimitz short of what he wanted for Detachment. The continuing urgency of not allowing the Japanese any respite nonetheless drove the operation ahead.

Setting aside the argument about the bombardment as a separate issue, planning a scheme of maneuver and outfitting the landing force naturally took into account all the experience gained in the fourteen months since Tarawa. The leading assault wave would be landed across seven beaches in LVT(A)s and drive quickly across the narrow waist of the island to split the defenders. As fast as reinforcements could be landed, the larger part of the assault force would wheel north and seize the high ground that over-looked the right flank of the landing beaches. On the other flank, one regiment had the job of seizing Mount Suribachi, the still fuming volcano that also overlooked the landing beaches. The first tanks would land only thirty minutes behind the first waves with artillery soon after. Landing times of successive waves were to be flexible, recognizing the congestion that inevitably built up on the beaches. Other preparations took into ac-count the unique features of Iwo Jima.

The planners knew the beaches consisted of volcanic ash, so unloading plans relied heavily on tracked vehicles. There were LVTs in large numbers plus a new tracked cargo vehicle known as the "Weasel." Rolls of steel Marston matting, usually used in airfield construction, were included as bridging material to cross the beaches. Sand sleds were constructed to be towed across the ash to firmer ground. One potent new weapon was avail-able to the Marines; a turret-mounted flame thrower had been developed for the Sherman medium tank and was ready for Iwo Jima. Assault troops also had a lighter model of the infantry flame thrower. The landing force included three battalions of Seabees to help keep the beaches clear and to get exits built. Lastly, since there was no known natural source of water on the island, providing an allowance of ten gallons per man for an in-vasion force of more than 70,000 men necessitated converting three fleet oilers to water tankers.

The planners expected heavy losses; they estimated 18 percent of the assault force would become casualties, with 20 percent of those killed.[4] Three hospital ships would accompany the task force as well as four hos-pital LSTs, one of which had a blood bank aboard. All transports were also expected to perform their usual roles as hospital ships. The Army provided rations and contributed three companies of DUKWs. Quarter-masters preloaded thirty-eight LSTs with essential supplies and stockpiled another thirty days' worth in the Marianas. At the recommendation of the Navy beachmaster, several bulldozers were fitted with armor plate to pro-tect the drivers and engines. Other preparations for clearing wreckage from the beach and fighting fires included the largest available tracked crane and seven diesel-powered fire pumps.

Including a Marine fighter squadron aboard one of the fleet carriers improved the prospects for good air support, at least to the Marines. Other squadrons assigned to the CVE *Wake Island* had the sole job of spotting for gunfire-support ships and artillery. By the first part of January, all the myriad details were worked out and operation plans issued. There re-mained only rehearsals and the long voyage to Iwo Jima.

Hawaii-based troops conducted rehearsals during the seven-day period

11–18 January. These exercises suffered somewhat because too few gunfire ships were available. The different task groups then began their passage to Ulithi and Saipan, where another rehearsal would take place the second week in February. Turner, Holland Smith, and Secretary of the Navy James Forrestal were in the AGC *Eldorado*; Harry Hill and Harry Schmidt were in the *Auburn*. The bombardment and support groups could call on the guns of six battleships, four heavy cruisers, one light cruiser, and sixteen destroyers.

The fast carriers of Task Force 58 came in, swelling the gathering at Ulithi. The constellation of admirals' stars increased by five when Nimitz joined Spruance in the *Indianapolis* for a final round of conferences among all the Detachment commanders. When the fleet finally sortied for Iwo Jima, the carriers and their screening ships needed more than four hours to clear the anchorage. The 233 ships of the amphibious task forces followed immediately, which took another three hours.

Shortly after the task force was at sea, Turner and the other commanders held a press conference aboard the *Eldorado* to brief the accompanying war correspondents. Holland Smith was somber in his remarks, making sure everyone understood Iwo Jima was going to be a hard task. Secretary Forrestal also spoke, expressing his confidence in the commanders and that all would work as planned. The correspondents were reminded to make no mention of kamikazes, napalm, or UDT operations.

There was a scary breach of security while the invasion force was on its final leg to Iwo Jima. An overheard radio conversation emanating from the vicinity of Saipan stated baldly, "We are going to Iwo Jima. It's a Jap island not far from here. We're leaving for there in the next day or so."[5] Turner's intelligence officers were no doubt near cardiac arrest, but the imminent invasion was no secret to the Japanese. For one thing, American carrier and land-based bombers had been overhead constantly for the previous two months. They had accomplished little, but all the attention surely signified a landing was close. Preparations to meet the Americans had continued apace.

Learning from previous battles, General Kuribayashi had forbidden counterattacks. He had no intention of exposing large numbers of his men to the destructive power of massed Marine artillery and naval guns. Insofar as possible, it was his intention to fight the battle from underground. Tunnels on a scale never before seen by the Americans linked defensive positions. The command post was seventy-five feet deep, far beyond the reach of the heaviest naval gun. The entire garrison could shelter beneath Iwo Jima's bleak surface and all ammunition, stores, and water were also underground. Artillery and mortars were registered on the probable landing beaches and their crews given strict orders that no gun was to fire until the first waves of troops were on the beach. Jeter Iseley summed up Japanese preparations on Iwo Jima:

> Expert military engineers had been imported from the homeland, and taking full advantage of the terrain . . . had fortified Iwo to near perfection. Where terrain dictated a blockhouse or a covered emplacement, there it was. Where fields of fire called for mutually supporting pillboxes to protect in turn a heavier defense, they were sure to have been built. Observers who had inspected German fortified areas in both world wars testified that never had they seen a position so thoroughly defended as was Iwo Jima. Comparisons are difficult, but it is probable that no other given area in the history of modern war has been so skillfully fortified by nature and by man.[6]

The defenders might not be able to stop the landing, but they could wait until so many men and so much equipment was ashore that every shell would cause maximum destruction. Kuribayashi was ruthless in replacing officers who insisted his tactics violated the offensive spirit of the Japanese military; he summarily replaced eighteen officers who objected to the plan. The Japanese had one advantage: American intelligence had underestimated the size of the garrison. Instead of the 14,000 enemy fighting men expected, the Marines faced almost 23,000, each pledged to take with him ten Americans.

Speculation became reality for the Japanese on 14 February when Spruance's carriers were spotted approaching the home islands. When the information reached Iwo Jima the next day, Kuribayashi ordered the garrison to take up defensive positions. There was no surprise then, when dawn of 16 February showed the island ringed by warships. The American amphibious juggernaut was off Iwo Jima in apparently overwhelming strength. The Japanese were not cowed; it would take considerably longer than the ten days expected by General Schmidt to overrun the island.

ASSAULT ON IWO JIMA: FEBRUARY–MARCH 1945

All supporting forces surrounding Iwo Jima were under the command of Rear Adm. W. H. P. Blandy, who flew his flag in the AGC *Estes*. His staff, which included a Marine officer specializing in naval gunfire, had worked long and hard to plan a scheme of bombardment that would best use the time allotted. Because of new air photos received at sea, a considerable amount of time was spent enroute from Pearl Harbor to make pen and ink changes to the op-plan. The constantly changing list of ships available, a state of flux resulting from the demands of the Philippines campaign, meant that gunnery officers from newly assigned ships had to be briefed after arrival in the Marianas. Each ship had a specific section of Iwo Jima, and all 724 targets categorized as posing either a primary or secondary threat to the landing were listed on a card index kept in the joint operations room aboard the *Estes*. The goal was a carefully controlled and observed bombardment, the effects of which would be listed daily in the card index.

Weather off Iwo Jima on 16 February was rainy and overcast. Since the success of the bombardment was predicated on deliberate firing at specific targets, little was accomplished the first day. Ships would fire when observation planes or their spotters could see targets. Unfortunately, those occasions were not frequent. Japanese AA fire was inaccurate but intense, keeping planes higher than needed for good spotting. The first day of Detachment thus did not bode well. Spirits lifted somewhat when the following morning brought clear weather and the opportunity for the bombardment group to really get to work.

The program for D − 2 included beach reconnaissance by the UDT teams. They were to make the usual checks for obstacles and to find out if the beaches were suitable for vehicles. Twelve LCI(G)s were to provide close-range support with three battleships lying farther off. As the landing craft carrying the UDT men and their supporting gunboats approached the eastern side of the island, the crew of at least one gun must have believed the actual landing was at hand. They opened fire and were quickly followed by several others. That the enemy soldiers were well trained was immediately made evident; they hit all twelve of the LCI(G)s, some badly. Typical was the experience of LCI(G) 466:

> when about 1200 yards from the beach we suffered at least three direct 6-to-8-in. enemy hits. The port and starboard 40mm guns were hit almost simultaneously. The third enemy hit demolished the interior of the pilot house . . . the ship was entirely out of control when [we were] ordered to retire. At 1200H, we maneuvered alongside the USS *Tennessee* and transferred our severe casualties.[7]

The supporting battleships helped the gunboats' withdrawal by putting down a barrage of smoke shells between the enemy gunners and the beach line. One gunboat was so severely damaged that she sank; the others were incapable of further action. Blandy later recognized their valor when he wrote, "The personnel of these little gunboats displayed magnificent courage as they returned fire with everything they had."[8] Lt. Rufus Herring, captain of LCI(G) 449, received the Medal of Honor for his conduct that day.

The gunboats suffered heavily but Japanese gunfire claimed only one UDT swimmer. They were able to report there were no mines or obstacles off the beaches nor was there any sort of incendiary barrier awaiting the marines. One bit of information they reported, that the beaches appeared suitably firm, would prove horribly wrong. Of immediate benefit to the landing force was the premature revelation by the defenders of numerous gun positions previously unknown to the Americans. Reaction by the bombardment force was swift and lethal: the *Nevada* moved in to point-blank range and pounded gun positions and bunkers for two hours. She smashed several batteries that would otherwise have delivered enfilading fire onto the landing beaches. Even so, the garrison reported to Tokyo that they had repulsed a landing attempt.

The battering received by the gunboats upset the bombardment timetable laid out for 17 February. Firing near the landing beaches had to be delayed until the damaged gunboats could clear the area. Once that was accomplished, some battleships resumed their long-range plunging fire while others closed in to shorter range. Bit by bit, the high explosives falling on Japanese positions reduced the number of AA guns, thereby allowing observation planes to get lower to see better what was happening. The fliers quickly reported that the bombardment was not making any significant inroads on the large number of positions capable of threatening the landing beaches. Blandy probably would have preferred better news but didn't hesitate to modify the plan.

As photo interpreters pored over the pictures taken on 17 February, they could see that camouflage had been stripped away from many additional enemy positions. There were clearly more emplacements than could possibly be eliminated in the single day remaining before the landing. Blandy therefore authorized all ships to expend their total outlay of bombardment ammunition less their allocation for supporting the actual landing. Rear Admiral Rodgers, commanding the gunfire task group, moved some ships from the western to the eastern side of Iwo Jima to beef up fire near the landing beaches. Four battleships and one heavy cruiser had instructions to pound those batteries posing the most direct threat. Rodgers set the tone for 18 February when he ordered his ships to close within 2,500 yards of the landing beaches and "get going." Weather again sided with the Japanese but the defenders did not go without damage.

Between breaks in the rain and low clouds that periodically swept over the island, carefully aimed fire blasted and crumbled positions that had taken the defenders months to build. Bombs joined the explosives cascading onto Iwo Jima, both from carrier planes and Army airmen flying from the Marianas. Half the enemy's heavy coast defense guns were destroyed, as were half of his heavy AA guns. Of 587 other defensive positions, fewer than 25 percent were destroyed.[9] The 500-pound bombs used weren't powerful enough to penetrate and accuracy was degraded by the low-hanging clouds. Naval gunfire was more effective, but the layer of volcanic ash absorbed some of its destructive power. Even the extra half hour of firing

Blandy ordered at the end of the day was not enough. Blandy notified Turner and Hill that another day of bombardment would be useful, but the landing could go ahead as planned on the nineteenth. Photos taken that day were quickly processed aboard the *Wake Island* and flown to Turner's flagship. All the commanders understood that much would depend on the final barrage scheduled just before the troops hit the beach.

While destroyers fired harassment missions throughout the night, the landing force made its final approach to the island and the transport areas ten miles off the beaches. A dawn nervously greeted by thousands of somber marines soon reverberated from the heaviest, most concentrated bombardment yet leveled at any landing area. Spruance had arrived off Iwo Jima in the *Indianapolis* during the night after racing south from Tokyo. He brought two 16-in. battleships with him and they added their destructive power to the barrage. Eight battleships, six heavy cruisers, three light cruisers, and ten destroyers were on hand to cover the landing.

Firing began shortly before 0700 and continued until just after 0800. A wave of Navy and Marine fighters then scoured the slopes of Mount Suribachi and the high ground on the right flank with bombs, rockets, and napalm. The Marine pilots of VMF 124 had particular motivation to do a good job; they were flying from a carrier in direct support of fellow Marines not because the Navy wanted them, but because there was a shortage of Navy pilots. They bored in noticeably low as they tried to make every bit of ordnance count. The assault troops were meanwhile embarking in their LVTs and approaching the line of departure 4,000 yards off the smoking, shuddering island.

Off Iwo Jima, the landing craft were preceded not only by the usual phalanx of LCI gun and mortar craft, but also by the new LCSs fitted with multiple rocket launchers. As the first wave was forming up, the latter vessels arced flaming volleys of more than 10,000 rockets onto and just behind the beaches. The bombardment ships also stepped up their rate of fire and, just before the first LVTs touched down, began rolling the barrage inland in 200-yard increments. To many marines crouched in the approaching LVTs, it seemed as if Iwo Jima must surely be atomized and would sink into the sea. Scant return fire came even as the first tractors began to heave themselves up from the sea onto the island. In only a few minutes, whatever frail hopes that the enemy had been blasted out of existence or into stunned helplessness were extinguished.

The first shock to the landing force came when they discovered that the beaches were in no way solid. Instead, they were covered with a deep, loose layer of black volcanic ash. The LVTs immediately began to flounder because they could get no purchase. Furthermore, wave action had formed the ash into steep terraces that were extremely difficult for either the tractors or men to climb. The hoped-for momentum of a large body of assault troops forging quickly inland immediately began to bog down. The infantry discovered that they sank into the ash to their shoetops, slowing them to a virtual crawl. The defenders meanwhile emerged from the safety of their shelters and began to loose a steadily increasing torrent of mortar and artillery fire onto the beach area, which was quickly filling with men. The well-choreographed schedule and hundreds of LVTs deposited more than 9,000 men on Iwo Jima in only forty-five minutes. Despite their numbers, the troops' progress off the seven invasion beaches was measured in feet and their very existence was in deadly peril.

Japanese artillery observers on Mount Suribachi and the heights to the right flank were extremely proficient in calling accurate fire onto the beaches. Casualties began to mount rapidly, despite the muffling effect of the volcanic ash. Not only was artillery and mortar fire assailing the marines in steadily growing volume, but unceasing small arms and machine gun fire was keeping them pinned down. Tanks and artillery were desperately needed; help seemed at hand when the first Shermans began to crawl off their landing craft at 1005. They too found the ash difficult to negotiate; some tanks managed to crawl over the terraces, others threw tracks and bogged down. Still others were disabled when they drove over mines. The tankers nonetheless did their best to support the infantry with fire from their 75-mm guns. These efforts quickly made them the focus of accurate antitank fire that knocked out several. In reality, the advance off the beaches of Iwo Jima was led by men with rifles, grenades, flame throwers, and demolition charges.

All the while, the beaches were turning into a tangled, confused mass of equipment bogged down in the ash or blasted into wreckage by Japanese fire. Many LVTs were hit, as were several LSMs bringing ashore the tanks. As Holland Smith had feared, the infantry suffered extremely heavy casualties. Nor was any other spot within the diminutive beachhead safe from enemy fire, as the casualties among the working parties struggling to unload supplies would show. Standing out above the confusion was a memorable beachmaster:

> [The beachmaster] and his four assistants were everywhere and must have had charmed lives, for in spite of heavy casualties among the beach parties they came through without a scratch. A Royal Navy liaison officer later said, "On the beach was an extraordinary character, almost as wide as he was tall, wearing the insignia of a navy captain, but delivering his commands in amazingly blasphemous language with a strong Scandinavian accent. He managed to get things done."[10]

Despite the carnage and enemy fire, the system of landing only ammunition, water, and medical supplies functioned as planned. Both LVTs and DUKWs were employed in the task. The amphibious trucks were also the means by which artillery landed, though the ash made that task far more difficult. Moving any kind of gun into position proved exceedingly difficult, as a vignette recorded by Marine combat correspondent T. Grady Gallant illustrates:

> "It'll have to go up trail first," the sergeant said. "That bank's too steep to go muzzle first . . . it'd plow into the dirt." The men swung the gun around, pointing the trail toward the bank. "Ready?" he asked. "All right, let's go." They pushed. The wheels hit the bank, sank into the gravel. The trail was elevated and the gun muzzle touched the beach. They pushed. The gun was immobile. The sergeant said, "Try it again. Ready? Heave!" The men pushed and pulled. The gun remained motionless.[11]

A few overloaded DUKWs carrying artillery pieces capsized or sank upon leaving their LSTs. Once ashore, some guns were heaved into position by gangs of sweating men while others were towed into position by LVTs, though not without difficulties.

One problem confronting the artillerymen was that many of their planned battery positions were unavailable because of the tight beachhead. Enemy counterbattery fire destroyed some guns but by late afternoon several batteries were ashore and firing in support of the infantry. Other support came from the carriers; the aviators flew more than 600 close-support sorties during the day. They were dropping napalm but most of the containers failed to detonate. With the impact of supporting arms relatively muted, what pushed the American line slowly forward was the tenacity and bravery of individual marines.

A twist in the weather made efforts to keep men and materiel flowing across the beaches even more difficult. The wind had shifted near midday, creating high surf on beaches that were not well suited for boats in the first place. The beaches were so steep that LCVPs bringing in the reserve battalions could not get sufficient purchase. It was thus difficult to hold them steady against waves and current. The rough surf would often rebound off the beach through the opened ramp, flooding the boat. Others were swung around by the strong current and flung onto the beach by the waves. So many boats flooded and broached by late afternoon that access to the beaches became difficult. Had less resolute troops or less experienced leaders been in command, the situation could easily have gotten out of control.

Both Admiral Hill and General Schmidt had a relatively good grasp of what was taking place on the beaches. Many difficulties common to amphibious landings affected the communications plan, including heavy casualties among the shore fire-control parties. But the quality of the radios had improved and sufficient communications personnel were included in the assault waves to make sure some word got back to the command ships.

One thing the commanders knew for sure was that casualties had been heavy; more than 1,200 men were evacuated from the beach the first day. They also knew the advance was not going as planned. Unlike Tarawa, however, no word came from the beach saying "issue in doubt."

As customary, the transports retired to sea during the night, but gunfire-support ships remained close inshore and fired continually throughout the hours of darkness. The naval shelling reassured the thousands of marines huddling uneasily in their holes. They had no way of knowing the Japanese planned no counterattack, but they were only too aware of the constant enemy shelling that fell throughout the night. The second day followed the first in its scale of unremitting violence and physical problems for the invaders. Vast quantities of supplies were to be landed the second day. The LSTs and LSMs that had the job of getting their loads of bulk cargo ashore not only had to run a gauntlet of enemy fire, but also to weave their way through and often over the tangle of debris cluttering the beaches. The wreckage punctured hulls and bent screws. Artillery fire hit several ships. As with their smaller cousins, the larger ships also had problems with the Iwo Jima beaches.

As an LST or LSM approached, she would drop a kedging anchor at an appropriate distance from her expected grounding point. The anchor would not only help keep the ship steady on the beach, but would serve to pull her off when the time came to retract. Unfortunately, the anchors could get no purchase in the soft bottom, making it difficult to hold the ships on the beach without broaching.[12] The weather made up so much on the second afternoon that nothing smaller than an LSM could even approach the beach, compounding further the unloading problem. Part of this slack was taken up by LVTs and DUKWs, which again proved their inestimable utility by shuttling continually between the transport area to the beach and back. They carried supplies inbound and casualties on the return trip. Without the amphibious vehicles, the flow of supplies to the infantry and evacuation of the wounded would have been seriously compromised.[13] The manner in which all the problems were overcome shows the polish and expertise of the amphibious forces.

Although there were enough newly commissioned transports and amphibious ships assigned to the task force for Turner to voice some concern, there was never any doubt that the assault would succeed. Weather, beach congestion, heavy casualties, logistical delays, and exceptionally stiff resistance were all met head on and overcome. Naval gunfire and air support contributed to the maximum extent; gunfire ships were assigned to support individual battalions and the control apparatus worked as planned. Japanese defenses based on caves again limited the effectiveness of naval gunfire as did the often too-close proximity of American lines to the enemy. Though there would be complaints about difficulties in getting timely air-

support missions, control personnel managed all the supporting arms better than ever. Navy and Marine fliers handled close air support until the first airfield went into commission. Army fighters then moved to Iwo and, by all accounts, delivered excellent support. A fire support coordination center was established to direct supporting fire and functioned well. The communications plan was generally held to be good, despite some badly overloaded channels.

There were problems with the organization of the shore party that affected the flow of supplies to the front lines. The general level of confusion caused some delay in landing the corps shore party, so divisional shore parties worked to exhaustion. The system of assigning infantry replacements to the shore parties also proved detrimental when the need to replace casualties at the front began cutting into the size of working parties on the beaches. Getting divisional dumps established took longer than anticipated. Handling pallets injected a certain level of difficulty to the logistical problem as they began to arrive on the beach before enough mechanical equipment was available. Bad weather combined with anchoring problems to make pontoons unusable. Weather continued to be a problem until beaches on the western side of the island could be developed and landing craft shifted to whichever shore had the most favorable wind and surf conditions. Johnny Huggins was then a young officer in the LSM 201. His ship made many deliveries of personnel and supplies to the beaches:

> On one occasion we beached on Blue Beach at night, carrying over 200 tons of airplane gasoline, 500-pound bombs and flame throwing fuel. That night, as was always the case, the Japanese fired at random from their [emplacements] up and down the beach and into the open bay. Every third round was a tracer and sometimes at night it appeared that each tracer was headed straight at you. We sustained no casualties at Iwo Jima and the only time we were hit occurred when we took in a part of the staff of General Cates of the 4th Marine Division. One of his staff member's rifles accidentally went off and shot out our spotlight.[14]

Even after the assault moved away from the beaches, the Marines were not the only ones taking casualties. The carriers that remained in the vicinity to deliver close air support and antisubmarine patrols became prime targets of kamikazes staging from Kyushu. They put the fleet carrier *Saratoga* out of action and sank a CVE. Several other ships took hits, reinforcing the dread that each succeeding operation would have to face a weapon so alien to Western minds.

For the Americans, the emotional highlight of the battle came on the afternoon of 23 February when a patrol from the 28th Marines reached the top of Mount Suribachi and raised the national colors. A second, much larger flag from the LST 779 was soon brought to the summit and attached

to a piece of pipe. Photographer Joe Rosenthal captured that raising in what many historians call the most famous combat photo of World War II. In keeping with the patriotism of a different era, no account of the battle fails to mention the emotional impact of the flag raising on the men who could see it.[15]

The battle for Iwo Jima lasted until 18 March, more than twice as long as forecast by General Schmidt. Progress was slowed by the complexity of the enemy's defenses and the steady attrition of Marine fighting strength. Despite enormous expenditures of artillery and naval gunfire, success depended mostly on squads of riflemen blasting the enemy out of his positions with flame throwers and grenades. It could have ended sooner had Holland Smith chosen to commit the 3d Marine Division in its entirety. Despite a request from Generals Schmidt and Erskine, he retained two regiments aboard their ships. Smith defended his decision on the grounds that there wasn't sufficient room on the island to deploy three divisions.

His fellow Marines expressed considerable disagreement about his decision; their question was if there were too many troops on the island, why not replace badly depleted battalions with rested ones? Given Smith's constant concern about casualties, his decision seems illogical. General Schmidt was blunt in his criticism; he said, "men would have been saved if they had been used," and that "there was no valid reason for holding them or for sending them back to Guam."[16]

Nimitz reduced fleet strength off Iwo as quickly as possible. The operation against Okinawa was looming large; ships and men needed a few days of upkeep and rest. Blandy and his support group went first, followed on 9 March by Kelly Turner. Holland Smith transferred to Admiral Hill's flagship, where he remained until 15 March before returning to Guam. He had gone ashore more than once to offer advice and suggestions, but was punctilious in allowing Schmidt to run the battle. The troops who fought the battle began leaving the island on 18 March; among the transports carrying them away was the *Zeilin*, fresh from repairs of kamikaze damage suffered off Luzon. Nimitz flew in from Guam to make his customary inspection of the recent battlefield. He came away with a new appreciation of Japanese skill on the defense. The cost for Iwo Jima was more than 6,000 marines, soldiers, and sailors killed and almost 23,000 wounded. Only 1,200 Japanese and Koreans became prisoners; more than 22,000 others were killed, including General Kuribayashi. Every American who fought on Iwo Jima was impressed by the skill of the defenders. All were intensely hopeful that there were no more generals of Kuribayashi's caliber in the Japanese ranks. There was also a growing sense of apprehension about the probable cost of having to invade Japan.

Press coverage of the assault had been comprehensive; among the civilian correspondents was Tarawa and Saipan veteran Robert Sherrod. He did an interview with Holland Smith that was published while the battle was still raging. That the fight was difficult was not kept from the home front. When the full extent of the casualty list for Detachment became known, however, both Nimitz and Holland Smith again came in for public criticism. The focus was once more on whether assaulting fortified positions like Iwo Jima was worth the cost. Again there was a call for Mac-Arthur to be placed in supreme command on the basis that his assaults had been far less costly. The question of why poison gas was not used was also raised. Holland Smith responded to the latter question by noting that gas was considered, but its employment was a decision beyond the authority of field commanders.[17] The furor over casualties was less easy to answer and caused him great personal bitterness. Because he had warned of high casualties before the operation began, he felt unfairly singled out as a scapegoat. He would soon leave the Pacific, tired and depressed. Nimitz also came in for his share of criticism. He spoke of his feelings in a letter to his wife:

> I am delighted with the news that Iwo has finally been conquered and I hope that I will not get too many letters cursing me because of heavy casualties. I am receiving two or three letters a day signed "a Marine Mother" and calling me all sorts of names. I am just as distressed as can be over the casualties but don't see how I could have reduced them.[18]

What became the centerpiece of the professional argument over Iwo was the length of the bombardment. Many Marines and naval officers believed the bombardment should have been delivered over a longer period. Samuel E. Morison wrote in his history of wartime naval operations, "There is no reason to believe that ten or even thirty days of naval or air pounding would have had much more effect on the defenses than the bombardment that was delivered."[19] One must question how Morison could have reached such a conclusion.

Nimitz's staff planners initially called for eight days of bombardment based on the intelligence available to them in the fall of 1944. Blandy's Action Report clearly states, "The bombardment by this force on 16 and 17 February also had less than the desired effect, due to . . . lack of thorough familiarity with the actual important targets, as distinguished from a mark on a map, or a photograph." He went on to say that what had been proved was the "need for ample time as well as ample ships, aircraft, and ammunition for preliminary reduction of defenses of a strongly defended position."[20] There seems little doubt that had a longer bombardment employing more heavy-caliber guns been carried out, Japanese resistance would have been reduced.

Turner's biographer hands ultimate responsibility to Spruance, but the evidence suggests Turner was feeling squeezed by a schedule that required him to invade Okinawa less than two months after Iwo. Had he permitted a longer bombardment at Iwo, there was every chance sufficient ammunition would have been unavailable for Okinawa, where the plan called for seven days of preparatory fire. Of course, hindsight is perfect. Mistakes are as much a part of war as the formulation of grand strategy on one level and a fire fight between squads of infantrymen on another. In the clear light of almost fifty years later, the less-than-adequate bombardment of Iwo Jima seems an avoidable mistake. The cost in lives for Iwo is always justified by the number of b-29s that made emergency landings on the island after being damaged over Japan. Nonetheless, the passionless ledger of lives lost versus lives saved cannot obscure the fact that the toll extracted for Iwo was too high. Twenty-one Marines and attached Navy medical personnel received the Medal of Honor for their actions on Iwo Jima, the highest total for any battle of the war. We can therefore only admire all the more the valor of the men who fought the battle.

ICEBERG: THE LAST DITCH, SPRING 1945

With an area of 485 square miles and a length of about 60 miles, Okinawa is the largest of the Ryukyu Islands. Since it lies only 350 miles south of Kyushu in the Japanese home islands, possession of the island would provide American forces with a perfect springboard for an invasion of Japan. Though Admirals Leahy, King, and Nimitz did not believe such an invasion would be necessary to defeat Japan, they came to accept the value of Okinawa as a base should an attack be mounted. Planning thus began in the fall of 1944, concurrent with plans to seize Iwo Jima.

Taking Okinawa promised to be a dress rehearsal for landing in Japan itself. The island was the largest yet targeted, had a sizable indigenous population that had been under Japanese control for more than sixty years, and had the largest garrison of any island yet assaulted. Eight divisions, three Marine and five Army, were assigned to the attack. Four divisions would make the assault, one would make a demonstration to draw enemy attention away from the main landing, one would take a group of outlying islands, one would remain in reserve, and the other would be put ashore as quickly as possible. The assault force was truly an army; because soldiers made up the bulk of the troops, command of the 10th Army went to Army Lt. Gen. Simon B. Buckner. His principal subordinates were Marine Maj. Gen. Roy Geiger, commanding III Amphibious Corps, and Army Maj. Gen. John Hodge, commanding XXIV Army Corps.

Spruance commanded the naval contingent. His certainty the previous fall that Okinawa represented a more profitable objective than Formosa had not gone unrecognized. An almost exhausted Kelly Turner remained in command of the amphibious forces; he was ably served by a corps of experienced flag officers who had learned their trade on the job. Admiral Blandy was on hand to reprise his Iwo Jima role with Rear Admirals John Hall and Lawrence Reifsnider. Hall had made landings in North Africa, Sicily, Italy, and Normandy, while Reifsnider had fought the Pacific amphibious war from Guadalcanal on. Air and gunfire support would come from task groups under Rear Admirals Morton Deyo and Calvin Durgin, both veterans of previous amphibious operations. Among the divisional commanders assigned to make the assault were veterans of the landings on Kwajalein, Bougainville, Saipan, and Leyte. Invading Japan still loomed in the future but in reality, Operation Iceberg would prove the most concentrated gathering of amphibious assault experience in the history of warfare.

The size of the fleet assigned to carry out the operation further reflected three-and-a-half years of amphibious warfare. Carriers of all classes were on hand for CAP duties and close air support. Gunfire-support ships from battleships to destroyers to yet another modification of landing craft into rocket-firing bombardment vessels were available in the thickest profusion. There were ammunition ships to feed what the planners expected to be the heaviest demand yet and forty oilers to keep the fleet in black oil and aviation fuel. The presence of six hospital ships and eight medically equipped LSTs signified the human cost of what was about to take place. The main battery of the assault, the infantry and their LVTs, was to be borne to Okinawa in almost 400 amphibians.

Gathering the necessary ships entailed staff work of the most polished kind; ships and troops had to come together at Ulithi from ports and camps on the west coast of the States, Oahu, New Caledonia, the Solomons, the Philippines, and the Marianas. If all facets of the plan worked, Operation Iceberg would completely overwhelm the garrison of Okinawa with almost 190,000 assault troops and the materiel to support them. In all, more than 500,000 soldiers, marines, sailors, and airmen would participate in the invasion of Okinawa.

Naturally, the Japanese defenders had no intention of being overwhelmed. They were led by Lt. Gen. Mitsuru Ushijima, a competent and energetic officer who had arrived on Okinawa the previous August with the specific brief of organizing the defenses against invasion. Imperial General Headquarters still considered Formosa the most probable target but recognized the likelihood of an attack on Okinawa could not be ignored. When Ushijima arrived at his new command, he found defensive preparations under way, including the building of fighting positions overlooking the beaches. Like Kuribayashi on Iwo Jima, he knew he could not keep the Americans from landing, so he ordered a reorientation of the defensive scheme into a concentration in the southern portion of the island, where the best airfield sites and harbors lay.

Mirroring what their countrymen had done on Iwo Jima, his men dug incessantly; they eventually bored more than 100 miles of tunnels through the island's soil. They built and interconnected every possible permutation of gun emplacement and fighting position. The Americans would have to face a densely interwoven network of positions and the heaviest concentration of artillery yet. Air raids by American carrier planes in the fall of 1944 and spring of 1945 caused considerable damage to surface installations and destroyed vast amounts of supplies but did not slow the construction effort. Ushijima had 77,000 Japanese and 39,000 conscripted Okinawans in his command; all were kept busy with the constant reminder that invasion was imminent. Preparations were also being made to greet the invaders from the skies as well as from underground.

Even at this late date, cooperation between the Imperial Navy and Army did not compare to that achieved by the Americans. Acting on its own, the Navy staff conceived Operation Ten-Go, a plan to overwhelm the invasion fleet with a concentrated kamikaze assault. They allocated more than 4,000 aircraft to conventional and Special Attack missions while gathering hundreds of explosives-laden boats at Kerama Retto, a small group of islands adjacent to Okinawa. Surviving fleet units, including the colossal battleship *Yamato*, were alerted for what could only be a one-way attack on the invasion force. The Americans got a foretaste of what was in store in mid-March when the fast carriers began a concentrated series of strikes against Okinawa; suiciders hit three carriers. Of all the facets of Ten-Go, the airborne arm would subject the amphibians to their greatest trial of the war.

American preparations were going ahead simultaneously. Because the operation was of great size and complexity, all the usual difficulties were present in profusion. First was the steady shifting of the scheduled landing date. The attack was originally slated for 1 March, then 15 March, and finally 1 April. These changes came about because of the conflicting demands of the Philippines and Iwo Jima. There were training difficulties because of the wide distances separating the assault troops. The planners also had to cope with the need to rest and rehabilitate the Army units recently released from the front lines in the Philippines. The Marine divisions had to deal with an influx of raw recruits as large numbers of experienced men rotated home to noncombat assignments. General Buckner and his staff logged thousands of miles traveling the Pacific to visit units and coordinate the planning process. Logistics specialists had to manage problems as diverse as providing three times the ammunition used in the Marianas to finding an adequate supply of snake-bite serum.

Problems were not confined to the assault troops or supply people. New ships were still commissioning in a steady stream and heading west after brief but intensive training periods. As the captain of the transport *Oneida* pointed out, the training period became all the more difficult when the Navy accepted the ship in less than perfect condition. After taking his newly commissioned ship through training at San Diego in January 1945, he had the following comments:

> The great handicap which prevents a ship from utilizing this splendid opportunity for training of inexperienced officers and men is the fact that these ships are commissioned in an unfinished condition with many vital items incomplete or unworkable for the duty for which intended. As a result, while the ship is going through a high-speed shakedown and training program, it is trying to finish those unfinished items . . . and this seriously interferes with getting the full benefit of the training program.[21]

Admiral Blandy had to handle problems involving veteran ships as well:

> Plans originally envisaged that ships . . . would assemble at Ulithi on 5 March and that the period from then until 21 March would be available for upkeep, logistics, training, and rehearsal. Actually, ships continued to arrive up to the day of departure. Many late arrivals, which came directly from Iwo Jima, badly needed upkeep, rest, and replenishment. In addition, many had received no plans at all prior to arrival.[22]

One element of shipboard training that received increased attention throughout the fleet was AA drills. With the advent of the kamikaze, the old naval dictum of "shoot the guns" had suddenly taken on greatly increased importance. The kamikaze could not be deterred; he had to be hit repeatedly and hard enough to drop him out of the sky. The problem for the amphibians, of course, was that they had so much other work to do. The amphibians were not helpless, but they were dependent on the CAP and the good shooting of the destroyer screen for their primary protection against the kamikazes.

Nimitz did what he could to alleviate the threat. The B-29 bomber force based in the Marianas was not under Nimitz's orders, but he could call upon them to support his offensive should the need arise. In mid-March, he asked Gen. Curtis Lemay to have the bombers saturate Japanese airfields on Kyushu. The general did not believe the airfields were proper targets for his bombers, but complied with Nimitz's request. Spruance also had the fast carriers raid enemy airfields on Formosa. The net result of the attempt to destroy the kamikazes before they could even take to the air was of little consequence: many enemy planes were destroyed on the ground and their airfields temporarily put out of action, but there were too many airfields and too many planes carefully concealed for the American effort to be decisive.

The assault force had meanwhile made its rendezvous in Ulithi, where the troops who would make the landing transferred from their transports to the LSTs that were carrying the LVTs. The minesweepers of Blandy's support force were the first to reach Okinawa, arriving on the morning of 24 March. Next came the destroyer transports carrying the UDTs and the bombardment group that was to deliver seven days of preparatory fire. They were closely followed by the ships carrying the 77th Infantry Division, whose task was to seize the islands of the Kerama Retto, off the southwestern coast of Okinawa. Kerama Retto featured an excellent anchorage in which auxiliaries could be stationed. The 77th Infantry Division landed on 26 March with little difficulty and secured all the islands by 29 March. One immediate benefit was the discovery of more than 300 concealed suicide boats. The long-range benefit was that the fleet had a sheltered anchorage near to hand that would be instrumental in saving several badly damaged ships.

ASSAULT ON OKINAWA: MARCH–JUNE 1945

The minesweepers arrived off Okinawa on 24 March, but the attack did not open auspiciously: the destroyer *Halligan* ran onto a mine on 26 March and blew up with heavy loss of life. Several fields were swept clear, allowing unfettered access to the landing beaches. The work of the UDTs likewise met with success as they cleared thousands of stakes imbedded in the reef fronting two segments of beach. Of questionable value was the effort poured into the bombardment.

Part of the controversy surrounding the length of the bombardment delivered on Iwo Jima resulted from the scale of what was done on Okinawa. Experience and the estimated size of the enemy garrison led planners to conclude that a landing would be fiercely resisted with accompanyingly high casualties. Furthermore, the five-mile-wide front of the landing was greater than anything previously attempted in the Pacific and perforce called for a greater scale of gunfire support. There can be no doubt that Turner's negative response to General Schmidt's request for a longer bombardment on Iwo Jima was colored by his knowledge of the plan for Okinawa.

Admiral Deyo's bombardment group had seven days to work over the landing area and its surrounding terrain. From 25 through 31 March, they fired at known and suspected targets, most often with benefit of air spotting. Throughout the entire period, there was no enemy fire in return nor did anyone spot any enemy soldiers. Numerous emplacements sited to defend the two airfields immediately behind the landing beaches were visible, but there was no sign they contained either guns or soldiers. There was a certain level of perplexity about the seeming absence of the enemy; memories of Iwo Jima were too recent to cut the bombardment short. Though there were some enemy soldiers near the beaches, the planners were seduced by Okinawa's size.

Although the various task groups of the support force didn't have to contend with resistance from the beach, they did absorb the first blows of the kamikazes. Japanese tactics of coming in low across the water just at twilight proved effective in evading radar detection and giving gun crews scant time to open fire. The enemy contrived to make these attacks despite a series of radar picket stations that Turner had established at regular intervals around Okinawa. Each picket consisted of a destroyer stationed 15–50 miles offshore, with a standing CAP during daylight. The picket destroyers and the CAP shot down many would-be attackers, but others managed to avoid detection and slip through the warning line.

Turner and the landing force arrived off Okinawa early on 1 April. In keeping with his pugnacious personality, Turner ordered the *Eldorado* to close the beach. Seeing this, Admiral Hall warned his own flag captain that he would be relieved if the task force commander got closer to the beach than Hall's flagship.[23] Typhoon season was fast approaching, but the morning of April Fool's Day was calm, a condition welcomed by the LVT and landing craft coxswains responsible for landing the assault troops. Turner issued the customary order, "Land the landing force," shortly after 0400; it took another four hours to load the troops and form the landing craft into the precise patterns called for in the op-plan. Under the cover of a last-minute barrage of gun and rocket fire, the leading wave amtracs headed for the beach.

The first wave landed on Okinawa just after 0830, only a couple of minutes behind the schedule laid out months before. Since opposition was sporadic and light, the elaborate control apparatus evolved through previous landings worked to perfection. Troops transferred from LCVPs into LVTs outside the reef while LCMs, LSMs, and LSTs brought tanks far enough onto the reef to wade ashore. More than 75,000 soldiers and marines with tanks and artillery landed by day's end and were driving steadily inland. There is little doubt that the demonstration carried out by the 2d Marine Division off the southern beaches of Okinawa was a waste of time and effort; the Japanese were not moving out of their interior defensive line regardless which beaches the Americans approached. The casualty figure of twenty-eight killed met with a certain level of incredulity; after Saipan, Peleliu, and Iwo Jima, it was hard to believe the Japanese were not putting up more of a fight.

As was always the case once the troops were successfully ashore, attention turned immediately to getting their supplies unloaded. The "hot cargo" system perfected in other landings was in effect at Okinawa, but the absence of opposition allowed general unloading to begin the afternoon of 1 April. The words left by one beachmaster illustrate why the unloading effort worked more smoothly than in previous operations:

> Upon arrival at the beach it was discovered that the only exit . . . was a narrow dirt trail. We were able to get two LCMs containing bulldozers in to the beach, and these bulldozers were immediately put to work widening . . . this road. By 1145 the road had been built up sufficiently to permit vehicles of all types to traverse it. Our next problem was to locate and mark a suitable channel for small boats to come directly to the beach through the reef. Swimmers were dispatched from the beach party and by 1300 a suitable channel had been located and buoys set out to mark it.[24]

A roadway parallel to the beach was quickly built, holes in the reef filled in and pontoon causeways erected. Early in the evening, the tide rose high enough to allow LCVPs to pass over the reef. Supplies could then be landed more easily. Weather caused high enough surf for unloading to be suspended for a few days. Once there were sufficient channels cut, LSTs, LSMs, and the many LCTs that had been piggy-backed to Okinawa as deck cargo otherwise had no trouble beaching. Despite the threat of air attacks, the amphibs worked cargo throughout the night of 2 April to ensure a maximum buildup ashore. As in the Philippines, the troops advanced so quickly that trucks and DUKWs had to travel much farther than anticipated to deliver their loads. There were other localized problems, but all were overcome quickly and efficiently.

The logistical achievements of the amphibians in supporting the Okinawa campaign are impressive by any standards. They brought to the island almost 194,000 combat and support troops with 1,256,000 tons of supplies.[25] The fleet supply train also contributed impressive numbers; the gunfire-support ships fired more than 25,000 tons of shells into Okinawa. To keep them supplied took five ammunition ships plying constantly between Okinawa and the Marianas; the newly developed technique of transferring ammunition at sea saw an average of 143 tons per day handled in the two months between 22 March and 17 May. There were a few anxious days for the artillerymen when kamikazes hit and sank two ammunition ships at Kerama Retto, taking 22,000 tons of ammo with them. Several LST-loads came up from Saipan, however, and a crisis was averted.

One veteran who was at Okinawa remembered that the work to get supplies ashore never seemed to end. Bud Farmer had recovered from the wounds he received at Omaha Beach and was assigned to the cargo ship *Tyrrell*. He recalled that the work he did off Okinawa was among the hardest he experienced in the Navy. The crew unloaded cargo throughout the day, interrupted by constant air raid alarms that sent them to the guns. In his quiet Tennessee drawl, Farmer remembered that while no one was overtly frightened, the kamikazes did "have us worried." He and his ship-mates found it hard to comprehend that the Japanese simply would not give up when they were so obviously beaten.[26]

The real test of combat for the fleet gathered off Okinawa began on 6 April when the Japanese launched the first of many massed kamikaze attacks planned for Operation Ten-Go. There had already been a steady dribble of attacks that had cost the Americans; among the amphibious ships, one LSM, an LST, and the transport *Henrico* were put out of action. Nothing yet experienced by the fleet compared to what was about to begin. Known to the Japanese as *kikusui*, or "floating chrysanthemums," the attacks sought to overwhelm American defenses and to inflict unbearable casualties to the fleet. Massing almost 700 aircraft for the first kikusui took several days. On the afternoon of 6 April, the real ordeal of Okinawa began for Spruance's and Turner's sailors.

The first of the attackers began to show up low over the water around 1600. They were greeted by the heaviest possible flak, and several turned into flaming pyres on the sea. Several more bored through and ripped into their desperately maneuvering targets. Before the day was out, they sank three destroyers, two Liberty ships, and an LST. Twelve more ships were hit, three so badly they were out of the war. Poor fire discipline among the transports elicited some comments from the captain of the *Charles Carroll*. After suggesting that the 3-in. guns his ship carried could hit a modern aircraft only through "the most happy of accidents," he went on to say, "it is believed that the batteries of transports, because these ships are usually in close formation, both while underway and lying to at anchor . . . constitute, unless gunnery personnel have reached the highest level of training, a distinct menace to friendly ships."[27]

The solution for the transports was to get them unloaded and away from Okinawa as soon as possible. Smoke screens were used to the maximum extent to hide those ships lying to while they unloaded. Bud Farmer remembered that with the constant air alarms, everyone quickly became exhausted. There was no looking back when the *Tyrrell* finished unloading and sailed away from Okinawa. For the destroyers manning the picket stations there was no such relief. As the pace of enemy attacks picked up, they came in for the heaviest share of attention and suffered accordingly. Turner attempted to relieve their travail by assigning LCS and LSM gunboats to beef up the fire power on each picket station. Although the amphibious craft didn't have the firepower or speed of the destroyers, their presence was welcomed by the destroyermen. It was far different kind of duty than the gunboats had trained for.

James Stewart was captain of the LSM(R) 189, which had already experienced several brushes with both air and surface kamikazes. As part of an antisuicide-boat picket line, she fought a brief skirmish with several enemy boats the night of 29–30 March. Air alarms became so frequent that the crew simply remained at battle stations; everyone ate and slept at the guns, never doffing lifejackets or helmets. On 12 April she was on radar picket station 14 with the destroyer *Mannert Abele* and LSM(R) 190. Just after 1300, the destroyer's air-search radar picked up many inbound contacts. The battle was joined in only a few minutes.

As Stewart and his horrified crew watched, one Japanese plane launched a smaller craft that headed for the *Abele* at a speed too fast for the gunners to track. The rocket-powered Okha flying bomb arrowed into the American destroyer and blew her midships out with such violence that she sank in only two minutes. For the next two hours, the two LSMs fought for their lives and the lives of the *Abele*'s survivors. The enemy airmen bombed and strafed both ships and the men in the water. The 189 disintegrated one plane with a direct hit from her 5-inch but then took a kamikaze that clipped her conning tower with one wing, then cartwheeled into the sea. Two sailors were swept over the side, injured but alive.

When the last of the enemy planes finally flew off, both LSMs quickly turned to the grim task of pulling the *Abele*'s wounded and injured from the oil-covered water. The two landing vessels managed to recover 258 men, the 189's two men who were knocked overboard, and the body of the Japanese pilot who had crashed the 189. The survivors were transferred to another destroyer that had answered the call for help. Stewart then sought instructions about what should be done with the body of the enemy flier:

> Our orders were to remove anything of intelligence value and to give him a proper burial at sea. We placed his body in a weighted bag, with his country's orange flag still under his blouse next to his heart, and mustered all hands not on duty stations to the fantail. We read from the Bible, said the Lord's Prayer, and eased his body over the side. The Christian service was the only one we knew. We trust we did no wrong. It was difficult for many on LSM(R) 189 to have a reverent and forgiving attitude toward the pilot, when he and so many like him were the instruments of destruction, injury and death for the DD 733, and the injured on 189. Yet the kamikaze pilots had performed their duty.[28]

Stewart's experience was repeated dozens of times over during the battle for Okinawa. Eight more amphibious ships were sunk, most of them on the picket stations. The Japanese launched ten separate kikusui at the American fleet, inflicting the most damage the Navy suffered during the war. The strength of the attacks eventually diminished, but the problem of stopping an airplane flying directly at a ship continued to bedevil the fleet until the final gun sounded. April, May, and June were months during which the sailors of the fleet fully shared the terrors experienced by the marines ashore. What had been stories of Japanese fanaticism heard secondhand became all too real as thousands of sailors perished in the gasoline-fed inferno of crashing kamikazes. That an attack on Japan would be costly beyond expectation was abundantly clear to all hands.

The land battle for the island was raging while the fleet was staving off the horror of the Divine Wind. General Ushijima's defensive plan worked as expected, forcing the Americans into a slow, slogging advance against well-dug-in and camouflaged positions. Naval gunfire was used in profusion, as was close air support. The first of the CVE-based Marine squadrons authorized by King saw action, as did planes based on the recently captured airfields ashore. The slow pace of the assault did breed some interservice controversy.

Nimitz and Marine Commandant Vandegrift made a visit to the island late in April and suggested that a flanking landing should be made behind the Japanese main line. Nimitz was supportive because he was worried about the steady casualties being inflicted on his ships by the kamikazes. Turner was equally supportive, but all were turned down by General Buckner, who had heard the same suggestion from his staff. Buckner's reasoning was that there were no suitable beaches and he didn't want another Anzio on his hands.[29] He insisted the battle had become an Army operation. Nimitz reportedly replied that although it was a ground operation, he expected to see some progress and soon. He also reminded the Army man that "if this line isn't moving within five days, we'll get someone here to move it so we can all get out from under these stupid air attacks."[30]

After clearing the northern part of the island, the 1st and 6th Marine Divisions went into the line next to their Army compatriots. Buckner's decision was not well received by the Marines but they dutifully carried out their orders. There was an amphibious end-sweep of sorts when two Marine regiments made a shore-to-shore movement and landed behind Japanese forces barricaded in a peninsula on the southeast coast of the island.

Spruance declared the amphibious phase of the battle over on 17 May, but it took until 21 June for the island to be declared secure. Nimitz recognized that his commanders were worn out, so Harry Hill relieved Turner and Halsey did the same for Spruance. Buckner did not live to be relieved or to see the final victory; an enemy shell exploded against a boulder near where he was standing on 18 June, mortally wounding him. General Geiger temporarily assumed command until Army Lt. Gen. Joseph Stilwell could reach the island and take over. When the battle was finally over, the toll in lives for control of Okinawa had reached an unprecedented high. More than 12,500 soldiers, marines, and sailors died. Another 36,631 soldiers, marines, and sailors were wounded. The Navy lost thirty-four ships sunk, nearly all by kamikazes. Estimates of Japanese military and Okinawan civilian losses vary, but 107,539 bodies were counted, including thousands of civilians. The toll was ghastly by any measure, foreshadowing what lay ahead in the home islands.

The argument can be made that the assault on Iwo Jima was the apogee of the amphibious war in the Pacific. Resistance at the beachhead was the most concentrated ever experienced, but the assault force prevailed. The landing on Okinawa was exemplary in the smoothness with which it was carried out and was also a logistical tour de force. Clearly, the difference is that there was no resistance of any consequence at the Okinawa beachhead. There can be no gainsaying the ferocity of the battle for Okinawa; all honor and respect is due the men who fought the battle and withstood the scorching fury of the Divine Wind. Iwo Jima nonetheless stands out as the culminating amphibious battle of World War II.

As had by then become commonplace, armchair commanders among the press scrutinized the strategy governing Iceberg. Headlines again questioned the terrific cost of assaulting Japanese-held islands and suggested that military leadership was negligent. Others asked why Marine suggestions for another amphibious landing were not carried out. Not eager to have another Saipan-like controversy on its hands, the Navy hierarchy from Secretary Forrestal on down bent over backward to praise Army performance on Okinawa. Nimitz held a press conference on Guam attended by seventy-six correspondents and backed Buckner's conduct, effectively silencing the critics. Nimitz realized that should the invasion of Japan be carried out, there could be no room for interservice battles. His efforts succeeded; the controversy quickly subsided.

During the months of the Iwo Jima and Okinawa campaigns, MacArthur's forces were pressing ahead in the Philippines. Admirals Barbey and Wilkinson directed ten amphibious landings between 28 February and 1 July 1945. Operations Victor I through V and Oboe I, II, and VI made landings on Palawan, Zamboanga, Zambales, Nasugbu, Corregidor, Legaspi, and Borneo. All were conducted with the speed and dispatch that typified III and VII Phib.

The effects of the long war were beginning to show during the Philippines campaign. One amphibious sailor, William Fox, wrote a memoir many years later. His recollection is in sharp contrast to the upbeat news accounts of the time. War weariness had become a distinct factor in strategic calculations that summer and Fox's account provides some insight into the low morale of some of the men: "Everyone thought . . . the war had been leveled directly at him personally and that he was the only one so abused. As far as the average man was concerned, he was forced to fight by the Government and must do so before he could come home again."[31]

Fox's ship participated in her first action during the landing on Palawan. He and his shipmates worked hard that spring and summer. By August, the crew of his ship, as well as every other American serviceman in the Western Pacific, was only too aware that what lay ahead appeared to be the invasion of Japan itself.

OLYMPIC AND CORONET: WHAT MIGHT HAVE BEEN

By midsummer 1945, the Japanese were desperate; the heart of sixty-six cities had been burned out by B-29s flying from the Marianas. Their supply of Bornean oil was cut off and 6 million tons of merchant shipping were sent to the bottom by American action. The Imperial Navy was reduced to a handful of ships incapable of contesting control of even home waters, all of which had been heavily mined by the Americans. With imports of food from the once-far-flung empire cut off, millions of Japanese were on the edge of starvation. Even with destruction and privation all around them, however, surrender was out of the question to Japan's military leadership.

A peace faction had quietly coalesced among a few retired military officers and civilian members of Japan's hierarchy, but they held no real power. Furthermore, to suggest surrender openly courted assassination at the hands of military extremists. As for the military, they were realistic enough to know that victory was out of the question. Their aim was a continuation of the basic strategy that had governed the conduct of the war: if the cost could be raised too high, the Americans might be induced to offer some terms. With invasion seemingly imminent, the defense of the homeland was intended to cost the invaders more than they could conceive. The Japanese concealed thousands of airplanes, torpedo craft, and explosives-laden boats as kamikazes. There also remained in the home islands a considerable body of well-equipped, well-trained, first-line army units. Millions of civilians were drafted into home-defense units and given training in suicide tactics. The military hierarchy, particularly the generals, was willing to sacrifice millions of lives rather than surrender.

There was a division of opinion among top American commanders about the need for an invasion. General Marshall believed that the only way to force unconditional surrender upon the Japanese was to invade their homeland. His thoughts reflected Clausewitzian and the Army's institutional ideas. He was supported by the Joint War Plans Committee, which said in October 1944 that the Japanese wouldn't surrender unless defeated in their homeland. By the summer of 1945, Marshall seemed to have precedent on his side. Although the Imperial Japanese Army had suffered heavily at the hands of the Americans, its command and organizational structure were intact within Japan. Despite the recent loss of Okinawa, they showed no inclination to end the war. Furthermore, more than 12,000 Americans had been killed and the fleet exposed to the incomprehensible fury of the kamikazes. To the Army men, there seemed no way to end the war other than invading Japan.

Admirals Leahy, King, and Nimitz, supported by Air Force commander Arnold, had other ideas. They believed the Japanese must inevitably succumb to the air and sea blockade that was surrounding Japan by the summer of 1945. To the naval and air leaders, the Japanese must surrender or starve. They held to their beliefs even after the Japanese government replied to a July demand for surrender by saying they would "kill [the demand] with silence." The realities of military planning had meanwhile already forced the hand of King and his supporters. As the summer moved toward August and the Japanese remained intransigent, preparations for the invasion of Japan were well under way.

THE PLAN

The Joint War Plans Committee submitted an invasion plan to the Joint Chiefs in September 1944. The plan called for the first landing to take place on Kyushu on 1 October 1945. If needed, a second landing would take place on Honshu on 31 December 1945. The plan called for a thirteen-division assault, backed by 7,200 carrier- and land-based aircraft. Almost 3,000 ships would be needed to lift and support the assault. Three landing sites would be used, all in southern Kyushu. Air and naval softening-up would begin during the summer of 1945 and focus on the invasion areas three days before the landing. Eight divisions in three separate corps would make the assault, followed by five more reinforcement divisions. Within forty-five days of the landing, the Air Force expected to have twenty-one groups of fighters and bombers based on Kyushu. British men-of-war were included in the invasion fleet, but no British ground units. This plan was modified somewhat during the following months, but remained the basic framework of the planned invasion. Command of the assault was the next problem to be confronted.

MacArthur naturally believed that supreme command of the invasion should fall to him. King and Nimitz, holding to their belief that naval forces should be commanded by naval officers, did not agree. A long debate followed throughout the fall of 1944 and spring of 1945. The resulting compromise gave command of all land and tactical air forces to MacArthur. Nimitz retained command of all naval forces, including those supporting the invasion. Both commanders would follow the directions of the JCS. Any operation already under way under the previous division of responsibility would continue within the same lines of command. Finally, the chiefs allowed the creation of a co-equal Air Force command to control the strategic bomber force. The B-29s would not be subordinate to either Mac-

Arthur or Nimitz, but would be available upon request. With command issues settled, the Joint Chiefs next agreed that preparing the invasion should begin. On 27 May, they told Nimitz and MacArthur to begin readying their forces for Operation Olympic.

There are no surprises found in the list of commanders assigned to Olympic. There has never again been such an accumulation of officers experienced in every aspect of amphibious warfare. Spruance had the 5th Fleet and the responsibility for making the assault. Turner had overall command of the amphibious forces. Under him were Ted Wilkinson and III Phib, Harry Hill and V Phib, and Dan Barbey with VII Phib. Halsey had the 3d Fleet and would support the amphibians with his fast carriers. With only small exceptions, the military forces assigned were similarly experienced.

Wilkinson's ships would lift XI Army Corps, which included the 1st Cavalry Division, the Americal, and 43d Infantry Divisions. They would land on the southeastern coast of Kyushu in Ariaka Bay. Hill's ships would lift the marines of V Amphibious Corps, consisting of the 2d, 3d, and 5th Marine Divisions. They would land on the western coast of Kyushu near Kaminakawa. Finally, Barbey's ships would lift the soldiers of I Army Corps, which included the 25th, 33d, and 41st Infantry Divisions. They would also land on the eastern coast of Kyushu, near Miyazaki. The 40th Infantry Division would seize some small islands off the southwestern coast that would be used for a fleet repair and supply base. The army reserve consisted of the 77th, 81st, and 98th Infantry Divisions, whose job was conducting a feint off the shore of Shokaku, which the planners hoped would draw Japanese attention away from Kyushu.

The Japanese were meanwhile making preparations of their own. Even before the fall of Okinawa, they anticipated that Japan would be next. Still, they refused to consider surrender. A monograph prepared after the war by Japanese army officers noted the attitude at Imperial Army Headquarters:

> We would be determined to drive the operation to final victory by making the most of any and every advantage inherent in fighting on our home ground. We would inspire the traditional superb morale underlying our system of universal military service and loyalty. . . . the whole nation would be called out for an all-out defense battle.[32]

Knowing that Iwo Jima and Okinawa had cost the Americans heavily, the military leaders continued to believe that if they could make the expected invasion incredibly costly, the United States government would allow them to ask for terms other than unconditional surrender. Their ideas were based, not unrealistically, on estimates of an American manpower shortage:

Recruiting of manpower . . . was considered one of their major bottle-necks. After having drafted a total force of some 11,500,000 [sic], it appeared they would have great difficulty in the future in supplying additional manpower to the industrial as well as the war fronts. There was a chance that a long, drawn-out battle might in the course of time breed hatred of war among their people . . . If they could be made "tired of war," their determination to continue the operation against Japan might relax.[33]

Information gathered after the war showed that the Japanese had a sound appreciation of possible landing sites. They expected an attack in November and massed the strongest of their units in the vicinity of the Miyazaki beaches. Throughout the summer of 1945, Imperial Army Head-quarters sent a steady stream of reinforcements south to Kyushu. Japanese army strength in the southern island increased from six to fourteen infan-try divisions. Seven infantry brigades and three armored brigades were also available. American intelligence estimated that 60 percent of the approxi-mately 500,000 Japanese soldiers on Kyushu were in the southern half of the island. In a switch from the tactics utilized at Iwo Jima and Okinawa, the Japanese plan was to defend Kyushu at the beaches. All units had orders to hold their ground and fight to destruction. Should the invaders gain a beachhead, a heavy counterattack was to be mounted within two weeks. Other plans included a massive kamikaze assault against the invasion fleet, especially the transports.

The Joint Intelligence Committee estimated that the enemy had 9,000 combat and training aircraft available for conventional and suicide mis-sions. In reality, there were more than 12,000, which the Japanese intended to send against the invasion fleet in waves of 300–400 at a time.[34] The Japanese were also preparing many suicide boats, one-man submarines known as *kaiten*, and a corps of suicide swimmers who would attempt to attach mines to the hulls of American ships lying off the beaches.

After almost four years of warfare with the Japanese, every American expected the worst should an invasion of Japan be carried out. The recent experiences of Peleliu, Iwo Jima, and Okinawa showed how high the toll could be. The question of casualties was therefore high on the agenda when the Chiefs met with President Truman on 18 June. Truman had been in office less than two months when the meeting took place. He listened to Marshall discuss the need for invading Japan, which King supported.[35] Truman wanted to know what casualties the planners expected. Marshall told the president that although casualties on Okinawa had been heavy, he expected fewer on Kyushu. Marshall explained that Okinawa had been a frontal assault with no maneuver room. Kyushu would be different because the Americans would have space to outflank the defenders. He therefore expected 63,000 casualties out of an initial assault force of 193,000 men.[36] Truman listened carefully before approving the assault. He withheld approval for any further operations until a later date. His "wait and see" approach no doubt rested on his knowledge that an atomic bomb was nearing its first test.

In the western Pacific, plans for Olympic were moving ahead. Halsey's carriers began the softening-up phase in July with a series of raids on Japan. They sank or immobilized the last few of the Imperial Navy's capital ships at their moorings and pounded every base within range. Halsey's battleships conducted a series of bombardments against selected targets along the coast. The Japanese offered little resistance, leading to speculation that they were hoarding their aircraft for the expected invasion. In Hawaii, the Marianas, and the Philippines, the troops who would make the assault were resting, refitting, and training.

One problem facing the assault divisions was the manpower shortage that was becoming steadily more serious. The United States had mobilized all the men it could while maintaining war production at home. Planners envisioned moving some units from Europe, but they would not be available in time for Olympic. Replacements were thus at a premium, especially for the Army divisions. Another concern was the fatigue of the divisions on hand. Except for the 81st and 98th Infantry Divisions, all had recently seen heavy or prolonged fighting. There was some high-level concern that morale might be a problem, especially among those men who had been overseas for extended periods.

Bud Farmer's memories no doubt speak for many others; he recalled that none of his shipmates on the *Tyrrell* relished the idea of invading Japan. His personal belief was that after surviving Omaha Beach, Olympic would be pushing his luck. "I knew my number would be up," is how he states it.[37] There was not much time for rest, however. A landing had to take place by 1 November or risk the onset of typhoon season. While the Olympic assault force was getting ready, the planners were shaping other schemes.

First was Operation Pastel, a deception plan intended to draw Japanese attention away from Kyushu. Part of the plan included deliberate intelligence leaks to the Japanese to make them believe that American casualties incurred on Okinawa were causing a delay in invasion plans. The deception would try to convince the Japanese that landings on the coast of China would occur before any landing in the home islands. There were other facets to the plan, but none were put into play. The other concern of the planning staffs was Operation Coronet, the second phase of the assault on Japan. Once a base of operations was in operation on Kyushu, attention would turn to a landing on Honshu. The primary targets would be the ports of Yokohama and Yokosuka, then Tokyo. Planners estimated that twenty-three divisions would be needed, with fourteen in the initial assault. Troops would have to be redeployed from Europe to do this job. The landing would take place in March 1946, if all went well on Kyushu. Operation Coronet was only in the earliest stages of planning when the atomic bomb made all the planning moot.

THE BOMB

Whether or not Truman was justified in his use of the atomic bombs has generated considerable comment. This narrative will touch only briefly on some of the issues. *Was using the bomb a message to the Soviet Union?* Possibly. Truman was convinced that the only way to deal with the Soviets was from a position of strength. The United States had the bomb and the means to deliver it. *Was using the bomb a political issue?* After an unprecedented and costly effort to develop the weapon, the pressure to use it was immense. One must remember that when World War II began, airmen were proscribed from dropping bombs on civilians. Five-and-a-half years later, British and American bombers incinerated the cities of Dresden and Tokyo, killing almost 200,000 people. With the progression in bombs from 250-pounders to 12,000-pound canisters intended to flatten a city block, the atomic bomb was only another, more powerful weapon.

Would the Americans have used the bomb on Germany? Had the war in Europe gone on long enough, there is no reason to think Truman would have shied away from using it. There is no argument that the clash of cultures intensified the war between Japan and the United States. Americans are pragmatic in their approach to war, however. Technology is central to American war fighting; American generals of the twentieth century have always preferred to send artillery shells and bombs in place of men. Truman's experience in World War I impressed upon him at first hand the cost in blood and suffering. In June, he heard Marshall say that invading Kyushu would cost at least 63,000 American casualties. Invading Honshu would probably cost as many more.

What about the option of blockading the Japanese into surrender? By the late summer of 1945, General Lemay reported to his superiors that there weren't enough targets left in Japan to properly employ the B-29s. The bombers had torched Japan's largest cities and made 8 million people homeless. A recurring theme in Japanese accounts of the time is how desperately hungry everyone was. Nonetheless, the Imperial Army in particular was trapped by its history of never having suffered a defeat and by the emperor-god myth it had helped create. Even with American control of the air and sea around Japan, the Imperial Army managed to reinforce its forces in Kyushu during the summer of 1945. There was a growing sense of hopelessness among many Japanese, but their soldiers were innured to hardship and came from a society with no tradition of individual dissent. If the generals said fight, they fought. The unyielding resistance they had shown in the face of completely overwhelming power had indelibly impressed itself on every American serviceman.

An invasion of Japan would have been the bloodiest battle of World War II. The Germans fought desperately in the forlorn defense of their homeland despite having no cultural proscriptions against surrender. One can hardly imagine the Japanese fighting any harder, but against Olympic they would also have had the added incentive of defending their homes. Using the battle for Okinawa as a scale and recognizing that the Japanese had no intention of moving civilians out of the battle zone, American firepower would have killed hundreds of thousands of Japanese noncombatants. The number of Japanese aircraft massed for kamikaze attacks would have wreaked untold casualties on the American fleet. With the body of experience available to the planners, there is no reason to doubt their projections of casualties among the infantry and supporting forces.[38]

The horror of the atomic bombs is manifest, but the war had to be ended. Truman was faced with an enemy who patently wouldn't quit; the casualty list stretching from Guadalcanal to Okinawa was convincing proof. No one could tell him how long a blockade would take, and maintaining the blockade would exact a continuing toll of American lives. The American public was growing increasingly anxious for the war to be over. Whether or not Americans had a predisposition to use ever-more-destructive weapons solely against the Japanese is moot. After almost six years of total war, the dividing line between what was acceptable and what was not had become vague. Lastly, Truman as president was motivated by a profound wish to save American lives. A device seemed to be at his disposal that would allow him to do so. He made the right choice.

DIMINUENDO AND FINALE

Save for airmen who delivered it, none of the millions of American fighting men gathered around the periphery of Japan had ever heard of an atomic bomb. After the news of Hiroshima and Nagasaki, they still didn't know what it was. They only knew it meant they were going home. William Fox, by then off LSM 168, remembered how the war ended for him:

> Away off to port there started a slight commotion that swelled and receded as it grew closer. Everyone, I think, knew what it was, but was not willing to believe it. I came . . . to the office where several enlisted men and officers had gathered. They said that an officer had run through the hut about ten minutes previously shouting that the war was over, but everyone just looked at him and thought to themselves that he had

just been over here too long. It finally dawned upon them; they could not believe it. . . . there was a great deal of noise, guns firing all over the base, shore patrol whistles shrieking, sirens screaming, and everyone talking and shouting at the top of his lungs. . . . I paused a short time to observe one of the most beautiful sights I ever expect to witness. Before me . . . stretched the immense Gulf of Leyte. I could not begin to estimate the number of ships in the area . . . it must have been literally in the thousands. Each ship was a blaze of light of all colors of the rainbow. Each ship had all its running lights, signal lights, colored recognition lights, and searchlights going full blast. Thousands and thousands of varicolored flares were shooting skyward each minute in a vast drapery of colored light. . . . the whole thing was just one mass of flowing, falling, shooting, colored lights, and fire. Men half-drunk and half-crazy lined the beach to see it. No man standing there would ever forget that night.[39]

The war was over but the amphibians were not quite finished. Their first task was to ferry the occupation force to Japan. War diaries record a movement carried out with the precision and caution of wartime. Though the enemy had agreed to quit, the Americans couldn't convince themselves that there would not be some treachery. They were relieved to discover that the Japanese had truly surrendered; landing the occupation force met with no resistance. Other amphibious ships remained busy for months transporting Japanese home from China and thousands of Chinese soldiers into the coastal areas formerly controlled by the enemy. Then, finally, came the long voyage home.

One by one, by the dozens and by the scores of dozens, the ships that fought the amphibious war were returned to their civilian owners, mothballed for possible future use, or sold for scrap. Hundreds of thousands of men who knew what it took to plan an amphibious assault or hold a heavily loaded LCM against the twist of tide and current took off their uniforms for the last time. In September 1945, there were 12.4 million Americans in uniform; by February 1947, there were 1.2 million. The greatest amphibious campaign ever conceived had become material for war college studies, memoirs of the participants, historians, and tales told to a generation of children then being born.

Allied success in World War II clearly hung on control of the seas. The hard-fought battles against the U-boats were crucial to keeping the British in the war and to the American buildup in England. The same applied in the Pacific; defeating the Japanese on Guadalcanal took six months because the Imperial Navy was able to contest control of the surrounding waters. The balance swung to the Allies in 1943 with the defeat of the biggest U-boat offensive and the arrival in the Pacific of the first *Essex*-class carriers. The amphibious war then took center stage. In Europe, the lead units of the armies that defeated Italy and Germany joined battle at the surf line of beaches from Sicily to Normandy.

In the South and Central Pacific, the amphibious war proved decisive on two counts. First in importance was the mobility and power of the amphibious forces. By striking where the Japanese were weakest, choices granted by control of the sea, the Americans succeeded in outflanking and cutting off much of the enemy's defensive strength. In those places like Tarawa and Iwo Jima where the attack was a direct, frontal assault, the ability of the amphibious forces to mass concentrated, overwhelming force carried the day. The Japanese had to admit that no matter how heavily they fortified an island nor how bravely their men fought, they could not stop an amphibious assault. Second, trying to stop the amphibious war caused the Imperial Navy to come out and fight. In the great sea battles off the Marianas and the Philippines, the U.S. Navy succeeded in destroying the last Japanese hope that they could halt the American advance on Japan.

American success in the amphibious war came at a cost, of course. The learning curve from Operations Torch through Galvanic to Iceberg was steep. Material and human losses were heavy, both through enemy action and the difficult nature of the problem. Amphibious doctrine and practice were never static, however. The uses to which the LCI was put, the ship itself an outgrowth of a specific amphibious need, are an example. The ship was conceived to land 200 or more infantrymen directly across a beach. In her various incarnations, the ship served not only in her intended role, but as a gunboat LCI(G), rocket ship LCI(R), force flagship LCFF, and as a redesigned support ship LCS. When the guns were finally quiet in August 1945, the U.S. Navy's amphibious forces were at the very doorstep of Japan. The ideas that first germinated in the early years of the century had become the most powerful amphibious force ever conceived. With the postwar drawdown, however, the amphibious fleet largely vanished and the doctrine itself came under question.

There were intense bureaucratic battles among the military services after World War II. Creation of an independent air force and unification of the services under the Department of Defense absorbed considerable energy. Another fight revolved around the existence of the Marines—many Army generals again wanted to do away with the Corps. They were thwarted, but the size of the Corps was drastically reduced. Yet another fight was the battle between the Navy and Air Force over the strategic roles to be played by each service. With regard to amphibious warfare, the airmen and some generals believed that the atomic bomb made large-scale amphibious operations impossible. The Marines meanwhile began experimenting with a new twist on amphibious assault designed to counter the bomb. The idea was called vertical envelopment. Using the first available helicopters with sufficient load-carrying capacity, Marine squadron HMX-

1 tested the concept of landing assault troops from the air rather than from landing craft. The personnel involved considered the tests a success; they would continue until the summer of 1950 and lead to the creation of a new manual, *Employment of Helicopters*. Testing was still under way when a new war erupted in Asia that would soon bring a classic amphibious assault to center stage.

On the western border of the Sea of Japan, Korea had been partitioned between American and Soviet forces after World War II. In June 1950, the Communist leadership of North Korea decided to reunite the country through military force. For the Americans, the war at first seemed a reprise of the early days of World War II. American forces were pushed steadily back until they held only a small portion of the Korean peninsula. Douglas MacArthur, still commanding the occupation forces in Japan, was also responsible for Korea. MacArthur, who had so masterfully used amphibious assault in his campaign against the Japanese, saw the geography of Korea as an opportunity to mount a counterstrike from the sea. His eye fell on the port of Inchon, far to the rear of the North Korean armies.

Getting the operation approved took some doing, especially since the naval commanders on the scene were not favorably disposed to the landing. Inchon was not easily accessible from the sea, was subject to a more than 30-foot tidal range, and was defended in unknown strength. Furthermore, the 1st Marine Division, which MacArthur wanted to use in the assault, was being hurriedly cobbled together from the few regular units available and from reservists recalled to the colors. MacArthur prevailed, in no small part due to a masterful presentation on his part that convinced most of the doubters. There was plenty of experience available to direct the assault; all the Navy and Marine commanders were veterans of the Pacific war.

Enough of the old skills remained for Operation Chromite to be organized and put into execution in only twenty-three days. Preliminary air attacks began on 10 September and the assault began the morning of the fifteenth. There were many of the old problems, something to be expected of an assault carried out on short notice with little training. By the end of the day, however, all had gone as planned.

Inchon was the last massed-amphibious assault carried out by American fighting men. It was executed in the familiar pattern of World War II, with equipment and doctrine of those days. There have been other amphibious operations since Inchon, including several combat landings during the Vietnam War. A large amphibious force was positioned off Kuwait during the Persian Gulf War but made no landings. While the basic problems of making an amphibious assault remain the same, technology has long ago consigned a massed fleet of troop-laden transports to the pages of history books.

Today's amphibious planners must cope with reconnaissance satellites, over-the-horizon targeting of guided weapons, cruise missiles, and the killing power of modern antipersonnel weapons. In his own arsenal, the amphibious planner has the ability to put thousands of troops ashore in minutes with helicopters and air cushion landing craft that can close the beach at 40 to 50 knots.

When asked whether technology had made amphibious operations obsolete, retired Marine Lt. Gen. Victor Krulak quietly told an interviewer, "Correct me if I am wrong, but more than 70 percent of the earth's surface is still covered with water, is it not?"[40] With the recent change in the Navy's focus from superpower confrontation to littoral warfare, amphibious warfare capability has taken on a new importance. The sailors and marines of today are inheritors of a long and successful tradition. How they handle the challenges of the nineties and the decades after is another story.

MAPS

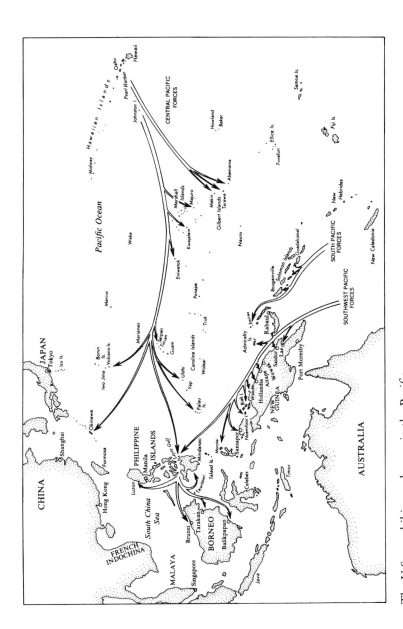

The U.S. amphibious advance in the Pacific

Source: Lt. Col. Merrill L. Bartlett, USMC (Ret.), ed., *Assault from the Sea: Essays on the History of Amphibious Warfare* (Annapolis, Md.: Naval Institute Press, 1983), 263.

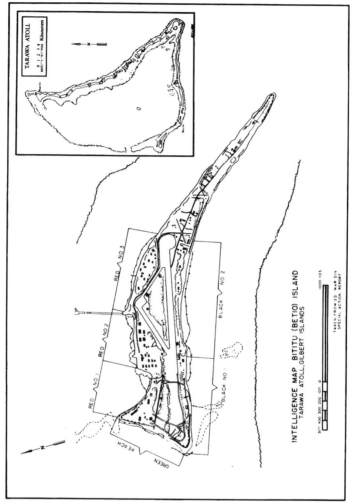

Operation Galvanic: Tarawa, November 1943
Source: Col. Joseph H. Alexander, USMC (Ret.), *Across the Reef: The Marine Assault of Tarawa,* Marines in World War II Commemorative Series (Washington, D.C.: Marine Corps Historical Center, 1993), 6.

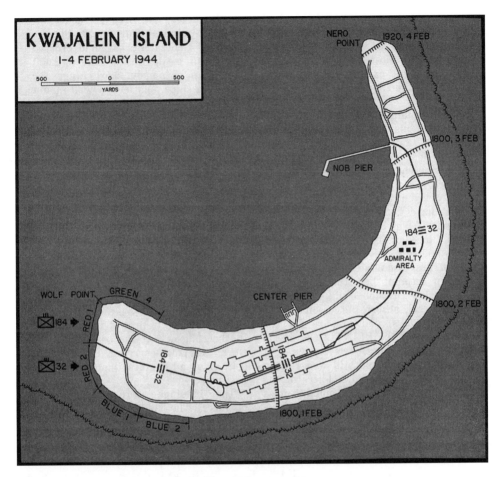

Operation Flintlock: Kwajalein, January–February 1944
Source: Henry I. Shaw Jr., Bernard C. Nalty, and Edwin T. Turnbladh,
Central Pacific Drive, vol. 3 of *History of U.S. Marine Corps Operations in World War II* (Washington, D.C.: Government Printing Office, 1966), 176.

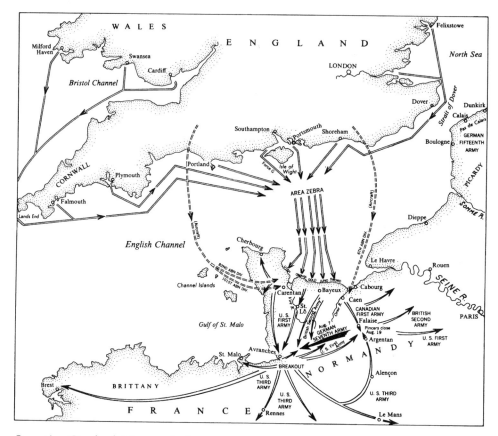

Operation Overlord: Normandy, June 1944
Source: Lt. Col. Merrill L. Bartlett, USMC (Ret.), ed., *Assault from the Sea:
Essays on the History of Amphibious Warfare* (Annapolis, Md.: Naval
Institute Press, 1983), 322.

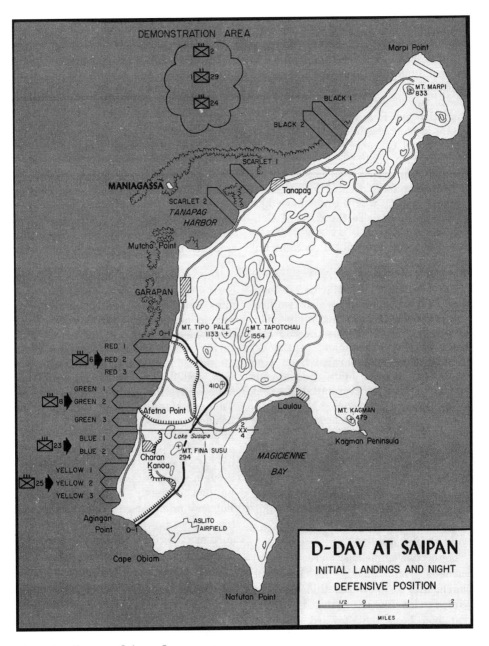

D-DAY AT SAIPAN

INITIAL LANDINGS AND NIGHT

DEFENSIVE POSITION

Operation Forager: Saipan, June 1944
Source: Henry I. Shaw Jr., Bernard C. Nalty, and Edwin T. Turnbladh,
Central Pacific Drive, vol. 3 of *History of U.S. Marine Corps Operations in
World War II* (Washington, D.C.: Government Printing Office, 1966), 265.

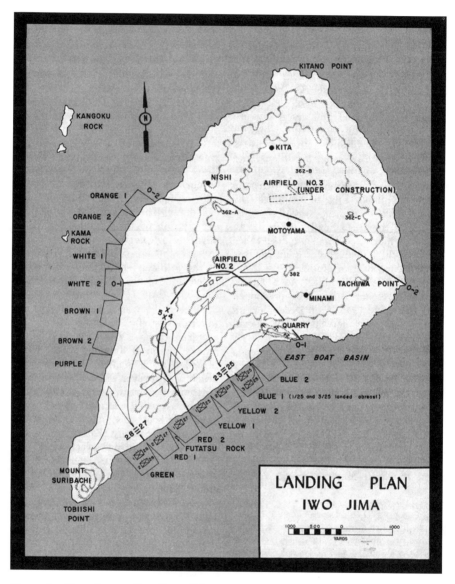

Operation Detachment: Iwo Jima, February 1945
Source: George W. Garand and Truman R. Strobridge, *Western Pacific Operations*, vol. 4 of *History of U.S. Marine Corps Operations in World War II* (Washington, D.C.: Government Printing Office, 1971), 470.

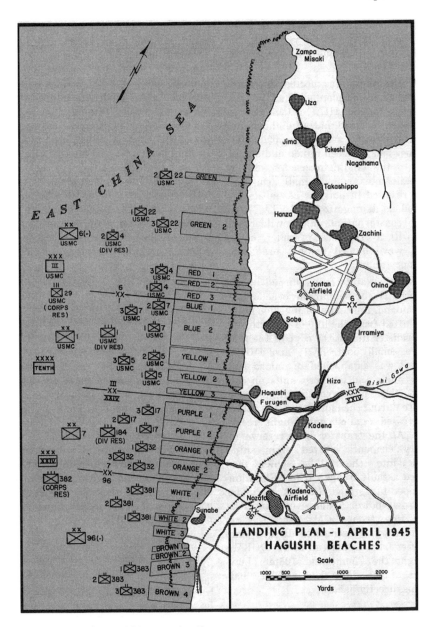

Operation Iceberg: Okinawa, April 1945
Source: Benis M. Frank and Henry I. Shaw Jr., *Victory and Occupation,* vol.
5 of *History of U.S. Marine Corps Operations in World War II* (Washington,
D.C.: Government Printing Office, 1968), 113.

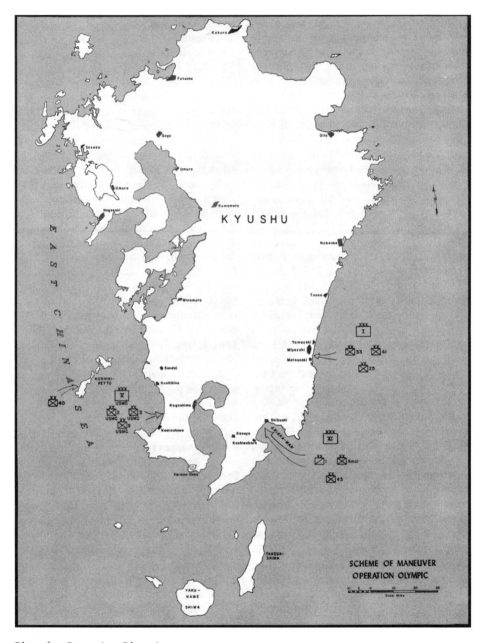

Plans for Operation Olympic, 1945
Source: Benis M. Frank and Henry I. Shaw Jr., *Victory and Occupation*, vol.
5 of *History of U.S. Marine Corps Operations in World War II* (Washington,
D.C.: Government Printing Office, 1968), 405.

NOTES

CHAPTER ONE   IN THE BEGINNING

1. Holland Smith, "Development of Amphibious Tactics in the U.S. Navy" (Washington, D.C., 1992), 20.
2. The occasion was the 1927 issuance of "Joint Action of the Army and Navy," a set of instructions governing how joint expeditions were to be conducted.
3. Jeter Iseley and Philip Crowl, *The U.S. Marines and Amphibious War* (Princeton, 1951), 31.
4. Ibid.
5. George Dyer, "Naval Amphibious Landmarks," *U.S. Naval Institute Proceedings, Vol. 92,* August 1966, 51.
6. Walter Ansel, *Reminiscences of Rear Admiral C. W. Ansel* (Annapolis, 1972), 37.
7. Dyer, "Naval Amphibious Landmarks," 52.
8. Victor Krulak, *First to Fight: An Inside View of the U.S. Marine Corps* (Annapolis, 1984), 12.
9. A. T. Mason, "Monograph on Amphibious Warfare," 9.
10. The boats would ground so far off the beach that the infantry often had to wade ashore in chest-deep water.
11. Krulak, *First to Fight,* 90–91.
12. Ansel, *Reminiscences,* 39.
13. Krulak, *First to Fight,* 91.
14. Richard Ketchum, *The Borrowed Years, 1938–1941: America on the Way to War* (New York, 1989), 558.
15. Thomas Buell, *Master of Sea Power: A Biography of Fleet Admiral Ernest J. King* (Boston, 1980), 149.
16. Ruthven Libby, *Reminiscences of Vice Admiral Ruthven Libby* (Annapolis, 1984), 53.

17. Ernest J. King, *Fleet Admiral King: A Naval Record* (New York, 1976), 413.
18. Holland M. Smith (General, USMC, Ret.), *Coral and Brass* (New York, 1949), 75.
19. Ibid., 53.
20. Norman Cooper, *A Fighting General: The Biography of General Holland M. "Howlin' Mad" Smith* (Quantico, Va., 1987), 76.
21. Smith, *Coral*, 92.
22. Krulak, interview.
23. Winston S. Churchill, *Their Finest Hour* (Boston, 1949), 244.

CHAPTER TWO　THE AMPHIBIANS GO TO WAR

1. Maurice Matloff, *Strategic Planning for Coalition Warfare—1941–1942* (Washington, D.C., 1953), 82.
2. Edward Beach, *The United States Navy* (New York, 1986), 470–71.
3. Buell, *Master*, 193.
4. George Dyer, *The Amphibians Came to Conquer*, 2 vols (hereafter *ACC 1/2*) (Washington, D.C., 1969), 253.
5. Matloff, *Strategic Planning*, 154.
6. Ibid., 182.
7. Ed Cray, *General of the Army: George C. Marshall, Soldier and Statesman* (New York, 1990), 309–10.
8. Daniel Barbey, "Manuscript for MacArthur's Navy," pt. II, 10.
9. George Mowry, "Landing Craft and the War Production Board," 11.
10. Cooper, *Fighting General*, 88.
11. Robert Heinl Jr., *Soldiers of the Sea* (Baltimore, 1991), 343.
12. Dyer, *ACC 1*, 270.
13. Samuel Milner, *Victory in Papua* (Washington, D.C., 1957), 30.
14. Iseley and Crowl, *U.S. Marines*, 90.
15. Dyer, "Landmarks," 59.
16. Joint Force Landing Board (hereafter JFLB #13–15), "Study of Training for Joint Amphibious Operations During World War II," A–11.
17. George Howe, *Northwest Africa: Seizing the Initiative in the West* (Washington, D.C., 1967), 14.
18. Robert Ghormley, *Events Leading Up to U.S. Attack on Solomons Islands*, 2.
19. Dyer, *ACC 1*, 286.
20. Ghormley, *Events*, 2–3.
21. Ibid.
22. George Dyer, *Reminiscences of Vice Admiral George C. Dyer* (Annapolis, 1973), 234–36.
23. Iseley and Crowl, *U.S. Marines*, 121.
24. WD, USS *Zeilin*, 7/21/42.
25. For example: officers were allowed one handbag while enlisted men were allowed only a knapsack. Post exchange supplies such as soap and cigarettes were allowed, but at least some space was saved by a complete proscription against candy.
26. AR, USS *Libra*, "Report of Landing Operations 7–9 August 1942, 2.
27. Dyer, *ACC 1*, 301.
28. Robert Leckie, *Challenge for the Pacific* (New York, 1965), 64.
29. Rev. Paul Moore, cited in John T. Mason, *The Pacific War Remembered* (hereafter *PWR*) (Annapolis, 1986), 129.

30. Dyer, *ACC1*, 346.
31. Iseley and Crowl, *U.S. Marines*, 125.
32. ONI Combat Narrative, "Miscellaneous Actions in the South Pacific," 66.
33. John Miller, Cartwheel: *The Reduction of Rabaul* (Washington, D.C., 1959), 232.
34. Though FTP 167 laid out specific divisions of labor between beach and shore parties, the problems experienced at Guadalcanal persisted in one form or another throughout the amphibious war. FTP 167 listed twenty-four tasks to be accomplished by beach and shore parties. Each transport and cargo ship was responsible for providing a beach party. Shore parties were to be provided by the marine or army units making the assault. (FTP 167, 34.) Assigning enough men to the shore party and giving them proper direction proved to be the single biggest problem.
35. Leckie, *Challenge for the Pacific*, 88.
36. Dyer, *ACC1*, 414.
37. Iseley and Crowl, *U.S. Marines*, 131–32.
38. Dyer, *Reminiscences*, 244.
39. James Merrill, *A Sailor's Admiral: A Biography of William F. Halsey* (New York, 1976), 73.
40. ComPhibForSoPac, "Report of Operations of TF 67 and TG 62.4," 3–4.
41. Dyer, *ACC1*, 414.
42. To Walter Ansel, Dieppe was also a message from Churchill to Roosevelt "that it couldn't be done: an invasion of the Continent was impractical" (Ansel, *Reminiscences*, 100).

CHAPTER THREE   ACTION IN AFRICA

1. Howe, 36.
2. Dyer, cited in John T. Mason, *The Atlantic War Remembered* (hereafter *AWR*) (Annapolis, 1990), 185.
3. Howe, *Northwest Africa*, 27.
4. Stan Newland, letter.
5. ONI Combat Narratives, "The Landings in North Africa," 5–11.
6. JFLB, A–23.
7. Kent Hewitt cited in *AWR*, 160–61.
8. ONI, "Landings," 12.
9. Philip Bucklew, *Reminiscences of Captain Philip Bucklew* (Annapolis, 1982), 44.
10. Samuel E. Morison, *History of U.S. Naval Operations in World War II*, 15 vols. vol. 2 (Boston, 1960), 41–42.
11. ONI, "Landings," 16.
12. Samuel L. Morison, *War: An Intimate View; The War Diaries of Rear Admiral Samuel Eliot Morison, USNR* (no date), 88–92.
13. ONI, "Landings," 16.
14. AR, USS *Charles Carroll*, 12/9/42, 5–6.
15. AR, USS *Harris*, 11/16/42, 4–5.
16. Combat Studies Institute, "Operation Torch" (hereafter CSI Torch) (Fort Leavenworth, Kans., 1984), 56.
17. Dyer, *Reminiscences*, 273.
18. Bud Farmer, interview, 5/31/92.
19. CSI Torch, 59.
20. Howe, *Northwest Africa*, 137.

21. Chester Eccleston, letter, 7/21/92.

22. JFLB, C-8.

23. AR, USS *Harris*, 4.

CHAPTER FOUR   CHOICES TO BE MADE: WAR ON MANY FRONTS

1. He had previously responded to a Roosevelt question about the difficulty of recon-
quering a Japanese-held island with the terse comment, "None will be easy to
reconquer once they are occupied."

2. Libby, *Reminiscenses*, 67–68.

3. Stephen E. Ambrose, *Eisenhower: Soldier, General of the Army, President Elect*,
vol. 1 (New York, 1983), 219.

4. Ansel, *Reminiscences*, 125.

5. Stetson Conn, *Guarding the United States and Its Outposts* (Washington, D.C.,
1964), 208.

6. WD, USS *Zeilin*, March 1943.

7. William P. Mack, *Reminiscences of Vice Admiral William P. Mack* (Annapolis,
1980), 128.

8. Libby, *Reminiscences*, 82.

9. Later in the day, the transport *Doyen* rescued a boatload of scouts who had become
lost in the fog and drifted out to sea. (WD, USS *Doyen*, 5/11/43).

10. Libby, *Reminiscenses*, 84–85.

11. WD, USS *Zeilin*, 5/12/43; AR, USS *Harris*, "Report of Operation Landcrab."

12. King introduced the practice of numbering U.S. fleets during these meetings;
Halsey's naval forces were thereafter known as the 3d Fleet and MacArthur's as
the 7th Fleet. Nimitz's forces were the 5th Fleet.

13. E. B. Potter, *Bull Halsey: A Biography* (Annapolis, 1985), 213.

14. Merrill, *Sailor's Admiral*, 86.

15. Raymond Tarbuck, *Reminiscences of Rear Admiral Raymond D. Tarbuck* (Annapolis, 1973), 122. Tarbuck's loyalty to Barbey is as laudable as the record of Barbey's
command. Although their accomplishments are manifest, nowhere in the South
Pacific did Barbey's men face a Tarawa or an Iwo Jima. To compare losses is to
compare apples and oranges.

16. Ibid., 84–85.

17. Ibid. Barbey's memoir corroborates Tarbuck's assertions: "Nowhere in the military
world were the interservice bickerings so bitter in the early days of World War II
as around Allied headquarters in Brisbane, Australia" (Barbey, Pt. II, 1).

18. Tarbuck, *Reminiscences*, 95–96.

19. Ibid., 97–98.

20. Barbey, Pt. II, 11–14.

21. Ibid., Pt. IV, 2.

22. Paul Dull, *Battle History of the Imperial Japanese Navy*, 182–83.

23. HQ Far East Command, Military History Section, "Imperial General Headquarters
Navy Directives," 118.

24. A September 1942 agreement gave to the Navy primary responsibility for amphibious training of all troops.

25. WD, LST Flotilla 5, March–April 1943.

26. Ansel, *Reminiscences*, 129.

27. Allen Pace, "LST—Large, Slow Target," *Naval History*, spring 1990, 20.

28. Ibid.

29. WD, LCI Flotilla 2, March–June 1943.

30. Richard Conolly cited in *AWR*, 284.

31. AR, "Western Naval Task Force, Sicilian Campaign," 42.

32. George Patton cited in *AWR*, 284.

33. AR, "Sicilian," 44.

34. Ibid., 18.

35. Carlo D'Este, *Bitter Victory: The Battle for Sicily, 1943* (New York, 1988), 176.

36. Morison, *History of U.S. Naval Operations*, vol. 9, 20.

37. R. Samuel Dillon, letter, 5/06/92.

38. "Story of the 345," no date.

39. Raymond Dabate, taped interview, no date.

40. AR, "Sicilian," 25.

41. Ansel, *Reminiscencces*, 147–48. Army Gen. Omar Bradley had already fought a similar battle with the Air Force during the planning process. The airmen originally demanded space in the initial lift for 660 vehicles, a requirement that Bradley reminded them was equivalent to an entire assault division. The fliers remained intransigent, saying that it was all or nothing. Bradley then informed them, "Very well then, you make the assault with your 660 trucks. Clear the beach for us and we'll come in on a later lift. It's either you or the infantry. There's not lift enough for both." The Air Force lowered its requirement to 234 vehicles (see also D'Este, *Bitter Victory*, 156–57).

42. AR, "Sicilian," 28.

43. Memo, USS *Florence Nightingale*, 7/5/43.

44. C. E. Cogswell, diary, 7/7/43.

CHAPTER FIVE   CLEARING THE ROAD: AMPHIBIOUS ADVANCE

1. One of many stories told at the LCT Association dinner, 5/30/92.

2. ONI, Combat Narratives, "Solomons Islands Campaign: Operations in the New Georgia Area, 21 June–5 August 1943," 14.

3. Susan Hall Godson, *The Development of Amphibious Warfare in World War II as Reflected in the Campaigns of Admiral John Leslie Hall Jr., USN* (Ann Arbor, Mich., 1979), 111–112.

4. ONI, Combat Narratives, "The Sicilian Campaign," 26–27.

5. Dell Ahlich, letter, 8/20/92.

6. Ibid.

7. D'Este, *Bitter Victory*, 285.

8. Ansel, *Reminiscences*, 135.

9. AR, "Sicilian," 40.

10. David Donovan, interview, 4/20/92.

11. AR, "Sicilian," 48–49.

12. Ibid., 16–17.

13. Dyer, *Reminiscences*, 328–29.

14. Ibid., 326–27.

15. AR, "The Italian Campaign, Western Naval Task Force Action Report of the Salerno Landings for September–October 1943," 96–97.

16. Martin Blumenson, *Salerno to Cassino* (Washington, D.C., 1969), 55.

17. Dyer, *Reminiscences*, 337.

18. Commander in Chief United States Fleet, "Amphibious Operations During the Period August to December 1943," 7-3.

19. Charles Adair, *Reminiscences of Rear Admiral Charles Adair* (Annapolis, 1977), 189.

20. AR, "Italian," 57.

21. Dyer, *Reminiscences*, 349.

22. Ibid., 77.

23. Bucklew, *Reminiscences*, 66–67.

24. Dyer, *Reminiscences*, 351.

25. Gunfire support was not usually among the duties assigned to an AGC; furthermore, the *Biscayne* had but a single 5-inch gun.

26. Dyer, *Reminiscences*, 359–61.

27. Blumenson, *Salerno to Cassino*, 92.

28. AR, "Sicilian," 152.

29. Bucklew, *Reminiscences*, 65. Clark's memoir says little about the whole issue.

30. Blumenson, *Salerno to Cassino*, 145–46.

31. Morison, *History of U.S. Naval Operations*, vol. 9, 170.

32. Robert Wallace, *The Italian Campaign* (Alexandria, Va., 1978), 73.

33. Commander in Chief U.S. Fleet, "Amphibious Operations for the Period August to December 1943 (hereafter COMINCH P-001), 3–17.

34. Ibid., 5–6.

35. Adair, *Reminiscences*, 194–95.

36. Ibid., 219–21.

37. Miller, *Cartwheel*, 239.

38. ONI, Combat Narratives, "Solomons Islands Campaign, the Bougainville Landing and the Battle of Empress Augusta Bay, 27 October–2 November 1943," 18.

39. Eccleston, letter, 7/21/92. Comments by the captain of the destroyer *Terry* reflect the lower level of amphibious experience in the Pacific compared to the Mediterranean. He suggested that instead of firing from 11,000 yards, the gunfire-support ships should be as close to the beach as the hydrography permitted. These were lessons already well known in the Mediterranean.

40. AR, USS *Libra*, 4.

41. On a lighter note, two LSTs were approaching Mono Island with barrage balloons streamed. Antiaircraft gunners on the island could see the balloons but not the ships, obscured by the terrain. They opened fire on what they took to be approaching Japanese airships. They scored no hits and the sailors quickly hauled down the balloons.

42. Iseley and Crowl, *U.S. Marines*, 211.

43. As previously noted, Nimitz wanted Smith in the position, but his appointment was subject to approval by the Marine commandant. Gen. Thomas Holcomb willingly gave his approval, saying of Smith, "He's the only general I've got who can shout louder than any admiral" (Heinl, *Soldiers of the Sea*, 406).

44. With the passage of time, both attacks have commonly come to be known by the names of their respective atolls, the practice this narrative has followed.

45. Thomas Buell, *The Quiet Warrior: A Biography of Admiral Raymond A. Spruance* (Annapolis, 1988), 195.

46. Henry I. Shaw, *Central Pacific Drive: History of U.S. Marine Corps Operations in World War II*, vol. 3 (Washington, D.C., 1966), 35.

47. The landings on Tulagi, Gavutu, and Tanambogo had been opposed but the defenses there were minimal compared to Tarawa.

48. Turner knew, of course, of the upcoming assault on the Marshalls. Because the

ships participating in the assault were also needed for the Marshalls operation, delaying Galvanic for a more favorable tide risked upsetting the timetable mandated by the JCS. With the subsequent furor over the tides, Turner's biographer went to great lengths to show that the admiral understood the problem of the tides. He ended his argument with the statement, "It was obvious that it was not anticipated at the command level that the LCVPs would land any marines dry shod." Dyer, ACC2, 719.

49. Smith, Coral, 117.
50. Cooper, Fighting General, 30.
51. With regard to the former figure, nowhere is Tarawa wider than 800 yards, and it is only 2 miles long.
52. Two hospital ships, the Relief and the Solace, were due to arrive in the Gilberts on 24 November.
53. During a postwar interview, Julian Smith told historian Jeter Iseley, "we never expected to encounter the type of defenses the Japanese had on Betio" (Iseley interview, 14).

CHAPTER SIX   TO THE OUTER GATE

1. Julian Smith, "Tarawa," U.S. Naval Institute Proceedings, November 1953, 1170.
2. Iseley and Crowl, U.S. Marines, 220.
3. Ibid.
4. COMINCH P-001, 3-7 & 3-8.
5. During his interview with Jeter Iseley, Julian Smith pointedly remarked that Admiral Hill "could never be reasoned with. He would never listen to the suggestions of anyone else, much less take advice." Smith also recalled that he, his chief of staff, and Hill's chief of staff pleaded with the admiral to continue gunfire support beyond the time when it was to be halted; "but when 0855 came around Admiral Hill threw his hands into the air and yelled 'Cease fire!' " (Iseley interview, 2–3).

The captain of the destroyer Dashiell later noted his disagreement with Hill's decision: "The necessity for continuing fire appeared to be quite obvious but it could not be continued because of a schedule and because apparently the Commanding Officers of Fire Support [section] 2944 [in the Dashiell] could not be depended upon to make a clear estimate of the situation when they were only 1500 yards from the scene of action and the controlling authority was over the horizon" (CO USS Dashiell cited in Dyer, ACC2, 708).

6. Radio traffic was badly hampered by mutual interference between the Maryland's transmitters, a side effect of not having enough space to accommodate the radios needed to control an amphibious operation.
7. COMINCH P-001, 3-4.
8. Shaw, Central, 67.
9. Ibid., 63.
10. WD, USS Zeilin, 11/21/43.
11. Shaw, Central, 79.
12. Ibid., 96–97.
13. Carl Moore cited in PWR, 177.
14. Cooper, Fighting General, 123.
15. Ibid., 124. Dyer says Holland Smith designated fire missions (Dyer, ACC1, 705).
16. COMINCH P-001, 3-10.
17. Julian Smith told historian Iseley in their 1948 interview that "the great stress on

the tank-flamethrower-infantry team best suited for overwhelming Betio was not made in the training period" (interview, 14).

18. Robert Sherrod, *Tarawa: The Story of a Battle* (New York, 1983), 138–39.
19. *Time*, 12/27/43.
20. HQ United States Army Forces Central Pacific Area, Office of the Commanding General, Re: Fifth Amphibious Corps, 27 December 1943.
21. Commandant of the Marine Corps, Re: Fifth Amphibious Corps, 11 January 1944.
22. Cray, *General of the Army*, 424.
23. King, *Fleet Admiral*, 518–19.
24. Cray, *General of the Army*, 436.
25. Adair, *Reminiscences*, 275–76.
26. Ibid., 254–55.
27. Dillon, letter.
28. Commander Task Force 18, "Action Report Operation Shingle," 9.
29. E. B. Potter, *Nimitz* (Annapolis, 1976), 282–83.
30. Ibid., 265.
31. Libby, *Reminiscences*, 111–14.
32. Commander in Chief, U.S. Fleet, "Amphibious Operations, the Marshall Islands, January–February 1944" (hereafter COMINCH P-002), 5-7.
33. The marines were particularly incensed because without gasoline to power the bilge pumps, the easily flooded LVTs were liable to sink.
34. WD, USS *LST 41*, 1/29/44.
35. Shaw, *Central Pacific Drive*, 141.
36. Iseley and Crowl, *U.S. Marines*, 272–73.
37. WD, USS *Wayne*, 2/1/44.
38. Philip Crowl, *Seizure of the Gilberts and Marshalls* (Washington, D.C., 1955), 313.
39. WD, USS *LST 226*, 2/1/44.
40. Control personnel had to deal with the continuing aggravation of poor radio equipment. The most common failure in the low-lying tractors was spray drowning out their radios.
41. COMINCH P-002, 3-16.
42. Cooper, *Fighting General*, 139; Morison, *History of U.S. Naval Operations*, vol. 7, 256–57.
43. Conolly ordered the ship so close to the beach that he was forever after known as "Close-in Conolly."
44. By now a ubiquitous workhorse, another LST was outfitted to serve as a floating repair and service center for DUKWs and LVTs.
45. One Japanese document read, "At the edge of the water scatter and divide the enemy infantry in their boats—attack and annihilate each one"; COMINCH P-002, 1-34.
46. Ibid., 5-20.
47. Cooper, *Fighting General*, 141.
48. Adair, *Reminiscences*, 286–91.
49. AR, USS *Brooks*, encl. A, 1.
50. In something of a turnabout from previous experiences with army officers, Admiral Kinkaid, MacArthur's naval commander, would later have to remind the general that there were some limitations on what could be accomplished by naval guns.
51. Adair, *Reminiscences*, 325.

52. Ibid., 306.

53. Ibid., 314.

54. Ibid., 317.

CHAPTER SEVEN   PIERCING THE WALLS

1. The naval component of Overlord was formally known as Operation Neptune. For simplicity's sake this narrative will use the all-encompassing Overlord.

2. King chose Kirk over Rear Adm. John Hall, whom Hewitt favored for the Overlord command. King did not waste Hall's experience, however. Hall and Rear Adm. Don Moon received command of the two American task forces participating in Overlord.

3. Gordon Harrison, *Cross Channel Attack* (Washington, D.C., 1951), 127; Cray, *General of the Army*, 446.

4. While he was struggling with landing craft figures, Eisenhower also had to contend with a request from Churchill for another meeting of the Combined Chiefs. None of the American chiefs wanted the meeting, especially not King. All believed that Churchill's main purpose would be to once again postpone Overlord. Roosevelt turned down the request.

5. Bucklew, cited in *AWR*, 344–45.

6. Commander, Western Naval Task Force, "Operation Normandy Invasion—Report of Naval Commander Western Naval Task Force," 14.

7. John Hall, cited in *AWR*, 378; Kirk cited in ibid., 353.

8. There were 266 army and navy doctors in the American task force. More than 2,600 navy corpsmen were also present.

9. In the midst of what any participant could see were preparations for momentous events, there is a certain air of incongruity to find that the mundane details of military life continued in their prescribed channels. The War Diary of LST 521 notes that on 24 May 1944, she hit and dislodged some planks from a fuel pier in the River Thames. As the Diary dutifully records, "This fact reported by letter to Port of London Authority via (1) COMLSTGRP 50, (2) COMLSTFLOT 17." WD, USS LST 521, 5/24/44.

10. Dwight Eisenhower, *Crusade in Europe* (New York, 1949), 243.

11. Bud Farmer and Harry Heckman, interview, 5/31/92.

12. Ibid.

13. Ambrose, *Eisenhower*, 308.

14. Ibid.

15. Heckman, interview.

16. Later study discovered that only one-third the weight of fire directed at Kwajalein was directed at Omaha Beach; Commander in Chief, U.S. Fleet, "Amphibious Operations, Invasion of Northern France Western Task Force June 1944" (hereafter COMINCH P-006), 2-19.

17. Farmer, interview. Farmer received the Silver Star for valor on Omaha Beach.

18. Carlo D'Este, *Decision in Normandy* (New York, 1991), 110.

19. John Morosco, "USS *Nevada* log of NGFS," 25.

20. WD, USS LST 288, 6/10/44.

21. Kirk AR, "Operation Normandy," 5.

22. Commander in Chief, United States Fleet, "Battle Experience: Supporting Operations for the Capture of the Marianas Islands (Saipan, Guam, and Tinian) June–August 1944" (hereafter COMINCH Battle Experience), 101.

23. No one wanted a repeat of the tragedy at Kwajalein when artillery fire struck a navy spotter and sent it crashing in flames.

24. Gene Watts, interview, 5/30/92. The War Diary of LST 226 notes that the first of these exercises that she carried out was "unsatisfactory." Words of a subsequent diary entry are a reminder of the different worlds that had to be mixed in amphibious warfare; in addition to training with the tractors, "The purpose of this . . . program was to . . . conduct tours for enlisted personnel of the Army and their officers to familiarize them with the LST and instruct them relative to its rules and regulations concerning Army personnel when on board" (WD, USS LST 226, 4/44).

25. WD, LST Flotilla 5, 6/2 and 6/6/44.

26. AR, USS *Doyen*, "Saipan Operation," 6.

27. AR, USS *Callaway*, "Assault on Saipan," 1–2.

28. COMINCH Battle Experience, app. 9, 5.

29. Morison, *War*, 425–26.

30. Draper Kauffman, cited in *PWR*, 240.

31. Commander in Chief, U.S. Fleet, "Amphibious Operations, Invasion of the Marianas, June to August 1944" (hereafter COMINCH P-007), 5-19.

32. One LST attempted to ease the handling problem by employing a cherry picker to lift the stretchers aboard from the landing craft (COMINCH P-007, 5-19).

33. Libby, *Reminiscences*, 119.

34. Kaufmann, in *PWR*, 244.

35. Commander Fifth Fleet, "Final Report on the Operation to Capture the Marianas Islands," app. 6, 2.

36. COMINCH P-007, 5-7.

37. Ibid., 3-13–3-14.

38. Nimitz and King would later try to have Sherrod's press accreditation revoked for his reporting of the incident. Nimitz was especially furious, but Marshall was able to prevail, contending that any such move would simply keep the controversy alive.

39. General Vandegrift wrote a scathing letter to Nimitz rebutting all of General Richardson's accusations against the Marine Corps. He took particular exception to Richardson's argument that amphibious operations were not a specialty and could be conducted by officers not specifically trained for the purpose. Vandegrift's reply was to the point: "This Headquarters believes most emphatically that he [Richardson] is not correct in these statements" (Vandegrift letter).

40. Admiral Wilkinson remained in command of III Phib Corps. In the South Pacific, MacArthur assumed command of all forces in the theater. Another change directed that all the amphibious force commanders in the entire Pacific theater answer directly to Kelly Turner. The practical aspects of amphibious warfare as used in the Pacific had also been codified in a weighty publication entitled *Transport Doctrine, U.S. Pacific Fleet*, which Turner's headquarters issued to the operating forces in April. Everything from loading to salvage to cargo handling to messing the troops was covered, a ready reference for all the novice amphibious sailors flooding into the Pacific.

41. AR, USS *Wayne*, "Landing on Guam, Beachmaster's Report of 7/28/44."

42. WD, USS *Zeilin*, 7/22–7/24/44.

43. WD, LCI(G) *466*, 9/5/44.

44. Cooper, *Fighting General*, 194–96.

45. ComFifthFlt, "Final," app. 6, 5.

46. CG, 1st Brig., 8–9.
47. AR, USS *Sumter*, "Occupation of Saipan," 10.
48. AR, USS *Harris*, Annex B, 2.
49. AR, USS *Sumter*, "Occupation of Saipan," 10.
50. Because pallets were too heavy to be manhandled, they required mechanical loaders to move them. They also took up more space and thus reduced the tonnage in any given load.

CHAPTER EIGHT   THE AMPHIBIANS ASCENDANT

1. Hewitt, in *AWR*, 426.
2. Nothing illustrates the amphibious planners' constant dilemma of not having enough ships as does the Overlord/Dragoon scenario. Had the attempt been made to launch the latter simultaneously with the former, there would have been insufficient ships. While Overlord was made possible by ships released from the Mediterranean, Dragoon was made possible only by some of the same ships being returned there.
3. AR, ComEighthFlt, 295.
4. AR, USS *Charles Carroll*, "Assault on the Beaches of Southern France," 8/23/44, 5.
5. The operation also included the planned seizure of Ulithi and Yap Atolls. Marine Maj. Gen. Julian Smith was commanding general, expeditionary troops for the entire operation. The operation was circumscribed by events elsewhere.
6. AR, USS *Wayne*, "Action Report of the Peleliu Operation," 10/2/44, 12.
7. The casualty situation at Peleliu was alleviated by arrival of the hospital ships *Samaritan*, *Bountiful*, and *Solace*.
8. Libby, *Reminiscences*, 135.
9. C. M. Blackford, "They Were All Giants at Peleliu," *U.S. Naval Institute Proceedings*, October 1950, 1117.
10. One extremely useful component of Stalemate was seizure of Ulithi Atoll, also part of the Carolines. The huge natural lagoon there proved vital to fleet operations in the Western Pacific for the remainder of the war.
11. Libby, *Reminiscences*, 86–137; George Garand, *Western Pacific Operation* (Washington, D.C., 1971), 287.
12. AR, USS *Wayne*, 25–35.
13. Morison, *History of U.S. Naval Operations*, vol. 12, 4. There was also, of course, MacArthur's personal pledge to the Filipinos that he would return.
14. Adair, *Reminiscences*, 317–72.
15. As an example of what costs the kamikazes were exacting from the amphibians, six LSTs would be sunk between 13 December 1944 and 13 January 1945.
16. AR, USS *Doyen*, "Lingayen Operation," 3–5.
17. Adair, *Reminiscences*, 394.
18. Ibid.
19. AR, USS *Doyen*, 8.

CHAPTER NINE   CRESCENDO AND DIMINUENDO

1. Readers familiar with modern underway-replenishment methods will no doubt wonder why supplying ammunition to the fleet while at sea was such a problem. Experiments had, in fact, been undertaken to develop the proper techniques. The procedure would be tried operationally for the first time off Iwo but was not yet part of Turner's repertoire during the planning stage.

2. Smith, *Coral*, 244.

3. Two different facets of Smith's association with Detachment must be considered: the lack of his customary vigor in pressing for a longer bombardment may be attributed to his being hospitalized between 5 November and 16 December. He later acknowledged that his mental faculties were impaired during that period. Second, Nimitz's biographer says point blank that Smith was ordered not to interfere with the operational management of Detachment. The general's biographer notes that Smith was "embarrassed" by the command setup but explained to the Commandant that he had been ordered to go: "I went to Spruance and Turner, and I discussed the situation from every angle. . . . I spoke with some heat and emphasis. . . . Both Spruance and Turner listened patiently, but insisted that they desired me to go along even if I took no part in the operation. They stated that as long as I was present, they had no apprehensions of the success of the operation" (Cooper, *Fighting General*, 223). It has been suggested that Smith was assigned to the operation to provide a marine officer of rank equal to Kelly Turner. Cooper also points out that Smith did not hesitate to offer advice and direction when he thought it was needed.

4. Garand, *Western Pacific Operations*, 479.

5. Ibid., 476.

6. Iseley and Crowl, *U.S. Marines*, 485–86.

7. WD, USS LCI(G) 466, 2/17/45.

8. Commander Task Force 52, "Operations of TF 52 in the Iwo Jima Campaign from 10 February to 19 February 1945," 7.

9. Iseley and Crowl, *U.S. Marines*, 473.

10. Harry Hill, cited in *PWR*, 298.

11. T. Grady Gallant, *The Friendly Dead* (New York, 1964), 64.

12. Attempts were made later to steady the landing ships with lines attached to bulldozers but nothing worked very well. Keeping the ship on the beach depended mostly upon the conning officer's skill with his engines.

13. The weather complicated the movement of casualties. It was sometimes difficult to get them off the beach, and their numbers overloaded the LST hospital ships. The *Doyen* reported that on the night of 22 February, she dispatched four of her boats to the hospital LSTs to begin transferring wounded to her own wards. Despite rough seas, "no casualties to either boats or personnel were suffered" (*AR*, 4). To help care for the large numbers of casualties, an army field hospital was established on Iwo by 25 February. Once the airfield was prepared, blood plasma was also flown from Guam and casualties evacuated by air. By D + 14, 9,500 men had been evacuated to the Marianas.

14. John Huggins, "Remembering Iwo Jima Forty Years Later," 8–9.

15. Including Johnny Huggins, who writes, "I have seen many flags since that day, but none prettier. This indeed was a day to be remembered" (ibid.).

16. Cooper, *Fighting General*, 233.

17. American forces were prepared to retaliate had either the Germans or Japanese resorted to poison gas. But the experience of World War I caused Roosevelt to forbid its offensive use by the armed forces of the United States. There is no doubt that gas would have helped reduce the complex system of caves and tunnels encountered on Iwo Jima. But even amid the appalling carnage of the island war, the president could not countenance the use of what he considered a morally revolting weapon.

18. Potter, *Nimitz*, 367.
19. Morison, *History of U.S. Naval Operations*, vol. 14, 73.
20. *AR*, CTF 52, 10. In keeping with his comments, Blandy made the specific recommendation that "future photographic plans have in mind fire-support requirements, and photographs be obtained which will, so far as possible, enable firing ships to thoroughly know their areas of responsibility." He further suggested that "intelligence officers aboard fire-support ships should become 'field fortification experts' and should be in a position to thoroughly brief personnel aboard" (ibid., annex B, 3).
21. Commanding Officer, USS *Oneida*, "Amphibious Training under Ship Training Group, Comments On," 1–2.
22. *AR*, Commander Amphibious Group One, "Operations against Okinawa Gunto etc.," A3.
23. Turner's biographer notes the episode, as does Hall's. The latter says the comment was made "jokingly" but Hall's own words give no sense that the comment was a joke (Dyer, *ACC2*, 1091; Godson, *Development of Amphibious Warfare*, 293).
24. AR, USS *Wayne*, Beachmaster's Report, 8.
25. Benis M. Frank and Henry I. Shaw, Jr., *Victory and Occupation: History of U.S. Marine Corps Operations in World War II*, vol. 5 (Washington, D.C., 1968), 242.
26. Farmer, interview, 5/31/92.
27. AR, USS *Charles Carroll*, "Invasion of Okinawa Jima," 12–13.
28. James Stewart, letter, 8/31/92.
29. Another amphibious operation took place when the 77th Infantry Division made an assault on the off-shore island of Ie Shima on 16 April. The enemy garrison of 4,700 soldiers was killed in a fight lasting six days.
30. Potter, *Nimitz*, 175.
31. William Fox, unpublished manuscript, 9; Potter, *Nimitz*, 23.
32. Headquarters Far East Command, Military History Section, "Imperial General HQ Army High Command Record," 210.
33. Ibid., 168.
34. V Amphibious Corps, "Japanese Plans for the Defense of Kyushu," 10.
35. King's 1952 autobiography states he "acquiesced" to Marshall's argument favoring invasion. He purportedly did so because the chiefs wanted to present a united front to the president (King, *Fleet Admiral*, 598). Although he still believed the naval blockade would prove decisive, he knew that plans and preparations must be made. An operation on the scale of Olympic would need considerable time to arrange. Once made, the plans could be canceled should they not be needed.
36. Frank and Shaw, *Victory and Occupation*, 403. According to information gathered postwar, the terrain favored the defenders once the initial penetration inland had been accomplished ("Plan," 25).
37. Farmer, interview. Farmer's comments were echoed by J. F. B. Johnston, who had been in the Pacific for the entire duration of the war (interview, 9/15/92).
38. The postwar study came to the following conclusions about the probable cost of Olympic: "In spite of counter measures the attacks directed against the task forces and transport areas would unquestionably have been serious and would have caused losses." Analysis of Japanese troop deployments also indicated a hard battle: "The strong concentration of Japanese divisions and the prepared plan to utilize the inland surrounding hills and mountains in the Miyazaki area, would have imposed heavy fighting on the I Corps." Despite many glaring weaknesses in Japanese

preparations and the disparity in firepower, the analysts agreed that "in theory the Japanese plan of defense was conceived to be and probably would have been, in the initial phase, a costly one for the invasion forces" ("Plan," 33–39).

39. Fox, pt. II: 30–31.

40. Krulak, interview, 6/19/92.

BIBLIOGRAPHY

BOOKS

Ambrose, Stephen E. *Eisenhower: Soldier, General of the Army, President-Elect.* vol. I. New York: Simon & Schuster, 1983.

Appleman, Roy, E. *United States Army in the Korean War: South to the Naktong North to the Yalu.* Washington, D.C.: Government Printing Office, 1961.

Baker, A. D. III. *Allied Landing Craft of World War Two.* Annapolis: Naval Institute Press, 1989.

Barger, Melvin D. *Large Slow Target: A History of the Landing Ships (LSTs) and the Men Who Sailed on Them.* Dallas: Taylor Publishing, 1989.

Bartlett, Merrill L. Lt. Col., USMC (Ret.), ed. *Assault From The Sea: Essays on The History of Amphibious Warfare.* Annapolis: Naval Institute Press, 1983.

Beach, Edward L. *The United States Navy: A 200-Year History.* Boston: Houghton Mifflin, 1986.

Belote, James H. and William M. Belote. *Typhoon of Steel: The Battle for Okinawa.* New York: Harper and Row, 1970.

Bennet, Ralph. *Ultra in the West: The Normandy Campaign of 1944–45.* New York: Scribner's, 1979.

Blumenson, Martin. *United States Army in World War II: Salerno to Cassino.* Washington, D.C.: Government Printing Office, 1969.

Buell, Thomas. *The Quiet Warrior: A Biography of Admiral Raymond A. Spruance.* Annapolis: Naval Institute Press, 1988.

———. *Master of Sea Power: A Biography of Fleet Admiral Ernest J. King.* Boston: Little, Brown, 1980.

Cannon, M. Hamlin. *United States Army in World War II: Leyte, The Return to the Philippines*. Washington, D.C.: Government Printing Office, 1954.

Churchill, Winston S. *The Second World War*. vol. 2: *Their Finest Hour*. Boston: Houghton Mifflin, 1949.

Conn, Stetson, et al.: *United States Army in World War II: Guarding the United States and Its Outposts*. Washington, D.C.: Government Printing Office, 1964.

Cooper, Norman V. *A Fighting General: The Biography of General Holland M. "Howlin' Mad" Smith*. Quantico: Marine Corps Association, 1987.

Cray, Ed. *General of the Army: George C. Marshall—Soldier and Statesman*. New York: W. W. Norton, 1990.

Crowl, Philip and Edmund G. Love. *United States Army in World War II: Seizure of the Gilberts and Marshalls*. Washington, D.C.: Government Printing Office, 1955.

D'Este, Carlo. *Bitter Victory: The Battle for Sicily, 1943*. New York: Dutton, 1988.

———. *Decision In Normandy*. New York: Perennial, 1991.

Dod, Karl C. *United States Army in World War II: The Corps of Engineers: The War Against Japan*. Washington, D.C.: Government Printing Office, 1987.

Dull, Paul S. *A Battle History of The Imperial Japanese Navy (1941–1945)*. Annapolis: Naval Institute Press, 1978.

Dyer, George C. *The Amphibians Came to Conquer: The Story of Admiral Richmond Kelly Turner*. Washington, D.C.: Government Printing Office, 1969.

Eisenhower, Dwight D. *Crusade in Europe*. New York: Doubleday, 1949.

Feifer, George. *Tennozan: The Battle of Okinawa and the Atomic Bomb*. New York: Ticknor & Fields, 1992.

Frank, Benis M. and Henry I. Shaw, Jr. *Victory and Occupation: History of U.S. Marine Corps Operations in World War II*. Washington, D.C.: Historical Branch, HQ, U.S. Marine Corps, 1968.

Frank, Richard B. *Guadalcanal*. New York: Random House, 1990.

Gallant, T. Grady. *The Friendly Dead*. New York: Doubleday, 1964.

Garand, George W. and Strobridge, Truman R. *Western Pacific Operations: History of U.S. Marine Corps Operations in World War II*, vol. IV. Washington, D.C.: Historical Division, HQ, U.S. Marine Corps, 1971.

Grover, David H. *U.S. Army Ships and Watercraft of World War II*. Annapolis: Naval Institute Press, 1987.

Godson, Susan Hall. *The Develpment of Amphibious Warfare in World War II As Reflected in the Campaigns of Admiral John Leslie Hall Jr., USN*. Ann Arbor: University Microfilms, 1979.

Harrison, Gordon A. *United States Army in World War II: Cross Channel Attack*. Washington, D.C.: Government Printing Office, 1951.

Hastings, Max. *OVERLORD: D-Day & The Battle for Normandy*. New York: Touchstone, 1985.

Heinl, Robert D. Jr. *Soldiers of the Sea: The United States Marine Corps, 1775–1962*, 2d ed. Baltimore: Nautical & Aviation Publishing, 1991.

Howe, George F. *United States Army in World War II: Northwest Africa: Seizing the Initiative in the West*. Washington, D.C.: Government Printing Office, 1957.

Iseley, Jeter A. and Philip A. Crowl. *The U.S. Marines and Amphibious War.* Princeton: Princeton University Press, 1951.

Ketchum, Richard M. *The Borrowed Years 1938–1941*: America on the Way to War. New York: Random House, 1989.

King, Ernest J. *Fleet Admiral King: A Naval Record*. New York: Da Capo, 1976.

Krulak, Victor H. Lt. Gen. USMC (Ret.). *First to Fight: An Inside View of the U.S. Marine Corps*. Annapolis: Naval Institute Press, 1984.

Langley, Michael. *Inchon Landing: MacArthur's Last Triumph*. New York: Times Books, 1979.

Leckie, Robert. *Challenge for the Pacific*. New York: Doubleday, 1965.

Leighton, Richard M. and Robert W. Coakley. *United States Army in World War II: Global Logistics and Strategy—1940–1943*. Washington, D.C.: Government Printing Office, 1955.

Mason, John T. *The Pacific War Remembered: An Oral History Collection*. Annapolis: Naval Institute Press, 1986.

———. *The Atlantic War Remembered: An Oral History Collection*. Annapolis: Naval Institute Press, 1990.

Matloff, Maurice. *United States Army in World War II: Strategic Planning for Coalition Warfare—1941–1942*. Washington, D.C.: Government Printing Office, 1953.

———. *United States Army in World War II: Strategic Planning for Coaliton Warfare—1943–1944*. Washington, D.C.: Government Printing Office, 1959.

Merrill, James F. *A Sailor's Admiral: A Biography of William F. Halsey*. New York: Thomas Y. Crowell, 1976.

Miller, Edward S. *War Plan Orange: The U.S. Strategy to Defeat Japan, 1897–1945*. Annapolis: Naval Institute Press, 1991.

Miller, John Jr. *United States Army in World War II: CARTWHEEL: The Reduction of Rabaul*. Washington, D.C.: Government Printing Office, 1959.

———. *United States Army in World War II: Guadalcanal—The First Offensive*. Washington, D.C.: Government Printing Office, 1989.

Milner, Samuel. *United States Army in World War II: Victory in Papua*. Washington, D.C.: Government Printing Office, 1957.

Morgan, Lt. Gen. Sir Frederick. *Overture to OVERLORD*. New York: Doubleday, 1950.

Morison, Samuel E. *History of U.S. Naval Operations in WWII*. vol. 2: *Operations in North African Waters*. Boston: Little, Brown, 1950.

———. vol. 4: *Coral Sea, Midway, and Submarine Actions, May 1942–August 1942*. Boston: Little, Brown, 1949.

————. vol. 6: *Breaking the Bismarcks Barrier, 22 July 1942–1 May 1944.* Boston: Little, Brown, 1961.

————. vol. 7: *Aleutians, Gilberts, and Marshalls, June 1942–April 1944.* Boston: Little, Brown, 1961.

————. vol. 8: *New Guinea and the Marianas, March 1944–August 1944.* Boston, Little, Brown, 1961.

————. vol. 9: *Sicily, Salerno, Anzio.* Boston: Little, Brown, 1954.

————. vol. 11: *The Invasion of France and Germany, 1944–1945.* Boston: Little, Brown, 1960.

————. vol. 12: *Leyte: June 1944–January 1945.* Boston: Little, Brown, 1961.

————. vol. 13: *The Liberation of the Philippines: Luzon, Mindanao, The Visayas—1944–1945.* Boston: Little, Brown, 1959.

————. vol. 14: *Victory in the Pacific—1945.* Boston: Little, Brown, 1961.

Morison, Samuel Loring, ed. *War: An Intimate View: The War Diaries of Rear Admiral Samuel Eliot Morison, USNR.* New York: Oxford University Press, 1994.

Morton, Louis. *United States Army in World War II: Strategy and Command: The First Two Years.* Washington, D.C.: Government Printing Office, 1962.

Newcomb, Richard F. *Iwo Jima.* New York: Holt, Rinehart and Winston, 1965.

Polmar, Norman and Thomas B. Allen. *World War II: America at War 1941–1945.* New York: Random House, 1991.

Pond, Hugh. *Salerno.* Boston: Little, Brown, 1961.

Potter, E. B. *Bull Halsey: A Biography.* Annapolis: Naval Institute Press, 1985.

————. *Nimitz.* Annapolis: Naval Institute Press, 1976.

————. *Seapower.* 2d ed. Annapolis: Naval Institute Press, 1981.

Russ, Martin. *Line of Departure: Tarawa.* New York: Doubleday, 1975.

Schofield, Vice Adm. B. B. *Operation Neptune.* Annapolis: Naval Institute Press, 1974.

Shaw, Henry I. Jr., and Douglas T. Kane. *Isolation of Rabaul: History of U.S. Marine Corps Operations in World War II,* vol. II. Washington, D.C.: Historical Division, HQ, U.S. Marine Corps, 1963.

————, et al. *Central Pacific Drive: History of U.S. Marine Corps Operations in World War II,* vol. III. Washington, D.C.: Historical Branch, HQ, U.S. Marine Corps, 1966.

Sherrod, Robert. *Tarawa: The Story of A Battle.* New York: Bantam, 1983.

Smith, Holland M. General, USMC (Ret.). *Coral and Brass.* New York: Scribner's, 1949.

Smith, Robert Ross. *United States Army in World War II: The Approach to the Philippines.* Washington, D.C.: Government Printing Office, 1952.

————. *United States Army in World War II: Triumph in the Philippines.* Washington, D.C.: Government Printing Office, 1963.

Steinberg, Rafael. *Return to the Philippines.* Alexandria: Time-Life, 1979.

Sweetman, Jack. *American Naval History, An Illustrated Chronology.* Annapolis: Naval Institute Press, 1984.

Vander Linde, Dean M. *Downfall: The American Plans for the Invasion of Japan in World War II.* East Lansing: Department of History, Michigan State University, 1987.

Wallace, Robert. *The Italian Campaign.* Alexandria: Time-Life, 1978.

Willoughby, Malcolm F. *The U.S. Coast Guard in World War II* (Revised). Annapolis: Naval Institute Press, 1989.

Winter, J. M. *The Experience of World War I.* New York: Oxford University Press, 1989.

ARTICLES AND ESSAYS

Alexander, Joseph H., Col. USMC. "Roots of Deployment—Vera Cruz, 1914," in *Assault From the Sea—Essays on the History of Amphibious Warfare,* Lt. Col. Merrill L. Bartlett, USMC (Ret.), ed. Annapolis: Naval Institute Press, 1983.

Berges, Charles. "Dieppe," *MHQ: The Quarterly Journal of Military History.* vol. 4, no. 2, spring 1992.

Blackford, C. M., LCDR, USCGR. "They Were All Giants at Peleliu," *U.S. Naval Institute Proceedings,* vol. 76, no. 10, October 1950.

Cosmas, Graham A. and Jack Shulimson. "The Culebra Maneuver and the Formation of the U.S. Marine Corps' Advance Base Force, 1913–14," in Bartlett (above).

Dyer, George C. VAdm USN (Ret.). "Naval Amphibious Landmarks," *U.S. Naval Institute Proceedings,* vol. 92, August 1966.

Fournier, Arthur F. "Influence of ULTRA Intelligence Upon General Clark at Anzio." U.S. Army Command and General Staff College, Fort Leavenworth, 1983.

Friedman, Norman. "Amphibious Fire Support," *Warship.* vol. IV. Annapolis: Naval Institute Press, 1980.

———. "Amphibious Fire Support: Post-War Developments," ibid.

Heinl, Robert D. Jr., Col. USMC (Ret.). "The U.S. Marine Corps: Author of Modern Amphibious Warfare," in Bartlett (above).

Hewitt, H. Kent, Adm USN (Ret.). "The Landing in Morocco—November, 1942," *U.S. Naval Institute Proceedings,* vol. 78, November 1952.

Honan, William H. "Bywater's Pacific War Prophecy," *MHQ: The Quarterly Journal of Military History.* vol. 3, spring 1991.

Leighton, Robert M. "Planning for Sicily," *U.S. Naval Institute Proceedings,* vol. 88, May 1962.

Pace, Allen and Marx Leva. "LST—Large, Slow Target," *Naval History,* vol. 4, spring 1990.

Perry, George Sessions. "Forty Hours Off a Sicilian Beach." *The Saturday Evening Post.* August 14, 1943.

Polmar, Norman and John J. Patrick. "Amphibious Command Ships: Past

Present, Future," parts I and II, *Warship*, vol. VI. Annapolis: Naval Institute Press, 1982.

Schriner, Charles W. Jr., Lt. Col. USMC. "The Dieppe Raid, 1942," in Bartlett (above).

Seese, Robert J. "Alligator by Roebling," *Naval History*, vol. 4, no. 2, spring 1990.

Smith, Julian. "Tarawa," *U.S. Naval Institute Proceedings*, vol. 79, no. 11, November 1953.

"Story of the 345," no date.

Weller, Donald M. Col. USMC. "SALVO-SPLASH! The Development of Naval Gunfire Support in World War II," part I. *U.S. Naval Institute Proceedings*, vol. 80, no. 8, August 1954.

———. "SALVO-SPLASH! The Development of Naval Gunfire Support in World War II," part II, *U.S. Naval Institute Proceedings*. vol. 80, no. 9, September 1954.

OFFICIAL DOCUMENTS

Barbey, Daniel, VAdm, USN (Ret.), "Manuscript for MacArthur's Navy."

Commandant of the Marine Corps, "Fifth Amphibious Corps," 1/11/44.

Combat Studies Institute. CSI Battlebook 3-A, "Operation Torch." Fort Leavenworth, 1984.

Commander Amphibious Force, South Pacific, "Report of Operations of Task Force SIXTY-SEVEN and Task Group 62.4—Reinforcement of GUADALCANAL November 8–15, 1942," 12/3/42.

Commander, Amphibious Group One. "Action Report, Operations against Okinawa Gunto Including the Capture of Kerama Retto and the Eastern Islands of Okinawa, March 21 to and including April 20, 1945," 5/1/45.

Commander Destroyers Pacific Fleet. "Destroyer Gunfire Support in Landing Operations," Serial 0495, 2/4/45.

Commander FIFTH Fleet. "Final Report on the Operation to Capture the MARIANAS Islands," 8/30/44.

Commander, Force U to Naval Commander Western Task Force. "Operation Neptune, Report of," 6/26/44.

Commander Gaffi Attack Group. "Action Report Sicilian Invasion Covering period 7/6/43 to 7/22/43."

Commander, Group 2 11th Amphibious Force. "Report of action between LST Convoy T-4 and enemy E boats 28 April 1944," 5/4/44.

Commander-in-Chief, U.S. Pacific Fleet and Pacific Ocean Areas. "Operations in Pacific Ocean Areas—June 1944," 11/7/44.

Commander in Chief, United States Fleet. P-001, "Amphibious Operations During the Period August to December 1943," 22 April 1944.

———. P-002, "Amphibious Operations, The Marshall Islands, January–February 1944," 20 May 1944.

———. P-004, "Amphibious Operations (excluding Marshall Islands Operations), January–March 1944." 1 August 1944.

———. P-006, "Amphibious Operations, Invasion of Northern France Western Task Force, June 1944," 21 October 1944.

———. P-007, "Amphibious Operations, Invasion of the Marianas, June to August 1944," 30 December 1944.

———. "Battle Experience: Supporting Operations for the Capture of the Marianas Islands (Saipan, Guam, and Tinian) June–August 1944."

———. "Medical Service in Amphibious Operations," 1/27/45.

Commander, Task Force 52. "Operations of TF 52 in the Iwo Jima Campaign from 10 February to 19 February 1945," 2/21/45.

Commander, Task Force 81. "Action Report Operation Shingle." 2/22/44.

———. "Supplementary Action Report—Operation Shingle," 5/17/44.

Commander, U.S. Atlantic Fleet. "Torch Operations: Comments and Recommendations," 12/22/42.

Commander U.S. EIGHTH Fleet. "Invasion of Southern France," 11/29/44.

Commander, Western Naval Task Force (CTF 122). "Operation Normandy Invasion—Report of Naval Commander Western Task Force (CTF 122)," 7/25/44.

Commanding General, First Provisional Marine Brigade. "Operations and Special Action Report," 8/19/44.

Commanding General, Third Marine Division, "Operation Report Forager, submission of," 8/19/44.

Commanding General, V Amphibious Corps. "Report of Galvanic Operations," 1/12/44.

Commanding Officer, USS *Alhena* (APA 26). "Report After Action," 8/11/42.

Commanding Officer, USS *Brooks* (APD 10). "Action Report, Landing Operations Los Negros Island, 29 February 1944," 3/2/44.

Commanding Officer, USS *Callaway* (APA 35). "Callaway; Casualty handling February 1–4, 1944," 2/8/44.

———. "Action Report, Assault of Saipan," 6/28/44.

———. "Action Report, Assault of Angaur," 9/28/44.

———. "Action Report, Assault of Leyte Island," 10/29/44.

———. "Action Report, Assault of Lingayen Gulf, Luzon Island," 1/13/45.

———. "Action Report, Reserve of the Assault of Iwo Jima, February to March 1944," 3/9/45.

Commanding Officer, USS *Charles Carroll* (APA 28). "Report on Torch Operations," 12/9/42.

———. "Contact and Action Report Operation Avalanche," 9/11/43.

———. "Action Report, Operation Neptune," 6/13/44.

———. "Action Report, Assault on the Beaches of Southern France, 15 August 1944," 8/23/44.

———. "Invasion of Okinawa Jima, Report of," 5/20/45.

Commanding Officer, USS *Doyen* (APA 1). "War Diary, supplement to and report of War Operations," 9/13/43.

———."Galvanic Operation, Report of," 12/3/43.

———. "Saipan Operation, Action Report on," 8/1/44.

———. "Leyte Operation, Action Report of," 10/44.

———. "Lingayen Operation, Report of," 1/12/45.

———. "Action Report, Amphibious Assault of Iwo Jima, 19 February 1945–6 March 1945," 3/9/45.

Commanding Officer, USS *Harris* (APA 2), "Attack on Safi," 11/16/42.

———. "Report of Operation Landcrab," 6/14/43.

———. "Report of Action, Kwajalein Operation," 2/14/44.

———. "Report of Action, Saipan Operation," 7/23/44.

———. "Report of Action, Leyte Operation," 10/31/44.

Commanding Officer, USS *Kephart* (APD 61). "Action Report, 6 December 1944 to 8 December 1944," 12/9/44.

———. "Action Report 12 December 1944 to 17 December 1944," 12/18/44.

———. "Action Report 4 January 1945 to 15 January 1945," 1/16/45.

Commanding Officer, LCI(L) 236. "Report of Amphibious Operations conducted against the enemy by this ship in Southern France during the period 9 August to 15 August 1944," 8/18/44.

Commanding Officer, USS *Libra* (AKA 12). "Report of Landing Operations 7–9 August 1942," 8/12/42.

———. "Action Report," 11/8/43.

Commanding Officer, LST 318. "Action and Damage Report," 8/14/43.

Commanding Officer, LST 372. "Action Report," 10/11/43.

———. "Action Report of Overlord Operation," 7/10/44.

Commanding Officer, LST 386. "Damage to ship and Destruction of secret matter, report of," 9/11/43.

Commanding Officer, LST 496. "Report of Action Taking Place morning of 28 April 1944," 4/30/44.

Commanding Officer, LST 507. "Loss of Ship, Report on," 5/2/44.

Commanding Officer, LST 511. "Report of Action Taking Place Morning of 28 April 1944," 4/30/44.

Commanding Officer, LST 515. "Action 28 April 1944, Report of," 5/3/44.

Commanding Officer, LST 583. "Action Reports, Submission of, 11/17/44 to 1/18/45."

Commanding Officer, USS *Oneida* (APA 221). "Amphibious training Under Ship Training Group, Comments On," 1/14/45.

Commanding Officer, USS *Roper* (APD 20). "Action Report, Landing on Ile du Levant," 8/16/44.

———. "Action Report, Suicide Plane Crash on USS *Roper* (APD 20), 25 May 1945," 5/31/45.

Commanding Officer, HMS *Saladin*. "Report of Proceedings," 4/29/44.

Commanding Officer, USS *Sumter* (APA 52). "Action Report, Occupation of Saipan," 6/28/44.

———. "Action Report, Landing on Angaur Island," 9/24/44.

———. "Action Report, Landing on Leyte Island, Philippine Islands," 10/23/44.

————. "Action Report, Landing on Lingayen Gulf, Luzon Island," 1/10/45.

Commanding Officer, USS *Wayne* (APA 54). "Action Report of the Landing on Guam," 8/25/44.

————. "Action Report of the Peleliu Operation," 10/2/44.

————. "Action Report, Leyte Island, Philippine Islands Operation," 10/27/44.

Executive Officer, USS *Harris* (APA 2). "Report on Activities of Ship's Personnel During Action While Debarking Troops and Cargo, November 8–11, 1942," 11/16/42.

Executive Officer, USS *Libra* (AKA 12). "Battle of Guadalcanal August 7–9, 1942," 8/12/42.

Executive Officer, USS *Wayne* (APA 54). "Report of Assault Operations Against Okinawa," 4/12/45.

Gavitt, James S. Lt. Col, USA. "The Okinawa Campaign: A Case Study," USAWC Military Studies Program Paper, U.S. Army War College: 1991.

Ghormley, Robert, VAdm. "Events Leading up to U.S. Attack on Solomons Islands, Etc." No date.

Hart, Franklin, Col. USMC. "Narrative Report of the Dieppe Raid," 8/27/42.

Headquarters Far East Command, Military History Section, Japanese Research Division. "Imperial General Headquarters Army High Command Record, Mid-1941–August 1945." No date.

Headquarters Far East Command, Military History Section. "Imperial General Headquarters Navy Directives." No date.

Headquarters United States Army Forces Central Pacific Area, Office of the Commanding General. "Fifth Amphibious Corps," 27 December 1943.

Headquarters, V Amphibious Corps. "The Japanese Plan for the Defense of Kyushu," 30 November 1945.

Hewitt, H. Kent. "Action Report, Western Naval Task Force, Sicilian Campaign," 12/31/43.

————. "The Italian Campaign, Western Naval Task Force Action Report of the Salerno Landings for September–October 1943," 1/11/45.

Iseley, Jeter A. "Conferences with Vice Admiral Harry W. Hill and Lieutenant General Julian C. Smith, Retired," 10/28/48.

Joint Landing Force Board Project No. 13–15. "Study of Training for Joint Amphibious Operations During World War II," May 1953.

Krulak, Victor H. Lt, USMC. "Report on Japanese Assault Landing Operations Shanghai Area 1937." No date.

Mason, A. T. Col. USMC. "Monograph on Amphibious Warfare," Office of the Chief of Naval Operations, 12/23/49.

Morosco, John A. "USS *Nevada* Log of NGFS." No date.

Mowry, George F. "Landing Craft and the War Production Board," War Production Board Special Study No. 11, 15 July 1944.

Office of Naval Intelligence, Combat Narratives. "The Aleutian Campaign, June 1942–August 1943," 1 March 1945.

————. "The Landings In North Africa–November 1942," 1944.

————. "Miscellaneous Actions in the South Pacific, 8 August 1942–22 January 1943," 1943.

————. "The Sicilian Campaign 10 July–17 August 1943," 1945.

————. Solomon Islands Campaign: I—"The Landing in the Solomons: 7–8 August 1942," 8 January 1943.

————. Solomon Islands Campaign: X—"Operations in the New Georgia Area, 21 June–5 August 1943," 1944.

————. Solomon Islands Campaign: XII—"The Bougainville Landing and the Battle of Empress Augusta Bay, 27 October–2 November 1943," 1945.

Senior Surviving Officer, LST 496. "Report of Action, LST 496, 11 June 1944," 8/3/44.

Smith, Holland M., Gen, USMC (Ret.). "The Development of Amphibious Tactics in the U.S. Navy," Washington, D.C.: History and Museums Division, HQ, U.S. Marine Corps, 1992.

U.S. Navy. FTP-167, *Landing Operations Doctrine, U.S. Navy*, 1938.

U.S. Navy Port Director, United States Naval Base San Francisco. "History of Navy Chartered Transports of World War II," 1 June 1946.

(Note: The following War Diaries are located in the Operational Archives of the Naval Historical Center, Washington, D.C. Navy Yard.)

War Diary, USS *Algorab* (AKA 8)

War Diary, Amphibious Group One

War Diary, USS *Barnett* (APA 5)

War Diary, USS *Brooks* (APD 10)

War Diary, USS *Charles Carroll* (APA 28)

War Diary, USS *Doyen* (APA 1)

War Diary, USS *Fomalhaut* (AKA 22)

War Diary, USS *Daniel T. Griffin* (APD 38)

War Diary, USS *Harris* (APA 2)

War Diary, USS *Kephart* (APD 61)

War Diary, LCI(G) 79

War Diary, LCI(L) 236

War Diary, LCI(G) 466

War Diary, LCI Flotilla 2

War Diary, LCI(L) Flotilla 13

War Diary, USS *Libra* (AKA 12)

War Diary, LSM 40

War Diary, LST 41

War Diary, LST 71

War Diary, LST 226

War Diary, LST 242

War Diary, LST 271

War Diary, LST 288

War Diary, LST 318

War Diary, LST 372

War Diary, LST 496
War Diary, LST 521
War Diary, LST Flotilla 5
War Diary, USS *Oneida* (APA 221)
War Diary, USS *Sumter* (APA 52)
War Diary, USS *Wayne* (APA 54)
War Diary, USS *Windson* (APA 55)
War Diary, USS *Zeilin* (APA 3)
Ware, Leonard, LCDR, USNR. "War Diary Force U, 31 May to 25 June." No date.

ORAL HISTORIES

Oral History Transcript, Lt. Gen. Victor H. Krulak, USMC (Ret.). Washington, D.C.: Historical Division, HQ, U.S. Marine Corps.
Reminiscences of Rear Adm. Charles Adair, USN (Ret.). Annapolis: Naval Institute, 1977.
Reminiscences of Rear Adm. C. W. Ansel, USN (Ret.). Annapolis: Naval Institute, 1972.
Reminiscences of Capt. Philip H. Bucklew, USN (Ret.). Annapolis, U.S. Naval Institute, 1980.
Reminiscences of Vice Adm. George C. Dyer, USN (Ret.). Annapolis: Naval Institute, 1973.
Reminiscences of Vice Adm. Ruthven E. Libby, USN (Ret.). Annapolis: Naval Institute, 1984.
Reminiscences of Vice Adm. William Paden Mack, USN (Ret.). Annapolis: Naval Institute, 1980.
Reminiscences of Rear Adm. Raymond D. Tarbuck, USN (Ret.). Annapolis: Naval Institute, 1973.

INTERVIEWS AND CORRESPONDENCE

Ahlich, Dell F.	*Frederick Funston*	letter 8/20/92
Alexander, Joseph Col. USMC, (Ret.)		letter 9/22/93
Andrews, Frank	LSM 280	
Boatwright, V. T.		letter 3/19/92
Brazier, Rogers	LCT 125, LSM 140	5/31/92
Campbell, Nelson	LST 345	letter 12/2/92
Cogswell, C. E.	LCT 201	letter, no date
Dabate, Raymond D.		taped interview
Davis, Sammy	2d Mar Div	interview 5/4/93
Dillon, R. Samuel Jr.	LCI(L) 235	letter 5/06/92
Donovon, David		interview 4/20/92
Eccleston, Chester	*George Clymer*	letter 7/21/92
Farmer, Bud	LCT Flot 17	5/30–31/92
Fox, William D.	LSM 168	unpub'd. manuscript

Friedrich, Richard	LSM 467	letter, no date
Gordier, Bob	LCT 66	interview 5/31/92
Heckman, Harry	LCT Flot 5	interview 5/30–31/92
Huggins, John A.	LSM 201	letter 10/28/92
Johnston, J. F. B., Capt USN (Ret.)		interview 9/15/92
Kaufmann, Erwin L.	LCT(A) 2124	letter, no date
Krulak, Victor H., LtGen USMC (Ret.)		interview 6/19/92
Newland, Stan	*Nightingale*	letter, no date
Pace, Allen	LST 386	letter 9/2/93
Paine, Donald C.	LSM 243	letter, no date
Slejko, Adolph	LSM 1	letter 3/30/93
Stansbury, Bob		interview 5/30/92
Stewart, John	LSM(R) 189	letter 8/31/92
Watts, Gene	LCT Flot 5	interview 5/30/92

INDEX

About the Author

John A. Lorelli, who holds a master's degree in history from California State University at Chico, has studied World War II naval history since childhood, when he came upon Samuel Eliot Morison's *History of U.S. Naval Operations in World II* in the library. In 1984 his first book, *The Battle of the Komandorski Islands,* was published by the Naval Institute Press.

Lorelli served on active duty with the U.S. Navy from 1966 to 1968, including one deployment to Vietnam in the USS *Ramsey.* Today he lives in Ventura, California, where he teaches history at the community college and manages the Santa Barbara City College Bookstore.